MULTINATIONAL BUSINESS SERVICE FIRMS

For my parents

Multinational Business Service Firms

The Development of Multinational Organisational Structures in the UK Business Services Sector

JOANNE ROBERTS
School of Social Political and Economic Sciences
The University of Northumbria at Newcastle

Ashgate

Aldershot • Brookfield USA • Singapore • Sydney

Published by
Ashgate Publishing Ltd
Gower House
Croft Road
Aldershot
Hants GU11 3HR
England

Ashgate Publishing Company
Old Post Road
Brookfield
Vermont 05036
USA

British Library Cataloguing in Publication Data
Roberts, Joanne
Multinational business service firms : the development of
multinational organisational structures in the UK business
services sector
1. Service industries - Great Britain 2. International
business enterprises - Great Britain
I. Title
338.8'871'000941

Library of Congress Catalog Card Number: 97-76945

ISBN 1 84014 154 9

Printed in Great Britain by The Ipswich Book Company, Suffolk.

Contents

Figures and tables   ix
Preface   xiii
Acknowledgements   xv

1 Introduction   1

1.1 Introduction   1
1.2 Aims and objectives   3
1.3 Method   4
1.4 The structure of the book   6

2 Internationalisation of services: conceptual issues and evidence   8

2.1 Introduction   8
2.2 Defining services   8
2.3 International service transactions   16
2.4 The extent of service and business service internationalisation   21
2.5 The value and significance of business services   30
2.6 Conclusion   32

3 International trade and foreign direct investment theories: 34
   application to services

3.1 Introduction   34
3.2 International trade theory and service trade   34

3.3 Foreign direct investment theory and service multinational enterprises   48

3.4 Foreign direct investment and intra-firm trade in services   65

3.5 Conclusion   66

4 Organisational theory of the firm and the international structure and strategy of service firms   **69**

4.1 Introduction   69

4.2 The organisation of the service firm   69

4.3 Strategy and structure in the development of service firms   75

4.4 The organisation of international service firms   82

4.5 Strategy and structure in the development of international service firms   84

4.6 Conclusion   89

5 The international business service firm: the evolution of an internationalisation framework   **92**

5.1 Introduction   92

5.2 Why does internationalisation occur?   93

5.3 How does internationalisation occur?   94

5.4 What factors influence the organisational structure of international service firms?   99

5.5 A framework for the internationalisation of service firms   102

6 Internationalisation of business services: an overview of advertising, accountancy and computer services   **105**

6.1 Introduction   105

6.2 Internationalisation of advertising services   105

6.3 Internationalisation of accountancy services   120

6.4 Internationalisation of computer services   132

6.5 Conclusion   141

7 The UK business services sector: survey framework   **144**

7.1 Introduction   144

7.2 The UK business services sector   144

7.3 Research aims and hypotheses   149

7.4 Framework of the postal questionnaire   155

7.5 Characteristics of the sample   156

vi

7.6 Conclusion   161

8 The internationalisation of the UK business services sector: **163**
   survey results

8.1 Introduction   163
8.2 Diversification and internationalisation   163
8.3 An evolutionary approach to internationalisation?   173
8.4 International clients - international business service firms?   184
8.5 Location and internationalisation   187
8.6 Ownership and autonomy of overseas establishments   187
8.7 Business service sector FDI: market-oriented or resource-   194
   oriented
8.9 Conclusion   196

9 Multinational structures and strategies in the business services   **199**
   sector

9.1 Introduction   199
9.2 Advertising firms   200
9.3 Accountancy firms   212
9.4 Computer service firms   228
9.5 Multinational structures and strategies in the UK business   240
   services sector
9.6 Conclusion   243

10 A model for business service firm multinationalisation   **245**

10.1 Introduction   245
10.2 An evolutionary approach to business service firm   246
   internationalisation
10.3 Explaining trade and FDI in business services   255
10.4 The role of intra-firm trade in the multinationalisation of   259
   business service firms
10.5 Multinational organisational structures in the business services   261
   sector
10.6 Conclusion   265

11 Conclusion   **268**

11.1 Introduction   268
11.2 The international competitiveness of the UK business services   269
   sector

11.3 The development of a theory for the internationalisation of   271
     service activity
11.4 Policy implications   274
11.5 Final conclusions   276

Appendices   **277**

Appendix 1: Research techniques and data analysis   277
Appendix 2: International Standard Industrial Classification: 283
     classification of business services

Bibliography   **284**

Figures and tables

Figure 4.1   Organisational structures   76

Figure 5.1   The internationalisation of service firms: a framework   103

Figure 9.1   Cordiant Plc. organisational structure   204

Figure 9.2   Gold Greenlees Trott Plc. organisational structure   210

Figure 9.3   Price Waterhouse UK national structure   215

Figure 9.4   The worldwide Price Waterhouse organisation   216

Figure 9.5   BDO Binder Hamlyn national structure   224

Figure 9.6   BDO international organisation   225

Figure 9.7   Sema Group Plc. organisational structure   233

Figure 9.8   Logica Plc. organisational structure   236

Figure 10.1   Internationalisation of business service firms   249

Figure 10.2   Paths of development in the evolution of a multinational   252
              business service firm

Figure 10.3   A framework for the multinational development of   267
              business service firms

Table 1.1   Research strategy   6

Table 2.1   Definitions of services: a classification   12

Table 2.2   Business services included in proposed reference list of   15
                industries

Table 2.3   International service transactions: a classification   20

Table 2.4   Growth in the value of world exports by major product   24
                group 1985-93

Table 2.5   Leading exporters and importers of world trade in   25
                commercial services 1993

Table 2.6   Industrial distribution of outward direct capital stock for   26
                selected countries in the late 1980s

Table 3.1   The nature of trade by sector   47

Table 3.2   The basis for trade: selected service industries   49

Table 3.3   The advantages and disadvantages of internalisation   57

Table 3.4   Illustrations of ownership, locational and internalisation   62
                advantages relevant to the activities of selected business
                service industries

Table 6.1   The top 30 UK advertising agencies in 1994   108

Table 6.2   The top UK advertising agency groups in 1993   109

Table 6.3   The world's top 30 advertising organisations in 1994   111

Table 6.4   The world's largest accountancy firms 1990-1   123

Table 6.5   Top 20 UK accountancy firms in 1994   124

Table 6.6   The UK's largest computer services suppliers 1994   135

Table 6.7   The world's top computer services firms 1993   136

Table 7.1   Numbers employed in the business services sector 1985   145
                and 1994

Table 7.2   Geographical distribution of employment March 1995: a   147
                comparison between the distribution of all employment,
                service sector employment and business services sector
                employment

Table 7.3   Employment in selected business service sub-sectors   148
                1985-1994 as a percentage of employment in the
                business services sector

Table 7.4   Foreign earnings in selected business services   148

x

Table 7.5   Estimated patterns of national competitive advantage in   150
               international business service industries

Table 7.6   UK business service sub-sectors surveyed and response   157
               rates

Table 7.7   Date of establishment   158

Table 7.8   UK and overseas employment for business service firms   159
               1989

Table 7.9   UK and overseas turnover for business service firms   159
               1989

Table 7.10   Company type   160

Table 8.1   Number of services provided by all firms   165

Table 8.2   Number of services provided by firms with an overseas   165
               turnover

Table 8.3   Business services firms: diversification by overseas   166
               turnover

Table 8.4   Accountancy firms: diversification by overseas turnover   166

Table 8.5   Number of firms delivering numbers of services to clients   169

Table 8.6   Number of firms with an overseas turnover in 1989   169
               delivering numbers of services to clients

Table 8.7   Number of services provided by firms established before   170
               1981

Table 8.8   Factors influencing diversification   171

Table 8.9   Age and size, domestic and international: correlation   175
               coefficients

Table 8.10   UK size and internationalisation: correlation coefficients 175

Table 8.11   How services are exported   178

Table 8.12   How services are exported by export only firms   178

Table 8.13   Overseas turnover and methods of exportation: 179
               correlation coefficients

Table 8.14   Overseas turnover and methods of exportation for firms   180
               with an overseas turnover of £5 million or less:
               correlation coefficients

Table 8.15   Factors as a source of competitive advantage   181

xi

Table 8.16   Merger and acquisition activity in the past 5-10 years   183

Table 8.17   Purpose of merger and acquisition activity   183

Table 8.18   Source of revenue: all firms   185

Table 8.19   Source of revenue: firms with an overseas turnover   185

Table 8.20   Revenue from MNEs and overseas turnover   186

Table 8.21   Location by internationalisation   188

Table 8.22   Domestic geographical spread and internationalisation   188

Table 8.23   Number of types of overseas presences   190

Table 8.24   Overseas turnover and the number of different types of   190
               overseas presences: correlation coefficients

Table 8.25   Overseas turnover and the international geographical   191
               spread of overseas presences: correlation coefficients

Table 8.26   Factors determining the form of ownership which an   192
               overseas presence takes

Table 8.27   Factors which determine the location of an overseas   195
               presence

Table 9.1   Price Waterhouse worldwide network locations 1985-   221
               1993

Table 9.2   Turnover by market sector: Sema Group Plc. and Logica   230
               Plc.

Table 10.1   Stages in the internationalisation of the firm   247

Table 10.2   A classification of international activities conducted by   251
               business service firms

Table 10.3   Conceptual framework: factors influencing the   254
               development of multinational business service firms

Table 10.4   Factors influencing the choice of organisational structure   265
               among business service firms

Preface

The development of the multinational enterprise (MNE) is a fascinating subject, and one that I have been attracted to since my time as an undergraduate student at the University of Lancaster. From both an economic and political perspective MNEs have a major impact upon the lives of individuals, and indeed, upon the role and activities of Nation States. On joining the Doctoral Programme on the Social and Economic Aspects of Information and Communication Technologies at the Centre for Urban and Regional Development Studies, University of Newcastle upon Tyne, I was introduced to the issues surrounding the impact of new information and communication technologies (ICTs) upon economic activity. The significance of the service sector became clear, as did its role in the economies of 'post industrial' societies. I became particularly interested in the international exchange of services, and within this the service sector MNE has a central function. This research has then evolved from a combination of long-standing interests with a more recently developed interest in the role of services. Information intensive services are of particular interest because, firstly, they have great scope for internationalisation, and secondly, new ICTs are having a significant impact upon the way in which they are produced and delivered.

Developments in ICTs have and will continue to have a major impact upon the structure of economic activity and more broadly on all types of human activity. This book does not attempt to address the general impact of ICTs, nor is it concerned with exploring the general restructuring of economic activity. However, consideration is given to the role of ICTs in the internationalisation of service sector firms.

Multinational enterprises in the manufacturing and primary sectors have received much attention from academics, whereas literature on the service sector MNE is in its infancy. Clearly, the general literature on the MNE does have relevance, however, given the significance of service activity, the development of multinational firms in this sector does warrant specific attention. The purpose of this book is to provide an in-depth analysis of the evolution of MNEs in the UK business services sector.

The empirical research for this book derives largely from the analysis of data gathered through a postal survey conducted in 1990. Additional secondary data has been collected in the intervening years. The research for this book was completed at the beginning of 1996. Clearly, the research findings, particularly those deriving from the postal survey have to viewed within the context of the late 1980s and early 1990s.

Compared to manufacturing activity, services are woefully under researched. With its role as a major source of both output and employment it is time that the service sector received an appropriate share of attention from researchers and policy makers alike. This book then, contributes to a small but developing body of literature. Rapid technological progress is changing the nature of services and economic activity in general. Within the information intensive services sector innovations connected with the Internet and electronic commerce will undoubtedly play a part in the future evolution of markets and firms. Such developments underline the need for further research to strengthen and extend our understanding of service sector activity.

Newcastle upon Tyne
August 1997

Acknowledgements

I would like to acknowledge all those people whose help and advice has been drawn upon in the writing of this book. Firstly, I am especially grateful to Dr Jeremy Howells, for his supervision of the research project. I would also like to thank all those members of staff at the Centre for Urban and Regional Development Studies at the University of Newcastle upon Tyne, both academic and administrative, who helped and advised me during my period of study there. Furthermore, I am particularly grateful to Professor Andrew Gillespie, Dr J Neill Marshall, and Professor Ian Miles, for their encouragement and advice.

This research has depended heavily on the goodwill of many people in the UK business services sector who took the time to complete my postal questionnaire in the Summer of 1990. I would like to thank everyone who participated in the survey, as well as those who gave freely of their time for interview purposes, and others who responded to my frequent requests for information. I am indebted to the Economic and Social Research Council for funding the research project (Grant No: A00428722021). The preparation of this book has been aided by assistance from the University of Northumbria's Small Research Grant Scheme (Project No: 871/P089).

Finally, I would like to acknowledge the love and encouragement of my family which has sustained me throughout. In particular, I am grateful to John for his unerring support.

1 Introduction

1.1 Introduction

The importance of the service sector in the domestic economy has been recognised for some time, with the share of gross domestic product (GDP) produced by this sector exceeding 60 per cent in most industrial countries, and accounting for more than 65 per cent of total employment in these countries (World Bank, 1996). The role of the service sector in the domestic economy has, consequently, been the subject of many studies (Fisher, 1939; Clark, 1957; Fuch, 1968; Lewis, 1973; Singelmann, 1978; Shelp, 1981; Gershuny and Miles, 1983; Kravis, 1983; Nusbaumer, 1987a; inter alia). Although services have come to dominate economic activity within the industrialised countries, whether they will achieve the same impact in the international economy is still open to question.

The US, which has the largest share of service exports (Broadman, 1994), was instrumental in raising awareness of the potential for the internationalisation of services with its call for the liberalisation of trade in services in the early 1980s. Service trade was subsequently included in the Uruguay Round of the General Agreement on Tariffs and Trade (GATT) negotiations which began in 1986 and concluded, after many delays, in 1993. One important outcome of the Uruguay Round has been the General Agreement on Trade in Services (GATS) which represents the first attempt to devise a multilateral, legally enforceable understanding covering trade and investment in the service sector.

The advanced industrialised countries face formidable competitive pressures from the Newly Industrialised Countries (NICs) in both traditional, and, even relatively new global markets. This competition has, since the 1970s, resulted in the decline of many traditional sectors. The advanced economies are, as a consequence, increasingly looking towards service industries as a means of securing future prosperity. However, for services to replace traditional industries, they must not

1

only have domestic potential but also international scope. As the advanced industrialised economies progress into Bell's (1974) Post Industrial era, will services come to dominate the exports of such countries? If countries become dependent on services as their main source of domestic economic activity, without a similar shift in international activity, they will experience a decline in their export capacity and hence a fundamental weakening of their economies.

Given the difficulties which arise in the export of services, the hope that they will take the place of manufactured goods as an export activity may appear to be a rather optimistic hope at the present time. However, technological advances are improving the scope for service internationalisation, with services increasingly being embodied in tangible form or delivered across telecommunication networks. In addition, there is the rapid growth of new information-based services that have developed as a result of new information and communications technologies (ICTs) which are highly tradable. Indeed, services have undoubtedly become more tradable in the past 20 years and are set to become increasingly so. It may well be then, that service exports do offer a real alternative to the export of manufactured goods.

Services already make up a significant and growing proportion of international trade. According to GATT (1994, p.2) world exports of commercial services in 1993 were valued at $1,020 billion, accounting for almost 22 per cent of all exports. The growing importance of service trade, together with rising interest in the internationalisation of services has stimulated a rapid expansion of the literature in this area (Sapir and Lutz, 1980; UNCTAD, 1983; Nusbaumer, 1987b; Krommenacker, 1984; Riddle, 1986; Tucker and Sundberg, 1988; Messerlin and Sauvant, 1990; Daniels, 1993; inter alia). Many of the studies conducted so far are of a general nature addressing conceptual issues and exploring trends in the internationalisation of the service sector. Such work is highly valuable, particularly, since this area was until recently almost completely neglected. However, given the heterogeneous nature of the sector, our understanding of the internationalisation of services can only be extended through the in-depth exploration of the internationalisation of individual service sector activities. It is the intention of this research to add to this body of literature in just such a way.

The focus of attention here is the business services sector which has experienced significant growth in the last 25 years, particularly among advanced industrialised countries. At a national level business services have increased their share of both employment and output, whilst at an international level both trade and investment in this sector have increased. Indeed some business services sectors are as large if not larger than many of the merchandise industries which were discussed in the Uruguay Round of GATT negotiations (UNCTC, 1990). Relatively little attention has been devoted to internationally provided business services, which are not only important in their own right, but also play a significant supportive role in the operation of the global production system.

2

1.2 Aims and objectives

The aim of this book is to explore the internationalisation of the service sector, through the analysis of the multinational development of UK business service firms. As a result of this exploration of a significant sub-sector insights will be gained into the service sector as a whole.

When exploring the internationalisation of services it is clear that both trade and investment need to be examined, as do the links between these two means of internationalisation. The objective of this research is to explore the internationalisation of business service companies and in doing so establish factors that influence the manner in which internationalisation occurs. Attention is focused upon the strategies of internationalisation which lead to multinational organisational structures through foreign direct investment (FDI) and other related means.

The central hypothesis is that FDI is the preferred manner of internationalisation, within the business service sector, despite the fact that advances in ICTs have made other methods, such as licensing, and indeed, even direct trade viable. It is further hypothesised that it is the information intensive nature of business services which necessitates such a method of internationalisation. Information is extremely difficult to protect, thus if a company is to secure its information assets, there is a need for a high degree of control over its subsidiary companies. Expansion of the firm through FDI, whether it be by way of a takeover or the setting up of a new firm, provides the basis upon which information can be internalised and thus protected within the boundaries of the firm.

The essential characteristics of business services therefore make direct trade very difficult. Even when services can be directly exported, the delivery system often requires a high level of back up necessitating a presence, temporary or permanent, in the local market. It is a contention of this book that, as a consequence, business service sector trade is often in the form of intra-firm trade, that is, services are transacted across national frontiers but this occurs within the boundaries of the firm.

More generally this research aims to:

1   Gain an insight into the internationalisation of the service sector through an exploration of the international development of the UK business service sector.

2   Review the explanatory value of international trade and FDI theory when applied to the case of international service transactions, in particular those in business services.

3   Assess the wider value of the theory of the firm when applied to the development of business service firms and in particular their multinational development.

4   Explore the interplay between trade and FDI within business service firms.

3

5   Explore, through empirical research, the internationalisation of UK business services, and in so doing to identify factors which influence the choice of multinational structure selected by business service firms.

6   Draw upon both theoretical and empirical research to develop a framework within which to explain the internationalisation of business services and more generally the service sector as a whole.

A vast body of literature exists concerned with international trade and FDI. However, the majority of this literature is concerned with the primary and manufacturing sectors, little has so far been published which focuses on the service sector. Given the growing importance of services within developed economies, this book seeks to make a significant contribution towards redressing this deficiency, both on an empirical and theoretical level.

On a practical level, the research will provide a framework within which to understand the internationalisation of service firms. It will be particularly useful for those decision-makers within the business services sector wishing to assess their firm's position in relation to internationalisation. The research will also be of use to those concerned with the regulation of business services and more generally the regulation of trade and FDI. Finally, this study will provide the foundations for future research into the internationalisation of services since it raises issues and questions that will require further investigation.

1.3 Method

This study was conducted in a number of stages and utilised a variety of research methods. It is useful at this point to briefly summarise the methodological approach. The first stage of the study involved a review of empirical and theoretical literature concerning the internationalisation of the service sector. The second stage of the research required the development of a substantial body of knowledge on the business services sectors derived from a multitude of secondary sources. During this phase it was necessary to select sub-sectors for further study.

A number of factors influenced the choice of sub-sectors. The research is primarily concerned with information intensive business services, furthermore, the central objective involves the exploration of the internationalisation of business services, thus it was essential to select sub-sectors which demonstrated both information intensiveness and a degree of internationalisation. From the sub-sectors which demonstrated these characteristics three were selected for in-depth research: advertising, accountancy and computer services. This selection was influenced by the desire to provide a cross section of the information intensive business services sector. The chosen sectors display different levels of growth and maturity, patterns of regulation, and organisational development. Accountancy, for example is a mature market with a high level of regulation, whereas computer services is a relatively new sector with an underdeveloped regulatory system, advertising whilst relatively mature is self regulating. Discussions were held with representatives of the trade and professional associations of the sub-sectors[1] with a view to confirming trends identified from the secondary information and exploring the research concerns with experts in the various fields.

The third stage of the research involved the construction and administration of a postal survey, together with the analysis of the data gathered. Hypotheses generated from the literature review, which are outlined in Chapter 7, were subjected to testing. The survey provided a broad overview of trends within a significant portion of the business services sector. This yielded valuable information and provided a context within which to set the in-depth case studies of individual firms which constituted the fourth stage of the research.

The choice of firms for case study research was informed by the survey results together with the availability of information on the firms and their willingness to participate in the research. The case studies were largely constructed from secondary sources including company annual reports and reviews, directory material, business services literature, press reports, trade papers and journals, confidential analysts reports and a host of other sources. These secondary sources were complimented by direct contact with the companies wherever possible. The case studies were useful in terms of confirming trends established from the postal survey, as well as providing detailed insights into the multinational development of business service firms. The four stages of the research process are summarised in Table 1.1.

The structure of the research methodology allowed the detailed exploration of the internationalisation of business service firms to be set within a broader frame of reference. The research concerns could be examined at the level of the market, both national and international, and at the level of the firm. Similarly, through the examination of the service sector, the business services sector, and the sub-sectors, the experience of the firms surveyed and studied in-depth could be contextualised. The review of literature provided an understanding of the wider environment within which the postal survey findings could usefully be interpreted. In turn these findings provide the context within which the case study research could be effectively analysed. Further consideration is given to the research methods in Chapter 7, where the postal survey is considered, and more generally in Appendix 1 where both the strengths and weaknesses of the methods utilised are discussed.

Having successfully completed the four stages of research it was possible to evaluate the framework for the internationalisation of service sector firms, developed from the review of theoretical literature, in the light of the experiences of business service firms. It must be recognised however that the business services sector is diverse, and that despite common features present among the sub-sectors studied there are also vast differences. Such diversity limits the extent to which a generally applicable framework may be developed. A less than complete

Table 1.1
Research strategy

Stage	Focus	Method
1	Internationalisation of services. Theoretical concerns: international trade; foreign direct investment; and organisational issues.	Review of theoretical and empirical literature.
2	Business service sector at an international and UK market level.	Literature survey and secondary data sources.
3	UK business service sector: sub-sector analysis.	Literature search, secondary data sources, interviews, and primary data generated by a postal survey.
4	Examination of the internationalisation of individual business service firms.	Literature and secondary data sources. Case study material gathered from primary and secondary sources.

framework is, however, a great improvement on no framework at all. It can be used as the foundation upon which future research may build.

1.4 The structure of the book

This introduction will be followed by Chapter 2 which will set the context of the research. Conceptual issues will be considered, in particular, the defining of services and international service transactions. The international significance of services in general, and business services in particular, will be revealed through the presentation of secondary data. The choice of the business services sector as the focus of the research will be elaborated upon.

An exploration of the relevant economic theory will be provided in the following two chapters. In Chapter 3, the theory of international transactions will be considered. The relevance of trade and FDI theories to the internationalisation of services and business services will be evaluated. In Chapter 4, the theory of the

6

firm, with particular attention being given to organisational theory, will be reviewed to assess its value in explaining the organisational structure of international service and business service firms.

This will be followed in Chapter 5 by the articulation of a framework within which to understand the internationalisation of service firms. This framework will draw on the theories explored in Chapters 3 and 4, together with the broad evidence presented in Chapter 2. Through this process of synthesis a more useful model for the appreciation the internationalisation of service firms will be developed.

Following on from this, Chapter 6 will provide a background to the internationalisation of the three business services sectors selected for in-depth study, namely: advertising; accountancy; and, computer services. An introduction to the UK business service sector is provided in Chapter 7 together with details of the development and operation of the postal survey, and a review of the survey sample. In Chapter 8 the results of the postal survey will be reported. Further support for these results is provided in Chapter 9 where the findings from case studies of six firms are considered. Particular attention is given to the organisational constraints within the internationalisation process. Chapter 10 will draw together the research findings from the previous two chapters. Moreover, the framework considered in Chapter 5 will be elaborated upon.

Finally, Chapter 11 will provide concluding comments, with consideration being given to the future of UK business services and the development of a theory for the internationalisation of service sector activity in general. Policy implications will be discussed and areas for future research will be outlined.

Note

1   These included discussions with the Advertising Association, the Institute of Practitioners in Advertising, the Computing Services Association and the Institute of Chartered Accountants in England and Wales.

2 Internationalisation of services: conceptual issues and evidence

2.1 Introduction

The purpose of this chapter is to investigate the internationalisation of the service sector, in general, and the business services sector in particular, through the examination of secondary information. The main data problems inherent in this analysis will be highlighted. The role of service transactions in international trade in goods will be considered, and an assessment of the significance of services as facilitators of global integration will be provided. Finally, the choice of the business services sector as the focus of this research will be discussed. However, prior to this it is necessary to address conceptual issues: firstly, how to define service sector activity; and secondly, to identify and classify international service transactions.

2.2 Defining services

The service sector includes a heterogeneous group of economic activities ranging from, for example, legal and banking services, to transport, communication, and cleaning services. It is only once the term services has been defined that it is possible to identify an international service transaction. There have been many attempts to characterise and classify services, a number of which will be reviewed in this section.

Early efforts to define services as a distinctive economic activity (Fischer, 1939; Clark, 1957) characterise them in terms of what they are not, rather than what they are. For example, Clark (1957) subdivides the economy into three categories, primary, secondary and a residual tertiary or service sector. A number of studies have identified the weaknesses of such a three sector typology (Browning and

8

Singelmann, 1975; Singelmann, 1978; Gershuny and Miles, 1983; Noyelle and Stanback, 1984; inter alia) and have proposed new classifications, which highlight the heterogeneity of the activities considered and categorise services into various subgroups. For example, Singelmann (1978) identifies consumer services, social services, producer services and distributive services. However such classifications remain based on Clark's fundamental distinction between primary, secondary and tertiary activities.

This definition of services by negation, is adopted in the International Standard Industrial Classification (ISIC) of all economic activities used in national income accounting. This approach, however, suffers from the defect that it defines a service as the output of non-manufacturing, non-mining and non-agricultural industry (Atinc et al., 1985). The point of reference is thus the nature of the industry rather than the nature of the output. Many manufacturing operations incorporate some service-related activities. For example, some large enterprises have their own internal units to provide services, such as computer or accounting departments. It seems, therefore, that statistical systems need to be refined to provide a more precise classification of economic activities with regard to their output. Castle and Findlay (1988) note that the residual definition is not helpful if we are seeking to understand how and why the structure of economic activity in society changes over time. For this purpose we need a definition of a more analytical nature, one which focus on general characteristics that seem significant rather than on sectoral descriptions.

An alternative method of defining the service sector is to concentrate on common features of industries as judged by the nature of their output. For example, a number of economists regard the service sector as comprising those industries with 'intangible' outputs. According to this definition, intangible outputs constitute the service and the industry producing them is therefore a service industry. While this may be a reasonable and useful description of a service activity, it fails to take account of certain industries whose tangible outputs are commonly regarded as being service related, for example, construction and publishing, (Atinc et al., 1985). Services, being intangible, have often been referred to as 'invisibles', although this may be confused by the fact that a service is often indistinguishable from the service provider who is visible (Nusbaumer, 1987a).

It is useful to make a distinction between goods and services, according to Hill (1977):

> A good may be defined as a physical object which is appropriated and, therefore, transferable between economic units.
>
> A service may be defined as a change in the condition of a person, or of a good belonging to some economic unit, which is brought about as the result of the activity of some other economic unit, with the prior agreement of the former person or economic unit. This definition .... is consistent with the underlying idea which is inherent

9

in the concept of a service, namely that one economic unit performs some activity for the benefit of another .... Whatever the producer of the service does must impinge directly on the consumer in such a way as to change the condition of the latter. Otherwise no service is actually provided (pp.317-18).

Three distinct characteristics of services can be drawn form Hill's analysis: firstly, services are consumed simultaneously with their production; secondly, services cannot be stored; and, thirdly, services are intangible. These features imply an extensive producer-consumer relationship, and consequently, have implications for the tradability of services.

With Hill's definition activities among the individuals comprising the household or within a firm, which relate to 'factor services', are a different type of transaction. For some analytical purposes a definition which included such activities would be appropriate, for example, when considering intra-firm service transactions. Furthermore, this perspective highlights the point that a service activity adds value to goods or other services belonging to other firms or other people (or to those people themselves).

If we take into account the impact of ICTs, then the characteristics of services defined by Hill are not universally applicable to all services. For example ICTs allow services to be separated both over time and space, with, for example, services being transferred across telecommunication networks or embodied in a tangible form such as a computer disk thus becoming storable.

In reality it is often difficult to distinguish between services and goods. Bhagwati (1984) talks of the 'splintering process' and the 'disembodiment effect' - as economies grow or change their structure, technical change and economies of scale interact to splinter services from goods and goods from services. Bhagwati (1984, p.139) notes that:

> With rapid technical change occurring in the information and communication networks, it seems increasingly clear now that the performance of a number of services, which would have required the physical presence of the provider of the service where they are used, is no longer critically dependent on physical presence. Traditionally, ... technical change in services has occasionally taken the form where this 'disembodiment' has taken the shape of the service in turn becoming embodied in goods, ... But we must increasingly contend with the fact that the disembodiment now takes place in a manner where services are simply 'transmitted over the wire' to the users.

'Splintering off' some activities shift out of the household or out of the firm into the market place and therefore come to be counted separately in various national accounting aggregates. What was formerly an in-house, legal or accounting, service

10

and hidden in goods production in the manufacturing sector is now bought from outside and identified as a service rather than a good (Castle and Findlay, 1988). It is important to note that the process also works in the opposite direction as firms expand through vertical integration. However, the growth in the 'externalisation' of service functions seems to be a part of a wider movement to new forms of economic organisation which are characterised by greater flexibility (Petit, 1986).

Nusbaumer (1987a) claims that the important thing about defining services is to see what economic functions they perform, and whether they may or may not be similar to the economic functions performed by goods. The frontier between services and goods tends to become increasingly blurred as manufactured products contain ever increasing amounts of services in the form of applied human capital and require more and more services to be used in the form of complementary software or staff training, maintenance and repairs. Many goods are an inextricable part of a total business deal which includes pre sale work in negotiating a contract, information and financing packages as well as after sales services. This sort of transaction certainly introduces severe measurement problems for domestic as well as international trade. Nusbaumer (1987a) suggests an alternative way to approach this increasing intermingling between material and non-material production is to speak of international trade as increasingly becoming trade in research and development (R&D) rather than trade in various kinds of commodities. This reflects the fact that an increasing proportion of the value added of traded goods consists of service products incorporated or embodied in those goods.

In the end, all production is geared to the final creation of utility at the individual or household level. What we call goods may be regarded simply as intermediates which produce a stream of services to households, and at least from that perspective, the distinction between the two is certainly blurred. At one level, all value added in an economy comes from services; that is, from factor services. Table 2.1 provides a classification of definitions, summarising the elements discussed above and also including additional definitions.

Such definitions as those given above are open to criticism, for example, Clairmonte and Cavanagh (1984) claim that they are analytically limited in that they embrace only formal economic aggregates, while ignoring corporate structures that in the last analysis are the providers and determinants of services. These definitions take no account of intra-firm service transactions, which in some areas account for a considerable proportion of international service transactions, in particular, 80-90 per cent of information service transactions are executed in this manner (Sauvant, 1986). Given that estimates suggest that the sales of the top 200 multinational corporations amount to more than one-third of world GDP (Clairmonte, 1986), definitions and classifications which fail to take this into account cannot reflect the reality of the economy. Thus, the changing relative importance of inter-firm and intra-firm transactions will have a major impact on the measurement of the value of goods and services, and this should be kept in mind

11

Table 2.1
Definitions of services: a classification

Defined By:	Proponents:
Sector: Tertiary/ Service Sector.	Fischer 1939; Clark 1957; Singlemann 1978; ISIC.
Characteristics of output: Intangible; Non-storable; Simultaneous consumption and production;	Hill 1977.
Invisible; Unproductive.	Balance of Payments Statistics. A.Smith; K.Marx.
Characteristics of production: Relatively low value of commodity content as intermediary input; High labour intensity; Low technological input.	Kravis 1983.
Economic function: Knowledge function; Linkage function; Communication function; Information function.	Nusbaumer 1987a.
Industry of origin/share of final demand.	Bhagwati 1984.
Degree of processing.	United Nations Standard International Trade Classifications.

when interpreting data (Stern and Hoekman, 1988; Clairmonte and Cavanagh, 1984).

It can be seen then, that many problems arise in any attempt to define services. Given the heterogeneous nature of the service sector it is not easy to provide a definition which will prove adequate for such a wide range of activities, indeed as Stigler wrote in 1956, "there exists no authoritative consensus on either boundaries or the classification of the services industries" (p.47). The above review of the existing approaches confirms the fact that there is still as yet no universally accepted theoretical framework for defining services.

With the progressive blurring of the distinction between services and goods, perhaps what is required is not an adequate definition of services but rather a reclassification of the whole production system. An alternative framework has been proposed by Bailly, Boulianne and Maillat (1987), which is founded upon the notion of the interdependence between services and goods production. This alternative framework should not necessarily replace the more traditional typologies but, rather, it provides a useful complementary approach for examining economic systems. This framework envisages a production system composed of a set of establishments, the principal role of each of which is to fulfil one of four major functions:

1 Fabrication: the transformation of raw materials or of semi-finished products.
2 Circulation: an intermediary role that facilitates the flow of material, of goods, of persons, of information, and of finances.
3 Distribution: the delivery of goods and services to the final demand sector.
4 Regulation: intervention in the operation of a production system so as to maintain, modify, regulate or control it.

Since the typology is based upon establishments rather than firms, the elements of a manufacturing firm that are not directly involved in fabrication are classed as performing circulation, distribution, or regulation functions. This establishment-based framework is well suited to analysing the structure and evolution of an economic system. It avoids many fundamental difficulties because it is not a simple reclassification of tertiary activities. It represents rather, a reconceptualisation of the notion of economic structure on the basis of the role of individual establishments in the production system. Moreover, by departing from the conventional forms of classification, this alternative typology emphasises the coherence of each activity in the context of the entire system.

It must be recognised that there are different ways of defining services the appropriateness of which will vary depending upon the purposes of the research being undertaken. Since the concern of this study is the internationalisation of the business services sector it is appropriate to use a definition which is relevant to transactions between economic units when referring to services provided by service firms to other firms, but also to define business services which are provided within one firm for another part of that firm. This is of particular relevance when considering intra-firm trade. It is important to be aware of the extent of service transactions, in particular business service transactions, which do occur within organisations. Given the heterogeneous nature of the service sector it may be futile to attempt to provide a general definition of services which will be of use to all the various activities which make up the sector. The most that can be achieved is to provide a list of common characteristics which represents the starting point from which all services may be defined with reference to a number of these common characteristics. This study focuses specifically on the business services sector hence attention will now turn to providing a useful definition of business services.

It is important to note at this point that business services are a part of the producer services sub-sector. Producer services[1] are those which are used ultimately by business firms and other productive enterprises. A great deal of the recent literature is concerned with producer services and stresses how a large portion of the recent growth of the service sector is accounted for by services directly or indirectly related to developments in production. Furthermore, producer services are increasingly recognised as a crucial element in economic development, as a factor that significantly influences the dynamics of growth, innovation diffusion, productivity increases and competitiveness across firms, sectors and regions (Marshall et al., 1987, 1988; Daniels, 1991; Perry, 1991; inter alia).

Business services are extremely diverse, including activities concerned both with handling tangible products, such as, machinery repair or catering, and with providing intangible expertise such as accountancy, market research or management consultancy. The range of activities falling under the title of business services can be seen from an examination of the ISIC, where business services are grouped within division 83 (Appendix 2).

Given the rapid development of the business services sector over the last 25 years it is useful to explore other definitions of the sector. Many business services are new and others are changing rapidly or evolving from other activities, thus difficulties arise in any attempt to provide an accurate definition of the sector. There is also the problem of the overlap between different business services. The business services included in a reference list of industries considered under the Uruguay Round of GATT trade negotiations are listed in Table 2.2. Again a diverse range of activities can be seen. The central characteristic of business services is that they are services purchased primarily by other producers, for use in further rounds of production (UNCTC, 1990). In addition, business services include a mix of activities some restricted to licensed professionals and others open to all.

Martinelli (1991) defines business services as a category which:

> ... groups all those services that are clearly directed to other firms, whether they operate in agriculture, manufacturing or other services: financial services, insurance, research and development, legal services, accounting and fiscal services, management consulting, engineering, architectural and other technical services, marketing services, advertising and public relations, electronic data processing (EDP) and related services, training services, photocopying and related services, special secretarial services, cleaning and security services (p.21).

14

Table 2.2
Business services included in proposed reference list of industries

Rental/leasing of equipment without crew
Transport: cars, trucks, aircraft, ships etc.
Non-transport: computers, construction/demolition etc.

Real estate service (not including rental of land)
Involving owned or leased property on a fee or contract basis (for example, property valuation, estate management, etc.)

Installation and assembly work (other than construction)

Maintenance and repair of equipment (not including fixed structures)

Services incidental to manufacturing

Professional services (including consulting)
Agricultural, forestry and fishing services
Mining and oil-field services
Legal services
Accounting and taxation services
Management and administrative services
Architectural services
Advertising
Market research and opinion-polling
Surveying and exploration services
Advisory and consultative engineering services
Industrial engineering
Engineering design services
Project management services
Urban planning services
Interior design services
R&D, laboratories, testing and certification
Computer-related services (including hardware-related consulting, installation, data processing, etc.)
Software development (including software implementation)
Travel agents and tour operators
Economic and behavioural research
Labour recruitment and provision of personnel
Investigation and security activities
Public relations services
Photographic services
Miscellaneous professional services

Business services not included elsewhere
Biotechnology services
Cleaning of building and similar activities
Packaging activities
Waste disposal and processing
Translation services
Exhibition management services
Printing and publishing
Other

Source: Uruguay Round, Group of Negotiations on Services, Reference list of sectors: note by the Secretariat (MTN.GNS/W/50, 13 April 1989), p.4.

15

Though this definition would appear to be valid it is important to note that firms which provide such services may also be providing the same services for final consumption. For example, a firm of lawyers may have both corporate and individual clients, as also might a public relations firm or an accountancy practice.

Martinelli (1991) goes on to argue that

> ... the growth of business services is most clearly related to the development of the productive system and its demand. The supply is largely private, either by firms or self-employed professionals. ... the amount of fixed investment required to carry out these services is generally lower than in distributive infrastructure, where as human capital and information are more crucial factors (p.21).

The focus of this research is on those business services which are information intensive, specifically advertising, accountancy and computer services and to a lesser extent management consultancy, public relations and market research services. These services have a number of common characteristics: the need for personal contact between producer and client; the importance of quality and reputation; a long term buyer/seller relationship; human capital and information intensiveness; and, the need for cultural sensitivity. In most business services local knowledge of regulatory and market characteristics may provide a considerable advantage to local suppliers. Additionally, the impact of new ICTs may have a major impact on both the production and delivery of such services, and indeed, upon the manner in which such service firms become international service providers. The three main sub-sectors will be explored in detail in Chapter 6.

2.3 International service transactions

International service transactions may take a variety of different forms. There have been many attempts to classify these various types of transactions (Sapir and Lutz, 1980, 1981; UNCTAD, 1983; Atinc et al., 1985; GATT, 1985; Sampson and Snape, 1985; Grubel, 1987; Stern and Hoekman, 1987; Vandermerwe and Chadwick, 1989; inter alia). A number of these studies will be reviewed in this section.

Sampson and Snape (1985) developed a classification system based on how and where the services are produced and traded. A 'residential' concept of national income is adopted - thus an international transaction is a transaction between the residents of one country and a resident of another. The transaction may take place entirely within one country. It is worth examining the four categories of international trade in services distinguished by Sampson and Snape (1985). Firstly, transactions may occur without the movement of factors of production or the receiver of the service, for example, consulting services, life assurance business and architectural design, which are handled through correspondence and produced in the exporting country. These are referred to as 'separated' services for they are separated from both factors of production and receivers. Secondly, transactions may occur as a consequence of the movement of factors of production, but not of the receiver of the service, for example, services produced by guest workers - construction teams, and services of imported financial capital. Thirdly, transactions may occur with the movement of the receiver of the service, but not of the provider, for example, tourism. Fourthly, transactions may occur with the movement of both factors of production and the receiver of the service, that is the transaction occurs in a third country, for example, where a surgeon and a patient meet in a third country. In their analysis, Sampson and Snape do not recognise that some services are not transacted internationally, they also fail to identify services provided through contractual relationships.

As a result of technological progress in telecommunications and international computer links, international transactions in some services may take more than one of the above forms. This is particularly so when the flow of information is an important feature of the service, as in the case of international banking, insurance, and telecommunications services (Atinc et al., 1985). As Bhagwati (1984) notes, the electronic transfer of information is enabling the separation of provider and receiver to develop rapidly. For some services such separation has existed for many years, for example, the design of bridges. Even with the use of new ICTs trade in services may require FDI in order to provide a delivery system for the services.

Grubel (1987) argues that services can cross international borders only if they are embodied in either material substances or people. It might be asked whether electronic signals are the exception? According to Grubel they are not, all international trade involving electronics results in the crossing of borders by material signals that in principle are recordable and measurable, much like books, letters and floppy disks.

Mobility provides the focus for Stern and Hoekman's (1987) classification of international service transactions. That is, whether the movement of the provider and demander of the service is required between countries. This allows the issues in services to be addressed in the context of international trade theory. Briefly, the four categories identified by Stern and Hoekman (1987) are as follows:

1 No movement of providers or demanders (separated services).
2 Movement of providers only (demander located services).
3 Movement of demanders only (provider located services).
4 Movement of providers and demanders (foot loose, non-separated services).

Each type of transaction can be further divided by distinguishing services that are related to goods, from services that are independent of goods.

One of the most useful classifications of international service transactions is that forwarded by UNCTAD (1983), which identifies five different types of transaction. These are:

> First, some services are provided and consumed by residents of a country and do not enter into the international market place. Second, other services are provided within national boundaries, but to non-residents. Third, some services are provided by resident firms or individuals across their national boundaries to non-resident firms or individuals abroad. Fourth, other services are provided through contractual relationships. Fifth, many services are provided through overseas affiliates of a parent company. In addition, several services can be provided to foreign markets either through direct export or through overseas affiliates (UNCTAD, 1983, p.6).

Atinc et al. (1984) appear to favour this definition using the last four categories in their own exploration of the internationalisation of services. In contrast to the above definition Sapir (1985) identifies only two categories of international service transaction: "International transactions in services result from either trade or foreign investment activity" (p.29).

A useful classification system of international service transactions is provided by Vandermerwe and Chadwick (1989) which is based upon two axes. These are: firstly, 'relative involvement of goods', that is, pure service/low on goods, services with some goods, or delivered through goods and services embodied in goods; secondly, 'degree of consumer/producer interaction' from lower to higher. This two way classification produces a six sector matrix within which services tend to cluster. Three main clusters are identified which relate to the internationalisation modes of: exporting; franchising, licensing, joint ventures or similar; and, wholly owned subsidiary. The value of this classification system lies in the way it links certain critical service characteristics with modes of internationalisation.

Bailly, Coffey, Paelinck and Polese (1992) provide a model for inter-regional trade in services, developed from their study of inter-regional trade in Canada. It highlights the importance of intra-firm trade within service producing firms, as well as intra-firm service trade within primary sector and manufacturing firms. Moreover, the interlinks between services and goods trade are recognised. This model can then be usefully applied to international trade in services.

Additional forms of international transactions can be identified when exploring individual services sectors, for example, Aaronvitch and Samson (1985, pp.152-3) determine seven types of international service transactions in relation to insurance. These are:

1   Branch establishment.

2   Establishment of subsidiaries registered in the host country as legal entities.
3   Equity stakes in foreign countries whether simply as 'trade investments' or to exercise some degree of influence or control. Such a stake may also be a prelude to a takeover bid.
4   Joint ventures such as Concorde-Minerve in Belgium or Norwich-Winterturn UK.
5   Collaborative/co-operative arrangements, such as AREA, UNISON or Campanie l'International d'Assurances et de Reassurance.
6   Correspondents or agencies. All major companies have a substantial network or correspondence and agents, frequently brokers and broking groups.
7   Underwriting business in other countries from home base to the degree that is possible or allowed.

The diversity found among the above definitions of international service transactions indicate the complexity of such transactions. It would therefore seem to be necessary to examine all service sectors individually in order to ascertain all the various types of international service transactions, a task which is beyond the scope of this study. However, when the internationalisation of specific business service sectors are considered later, there will be an attempt to distinguish the various methods through which such international service transactions occur. For now though it is possible to summarise international service transactions into: firstly, those which are non-traded; secondly, those which are traded; and thirdly, those which involve factor movements (Table 2.3).

Not all services are provided through every mechanism. Castle and Findlay (1988) claim that services consumed by households tend to be provided by FDI or through the movement of the consumer. Producer or intermediate services are provided through the movement of the service provider, which may or may not involve a permanent base in the consuming country. Data on the relative importance of FDI in services as compared to other forms of service exchange reveals that the FDI mechanism is by far the more important vehicle for delivery of services to foreign purchasers for the developed market economies. It is 1½ times as important as sales from the home base ('service exports') for these countries, which account for over 80 per cent of total service exports and over 90 percent of total sales by foreign service affiliates (Sauvant, 1986). For the developing countries, sales of services by exports are much more important than sales through affiliates.

For business services pure cross border trade means the provision of a service by, for example, a letter, a report, a telephone conversation, computer to computer transfer of electronic information via a telecommunications network, software on a disk or similar means. In practice, however, business services are rarely transacted in this fashion alone, (that is apart from intra-firm trade), but more often in

19

Table 2.3
International service transactions: a classification

1. Non-traded services:

Provided solely to country's permanent residents e.g. certain government services.

2. Traded services:

a) Market trade in 'separated', 'embodied' or 'over the wire' services.

b) Investment related: (i) market trade - with local support services; (ii) intra-firm trade.

c) Contractual arrangements associated with fees, royalties and licensing agreements (export of intangible assets or rights).

d) Purchase by foreign individuals or companies of services in the home country.

3. Factor movement related international service transactions:

a) Personnel travelling overseas:(i) temporary project work; (ii) permanent.

b) FDI in branches or subsidiaries.

c) Joint ventures or equity stake.

d) Franchising.

e) Movement of provider and purchaser to a third country.

conjunction with other methods. The cross border movement of consumers or factors of production are necessary. For a number of services the movement of the consumer is not an option. Most of these services are knowledge and skill intensive rather than capital intensive. The competitive advantage of such firms are rooted mostly in intangible assets such as human capital, firm specific experience and accumulated technological information, or goodwill. Thus internationalisation will frequently necessitate the movement, (temporary or permanent), of highly skilled professional staff abroad. Given that the firm's assets are primarily incorporated in personnel the costs of setting up a presence overseas are relatively low when

20

compared to a firm in the manufacturing sector. All that is required is an office to accommodate the appropriate personnel.

A study produced in 1985 by the Office of Technology Assessment of the US congress (Washington DC 1986 "Trade in Services: Exports and Foreign Revenues", quoted in UNCTC, 1990, p.156) suggests that with the exception of legal services, US business service firms service foreign markets primarily through foreign affiliates. This results from a combination of technological, economic and regulatory factors. Firstly, despite the application of new ICT, much of the process of production in business services remains embedded in the direct relationship between client and producer. Secondly, whereas in some cases business services can be rendered indifferently through the movement of customers or that of the producers, in others the producer has no choice but to move to the customers location. Thirdly, in a world in which attention to quality, service and local tastes has become a formidable competitive weapon, business services producers simply are unable to compete as effectively as they should, unless they have people deployed in the market place. Finally, certain forms of international transactions, not only pure cross border trade, but also transactions based on the temporary movement of professionals, are at times not possible, simply for regulatory reasons. For example, most countries do not allow auditors from other countries to practice locally, unless they have gained relevant local qualifications (UNCTC, 1990).

Furthermore, Noyelle and Dutka (1988, p.53) identify restrictions impeding the international expansion of business service firms in the following areas: local ownership and rights of establishment; international payment transfers; the mobility of personnel; technology transfer; transborder data flow; procurement policies; restrictions on the business scope of firms; and restrictions on the use of the firm's name. Thus it can be seen that when considering the methods of service internationalisation it is important to explore not only what is possible from a practical perspective, but also what is feasible given market competitive conditions and regulation. The regulation of investment and migration are important influences since much internationalisation is brought about through the movement of capital or people.

2.4 The extent of service and business service internationalisation

Data difficulties

Prior to an examination of the extent of service internationalisation it is necessary to highlight the problems which exist with the available data (UNCTC, 1990; Stern and Hoekman, 1987; Ascher and Whichard, 1986; inter alia). The first of these derives from the difficulties inherent in defining services, which of their nature create problems for the measurement of the service sector. The systems of measurement most commonly used tend to measure services as a residual factor, consequently, there can safely be said to be under-accounting. Further under-accounting occurs since services provided in the home and within organisations, together with those provided in the black economy, are not measured, activities in these areas tend to be more service than manufacturing orientated.

The second problem concerns the difficulty of measuring international transactions in services. In contrast to goods, services are usually intangible and are thus difficult to measure. For example, customs agents typically cannot observe flows of services across the frontier, since they are usually embodied in an information flow, a person, or a good. Difficulties also arise in the measuring of output in the service sector, for example, output often has to be measured in terms of inputs. Problems therefore arise in determining the service sector's share in total output as well as total output itself. Moreover, the blurring of the distinction between goods and services introduces severe measurement problems for domestic as well as international service transactions.

The third problem relates to the reliability of data. Existing procedures for the classification and collection of statistics were designed chiefly for goods, reflecting the fact that until recently there was no great demand for tracking the development of service sector activities. Carter (1987) notes further measurement problems introduced by the degree of aggregation used in compiling official statistics because of, to some extent, the slowness to appreciate the nature of the structural changes occurring in economies, but also because the conceptual basis for gathering statistical data remains rather confused for many countries. As a result, both cross country and cross time comparisons must be treated with caution. Over time technological changes and increasing specialisation associated with economic growth may lead to the creation of new services that are not captured in existing classification systems. There is also the process of internalisation and externalisation of services by both firms and households which leads to some services no longer being registered in the national accounts while others are added to the figures.

When considering international transactions it is necessary to consider factor movements, this gives rise to a fourth problem. Global data on FDI are poor, and country data, if reported at all, are usually at a high level of aggregation. The basis for FDI figures varies widely, and statistics are usually not readily comparable across countries. Furthermore, since information on the sectoral breakdown of employment of foreign workers is not available, it is impossible to ascertain the movement of labour associated with the cross border delivery of services.

The pattern of service internationalisation

GATT (1994, p.2) estimated the value of commercial services exports to have been $1,020 billion in 1993, compared to merchandise exports valued at $3,640 billion. Commercial services accounted for almost 22 per cent of total world exports in that year. It is also interesting to note the strong growth in commercial services exports

22

compared to growth in merchandise exports (Table 2.4). Both sectors experienced a slowdown in 1993, although trade in commercial services continued to grow marginally faster than merchandise trade. A breakdown by sector for the ten largest traders of commercial services for which data are available, indicate moderate decreases in the export of transportation and travel services which are, however, offset by a rise in other services (comprising communications, financial services, insurance and business services; GATT, 1994, p.2).

Hoekman (1990, p.34) examining the relative importance of the components of private services in world trade for 1987 found that exports of transport services and expenditures by travellers in host countries each made up somewhat less than one-third of global private service credits. The remainder was a mix of business and professional services, construction, and exports of labour and intangible property, such as know-how and trademarks. Industrial nations dominate credit flows associated with sales of intangible property, which largely consist of fees for licensing and franchising arrangements, trademarks, and technology. These countries also have a much larger share in world credit flows associated with the temporary movement of labour. It is widely assumed that industrial countries generally register surpluses in trade in invisibles and that developing countries tend to run deficits, such generalisations can be misleading. For example, in 1987 roughly four out of ten developing economies registered a surplus or were in approximate balance - a figure not much different from that for developed countries (Hoekman, 1990, pp.37-9). A breakdown of exports and imports of commercial services by selected region and economy for the years 1983-93, provided by GATT (1994, p.102), shows that 70 per cent of these world exports derive from North America and Western Europe whilst these same areas account for 65 per cent of world imports of commercial services. Clearly, then the majority of world trade in commercial services occurs between developed countries. In Table 2.5 the top 20 countries are ranked by their level of exports and imports of commercial services in 1993. It is interesting to note that these 20 countries accounted for 78.3 per cent of exports and 79.5 per cent of imports of commercial services in that year. In addition, the UK is a major contributor to international trade in services being the fifth largest exporter of services and the sixth largest importer.

Since a commercial presence of the foreign provider in the country of the consumer may be a precondition for the provision of services, and a temporary or long term movement of factors of production may be necessary, it is essential to examine the level of factor movements associated with international service transactions. Since sector specific data is unavailable on the cross border movement of labour, attention here is focused on FDI data. As of the mid-1980s about 40 per cent of the world stock of FDI and approximately 50 per cent of the annual (new) flow of FDI was in services (Sauvant and Zimney, 1987). In countries that reported data, FDI in services has almost invariably become more important over time. The distinguishing characteristics of service provision are probably one of the driving forces underlying this increase. Because physical proximity is often a

Table 2.4
Growth in the value of world exports by major product group 1985-93
(Billion dollars and percentage)

	Value	Average annual change			
	1993	1985-90	1991	1992	1993
I. World merchandise exports[a]	3640	12.3	1.5	6.3	-0.4
Agricultural products	438	10.1	1.1	6.8	-2.1
Mining products	433	2.5	-5.0	-1.8	-2.7
Manufactures	2668	15.5	3.0	7.9	0.1
II. World exports of commercial services	1020	...	5.5	12.5	0.5

[a] Including unspecified products.
Note: The statistics for commercial services and for merchandise trade are not directly comparable because (i) the country coverage of available data on commercial services trade is less comprehensive than that for merchandise trade, and (ii) the data on commercial services are subject to other sources of (primarily downward) bias.

Source: GATT (1994, p.2).

necessary condition for provision, FDI of some sort may be required. The increase in the relative importance of FDI in services occurs in both industrial and developing economies, although the increase is more marked for the former. Much of the services FDI in developing countries is related either to investment in offshore financial centres and tax havens or to investment in flags of convenience. Even when these are excluded, however, the share of services in total FDI rises in these countries (UNCTC, 1988).

In the case of services the motivation for foreign investment is usually the ability to provide a service with a view to satisfying local demand, rather than to provide a base for re-export. Kravis and Lipsey (1988) have shown that the export propensity of US service affiliates is quite low. Data on the sectoral composition of FDI in service activities is limited. According to UNCTC (1993, p.78) finance and trade-related activities account for two thirds of the stock of FDI within the service sector for developed countries and the majority of the stock in many host developing countries. Table 2.6 shows the sectoral distribution of outward direct capital

Table 2.5

Leading exporters and importers of world trade in commercial services 1993 (Billion dollars and percentages)

Rank	Exporter	Value	Share	Annual change	Rank	Importer	Value	Share	Annual change
1	United States	169.9	16.7	4	1	United States	116.4	11.8	9
2	France	101.3	9.9	-2	2	Germany	111.9	11.3	-3
3	Germany	61.7	6.0	-8	3	Japan	100.7	10.2	3
4	Italy[a]	57.6	5.7	...	4	France	83.0	8.4	-2
5	United Kingdom	53.5	5.2	-5	5	Italy[a]	57.2	5.8	...
6	Japan	53.2	5.2	7	6	United Kingdom	44.4	4.5	-5
7	Netherlands	37.0	3.6	1	7	Netherlands	35.9	3.6	-2
8	Belgium-Luxembourg[a]	36.7	3.6	...	8	Belgium-Luxembourg[a]	32.3	3.3	...
9	Spain	31.7	3.1	-12	9	Canada	27.1	2.7	1
10	Austria	29.7	2.9	-1	10	Chinese Taipei	21.3	2.2	11
11	Hong Kong	28.9	2.8	16	11	Austria	21.1	2.1	6
12	Singapore	20.8	2.0	11	12	Spain	19.3	1.9	-13
13	Switzerland	19.7	1.9	0	13	Switzerland	16.8	1.7	-6
14	Canada	16.7	1.6	3	14	Korea, Rep. of	16.5	1.7	13
15	Korea, Rep. of	15.4	1.5	20	15	Hong Kong	16.0	1.6	13
16	Mexico	14.3	1.4	6	16	Saudi Arabia[b]	14.8	1.5	9
17	Chinese Taipei	13.1	1.3	23	17	Norway	13.9	1.4	-6
18	Denmark	12.8	1.3	-14	18	Sweden[a]	13.3	1.3	-30
19	Norway	12.6	1.2	-6	19	Australia	13.1	1.3	-5
20	Sweden	12.4	1.2	-23	20	Singapore	11.5	1.2	14
	Total of above	799.1	78.3	-		Total of above	786.7	79.5	-
	World	1020.0	100.0	1		World	990.0	100.0	0

[a] GATT Secretariat estimates.
[b] Refers to 1992 data.

Note: When considering the ranking of the countries, it should be kept in mind that data are not always fully comparable across countries.

Source: Complied from GATT (1994, p.9).

Table 2.6
Industrial distribution of outward direct capital stock for selected countries in the late 1980s (percentages)

	Developed countries							Developing countries				
	Canada (1989)	France[a] (1989)	Germany (1989)	Italy (1989)	Japan[b] (1989)	UK (1987)	US (1989)	China[c] (1988)	Colombia (1988)	India (1988)	Korea[d] (1989)	Thailand (1989)
Primary	6.4	13.4	2.7	8.2	6.7	27.0	16.7	26.0	3.7	3.1	42.3	0.3
Agriculture	neg	0.2	0.4	0.3	0.7	1.0	0.1	10.2	3.0	3.1	9.1	0.2
Mining & quarrying	6.5	neg	0.5	neg	6.0	nsa	1.3	8.4	0.6	neg	33.3	0.1
Oil	neg	13.2	1.8	7.9	neg	26.0	15.3	nsa	nsa	neg	neg	neg
Secondary	51.6	39.9	41.7	33.6	26.0	34.3	41.0	45.0	17.8	81.7	32.8	17.4
Food & drink products	6.1	7.7	0.6	2.2	1.3	6.8	4.9	1.1	15.4	3.8	4.5	13.1
Chemicals & allied products	7.2	6.7	15.6	8.8	3.4	9.4	9.5	1.2	nsa	21.2	2.3	0.2
Metals	16.1	9.2	2.3	2.3	3.5	0.7	2.2	12.1	0.1	13.0	11.3	0.3
Mechanical engineering	nsa	1.5	4.0	6.3	2.6	1.6	7.1	0.2	0.5	6.4	0.4	neg
Electrical & electronic goods	nsa	5.4	6.9	nsa	5.8	3.8	3.1	4.4	nsa	1.3	2.2	0.1
Motor vehicles	nsa	2.5	6.1	2.6	3.5	1.1	5.9	neg	nsa	nsa	1.4	nsa
Textiles, clothing & leather goods	nsa	0.8	1.0	1.1	1.3	nsa	0.5	4.6	0.1	15.5	6.8	neg
Paper products	11.7	1.1	0.9	nsa	1.1	2.9	2.3	0.6	0.7	11.5	nsa	3.6
Rubber products	nsa	0.5	1.3	nsa	nsa	nsa	1.7	0.4	0.9	1.2	nsa	neg

26

Table 2.6 continued.

	Canada (1989)	France[a] (1989)	Germany (1989)	Italy (1989)	Japan[b] (1989)	UK (1987)	US (1989)	China[c] (1988)	Colombia (1988)	India (1988)	Korea[d] (1989)	Thailand (1989)
Coal & petroleum products	7.0	nsa	0.1	nsa	nsa	nsa	3.5	0.2	nsa	1.9	nsa	neg
Other manufacturing	3.5	4.5	2.9	11.3	3.5	nsa	2.8	20.2	0.1	5.9	3.9	0.1
Tertiary	42.0	46.7	55.6	58.2	67.0	38.6	42.3	29.0	77.8	15.3	24.9	82.3
Construction	nsa	1.8	0.4	nsa	0.8	1.8	0.3	2.7	0.2	1.2	3.4	0.1
Transportation & communication	2.1	1.3	0.9	0.8	6.0	2.1	0.8	3.7	nsa	nsa	0.3	3.5
Trade & distribution	4.8	5.2	19.6	7.2	9.9	9.0	11.7	5.6	3.4	1.9	9.4	2.0
Real estate	nsa	4.4	9.7	nsa	13.7	nsa	0.7	1.5	2.0	2.7	2.8	neg
Finance & insurance	27.6	26.1	17.9	44.7	22.6	13.4	26.5	nsa	67.5	nsa	nsa	77.1
Other services	7.5	7.9	7.1	5.5	14.0	12.3	2.3	15.5	4.7	9.5	9.0	-3.2
Total	100.0	100.0	100.0	100.0	100.0	100.0	100.0	100.0	100.0	100.0	100.0	100.0
Value national currencies	$C	FF	DM	L	$	£	$	Yuan	$	R	Won	B
(billion)	79.9	433.1	206.6	63407	253.9	86.7	380.0	1.7	0.37	1.2	765.6	6.6

[a] Cumulative direct investment flows since 1972. [b] Cumulative direct investment flows since 1951.
[c] Cumulative direct investment flows since 1979. [d] Cumulative direct investment flows since 1962.
nsa not separately available. neg negligible.
Source: Compiled from Dunning (1993a, pp.30-31).

stock for selected countries in the late 1980s. It can be seen that 38.6 per cent of UK FDI was in the service sector in 1987 and 12.3 per cent of FDI in the 'other services' category which includes business services.

A significant portion of the stock of existing FDI in services reflects the establishment of service affiliates by firms whose primary activity is industrial in nature. In large part these investments are directed towards financial and distribution-related activities and are intended to support production and sales by parent firms. Thus, much of the investment in finance and distribution is not independent. In the US, for example, whilst 49 per cent of the total stock of FDI in 1989 was in services only 22 per cent of the total stock of FDI was controlled by service sector MNEs. Similarly, for the Federal Republic of Germany in 1990 the figures were 56 per cent and 46 per cent respectively (UNCTC, 1993, p.78). Presumably this indicates that services required by the MNEs involved are not available abroad, are of insufficient quality, or are too costly. Furthermore, they are either not tradable separately or are too costly to trade. It would be interesting to know the relative roles of barriers to trade, market structure, and technological constraints in this regard. For industries such as retail banking, distribution, and hotels and restaurants FDI will clearly be required if services are to be provided. For other services national regulations may require establishment; insurance is a typical example. The pattern of international trade and production will be, in part, a function of the incentives and disincentives created by national governments, tax regimes and performance requirements are prime examples.

Turning now to the extent of internationalisation in the business services sector, for 1987 the world revenues for accounting and auditing, management consulting, software and data processing and advertising (measured in billings) were estimated, respectively, at $50-60 billion, $80-90 billion, $100-120 billion and $215 billion (UNCTC, 1990, p.144). In many business services industries the US market accounts for half or more of the world market in percentage shares. However, since the mid 1980s the market for business services has typically grown faster outside than within the US. It should also be noted that the growth in business services is no longer overwhelmingly concentrated in the advanced economies, as was once the case. There is considerable evidence that business services have already taken on a central role in the economy of many developing countries. Also, as noted earlier, some business services are as large if not larger than many of the merchandise industries discussed in the Uruguay GATT Round (UNCTC, 1990).

Growth in recent years has not been evenly distributed among business services, for example, advertising increased by 45 per cent in the US between 1983-7, whilst computer software and data processing increased by over 70 per cent in the same period. Such increases explain why business service firms in some of the relatively slower growing industries, such as auditing and advertising have sought to diversify into faster growing ones, respectively, management consultancy and computer software services, and public relations and direct marketing (UNCTC, 1990, p.145).

As GATT (1994, p.2) notes worldwide exports of business services are increasing. For the twelve members of the European Union (EU) up to 1995, exports of business services[2] to the rest of the world increased from a value of Ecu 7,392 million in 1983 to Ecu 11,915 million in 1992, an increase of 61 per cent on the 1983 figure (EUROSTAT, 1994, p.16). Business services also increased their share of total EU exports in this period. For the US exports of business services to the rest of the world rose from Ecu 2,972 million in 1986 to Ecu 6,733 million in 1992, an increase of over 126 per cent on the 1986 figure (EUROSTAT, 1994, p.86). Between 1986 and 1992 business services more than doubled their share of total US exports.

Although the internationalisation of business service firms dates from the late nineteenth century and early 1900s, this phenomenon has clearly gained speed and magnitude during the 1970s and 1980s. UNCTC (1990) identify this international expansion as resulting from both demand and supply driven forces. With the increasing globalisation of economic activity, business service firms have come under growing pressure to follow their multinational clients; this accounts for the demand driven internationalisation. As the market for their services has widened to include a growing number of medium and small size business customers, however, business service firms have felt under increasing pressure to expand their presence in many countries, partly in order to generate the scale economies needed to bring down the costs of their services, and in turn, to make them attractive to a wider base of customers. In this respect the multinational expansion of business services can be seen as supply driven, in the sense that firms have sought to reach out to a wider, and thus domestic rather than a multinational, client base.

In addition, UNCTC (1990) highlights a number of factors which have driven the development of major business services. These include: a search for new and greater economies of scale, which has resulted from the application of new ICTs; a search for greater economies of scope; the opportunity to leverage further the business name and reputation of the firm by diversifying into new areas; a search for exclusive access to privileged information, (to make it costly for clients to change suppliers by increasing the opportunity cost of such changes); and, the desire to raise costs of entry for potential competitors. The strategy used to reach those goals involves the creation of special linkages, both geographical and institutional, that encourage clients to use an ever expanding diversity of business services from the same supplier, while making it costly for them to switch over to competitors or to multiply the number of their suppliers. Together these factors have helped in the formation of large multinational firms in the sector. Although, as highlighted earlier, FDI in the service sector is dominated by financial and distributive activities, FDI in business services is increasing. The impact of this growth, however, is limited since firms in this sector tend to be relatively small and are generally skilled labour intensive as opposed to capital intensive. Moreover, in certain sub-sectors multinational expansion occurs through mechanisms other than FDI.

It is often claimed that services provide the 'oil' of the economy. It is important, therefore, to examine the growing significance of services as a facilitator of economic integration. It is estimated that the contribution of the service sector to world value added was about $13,000 billion in 1986 (Hoekman, 1990, pp.42-3), of this total government services accounted for 15 per cent, distribution accounted for 13 per cent, business services for 10 per cent, construction for 7 per cent, transport for 5 per cent, and finance for 4 per cent. It is important to note that some 36 per cent of the service sector contribution to world value added was goods related.

Distribution and communication services have always been fundamental to the operations of the world economy, providing the infrastructures through which goods are transacted across national borders. With developments in ICTs this function is becoming more complex. However, the role of services is not confined to the operation of a global infrastructure. In particular, business services are a significant contributor to world value added. They have come to play a key role in the competitive process. Trade in these services has been one of the most dynamic components of trade in invisibles, and is consequently of great current policy interest. It is clear that services have a role, not only as a facilitator of trade in goods, but also, in determining the international competitiveness of goods.

2.5 The value and significance of business services

The business services sector has been selected as the focus of this study for a number of reasons. Firstly, business services account for a significant and increasing portion of service sector activity in terms of both output and employment. The Commission of the European Community (1988) estimate that business services account for about 5 per cent of the GDP of the European Union and that their output makes up 5-10 per cent of all intermediate inputs into the productive branches of the economy. In the US, during the period 1982-87, employment in business and professional services and legal services (which together accounted for 20 per cent of service employment) grew at 6 per cent or more a year; employment in services in general grew at about 3 per cent per annum and employment in the goods producing sector at 2-5 per cent per annum (Sinai and Drury, 1988). In four other industrial economies (Belgium, France, Federal Republic of Germany and Sweden) employment growth rates in business services were 25 per cent or more during the period from 1979 to 1986, as against growth rates of 10 per cent or less in total employment (UNCTC, 1990, p.143).

Secondly, as demonstrated above, the importance of business services in international trade and investment is increasing. In addition, business services clearly have an important role in the competitiveness of other sectors of the economy since they have an impact on the economic performance of their clients (O'Farrell and Moffat, 1995a). Thirdly, then, there is the function of business services in the economy. The growth of the sector can be seen as the result of both, the externalisation of service activities, and, the growth in services which add to industrial activity, for example, R & D or design services. Furthermore, the growth of economic activity in general also stimulates business services sector expansion.

Growth resulting from externalisation can be seen as part of the changes in economic activity, that is, the move from huge industrial concerns towards more flexible organisations as firms refocus their activities on core areas. The transition from Fordist production systems typified by mass production towards the Post Fordist or Neo Fordist systems of production is characterised by the adoption of such features as small batch production, Just In Time (JIT) and lean production systems (Aglietta, 1979; Scott, 1988). The result has been the emergence of more flexible firms, part of this flexibility being achieved by the externalisation of service activities (Petit, 1986; Perry, 1992).

Fourthly, business services are information intensive in their nature. They lend themselves to the application of new ICTs, which may be used to achieve growth, efficiency and internationalisation. ICT has perhaps had less of an impact in terms of making services more tradable than in terms of facilitating the easier management of diverse geographically located subsidiaries. Although, new ICTs do enable the exportation of business services in the traditional sense, this does not appear to be occurring in any major way, that is, there has not been a wholesale shift towards exports of information intensive business services. This is perhaps due to the importance of personal contact and customisation of the service at the point of delivery. As technologies develop there may be an increasing use of exportation. At present a great deal of international trade in the business service sector would appear to take the form of intra-firm trade, however, unfortunately there are no accurate figures for this type of trade.

The development of certain technologies has proved to be an important factor accounting for the growth of the business services sector. For example, the increased use of computers has given rise to economies of scale in the production of information intensive services. As a result, business service firms are able to provide services at increasingly competitive prices. Thus business services are fundamental to the competitiveness of other sectors of the economy. They not only, for example, facilitate trade in goods, but they are a factor influencing the international competitiveness of a country's manufacturing sector.

Finally, the business services sector is highly regulated in many countries making local knowledge very important, and, also reducing the ability to provide such services internationally. There are then barriers to both trade and investment in this sector. Changes in the regulatory environment may give rise to increased internationalisation. Regulation or differences in regulation will, in many cases, be an important factor determining the competitive advantage of countries in the provision of such services.

2.6 Conclusion

This chapter has provided the context against which the study of the internationalisation of the UK business services sector may be set. The internationalisation of the service sector in general, and the business services sector in particular have been explored. Problems have been identified with regard to defining services with a variety of alternative approaches being considered. The difficulty of separating service from non-service activities, as the distinction between the two becomes increasingly blurred, has been highlighted. Classifying international service transactions also presents difficulties. Drawing on earlier efforts to analyse cross border service activity a classification of international service transactions has been presented (Table 2.3).

The internationalisation of services and business services has been examined using secondary data and the significance of both trade and FDI as a means of internationalisation have been highlighted. The problems inherent in the available services sector data have been outlined. The analysis indicates the growing importance of services and business services to general levels of economic activity. Services account for almost 22 per cent of exports and 50 per cent of annual FDI flows. Within the sector business service activities are making an important contribution to overall growth. The expansion of business services can partly be attributed to the restructuring of economic activity with firms increasingly focusing on their core activity and buying in producer services.

The increased level of international business service activity can be seen as a part of the general trend towards increasing levels of globalisation among firms. Increasingly businesses are seeking out new and larger markets in the search for economies of scale. As firms in general become more international then there is pressure upon the suppliers of business services to follow their clients into overseas markets. In addition, through expansion business service firms can gain both economies of scale and scope enabling them to provide services at a lower cost to their clients and thus improving the competitiveness of such clients. Business services then play an important role in the efficient production of goods and services both in the domestic and global market.

To fully appreciate the internationalisation of the UK business services sector it is necessary to explore the theory of international transactions, and to assess its explanatory value in terms of accounting for the existence, and pattern of international transactions in services and, business services. It is this to which attention will be given in the following chapter.

Notes

1   Producer services may be more thoroughly defined as all those activities (that is labour phases) which do not involve direct material production or transformation but are necessary to carry out the full cycle of production in any type of industry. They include activities related to the mobilisation of resources, the conception and innovation of products and processes, the actual organisation and management of production, production itself, the promotion and distribution of products. They must therefore be considered production inputs in the same way as other intermediate goods: their value adds to the cost of production and is transferred into the price of the final output in final markets (Martinelli, 1991, p.22).

2   EUROSTAT (1994 p.8) includes under the title of business services a large number of services concerning the exchange of know-how; technical services (engineering, architecture, technical studies), computer services (software design, database management, maintenance), other professional services (legal, accounting, consultancy and management, etc.). However, advertising services are listed separately.

3 International trade and foreign direct investment theories: application to services

3.1 Introduction

With the service sector now accounting for the largest part of both employment and output in advanced industrialised countries, the question arises as to whether trade and FDI in services will come to dominate international economic activity. As demonstrated in the previous chapter, international service transactions already make up a significant and expanding share of total international transactions. Which countries and which companies will succeed in securing a share of the evolving global market for services? How can countries best prepare themselves for future prosperity based as it may be upon successful service sector export performance? In order to address these questions it is essential to have an appreciation of the reasons for trade and FDI in services. This chapter will provide such an understanding through a critical exploration of the theories of trade and FDI, and an assessment of their relevance to service transactions. Previous attempts to apply international transactions theory to services will be examined and elaborated upon.

3.2 International trade theory and service trade

Introduction

The failure of international trade theory to consider services is largely due to the traditional view of them as being 'non-tradable'. Since services are generally produced and consumed simultaneously they cannot be stored and consequently cannot be traded internationally. However, as illustrated in Chapter 2, there are a variety of trade mechanisms through which services can be transacted across

34

national borders. Indeed, some services, for example, shipping, have been exchanged internationally for many centuries. With the development of ICTs the scope for service trade is growing, with services increasingly being provided at a distance through telecommunication networks.

International trade theories vary in their ability to explain trade in goods, however, despite this, the application of these theories to international service transactions is a useful exercise. It provides a starting point from which a theory of international service transactions can be constructed. When examining the relevance of trade theories to services it is important to note that services are different to goods, in that all goods can be traded whilst not all services can. Although, one might argue that some goods are non-tradable due to prohibitive costs (for example, roads and buildings). According to Sampson and Snape (1984) 'non-separation' is the essential difference between trade in goods and trade in services.

Absolute and comparative advantage

The theory of international trade begins with Adam Smith's (1776) theory of absolute advantage.[1] Although superseded in the early nineteenth century by Ricardo's (1817) theory of comparative advantage, the theory of absolute advantage does provide the basis for trade in certain services. The production of many services is knowledge or information intensive. One country may have an absolute knowledge advantage over another country, that is, a country may have sole access to a certain body of knowledge. Trade in a service which uses this body of knowledge in its production will be on the basis of an absolute advantage. According to Nusbaumer (1987b) services can be divided into those which are differentiated, requiring specialised knowledge in order to cater to the specific needs of consumers; and those which can be more readily standardised in terms of their knowledge input and the identification of separate units. Trade in the specialised knowledge category of services would be determined more by absolute advantage. Whereas trade in the standardised knowledge category of services would be determined more by the comparative advantage conferred by primary factor endowments.

The theory of absolute advantage may be of particular relevance to business services, as they are highly differentiated and often embody specialised knowledge. Business services are customised to the needs of individual clients and are heavily dependent on client specific knowledge in combination with specialised firm specific knowledge assets. However such specialised knowledge may not be confined to one country as the business service firm may operate in a number of countries. Thus it may be more appropriate to talk of firms having absolute competitive advantage rather than countries. It is important then to make a distinction between the absolute or comparative advantages of nations and the competitive advantage of companies.

Ricardo's (1817)[2] theory of comparative advantage in its extended form of the Heckscher-Ohlin-Samuelson model (H-O-S model), remains the most widely accepted explanation of international trade. A central weakness in the original model is the assumption that differences in labour productivity exist and are responsible for differences in comparative costs. Despite this many authors accept that the theory of comparative advantage applies to services (Sapir and Lutz, 1981; Shelp, 1981; Bhagwati, 1984; Hindley and Smith, 1984; Sampson and Snape, 1984; Krommenacker, 1984; inter alia). Hindley and Smith (1984), for example, state:

> That services are different from goods - whatever that means in a particular context - does not in itself provide any basis for a supposition that the theory of comparative advantage (which is also referred to as the theory of comparative cost) does not apply to services. For that, it is necessary to point to the differences which make the *logic* of the theory inapplicable to services, a much more stringent requirement than mere 'differences' (p.370).

They point to the fact that economists concerned with testing theories of trade flows have found it necessary to extend the basic H-O-S model to take account of additional factors of production, such as skilled labour. Also new theories have been developed which focus on such variables as technological differences, economies of scale and market imperfections. They go on to argue that "difficulties in empirical testing of theories do not provide intellectual justification for ignoring the normative component of the theory of comparative costs"(p.371).

Hindley and Smith (1984) assume that the free trade theory developed in the field of goods is applicable to all fields of economic activity, including services. However, they fail to explain why this should be the case. They do, however, identify characteristics which raise doubts about the applicability of the Ricardian proposition to services. Firstly, many service industries are subject to fiduciary regulation, and in many others, sellers are required to possess appropriate licensing and/or qualifications. Secondly, in some service industries, foreign markets are most efficiently served by a permanent presence in the market.

Although they give no useful explanation as to what determines comparative advantage in services, Hindley and Smith (1984) do make some observations about the likely pattern of comparative advantage between developed and developing countries. Firstly, services and service related investment, tend to flow from developed to developing countries. Secondly, service industries engaged in international transactions tend to be organised around information and its exploitation. This strongly suggests that countries with a relatively large skilled labour force will have a comparative advantage in the production of services. In general it can be concluded that developed countries have comparative advantage whilst developing countries have comparative disadvantage.

36

Hindley and Smith (1984) conclude that one of the most important features of services is their role as an intermediate good. It would be useful then, to explore theories of trade which are relevant to intermediate goods. Since such goods are often internationally transacted within the firm an appreciation of intra-firm trade would contribute to the understanding of international services transactions. An appreciation of trade in intermediate goods and services is of vital importance to the understanding of international transactions in business services which are primarily intermediate in nature. It is also important to recognise that trade in intermediate goods and services may be significant in determining the comparative advantage of final goods and services.

The acceptance of comparative advantage as the basis for trade in services seems to be largely an acceptance in the absence of evidence to the contrary. Comparative advantage does not explain trade in certain goods, so why then does it necessarily explain trade in services? A number of more rigorous studies of trade in services have been completed using the H-O-S model, these will now be considered.

Heckscher-Ohlin-Samuelson model

The Heckscher-Ohlin-Samuelson model (also known as the factor proportions model), developed by Heckscher (1919), Ohlin (1933)[3] and later by Samuelson (1948), builds upon Ricardo's theory of comparative advantage. It is recognised that countries are endowed with many factors, but in different proportions. As long as there are international differences in relative factor endowments, this alone is sufficient to explain differences in comparative cost and the basis for international trade and specialisation.

Testing of the H-O-S model has produced various results, some which fails to confirm its predictions (Leontief, 1953), whilst, others provide support for the significance of factor proportions in the determination of trade patterns (Leamer, 1984). The assumptions[4] upon which the model is based provide the focus for much criticism since they reduce its value in terms of explaining trade in the real world. As a result, there have been many attempts to extend the H-O-S model by relaxing various assumptions. In this way the implications of for example: imperfect competition; changing factor endowments; the existence of intermediate goods; the international mobility of factors; differences in demand conditions across countries; differences in production functions; and product differentiation can be explored. Further extensions can be made if the range of factor endowments is expanded to include technology, R&D and human capital. In addition, the static analysis has been extended to comparative statics and some attempts at dynamic analysis.

By taking into account economic growth changing factor endowments can be incorporated into the H-O-S model. Economic growth generally involves relative growth in the stock of capital, rather than the isolated growth of the labour supply. According to the Rybczynski theorem (1955) countries experiencing such growth should expect to see the size of their labour-intensive industries contract. The implication of this theory is that comparative advantage is not something given once and for all.[5] It is useful to view comparative advantage in a dynamic setting in which some common and recurring characteristics of development influence the evolution of the composition of a country's trade (Williamson and Milner, 1991).

It should also be recognised that factors of production may be mobile internationally. In particular, capital may move from high-wage industrial countries to developing countries to take advantage of lower wages for labour-intensive stages of production. Such fragmentation of industrial processes and geographical spread of activities is profitable where the specialisation and wage cost advantages exceed the additional transport costs incurred, provided product quality is maintained. Thus the basic H-O-S model of trade needs to be further extended to allow for trade in intermediate goods and 'footloose industries'. The model must be related to processes rather than to products. The outputs of one country can be the inputs in production processes in other countries. The pattern of international production and trade may in these circumstances differ from those predicted by the 'classical paradigm' of trade in final goods only. In order to understand this type of trade it is necessary to examine the theory of FDI together with intra-firm trade (Caves, 1970; Helpman, 1985,1984) to which consideration will be given later in this chapter.

Deardorff (1985), in his examination of trade in producer services, employs a H-O-S model where there are two countries, two factors, one good and a service. The service is not tradable and the factors of production are labour and management. If country A has relatively lower labour costs and services are labour intensive, then managers from country B will have an incentive to join with labour in A in order to supply services in country A. Deardorff suggests that this result contravenes the principle of comparative advantage since the "Labour-scarce Country B exports labour-intensive services in spite of the fact that these services cost more in Country B than in Country A in autarky" (Deardorff, 1985, p.65). However, there is, possibly some confusion here, for trade in services is defined by Deardorff as the production of services in A by managers located in country B, rather than as the export of factor services. Moreover, it should be noted that there is no reason to call the non-traded sector a service at all in this model. Country B would still supply management services if the non-traded sector produced a good rather than a service. Deardorff notes that the principle can be rehabilitated if it is reinterpreted to apply to the supply of management services. In this case country B has the comparative advantage since the relative salary of management in B is lower in autarky.

Deardorff (1985) claims, that such a reinterpretation will lead to problems if the comparative advantage in country A is based upon a technological advantage in the production of services. In this case, although country A has a higher autarky return to management, it will export management services as long as its technological superiority outweighs the relative costliness of its management.

The apparent contravention of the principle of comparative advantage arises because the technological advantage is specific to the management factor in country A. Markusen (1983) demonstrates this in a model where both goods are traded and the factor employed intensively in the technologically superior industry enjoys a relatively high return. If management is used intensively in the technologically superior sector, and both factors are mobile, then managers will migrate to country A until returns are equalised. In Deardorff's model, however, the managers from country B do not become technically more capable when they provide services in country A and their effective return is lower because while the return per manager in country A is higher, the return per effective management unit is lower. Consequently, country B can only reap the benefits of country A's superior technology if it rents the technically superior management services from A in return for goods. The appropriate measure of comparative advantage in this model is not the return to the management service, but rather the return per effective management unit. As Ryan (1988) notes, this model highlights both the importance of defining the service activity appropriately and the importance of choosing the appropriate indicator of comparative advantage when analysing trade in services.

Deardorff (1985) finds it necessary to introduce differences in technology with identical factor endowments, thus departing from the traditional H-O-S model, which assumes different factor endowments but identical production technology. Although, later developments of the theory of comparative advantage have put increasing emphasis on technology and knowledge factors in explaining trade flows. Deardorff's example is further complicated by the fact that the management services exported by the first country with the technological superiority are in fact 'traded' by way of a movement of factors from the first to the second country. However, movements of factors cannot be used as an explanation of trade in the traditional sense of the word, since one explanation for trade is precisely that it substitutes for movements of factors from one production area to another.[6] If it is true that there is likely to be trade in management services between the technologically advanced and the technologically poor countries, it is more likely to be because managers exporting their services have an absolute advantage for which users in the second country would probably be ready to pay almost any price, and in any case a higher price than the first country. When dealing with trade in services in the form of factor movements, therefore, it is not necessary to refer to the principle of comparative advantage to explain such flows.

Melvin (1989) illustrates an important result that follows from this model. If one country is relatively well-endowed with a mobile service factor and the industry producing the tradable good uses this factor intensively, efficient world output is possible. The trade pattern will not, however, be as predicted by the H-O-S model. The country that is relatively well-endowed with the immobile factor will be observed to be exporting the good that is intensive in the mobile factor.

Deardorff's model (1985) reveals that trade in services can lead to greater gains from trade, to a violation of the H-O-S theory, and it can be further shown that tariffs can lead to a fall in welfare even for large countries. However, there are problems with this model, Nusbaumer (1987b), for instance, notes that a difficulty with Deardorff's example is that it completely separates out services and goods as if efficient services had no impact on the technological content, quality, mode of production, and price of goods.

Transport services have received considerable attention in the trade literature (Samuelson, 1954; Mundell, 1957b; Falvey, 1976; Cassing, 1978; Casas, 1983; Kierzkowski, 1986). This is not surprising given that the value of transportation services may be as much as 13 per cent of the value of world merchandise trade (Kierzkowski 1986). Falvey (1976) and Cassing (1978), for example, incorporated the transport services sector into the traditional H-O-S model. By considering transportation as just another production sector, Falvey is able to allow market conditions to determine which country will supply services. As with any H-O-S model, the result will depend upon the relative factor intensities of the three sectors (two goods and one service - transportation) and the factor endowments of the countries. If the service sector is more capital intensive than both of the goods sectors then the capital-rich country will produce services. If transportation is more capital intensive than only one of the goods, then it is not possible to predict a priori which country will supply the transport services.

The first attempt to explain trade in services in a systematic manner was made by Dick and Dicke (1979). The focus of their study was on aggregate measures of trade in knowledge-intensive services, which they defined as consisting of shipment, other transport and other private services (including property income from intangible assets, that is, patents and licences). In order to test the theory of comparative advantage, they regressed various indicators of revealed comparative advantage on variables measuring factor endowments. The results of their cross-section estimates for 18 OECD countries found no evidence of the role of comparative advantage in determining the pattern of trade in services. Although the result was partly attributed to non-tariff trade barriers, the authors seemed to accept the then widely held view that "regardless of trade distortions, it is imaginable that factor endowments have no significant influence on trade in services" (Dick and Dicke, 1979, p.346).

This view has been challenged by Sapir and Lutz (1981). Using a simple econometric model, they found that the main factors shaping comparative advantage in services were the availability of physical and human capital. Sapir and Lutz (1981) explained the relative position of developing and developed countries in international markets for main categories of services on the basis of their relative endowments in such forms of capital. The development of new ICTs may lead to the appearance of new comparative advantages based on the 'disembodiment' of certain services. This would entail standardised and labour-intensive tasks being performed in labour rich countries, whilst the high skill intensive and differentiated tasks, which are not transferable abroad without at the same time transferring the factors possessing the required skills, would continue to be performed in capital rich countries (Hindley and Smith, 1984). An example of this is the location by computer service companies of data entry activities in developing countries. Although, it is apparent that some of these countries are developing the capability to produce high skill intensive services. India, for example, is now an important producer of computer software because it is well endowed with mathematical and programming skills.

Given the importance of human capital in services production, trade theory that relates to the literature on the formation of human capital would appear to be relevant to trade in services. Findlay and Kierzkowski (1983) developed a model where there are two goods, X and Y, and two factor inputs, skilled and unskilled labour. Unlike the traditional H-O-S model, the endowment of these two factors is not determined exogenously, but rather the quantity of skilled labour is an endogenous variable. They conclude that in a world with free trade in goods, the country with the higher stock of educational capital can be expected to export the skilled-labour-intensive good and import the unskilled-labour-intensive good. These conclusions might also be extended to services, when considering skilled labour intensive services and unskilled labour intensive services.

In his analysis of the sources of comparative advantage, Leamer (1984) has also addressed the problem of differences in technology and knowledge and their relation to the static theory of comparative advantage. Referring to Ricardo, he began by stating that "...the technological differences in the Ricardian model can be thought to arise from different endowments in knowledge capital" (p.1). In the static comparative advantage model, human capital and machinery can be treated as fixed inputs or factor endowments because they are not fungible in the short run, and at any given point in time they are, as Leamer observes, the current result of past saving decisions. From Leamer's analysis, we can draw the conclusion that the main reason why it is intuitively difficult to use the H-O-S theory to explain international trade in services is precisely that the fastest developing sectors of this trade are those where the most dynamic changes in production methods and consumption patterns are taking place, which the static H-O-S theory of comparative advantage is ill-equipped to deal with. The fundamental question, therefore, is perhaps not whether in the dynamic world of services the H-O-S theory can provide useful insights into the determinants of trade, but rather what elements of the theory retain their explanatory power for services, and in what circumstances.

The answer to this question depends on how the services concerned are produced. It should be noted in this connection that even in the field of goods, the traditional theory of comparative advantage has been found difficult to apply when dealing with technologically advanced goods produced only in certain countries. For this reason technology and knowledge have been introduced as specific factors into the basic theoretical framework in an attempt to extend its applicability (see for

41

example: Kravis, 1956; Hufbauer, 1966; Vernon, 1970; Machlup, 1984; Rada, 1984; and Edvinsson, 1985).

In a field such as services, where trade performance is not readily quantifiable, it is necessary to rely on business experience of market competition rather than on statistical calculations to assess the relative competitiveness of different producers. The one, and perhaps only basis on which comparative advantage in services can be analysed is the so called revealed comparative advantage (RCA) index developed by Balassa (1979). An analysis of the comparative advantage of major trading countries in a number of service sectors has been carried out on a similar basis by Peterson and Barras (1987). However, as Peterson and Barras (1987) admit, the RCA index measure is severely limited in aggregating all service sectors in one index, due to data limitations, and it gives no indication of the source of variation. Given the difficulties in assessing the level of comparative advantage, together with its questionable relevance to many service sector activities, it is necessary to explore alternative theories in the search for an adequate explanation of international trade in service.

Demand factors, increasing returns and intra-industry trade

The classical and neoclassical trade theories focus predominantly on supply-side differences between countries as the major determinant of international trade. However, differences in demand conditions between countries do influence trade patterns at least at the detailed product level. Linder (1961) drew a sharp distinction between trade in primary products, which he argued would be determined on the basis of factor endowments, and trade in manufactures. In the case of the latter, he argued that factor intensities were much the same and that the principal determinant of the pattern of trade was to be found in the structure of demand, especially in trade between high-income countries.

The Linder thesis is often viewed as being predominantly concerned with intra-industry trade, but it was not intended to be exclusively so. Linder's theory competes with the neoclassical paradigm by providing a rationale for trade between similar economies. It is true that the trade between similar economies tends to be of an intra-industry nature, while trade between dissimilar economies, where factor endowment explanations are more appropriate, tend to be predominantly of an inter-industry nature. Factor proportions may, however, also be of relevance in the understanding intra-industry trade. If different varieties, especially different qualities, of a given product or service require different factor intensities, then differences in countries' factor endowments may push a country's comparative advantage towards a specific variety. It may export those varieties that incorporate its abundant factor most intensely and import those varieties that are intensive in the country's relatively scarce factor. Clearly, intra-industry trade of this type can be seen in the area of tourism where the nature of the service provided depends on

42

factor endowments such as climate, scenery, historical sites, or indeed, the location of man-made tourist attraction such as Disney World.

The theory of intra-industry trade (Grubel and Lloyd, 1975), by contrast, abstracts from the role of inter-country differences in factor endowments and concentrates on the role of influences such as non-competitive market structures, product differentiation and increasing returns to scale. The demand for variety and the relaxation of the constant costs assumption provide sufficient conditions for intra-industry trade, and these can be modelled under all kinds of market structures. What emerges is that market structure, economies of scale and product differentiation can generate trade, including two-way trade, independently of the classic sources of trade. Krugman (1983) notes that this theory explains trade best when scale economies are important and factor endowments are similar, hence its power is explaining trade in manufactures between economically advanced countries.

Economies of scale are clearly evident in capital intensive services, such as shipping and telecommunications. However, they are less important in the production of many services, for example professional and business services, where customisation and quality, rather than standardisation and low price, are required by consumers. Although the application of new ICT is certainly increasing the capacity for economies of scale and scope in many areas. It can, however, be argued that product differentiation is a key phenomenon in many service areas. Certainly theories based upon it will often be of more relevance to such services than those based upon comparative advantage, which assumes a single, homogeneous product.

Zweifel (1986) suggests that the inability to combine services linearly implies that services are more likely to be traded than goods. Since services cannot be combined to yield the desired characteristics, the need for variety is greater. It follows that, since international trade facilitates greater variety when differentiated products are produced under increasing returns to scale, services are more likely to be traded than goods. The theories of intra-industry and overlapping demand appear then to hold some relevance to trade in services.

Most industrial products are sold in markets characterised by imperfect competition, including oligopolistic and monopolistic conditions. The theoretical trade literature on constraining domestic monopoly has focused on goods, however, it also applies to services. For example, Markusen (1987) notes that many producer services, such as engineering and management consulting, require a high initial investment in learning. However, these services can be provided to additional users at a very low cost. Markusen develops a model, similar to that of Either (1982), in which the output of a good is modelled as the assembly of components, and these components are producer services. Since these components are produced with a fixed cost and a constant marginal cost, increasing returns to scale exist. The market structure, therefore, is assumed to take the form of monopolistic competition. Markusen shows that allowing trade only in goods is an imperfect

43

substitute for trade in services, because the gains from specialisation in services cannot be realised. Kierzkowski (1986) suggests that since many services such as shipping and telecommunications are characterised by oligopolistic market structures, it would be more appropriate to use a version of the intra-industry trade model such as those employed by Brander and Krugman (1983) and Brander and Spence (1984). Building on such models Kierzkowski constructs a duopoly theory of international service trade.

The trade theories discussed in this section are clearly of value when used to examine trade in services. The importance of product differentiation in certain specialist service sectors has been highlighted, and hence the relevance of theories which acknowledge such differentiation. The theories based upon increasing returns and market concentration would also appear to be relevant to those service sectors where economies of scale arise, for example, the telecommunications and transportation sectors. Business services, however, are less likely to experience increasing returns to scale, although a high level of service differentiation is evident in the sector.

The product cycle theory

The H-O-S model takes technology to be both exogenous and fixed. The technology gap theorem (Posner, 1961; Hufbauer, 1966) proposes that 'temporary' differences in industry-specific knowledge determine trade. A country will export the goods of those industries in which it has a technology advantage over other countries, even though both exporting and importing countries may have similar factor endowments.

The product cycle theory, developed principally by Vernon (1966), seeks to incorporate technology gap principles into a framework in which there are factor endowment differences between countries and in which multinational production is possible. Vernon (1966) argued that innovation and new products are more likely to occur in a high wage, capital abundant country. In the early stages of development, new products will be manufactured close to the market. As the product matures, an increasing amount of total production is likely to be exported, primarily to other capital rich countries, and relative production costs become increasingly important. As the product becomes standardised and knowledge becomes more freely available, potential competition may threaten in export markets encouraging the location of production within major overseas markets. In the final stage full standardisation is achieved, and the location of production may shift yet again, in this case to labour-abundant economies where labour costs are relatively low. Thus over time exports from the innovating country will decline, and may indeed be replaced by imports.

This model of technological change as the basis of trade provides some interesting insights into the dynamics of the way in which comparative advantage can shift over time. The empirical evidence does give support for the view that technological

44

know-how is, among other factors, significant in explaining cross-country variations in export performance. This may, however, be consistent with an extended version of the H-O-S model in which more factors of production are recognised, specifically, in this case technology or human capital.

The product cycle theory provides a framework within which the early post war expansion of US investment into Europe can be interpreted. However, the sequential development process assumed may still have some applicability: for firms which are expanding abroad for the first time; for MNE activity associated with the final product type; and, for the development of offshore export platforms in LDCs. It may be less applicable now for established MNEs: the model of planning products for one market before selling these abroad does not adequately describe the complex global strategy employed by many experienced MNEs. The theory does not per se explain the source of the MNE's ownership advantage, and must be considered in conjunction with the ownership-specific advantages discussed later in this chapter.

An aspect of the product cycle theory which is questionable when applied to services is whether service products and processes move abroad first through export and then by investment, and whether this is caused by standardisation. The product cycle is only applicable at this stage if the service is exportable, that is, can the service be provided through a trading mechanism. The final phase of Vernon's product cycle theory occurs when the overseas affiliate begins to export its products to third markets or back to its home base because of differences of labour or other factor costs. This stage is much less likely to occur because of the nature of overseas service production which is more likely to be market-oriented rather than resource-oriented. In relation to this Shelp (1981) comments:

> For services that are easily traded, patterns in which affiliates export back to home markets are not easily discernible. The reason for this seems to lie in the structural differences between goods trade and service trade and particularly what determines competitiveness in each. For example, it is difficult to visualise the overseas affiliate of a multinational bank or accounting firm competing with its parent or replacing the original facility in providing services to home clients. However, it is not inconceivable that affiliates could displace other firms by developing clients in neighbouring third countries because of their proximity or the trade patterns between the host country and third countries (p.92).

Examples of service activities being exported back to the country of origin are, however, becoming increasingly common, for example, in the computer services industries, in R&D activities and intra-firm trade in services.

At this point the existence of a reverse product cycle in service industries should be noted. Barras (1986) identifies three phases in the reverse product cycle: firstly, when new technology is introduced to increase the efficiency of delivery of existing services; secondly, when the technology is applied to improving the quality of services; and lastly, when technology assists in generating wholly transformed or new services. The existence of such a cycle in the service sector has implications for the validity of Vernon's product life cycle to internationally traded service. The combination of the two cycles would suggest that services would be sold internationally as they evolve, rather than there being a period during which they are sold only in the domestic market. This would seem to be especially the case if the service uses new ICT in its production.

With modification of the product cycle theory Vernon (1979) brings the hypothesis closer to the Hymer-Kindleberger model of international production. Emphasis is placed on the oligopolistic structure in which most MNEs operate, and their attempts to forestall entry into the industry by new firms. The three stages of the cycle are viewed here as those of, innovation based oligopoly, where there are strong economic incentives to locate production in the country where the innovation was developed in order to coordinate the production process with the R&D and marketing function. The second stage is mature oligopoly, here the assumption is that production and locational strategies are based upon the actions and reactions of other MNEs. At this stage the predictions of the model are very similar to the 'follow the leader' practice observed by Knickerbocker (1973), since firms set up production operations in their competitor's major markets to strengthen their bargaining position. In the final stage of senescent oligopoly, competitive pressures are assumed to re-emerge, as barriers to entry weaken. Production locations are then more closely determined by cost differentials than by adjacency to markets or oligopolistic reactions. This modified interpretation of the product cycle clearly holds some relevance to those service sectors characterised by concentrated market structures. Its focus on international production makes it more appropriate to those service which are non-tradable with international transactions occurring through the establishment of MNE's.

The product cycle model yields many interesting insights into the process of global competition. However, its over deterministic and programmatic nature are features which have to be modified in view of the increasing sophistication of global competitive interaction (Giddy 1978). According to Buckley and Casson (1985) in the analysis of the strategy of established MNEs, the product cycle approach splits three decisions which are interdependent: (i) investment in product development; (ii) the method of servicing of foreign market; and (iii) the firm's competitive stance relative to foreign firms. These elements need to be considered simultaneously by MNEs.

The value of the product cycle model is its focus on the dynamic growth of trade and MNEs. It would seem that much of the product cycle theory could successfully be applied to international transactions within certain service sub-sectors, particularly where services are tradable, however, if the service is produced and delivered with new ICT then the relevance of this theory is questionable.

Table 3.1
The nature of trade by sector

Basis of trade	Sector		
	Extractive	Manufactur -ing	Service
Absolute advantage.	X	X	X
Comparative advantage.	X	X	X
Intra-industry trade and increasing returns.		X	
Product life cycle.		X	
Intra-firm.		X	X

X denotes highly appropriate. Absence of X does not exclude this category.

Conclusion

The immediate cause of international exchange of commodities is the existence (pre-trade) of inter-country differences in the price or quality of competing goods. Given the complexities of the real world, there are likely to be a large range of inter-country differences in supply conditions that simultaneously influence relative costs of production. Empirical studies (for example: Hufbauer, 1970; Leamer, 1974) demonstrate that the commodity composition of the exports of developed and developing countries is significantly correlated with a range of national attributes such as resource endowments and technological factors. Indeed, this evidence might be interpreted as supporting the view that actual international flows are 'explained' by an amalgam of theories. Specific theories tend to concentrate, however, on a single source of dissimilarity or comparative advantage (Williamson and Milner, 1991). It is quite legitimate to employ the H-O-S model to explain the broad patterns of comparative advantage, that is, the balance of comparative advantage between manufactured and agricultural goods or between labour- and capital-intense goods or services, and to employ alternative models to explain patterns of specialisation and trade within sectors of an economy. Inter-industry trade between dissimilar economies is probably best viewed within a H-O-S framework, while intra-industry trade between similar economies is better explained by a Linder-type framework or models of intra-industry trade.

Landesmann and Petit (1995), for example, use the H-O-S model to account for trade at the broad level of producer services as a whole, and in particular to characterise trade between countries at different levels of economic development. Whilst they find an organisational approach based on the presence of economies of scale, economies of scope and transaction costs to be more relevant when examining trade in producer services at the detailed level. Table 3.1 provides a summary of the nature of trade by sector, whilst Table 3.2 focuses on the basis of trade for a selection of service industries.

From the above discussion it would seem that the traditional trade theories can be meaningfully applied to services, and that they are as relevant to them as they are to goods. For specific sub-sectors the theories may require modification or indeed totally new theories, for example, where services are non-tradable in the traditional sense. The importance of regulation in the service sector also has implications for the pattern of trade. It is clear however, that to have a full understanding of international service transactions it is necessary to examine not only trade theory but also FDI theory to which attention will now turn.

3.3 Foreign direct investment theory and service multinational enterprises

Introduction

The rising importance of FDI in the form of the MNE since 1945, has attracted a great deal of attention from economists (Hymer, 1960; Kindleberger, 1969; Caves, 1982; Vernon, 1966; Dunning, 1981; Buckley and Casson, 1976; Rugman, 1981; inter alia). Foreign direct investment involves the establishment by a company of an overseas subsidiary or the acquisition of a controlling interest in an overseas company. It is more than a transfer of money capital, entailing a package of resources, which includes ownership, control, management, technology and other resources.

The MNE has been variously defined.[7] Hood and Young (1979), for example, define a MNE as "a corporation which owns (in whole or part), controls and manages income-generating assets in more than one country" (p.3). Whilst, Caves (1982) drops the ownership requirement defining a MNE as "an enterprise that controls and manages production establishments - plant - located in at least two countries" (p.1). UNCTC (1984) gives the following definition:

> ... an enterprise (a) comprising entities in two or more countries, regardless of the legal form and fields of activity of those entities, (b) which operate under a system of decision-making permitting coherent policies and a common strategy through one or more decision-making centres, (c) in which the entities are so linked, by *ownership or otherwise*, that one or more of them may be able to

Table 3.2
The basis for trade: selected service industries

	Absolute advantage	Comparative advantage	Intra-industry increasing returns
Advertising	Reputation; creative skills.	Abundance of skilled labour.	
Accountancy	Specialised know-ledge; reputation.	Abundance of skilled labour.	
Computer services	Specialised know-ledge; reputation.	Abundance of skilled labour.	
Financial services	Specialised know-ledge; reputation.	Abundance of skilled labour; location, e.g.: centres of agglomeration where input costs lower.	
Air transport	Monopoly rights to certain routes.		Economies of scale; differentiated services.
Tourism	Unique tourist attraction.	Abundance of tourist attractions; natural and man-made.	Trade in differentiated holidays between developed countries.

exercise a *significant influence* over the activities of the other, and, in particular, to share knowledge, resources and responsibilities with others (p.2).

Here, neither ownership or control in the traditional sense is required. UNCTC then, provides a broad and therefore useful definition which reflects the variety of ownership and organisational forms apparent among MNEs today. The numerous definitions are accompanied by a diverse range of theories developed to explain the MNE.

Although the definitions considered here may be applied to service MNEs, the conceptual and theoretical analysis has failed to keep pace with the growth in service sector multinational activity. This section attempts to address this failure by applying theories developed to understand MNEs in the extractive and

49

manufacturing sectors to those in the service sector. In doing so it will add to a small but expanding body of literature on service MNEs (Dunning and McQueen, 1981; Boddewyn et al., 1986; Rimmer, 1988; Terpstra and Yu, 1988; UNCTC, 1989; Enderwick, 1989; Daniels, Thrift and Leyshon, 1989; Dunning, 1989, 1993b; inter alia). Firstly, though, it is useful to highlight some distinctive characteristics of service sector MNEs.

Service MNEs are a widespread phenomenon, they arise in the international provision of: consumer services; retail and distribution services; and producer or intermediate services. Examples range from McDonald's to American Express. Dunning (1989) attributes the growth in multinational service activity in the last two decades to a number of factors: the growth in demand for consumer services following a rise in real incomes; technological advances which have increased the demand and supply of services and their tradability; the expansion of telecommunication and other service support facilities as goods have become technically more complicated; the expansion of trade in goods associated with increased geographical process or product specialisation; the increasing complexity and uncertainty of modern society leading to the need for insurance and professional advisory services; the increasing specialisation and round-aboutness in production; and the increasing role of government.

Since exporting is not always a feasible option for service firms they cannot always move gradually into foreign markets, firstly through exporting and later through foreign production. This explains the use of franchising and licensing in certain service areas. However, problems arise with such forms of foreign involvement in relation to the protection of knowledge and the quality of the service provided. The risks involved in franchising and licensing may however, be outweighed by the market knowledge possessed by the local producer.

Apart from those in the banking sector, service MNEs are generally small by comparison with their manufacturing counterparts and display greater product specialisation. A number of factors account for this. Firstly, economies of scale appear, in most cases, to be less important for service firms. Secondly, the immobility of many services implies that concentration of production and dependence on mass distribution is not a viable growth strategy for much of the service sector. Thirdly, small size is also likely to be related to the relative immaturity of many service MNEs. It is important to note that some of the large traditionally manufacturing MNEs have ventured through diversification into service sector activities.

Hymer-Kindleberger approach

The Hymer-Kindleberger (Hymer, 1960; Kindleberger, 1969) approach forms the basis of the theory of the MNE. Foreign direct investment is viewed as a product of imperfections in good and factor markets throughout the world. It could not exist in a perfect market since local firms would always be able to out compete foreign entrants. Thus, in order to compete with indigenous firms foreign entrants must have some compensating advantage. Kindleberger (1969) examined four main areas of internationally transferable advantage. First, departures from perfect competition in good markets; second, departures from perfect competition in factor markets; third, internal and external economies of scale; and finally, government intervention. Such advantages enable the foreign entrant to overcome its lack of knowledge of local conditions, and also serve to compensate for the foreigner's cost of operating at a distance. All four areas of internationally transferable advantage discussed by Kindleberger (1969) may be viewed as relevant, to a greater or lesser degree, in the case of service sector FDI.

Early theorists of FDI focused their attention on one of a number of ownership advantages which the MNE was believed to acquire within an imperfectly competitive environment. A number of ownership advantages, which have proved most useful, especially in terms of their relevance to service MNEs, will be discussed in the following section.

Ownership specific advantages

Ownership specific advantages, (also known as firm specific advantages), can be broadly applied to service MNEs, however, additional advantages need to be considered which are specific to service firms. As mentioned above, many MNEs provide both goods and service; in such cases the advantage in services may arise from the firm's goods production activities. For example, companies like Unilever and Royal Dutch Shell are active in the freight shipping business because of the nature of the products produced and transported, and the perceived advantages of logistical management (Van Rens, 1982). In this study the focus is upon pure service MNEs, primarily providing services, however, even here some involvement in goods provision may be required. For example, the supply of specialist information may depend upon the capacity to provide computer terminals and other hardware necessary for the construction of information networks.

Service firms may acquire ownership advantages through their use of technology. Their competitive assets are more often likely to be of low technological complexity in the general sense, although, technological advantages in the broad sense are particularly important. Such advantages include product and production secrets, management organisational techniques and marketing skills, including product differentiation and brand names. Ownership advantages may derive from the use of ICT, for example, passenger airlines are able to derive competitive advantage from the development of computer reservation systems.

A technological or 'knowledge' advantage, must be easily transferable within the firm and across national boundaries, having the characteristics of a 'public good' within the organisation (Johnson, 1970). But be less easily transferable between different firms, whether in the same or in different countries. Without this qualification a knowledge advantage would be of little significance to FDI since it would dissipate too rapidly to justify long term investment.

Caves (1971) suggests that the critical ownership advantage is the ability to differentiate a product, thus enabling the firm to service simultaneously several international markets. Given the highly differentiated nature of business services this would appear to be an important source of competitive advantage for firms in this sector. Brand names and trademarks are of special importance to service MNEs. All services are embodied either in goods or people, and their quality displays more variation than that of 'pure' goods. Similarly, many services are 'experience' commodities whose performance can only be assessed after consumption. For these reasons branding may form a powerful competitive weapon conveying as it does, valued information to potential consumers. A reputation for quality and consistency is an important ownership advantage for service firms and this is embodied in the company's brand name or trademark. The generation of goodwill and corporate identity is encouraged by the product specialisation characteristic of many service firms. Even where a policy of diversification has been pursued this tends to focus on related business areas. The role of economies of learning and doing are particularly important in multinational services like banking (Yannopolous, 1983). Product specialisation and the diffusion of corporate identity are particularly valuable in industries characterised by supplier-client confidentiality such as business services.

Innovation as a competitive factor can also be classed as an ownership advantage. In many cases innovations which form the competitive advantage of service MNEs are relatively unsophisticated, when compared to the technological achievements of some manufacturing firms, and typically they are incremental. They tend to be related to the application of modern managerial methods. Although, in some cases significant innovations based upon the conjunction of goods and services have provided a competitive edge, for example, the provision of educational services embodied in videos or CD ROMs. The quality of labour and investment in training is an important element in the development of the knowledge and trademark of a MNE, helping to consolidate and improve market share. Dunning and McQueen (1982) liken investment in training among service firms to the importance of R&D to manufacturing MNEs.

Another ownership advantage is that deriving from industrial organisation, that is from an oligopolistic market structure and behaviour. Knickerbocker (1973) has gone furthest in developing an oligopolist model of MNE, he found a close relationship between oligopolistic reaction (demonstrated by the 'bunching' in the time of entry into a particular market by oligopolistic firms) and industrial structure. Evidence in the service sector of this type of oligopolistic reaction can be seen in the entry of Japanese merchant banks into the British financial sector in response to deregulation in the 1980s.

Further advantages which derive from large size in oligopolistic markets are: firstly, the availability of economies of scale; secondly, that market power enables the profitable exploitation of technology; and, finally, the scope for product differentiation. The emphasis on the importance of economies of scale and large size of the company fails to explain the existence of small MNEs which arise when output is dependent upon small scale production, either because of quality control or the size of the market.

According to Shelp (1981) many services sectors do not exhibit the same negative characteristics as manufacturing or extractive industries, such as, oligopolistic market structures. Economies of scale are less important to services in general; though they are significant in those sectors characterised by high fixed costs and comparatively low variable costs of operation, (for example, airlines, shipping and telecommunications). In banking and finance large size bestows advantages of risk spreading and arbitrage. Economies of scope, which are a function of the spread rather than scale of a firms activities (Panzar and Willig, 1981), provide competitive advantages in some service industries. These economies are becoming increasingly important in a number of business services. The spate of mergers and takeovers during the late 1980s among accounting firms, advertising agencies and management consultants was partly driven by the search for scope economies and the desire to provide one-stop-shops for clients.

A requirement for a particular raw material may clearly be a country-specific factor influencing the location of overseas activities. However, if a MNE has privileged access to such raw materials, then this becomes an ownership advantage. Such privileged access may arise from: control over production of the material; control over processing; control over the market for the material; or control over the distribution of a product.

For service MNEs an ownership advantage may result from favoured access to inputs, for example, in the airline business the acquisition of rights to particular routes is an important property right, indeed, essential if flights to a particular location are to be provided. Similarly, the ownership of a government licence or franchise securing the right to provide a certain service is an important ownership advantage in some sectors, for example, in the provision of commercial television in the UK. Favoured access to inputs may in some cases result from the firm's size and reputation, for example, the top accountancy firms are able, by virtue of their reputation, to recruit the highest quality graduates for their training programmes.

Control over a raw material, in the traditional sense, is perhaps of less relevance to a service sector MNE, although, differential access to, and ability to process, control and apply information is clearly of relevance. Information has a number of significant economic characteristics. It often requires considerable investment in indivisible assets; offers considerable economies of learning, scale and scope in its production; and lends itself to specialisation and economies of integration in the different stages of production. The existence of such economies in the production and processing of information suggests first mover advantage. There may also be an interaction between multinationality and the establishment of competitive assets. That is, multinationality achieved on the basis of advantages of differential access

53

to information is likely to reinforce such advantages creating barriers to competitive entry and allowing incumbents a considerable degree of immunity from competitive threat. Advantages based on access to information are likely to be particularly important to services such as stock broking, foreign exchange and securities dealing, commodity broking and data-providing services.

The relationship between service MNEs and the client industries are of interest. A number of studies suggest that around one third of tertiary sector output is in the form of intermediate services (Gershuny and Miles, 1983, p.30). Multinational services provide the infrastructure that facilitates trade. They may, however, be somewhat dependent on trade activity in goods. Firms providing intermediate services have found it imperative to go where their customers do business or risk losing them. This principle has been recognised in banking where some banks were led reluctantly into multinational operations by their major customers (Yannopoulos, 1983). The relationship between service firms and their clients can be regarded as an ownership advantage in the sense that the service firm has favoured access to a particular market, or clients base. Indeed, this advantage may be crucial in the decision to become multinational.

It can be seen then that service sector MNEs have ownership advantages which enable them to compete in foreign markets with domestic firms. Largely these ownership advantages are the same as those applying to the manufacturing sector, however, as has been seen, some ownership advantages are distinctive to the service sector.

Given the existence of an ownership advantage, what is it that leads the firm to use FDI as a means of exploiting this advantage abroad? The basis of the FDI decision, according to the Hymer-Kindleberger proposition, is profitability. In many cases direct investment will be preferred to either exporting or licensing an advantage to a host country firm. Exporting will in many cases be hindered by tariffs and transport cost barriers, or by the very nature of the product or service. Also, a local producer may be better able to adapt the product or service to local conditions, and indeed, a local presence may have the effect of stimulating demand. Hymer (1960) argues that firms will often prefer FDI to licensing because the advantage possessor cannot appropriate the full return from its utilisation as a result of imperfections in the market for knowledge. Further, factors which favour FDI over licensing are the desire to control by the advantage possessor, together with the danger that the buyer of the advantage may become a competitor, or may use the advantage in 'ways which have not been paid for'. Licensing then, may incur heavy firm to firm transfer costs, including costs of 'policing' the transferred property rights (Davies, 1977), costs which do not arise in the case of transfer from parent to subsidiary.

It is arguable that the Hymer-Kindleberger approach is not as applicable to the established MNE as it is to the firm becoming multinational. Established MNEs have gained worldwide dominance and have developed techniques to 'learn in advance' local conditions. Product processes, management style, and marketing techniques are continually adapted to local markets. The ability of the MNE to forecast and adapt is one of the major competitive skills. According to Buckley (1983) the whole concept of firm specific advantage must be questioned. He claims that the concept is artificially attenuated at the point where the firm first crosses national boundaries. Firm-specific advantage is a reflection of this cut-off point as a snap shot in time of a dynamic process. The concept of ownership specific advantage can thus, be classed as a short run notion, when endowments of proprietary knowledge among firms are fixed. In the long run, the investment policy of the firm is crucial, and a dynamic reformulation of industry barriers to entry is required to bring about an approach integrating the life cycle of the firm to expansion paths over time (Magee, 1977; Buckley, 1983).

Internalisation theory

The existence of ownership advantages does not per se explain why a domestic firm should choose to exploit its monopolistic advantage by foreign production rather than by producing at home and exporting, or by licensing a manufacturer abroad. The resolution of this dilemma lies in the theory of internalisation, which is now widely accepted as a key element in the theory of the MNE (McManus, 1972; Buckley and Casson, 1976; Dunning, 1979; Rugman, 1981).

Internalisation is in fact a general theory of why the firm exists. Its origins can be found in an article by Coase (1937) which gives an explanation of the origins and equilibrium size of the firm. The market, it is argued, is costly and inefficient for undertaking certain types of transactions. The 'transaction costs'[8] of using the market are: the cost of finding a relevant price; the cost of defining the obligations of both parties to a contract; the risk associated with accepting such contracts; and the taxes to be paid on market transactions. Wherever transactions can be organised and carried out at a lower cost within the firm than through the market, they will be internalised and undertaken by the firm itself. A MNE exists as a result of the internalisation of transactions across national boundaries. In this way the MNE is able to capitalise on the possession of its unique advantage. Imperfections in the external market provides the incentive for internalisation; where markets are perfectly competitive, internalisation could not improve upon the external market allocation.

The first systematic attempt to incorporate the internalisation model into the theory of the MNE was that of Buckley and Casson (1976). They include in their analysis activities such as: R&D; marketing; the training of labour; and, the building of a management team. Activities which are considered to be interdependent and connected by flows of intermediate products. These intermediate products are not just semi-processed materials, but more often are types of knowledge incorporated into patents and human capital. Imperfect competition in these markets is as important as in final markets, and the profit maximising firm facing such imperfections will attempt to internalise the intermediate products and services within its organisation. A number of such imperfections are considered to be particularly important in stimulating internalisation, for example, government intervention in the form of tariffs, taxation, dividend remittance and exchange rate policies, provide a rationale for internalisation, since in this way the firm has the opportunity, through transfer pricing to minimise tax payments and so on.

It is suggested (Hood and Young, 1979) that the incentive to internalise depends on the relationship between four groups of factors: (i) industry specific factors, such as the nature of the product, external market structure and economies of scale; (ii) regional specific factors, such as geographical distance and cultural differences; (iii) nation specific factors, such as political and fiscal factors; and (iv) firm specific factors, such as management expertise. The main emphasis is on industry specific factors, and within this group the knowledge factor is considered to be of major importance, for several reasons. Firstly, knowledge provides a monopoly advantage which can best be exploited through discriminatory pricing by the firm itself, rather than, for example, by licensing. Indeed, Caves (1971) argues that direct investment was preferable to licensing since know-how could not be transferred independently of the firm and its management. Secondly, the production of knowledge require long term R&D and at any stage before a project is complete the value of the knowledge obtained may be difficult to establish, if the firm were contemplating selling. Licensing a foreign producer would be as profitable as direct investment only in specific cases, where, for example, the advantage of the present firm lies in some once and for all innovation. Alternatively, a small firm might settle for licensing, since the extra control and communication costs of operating abroad might prove prohibitive at the company's scale of output.

According to internalisation theory, it is not the possession of a unique asset per se which gives a firm its advantage, rather, it is the process of internalising that asset which gives the MNE its unique advantage. Internalisation gives rise to both advantages and disadvantages the most significant of which are summarised in Table 3.3. For internalisation to occur the costs involved must be more than offset by the benefits.

In a number of service industries there are strong incentives to internalise overseas market servicing through affiliate production. Information intense industries, such as banking and business services, generate considerable knowledge which is better protected and more profitably applied within the organisation. Among many service sectors horizontal integration occurs as firms seek to maintain quality and protect investments in goodwill and brand names or trademarks.

Enderwick (1989) refers to economies of governance which arise from the efficient integration of economic resources with an accompanying reduction in transaction costs as exchange is hierarchically managed; that is, when transactions are internalised. In the service sector, such economies may be considerable and arise because of a high cost of market transactions in information. Again, the reasons for this are to be found in both the nature of services as economic

Table 3.3
The advantages and disadvantages of internalisation

Advantages of internalisation	Disadvantages of internalisation
1 The increased ability to control and plan production, and in particular to coordinate flows of crucial inputs.	1 Increased accounting and control information is required.
2 The exploitation of market power through discriminatory pricing.	2 Communication costs rise.
3 The avoidance of bilateral market power.	3 With a dislike of MNE in many host countries, there are also the costs of political discrimination to be taken into account.
4 The avoidance of uncertainties in the transfer of knowledge between parties.	
5 The avoidance of potential government intervention by devices such as transfer pricing.	

commodities and in their markets. Services are characterised by considerable quality variations; they may require significant customising; and much knowledge is tacit. The markets for services are often segmented and there may be difficulties in protecting core knowledge. These incentives to internalise transactions are reinforced by the high frequency of transactions for services of an intangible or transient form. For all these reasons there are significant incentives to internalise the market for services.

In the case of knowledge-based innovative services there are further incentives to internalisation. When innovators must undertake market making expenditures, demand creation and diffusion require buyer education. Innovators, often with unique knowledge of their services may be best equipped to undertake buyer instruction. This suggests at least vertical integration of production and sales. The proportion of benefit innovators can appropriate falls as diffusion occurs, this implies the need to provide potential innovators with some form of protection, for example, patents, or in the case of many services, copyright. One of the drawbacks of such a system is the incentive it provides for premature innovation. For those service activities where quality considerations are paramount, alternative forms of protection may be necessary if services of the requisite quality are to be developed. In these cases internalisation is an economically efficient solution, since simple patents or copyrights are unlikely to cover the nebulous knowledge released by diffusion. A further advantage of a significant overseas presence is the possible strengthening of protection over intangible assets such as trademarks and copyrights.

Internalisation of service outputs may also bring advantages to potential buyers. Multinational branding of services conveys valuable information about the quality and performance of services. Similarly, existing customers in one market face lower search and transaction costs if they wish to purchase the same service in a second market where this market is supplied by the same service MNE.

Licensing is discouraged by a number of facets of service sector activity. There are problems of separating out the technology package of many services. For novel or differentiated service products, valuation differences between buyer and seller will raise the costs of market exchange and discourage licensing. For differentiated and branded quality services there is a danger of under performance by a potential licensee, which impose potential costs on the licensor.

It is likely that technology transfer within some services will take the form of franchising, a variant of licensing, which allows the franchisor to retain a greater degree of control over service and systems inputs facilitating quality maintenance. Examples of franchising can be seen in the retail and restaurant sectors, for example, Body Shop and Pizza Hut respectively. Management contracts are also prevalent in areas, such as, international medical services and hotel management. Where knowledge is codifiable the use of contracts may be a suitable alternative to wholly owned subsidiaries. Franchising and non-equity agreements together with joint-venture, do then exist in a number of service sectors. They are of particular appeal where services require customisation to suit local preferences; where risks must be shared; where complementary assets are required; or where investing firms are too small or too immature to undertake the necessary investment.

Dunning (1989) identifies three groups of services which tend to be supplied across borders via FDI rather than by contractual relationships. The first include banking and financial services and most kind of information-intensive business services and professional services. Here the main reasons for integrating either vertically along, or horizontally across, the value-added chain are because:

1 Much of the proprietary knowledge and information is tacit, expensive to produce, complex and idiosyncratic, but easy to replicate.
2 There are significant synergetic advantages to be gained from geographical diversification of productive activities which can be achieved most efficiently within MNE hierarchies.

The second group of services contain firms which engage in forward integration to ensure productive efficiency, and/or to protect the quality of the end product. Often such companies are known by their brand name or image. The third group are trade related service affiliates which are frequently owned by non-service MNEs, their purpose being to obtain inputs for parent companies on the best possible terms or to develop markets for goods produced and exported by parent companies. In the first case, the protection of the supply position of the importing company and the assurance of the right quality at the right price is the dominant motive for internalisation; in the second case, it is the belief that fully or majority-owned subsidiaries are likely to be more efficient and better motivated to serve the exporting country's interests than independent sales agents (Nicholas, 1983).

Internalisation occurs within service MNEs in the same manner as it occurs within manufacturing MNEs. Similarly the most significant reason for internalisation is the protection of knowledge and other intangible assets. Internalisation is then of particular relevance to knowledge intensive services. Further consideration to the internal operation of service MNEs will be given in the next chapter which focuses on the international organisation of service sector firms.

Locational theory

It is fair to say that the theory of the MNE neglects the area of locational theory. Yet any viable explanation of their growth pattern and organisation of inputs and market servicing policies must include elements of locational theory. MNEs can be seen as simply a major vehicle for the transfer of mobile resources to areas with immobile complementary inputs. Thus, locational theory can be closely linked with the factor endowment theory of international trade.

The existence of an ownership advantage together with the need to internalise that advantage does not account for the choice of the location of FDI. The inclusion of locational factors relating to the host country enables a more complete explanation of why a firm will take the trouble, and accept the risk of organising production operations abroad.

A location specific advantage can arise as a result of differences in labour costs due to the immobility of labour. As technology becomes standardised, production may be transferred to the source of cheap labour input. The presence of raw materials in the host country will be an important locational factor in vertical FDI and indeed it explains the early development of MNEs in the extractive sector.

The importance of location specific advantages will vary depending on the type of service being produced. For location-bound services where consumption and production must occur at the same time and place, a foreign presence is inevitable. In this case the existence of a viable market is likely to encourage the establishment of an overseas presence. For firms providing such services growth will be based on multiple representation. Clearly, for some services production can be centralised and economies of scale achieved. For example, film processing and dry cleaning services can be centralised with only distribution outlets being located in close proximity to the customer. However, even in such cases, Quinn and Dickson (1995) have identified a tendency towards decentralisation of production with the introduction of new information technologies which facilitate cost efficient small batch production allowing the colocation of both production and distribution. The choice of location is considerably greater for foreign-tradable services and as such will be determined by other factors.

Economies of agglomeration can be important, because locations where a number of competitors are spatially concentrated may give rise to opportunities for the provision of innovative new services that can be supplied only because of the degree of market development. A good example derives from international banking where the concentration of several similar competitors in major financial centres may allow the creation of an inter bank market. Here incumbent firms enjoy a clear competitive advantage over non-participants (Enderwick, 1989). The behaviour or anticipated behaviour of competitors may also affect locational decisions in oligopolistic service sectors, note the example of Japanese banks moving into Britain mentioned earlier.

The availability of key human and/or natural resources may be crucial in some service sectors. Many business service MNEs require a highly educated workforce, consequently, a ready supply of such labour would provide an important location specific advantage. Other services such as the provision of hotel accommodation may depend on locationally specific factors such as scenery or climate.

Market characteristics, including size, rate of growth and the presence of local competition are important to the location of service MNEs. In addition, the level of development is significant and reflected in the fact that 84 per cent of the stock of service FDI by service MNEs is located in developed countries, compared with 75 per cent of all kinds of investment (Dunning, 1989, p.20). Developing countries, with the exception of tax havens and offshore banking centres, host little service investment. The cultural characteristics of a market are likely to be of particular importance to the service MNE, the competitive provision of many services being based as it is on close cooperation and understanding between client and producer.

Again, as with manufacturing MNEs, the general investment environment will be important, as will government regulation. The role of government in influencing the location of certain service MNEs may be particularly significant. It is generally recognised that the regulation of services is greater than that of goods, although there have been moves towards deregulation in recent years, for example in the telecommunication and financial services sectors. The same kind of incentives, controls and regulation that affect trade and FDI in goods also abound in services. Indeed, some governments are making deliberate attempts to attract inward investment in services, particularly in infrastructure projects. In other, strategically and politically sensitive service sectors, (e.g. transport, telecommunications, banking and community services), governments may impose strict controls on foreign investment by a variety of discriminatory measures or non-tariff barriers. Regulation not only encourages foreign investment by restricting international trade, but also creates opportunities for those enterprises located in unrestricted or less heavily regulated regions, for example, in international banking and shipping.

Future standardisation of regulation between countries, brought about by initiatives such as the Single European Market and the General Agreement on Trade in Services, will no doubt have implications for the location of service MNEs. Dunning (1989) argues that the most significant features affecting the changing location of service activities by MNEs in recent years have been: changes in regulatory patterns, and; advances in the technology of transborder data flows.

A general theory of the multinational enterprise

In the search to provide an improved theoretical explanation of the MNE there have been attempts to produce a synthesis of the elements discussed above, with the aim of creating a general theory of the MNE. Rugman (1981), for example, presents internalisation as a general theory. In this analysis both ownership and locational advantages are incorporated under the benefits from internalisation in the sense that the benefits from various sources only accrue to the MNE through the process of internalisation. In contrast to this, Dunning (1981) has developed an eclectic approach. As with internalisation theory, the central theme of the eclectic approach is the cost of transactions in external markets, to which is added an analysis of location costs. According to Dunning (1981) the ownership advantage is a useful concept because it helps to predict who internalises transactions. The internalisation theory elaborates on the causes of impediments to trade and transaction costs, however, fails to explain the direction internalisation takes. The addition of locational factors is necessary to make the theory operational.

Although the eclectic paradigm enhances the understanding of the nature and process of international production, it does not, as yet, amount to a theory of international production. It does, however, provide a useful base for further theoretical work. As such, the eclectic approach is clearly of value when exploring service sector MNEs. Examples of ownership, location and internalisation advantages for a selection of business service industries are provided in Table 3.4. Clearly it is possible to highlight the importance of all three elements for many services, however for knowledge intensive activities, including business services, internalisation is of particular significance.

Conclusion

The theory of the MNE is of value to the understanding of service MNEs, however, certain service characteristics need to be taken into account and as a result the theory does require a degree of adaptation. It would appear that the motive for overseas service investment is considerably more complex than the simple following of, and support for, manufacturing MNEs. Although, some service firms have become multinational in order to retain clients, this does not hold true for all service providers. Indeed, the initial internationalisation of services through the need of service producers to follow their clients has created international markets

Table 3.4

Illustrations of ownership, locational and internalisation advantages relevant to the activities of selected business service industries

Industry	Ownership (competitive advantages)	Location (configuration advantages)	Internalisation (coordinating advantages)	Foreign presence index[*] (United States data)	Organisational form
Accounting/ auditing	Access to transnational clients Experience of standards required Brand image of leading accounting firms	On-the-spot contact with clients Accounting tends to be culture-sensitive Adaptation to local reporting standards and procedures Oligopolistic interaction	Limited interfirm linkages Quality control over (international) standards Government insistence on local participation	High (92%) Little intrafirm trade	Mostly partnerships or individual proprietorships Overseas subsidiaries loosely organised, little centralised control Few joint ventures
Advertising	Favoured access to markets (subsidiaries of clients in home markets) Creative ability; image and philosophy Goodwill Full range of services Some economies of coordination Financial strength	On-the-spot contact with clients Adaptation to local tastes, languages Need to be close to mass media Import restrictions on foreign commercials	Quality control over advertising copy Need for local input National regulations Globalization of advertising-intensive products To reduce transactions costs with foreign agencies	High (85%) Some intrafirm trade	Mainly 100% ; some joint ventures; limited non-equity arrangements
Computer software/ data processing	Linked to computer hardware Highly technology- or information-intensive Economies of scope Government support	Location of high skills and agglomerative economies often favour home country Government incentives to encourage offshore data entry	Idiosyncratic know-how; need for protection against dissipation Quality control Coordinating gains		

62

Table 3.4 continued.

Industry	Ownership (competitive advantages)	Location (configuration advantages)	Internalisation (coordinating advantages)	Foreign presence index* (United States data)	Organisational form
Information services: data transmission	Highly capital- and human skill- intensive Sometimes tied to provision of hardware Considerable economies of scope and scale Quality of end product/service provided	Varies according to type of information being sold and transmission facilities between countries Where people-based clients may visit home country or firms supplying services in client's countries News agencies are location-bound, i.e. where news is	In case of core assets, need for protection from dissipation Quality control Substantial gains from internalising markets, to capture externalities of information transactions Cognitive market failure, asymmetry of knowledge	Balanced (50%) Some intrafirm trade	Mixture, but 100% where market failure pronounced
Management consultants and public relations	Access to market Reputation, image, experience Economies of specialisation, in particular, levels of expertise etc., skills, countries	Close contact with client; the provision is usually highly customer specific TNC clients might deal with headquarters Mobility of personnel	Quality control, fear of under performance by licensee Knowledge sometimes very confidential and usually idiosyncratic Personnel co-ordinating advantages	Balanced (55%) Some intrafirm trade headquarters often co-ordinates assignments	Mostly partnerships or 100% subsidiaries A lot of movement of people

*The percentage in brackets represents the promotion of sales of United States foreign affiliates to United States exports plus sales of foreign affiliates, as reported by the United States, Office of Technology Assessment (1986), Trade in Services: Exports and Foreign Reserves, Washington, DC: Government Printing Office.

Source: Compiled from Dunning (1989).

in services where formerly they did not exist. The motives of service firms now entering these international markets are likely to differ from the motives of the initial entrants. In fact, the growth of both final and intermediate demand for services suggests that the dependence of service MNEs on their manufacturing counterparts is less than complete. Similarly, evidence on the possession of ownership and location specific advantages implies that service firms may undertake foreign investment for profit seeking motives rather than as a defensive strategy. Changing strategies among service sector MNEs are related to the development of new forms of economic organisation with the trend towards more flexible firms and the externalisation of many service functions.

The theories discussed above do give some insight into the MNE, however, they fail to adequately explain their development after the initial step into multinationality. In addition there is a need to take into account the rising importance of other forms of foreign involvement besides FDI, for example licensing, franchising and management contractual arrangements together with joint ventures.[9] As technology advances, other means of foreign production may become more significant as, for example, improvements in communications technology enable firms to monitor more closely the activities of its foreign producers in order to maintain quality and prevent the dispersion of knowledge advantages. Furthermore, a closer examination of intra-firm trade is required given its significance in terms of global trade and the fact that much intra-firm trade is in intermediate services.

Western MNEs are the prime focus of the theory, however, it is essential to consider MNEs from other parts of the world, especially from LDCs and Japan. Indeed, Kojima (1978) claims that the understanding of Japanese multinationals requires a distinct approach. Of particular relevance to the study of service MNEs is an appreciation of the giant Japanese general trading companies, the 'sogo shosha', which are involved in a vast array of activities including mining, agriculture, manufacturing as well as services. A number of valuable studies have been completed (Kojima and Ozawa, 1985; Yoshino and Lifson, 1986; Young, 1979; inter alia) which find the sogo shosha to be a uniquely Japanese institution with deep historical, cultural and social roots.

Finally, although, the theory of the MNE does provide a basis for the understanding of the service MNE it is important to note that it does not fully explain the existence of MNEs in the manufacturing sector. Even the recent attempts to synthesise a general theory have proved less than satisfactory. To provide a full explanation for the MNE it is necessary to draw upon many areas of economic analysis. Useful contributions from organisational theory have been made by Williamson (1981) and Kay (1984). Indeed, it may be necessary to draw upon other disciplines such as international politics and law, if the MNE is to be fully understood. Consequently, given the characteristics of service sector firms, the theory cannot be expected to give more than a rudimentary understanding of service MNEs.

3.4 Foreign direct investment and intra-firm trade in services

International transactions theory must recognise the significance of intra-firm trade. According to UNCTC (1988, p.91) between one fifth to over a third of the exports and imports of the major developed market economies is internal to the firm. Such trade is likely to grow in line with the volume of international production by MNEs.[10] It is fair to assume that a proportion of such trade is in services, for example, head office services, R&D activities, trade in intangible knowledge advantages and other non-visible services.

Coffey and Polese (1987) note that the services most often traded via intra-firm channels are generally office based activities, specifically legal, accounting and insurance services. The MNE promotes international trade in services due to the centralisation of service provision within its organisation (Rugman, 1987). Furthermore, MNEs which have contracted out their service provision wish to be supplied with services of a known quality and uniform standard around the world. "As service companies have responded to meet the demand for such global services, they have created global service networks that now serve as efficient channels of trade for such services" (Feketekuty, 1985, p.205). Intra-firm trade is then an important means through which services are transacted across national boundaries both within manufacturing and service MNEs.

The level of intra-firm trade within the services sector may however be less than that in the manufacturing sector, as UNCTC (1988, pp.466-7) notes:

> ... intra-firm trade in the service sector is considerably lower than in the manufacturing sector; in other words, the type of trade is low that would be high in industries that can split their production processes among locations. Except in a few cases, service firms cannot detach low-skill operations and shift them to developing countries, while keeping high skill operations at home. As a result, foreign affiliates in many service industries tend to be more similar to their parent firms in terms of physical capital intensity and skill intensity. Thus, the lower tradeability of many services may mean that a given level of FDI in services represents more transfers of skills and physical capital than the same level of FDI in manufacturing. In sum, foreign service affiliates tend to be more complete and more free standing than foreign manufacturing affiliates.

Since the type of international production present within multinational manufacturing firms is rare among service firms it may be fair to assume that intra-firm trade within service firms is likely to be less. However, its existence must be noted, as indeed, must the potential for the growth of this type of trade. For service firms intra-firm trade may be used as a means of delivering a service across borders rather than within a system of international production as such. To fully appreciate the links between parent firms and their subsidiaries it is necessary to explore the organisation of the international firm which is considered in the next chapter.

3.5 Conclusion

Until recently the service sector had suffered from an almost total neglect in the literature on international transactions. It has been shown here that the theories of international trade and FDI can, in certain circumstances be successfully applied to international service transactions. However, a number of problems must be highlighted.

Firstly, there is the static nature of much of the theory which makes it particularly difficult to apply to some of the rapidly developing service activities such as, information intensive services where developments in ICTs are having a major impact. It is also clear that much of the theory is of questionable value in terms of providing an understanding of trade and FDI in goods, so it is also likely to be of limited value to the understanding of international service transactions.

Secondly, the theories fail to adequately explain why international transactions in services may occur through a foreign presence even though it is possible for a service in some cases to be exported in the traditional sense. The problems of defining services and international service transactions also give rise to difficulties in terms of applying traditional theories. As does the high level of regulation which is a common feature in many service markets.

Having explored trade and FDI theories in relation to services it is clear that to fully appreciate the activities of service sector firms it is necessary to look beyond these theories. The interaction between trade and FDI must be recognised, and, in particular, the importance of intra-firm trade in services. To fully appreciate the internationalisation of services it is necessary to explore the organisational development and structure of international service firms. In this way a thorough comprehension of the dynamics of international service transactions can be gained, with light being shed on the structure and strategic growth of service sector firms. Thus before exploring the internationalisation of business services an examination of organisational theory and its relevance to service sector firms will be provided in the next chapter. Once this has been completed it will be possible to move to a sub-sectoral level with a full appreciation of the theoretical issues.

Notes

1   According to Smith (1776) if free trade were permitted then it would be based on 'absolute advantage', that is, the capacity of a country to produce its export commodities at an absolutely lower cost in terms of real resources

used at home than abroad, and to import those commodities that another country can produce at an absolutely lower real cost.

2 According to Ricardo (1817), under conditions of free trade, a country will specialise in the production and export of those commodities it can produce with greatest comparative advantage, that is, those commodities for which its costs are comparatively lowest, and will import commodities in which it has a comparative disadvantage, that is, those commodities it can produce only at high relative cost. Ricardo used a simple model with two countries, two commodities, and one factor of production, labour. Constant costs and perfect competition were assumed. The comparative productivity of labour is identified as the source of comparative differences in real costs. If the number of commodities and number of countries are increased, the model becomes more complicated, but the logic remains the same (Dornbusch et al., 1977). Any number of commodities in any number of countries can be arranged in a chain of declining comparative advantage (Bhagwati, 1964; Findley, 1970).

3 Heckscher and Ohlin developed a $2 \times 2 \times 2$ model in which there exists two goods, two factors of production and two countries. In addition, a number of assumptions are made: products are homogenous; each country faces identical production functions; countries enjoy equal access to the same body of technological knowledge; consumer preferences are assumed to be identical in all countries; factors of production are perfectly mobile within countries but immobile between countries; product markets and factor markets are perfectly competitive; there are no transport costs; and, no barriers to trade.

4 See note 3 above.

5 Evidence of a changing pattern of comparative advantage, with the structure of exports developing in line with changing relative factor endowments, has prompted what has been referred to as a 'stages approach' to comparative advantage (Balassa, 1979).

6 The H-O-S model illustrates the principle that when factors are not freely mobile between countries but trade is unrestricted, the factors in effect move in the guise of commodities traded leading to factor price equalisation (Samuelson, 1948,1949). Commodity trade therefore tends to be a substitute for international factor movements (Mundell, 1957a).

7 For a comprehensive examination of the definitional problems see, for example, UN Economic and Social Council, 1978, Annex I, pp.158ff.

8 The term 'transaction costs' does not appear in Coase's (1937) article, it was first used by Arrow (1969).

9 For a review of alternative forms of foreign involvement see Young et al. (1989).

10   For a review of the extent of intra-firm trade see for example Chudson
      (1981) or Helleiner (1981).

4 Organisational theory of the firm and the international structure and strategy of service firms

4.1 Introduction

For many service sector firms international trade is limited, or simply not an option. International expansion for these firms requires the extension of their organisations beyond national boundaries through FDI or other related means. To fully appreciate the internationalisation of services it is then necessary to explore the organisational development of international service firms. It is the purpose of this chapter to achieve this through an examination of the organisational theory of the firm. A review of the wealth of organisational literature is beyond the scope of this study, attention here will be focused on economic approaches to organisations. The chapter will begin with a brief review of organisational theory of the firm and an assessment of its relevance to service firms. This is followed by an exploration of the organisation of international service firms. Conclusions will be drawn with regard to the value of organisational theory as an explanation of the organisational development of international service firms.

4.2 The organisation of the service firm

Organisational theories explore the firm as a social organisation made up of individuals who often have different objectives, motivations, information sets, and contractual obligations (Thompson and Wright, 1988). This then goes beyond the neoclassical economic treatment of the firm as a 'black box' operating in an environment free from uncertainty and whose actions are determined by the entrepreneur in pursuit of profit maximisation.

It is only since the 1960s with the writings of behavioural and managerial theorists (Cyert and March, 1963; Baumol, 1959; Marris, 1964; Williamson, 1964), with their attention on decision taking within the firm, that there has been considerable theoretical and empirical efforts by economists to determine the properties of alternative internal organisational forms. With this has come a renewal of interest in Coase's (1937) explanation as to why firms exist. Coase argued that:

> The main reason why it is profitable to establish a firm would seem to be that there is a cost of using the price mechanism. The most obvious cost of 'organising' production through the price mechanism is that of discovering what the relevant prices are ... The costs of negotiating and concluding a separate contract for each exchange transaction which takes place on the market must also be taken into account (1937, pp. 390-1).

Since using the market is costly, an authority (the entrepreneur) may choose to direct the allocation of resources within the firm. Coase provides a reason for the existence and size of firms but fails to give any insight into the organisational structure of the firm.

In contrast to Coase, Alchian and Demsetz (1972) argue that the only major difference between the firm and the market is the importance of team production, and the consequent difficulty of metering and rewarding the individual contribution to the collective effort. They argue that there is a need for a monitor to minimise shirking amongst the workforce. The necessity of monitoring is also highlighted by Jensen and Meckling (1976) who regard the theory of the firm as a special case of the theory of agency relationships. The principal (shareholder in the case of a firm) engages the agent (manager) to perform some task, however, agents will not necessarily work in the interests of the principal, thus monitoring costs arise. The problem of monitoring can be viewed as the driving force of organisational design.

Williamson (1985) extending the Coasian notion of the firm has developed his central thesis that economic institutions such as firms "have the main purpose and effect of economizing on transaction costs" (p.1). Williamson however, fails to adequately clarify the meaning of transaction costs, and instead quotes Arrow's (1969, p.48) definition of transaction costs as the "cost of running the economic system". As Fischer (1977, p.322) notes:

> Transaction costs have a well-deserved bad name as a theoretical device, because solutions to problems involving transaction costs are often sensitive to the assumed form of the costs, and because there is a suspicion that almost anything can be rationalised by involving suitably specified transaction costs.

In Dahlman's (1979) view, all forms of transaction cost reduce to one: principally a cost incurred due to lack of information. The difficulties incurred in defining transaction costs by their very nature give rise to measurement problems. The value of a theory based on such an ill defined concept is open to debate. To operationalise the theory it is necessary to employ further assumptions.

However, transaction cost economics has, in recent years, come to dominate discussions of the nature and organisation of the firm. This framework is not without its critics, Dietrich (1994), for example, argues that its comparative static methodology is least effective in explaining the dynamic aspects of a firm's behaviour. Despite the problems associated with the transactions cost approach, it does offer some useful insights into the nature and organisational development of the firm. It is best viewed as a basis from which the construction of a general theory of the firm can be attempted.

It is useful then to explore Williamson's (1975, 1985) markets and hierarchies approach to economic organisations and to evaluate its explanatory value when applied to service sector institutions. Williamson views external trading and internal organisations as competing modes of handling transactions. In his 'organisational failures' approach he set out to identify key factors which influenced the transaction costs and so determined which mode or, governance structure, was most appropriate. Individual *opportunism* - the tendency of individuals to pursue self interested behaviour, and *bounded rationality* arising from the limited information-processing and decision making capacity of human agents (Simon, 1955), are assumed together with an economic environment characterised by uncertainty and complexity. According to Williamson, the conjunction of uncertainty and opportunism is likely to lead to the exploitation of *informational asymmetries* with attendant problems for market transactions. The asymmetric distribution of information and skills among opportunistic traders can lead to *small numbers* of potential buyers or sellers with the consequent costs of bilateral monopoly. Also, Williamson notes that non-economic factors influence our willingness to transact.

Further to this Williamson (1979) has suggested that asset specificity[1] and the frequency of transactions determine the broad characteristics of contracting arrangements (governance structures). This is because idiosyncratic investments in physical or human capital together with frequent trading raise the hazards of becoming involved in an exchange relationship. Hierarchy thus becomes the best, though not only, means of resolving governance costs. The notion of governance structures significantly develops the theory of organisational choice beyond a simple market-versus-hierarchies dichotomy to encompass intermediate forms.

Such a framework can be usefully applied to service sector organisations. Service firms benefit from economies of common governance (Enderwick, 1989) which reduce transaction costs as exchange is hierarchically managed. When attempting to identify the factors which influence the transaction costs incurred by service sector firms, then Williamson's focus on opportunism, bounded rationality, uncertainty and small numbers would appear to be equally relevant. The problem of asymmetric information may have even more relevance to service sector enterprises.

Many of the inputs into the production of both goods and services take the form of services. The transaction of such intermediate services within the market may give rise to high costs. Since service firms are likely to incorporate a higher proportion of service inputs than manufacturing firms, then the costs involved in these intermediate transactions will be more significant to the overall structure of a service firm.

The following factors lead to high cost for market transactions in services:

1 Services are an experience product, as such their quality cannot be determined prior to consumption and therefore purchase.

2 Services suffer from a higher degree of quality variation when compared to manufactured goods or components.

3 Many services are information intensive which gives rise to additional problems: market transactions in information incur a high level of risk since information can be easily replicated and rapidly disseminated. This is particularly true of information which is tacit and non-codifiable. Difficulties arise then in the protection of core knowledge.

As a consequence of these factors, there is scope for contracting parties to act opportunistically. For example, a seller of a service may hide the true quality of a service, whereas a buyer may use information services in ways which have not been paid for by, for example, reproducing and selling such services to other parties. There are then problems of adverse selection and moral hazard[2] which arise in the exchange of services which may prevent such transactions occurring in the open market. By internalising the transaction within the boundaries of the firm the difficulties and costs involved in policing service transactions in the market are immediately eliminated.

The difficulties incurred in the market transaction of services and information are accentuated by the inadequacies of the patent system to protect information assets, which are often difficult to codify since their substance may be of a nebulous nature. Copyright is useful in some circumstances, but in others the best form of protection is to keep the information asset within the boundaries of the firm, thus preventing its use and abuse by unauthorised parties.

It is also interesting to note the role of asset specificity and frequency of transactions in determining the manner in which the production of services is organised. The investments made by service firms are generally in human capital and intangible assets. Although in some sectors such as transport and communications investments are dominated by capital assets. Intangible assets include brand names, trademarks, goodwill, reputation, idiosyncratic ideologies and methodologies together with unique organisational systems. These are clearly firm specific in their nature. Increasingly, in information intensive sectors these intangible assets are supported by information networks, the hardware of which can be regarded as a capital asset with low specificity. The most important element of

72

an information network is, however, its operating system which may be designed or customised for the particular needs of the firm and therefore can be regarded as firm specific.

On the whole the capital equipment used by many service firms is not firm specific. For example, office equipment and premises employed by professional or business service firms, are not firm specific assets, or indeed even sector specific. Such equipment can be easily purchased in a competitive market or obtained on a contractual basis through leasing arrangements.

Exploring firm specific assets in more detail it can be seen that they are best exchanged within the boundaries of the firm, particularly if frequent transactions would be required under market arrangements. Take a brand name, for example, this may initially be bought in the market in the sense that a firm might employ a market research company or advertising agency to develop and establish a brand name. However, once it is associated with the firm for which it has been designed it becomes an integral part of that firm. A brand name can only be sold on to another company with accompanying assets including information assets necessary for the production of the good or service with which it is identified. A brand name informs customers of the quality of a product or service which they can expect to receive from a particular firm. The exchange of the right to use a brand name in the market raises the risk that purchasers may act opportunistically by free riding and supplying an inferior product or service. Such action would damage all the firms which use the brand name, since customers' expectations will be down graded. Protecting against such an eventuality is best achieved through the internalisation of a brand name within the boundaries of the firm. Where brand names are exchanged through contractual relations, such as licensing or franchise operations, this is often accompanied by a high level of supervision from the owner of the brand name.

One of the most important assets for a service firm is its personnel. Investments in human capital will tend to be firm specific, although labour may be fairly mobile within the sector. The internalisation of key personnel is crucial to the service firm. The firm may invest heavily in training and in order to reap the benefits of such investments staff must be employed on a long term basis. Internalisation of key staff is particularly important if they are closely associated with the firms brand name, image, or reputation. Retaining such staff is essential to the success of the firm. Favourable remuneration packages and good promotion prospects will be used in an attempt to lock staff into the firm. In addition, the maintenance of a good reputation together with high performance back up systems, for example information networks, will also be useful factors helping to retain staff. Without securing key staff there is the danger that they may leave to join a competitor taking with them clients and knowledge assets. Alternatively, they might set up in competition with their former employer, for example, Maurice Saatchi's establishment of the New Saatchi Agency after leaving the Saatchi and Saatchi Company in December 1994.

There is much scope then for labour to act in an opportunistic manner, this scope is further extended if labour is employed on a contractual basis. Despite this many service firms do employ labour on such terms. For example, to complete a particular project an advertising firm or computer services firm may contract a specialist in design or software production respectively. If such labour is essential to the long term success of the firm then it will be internalised. However, when labour is highly specialised and only required on a short term basis, perhaps only for the life of a particular project, it will usually be obtained through a contract. Labour obtained in such a manner can be used to complement and supplement the internal resources of the firm on a temporary and flexible basis.

It is important to note that technological developments are leading to a period of rapid evolution within the field of organisational design in all sectors of the economy. The speed and accuracy with which information may be collected, collated, analysed and distributed throughout the firm's structure has implications for the viability of contractual relations since it can service to alleviate the problems of asymmetric information. Thus both monitoring costs and uncertainty may be reduced.

The boundaries of the manufacturing firm are being eroded by the growth of inter-firm collaborative agreements which are undermining the distinction between markets and hierarchies. The increased focus on core activities and outsourcing of non-strategic activities is leading to the development of 'hollow corporations' (Business Week, 1986) with more compact organisations and fewer hierarchical levels. An example is Benetton a designer and retailer of clothing, which is produced through contractual arrangements with clothing manufacturers. These developments have implications for the growth of services, in particular business services, due to the process of externalisation (Martinelli, 1990). Moreover, it is possible to see formerly manufacturing enterprises becoming in effect service organisations. The vast majority of systems costs, value-added, profits, and competitive advantage for companies such as those in pharmaceuticals, computers, clothing, oil and gas, food, office or automation equipment, derive from service activities (Quinn, Doorley and Paquette, 1990).

This pattern of disintegration with firms focusing on their essentially core specific activities may follow in the service sector. However, given the high level of transaction costs among service firms particularly those in the information intensive sectors, unified governance structures are likely to persist for some time. Indeed, the pattern of development among service sector firms appears, at present, to be inclined towards integration rather than disintegration. For example, in the financial, retail and business services sectors, firms have been extending the range of services they produce in search of economies of scale and scope.

4.3 Strategy and structure in the development of service firms

Organisational structures evolve over time, as events place strains upon an existing structure, informal processes and communication networks develop. Eventually a rationalisation of the formal structure is undertaken which tends to legitimise the trends that have emerged informally. As firms grow in size and complexity they generally develop a hierarchical form. An alternative is the peer group organisation which exists when a group of people work together without a hierarchy. However, once such a group grows beyond a certain size a manager may be elected to coordinate activities, and a simple hierarchy is established. Since many service firms are small, there is likely to be a high occurrence of simple hierarchical forms within the sector. Furthermore, given the nature of many professional service providers, such as accountants, consultants, lawyers and doctors, small firms in these areas are likely to be characterised by peer group organisational forms such as partnerships.

Many service firms may not develop beyond the simple hierarchical stage. Serving locationally defined or niche markets, with little prospect of gaining economies of scale or scope such firms remain small. The service sector is characterised by large numbers of small firms, from hairdressers and plumbers to accountants and corner shops. Increased levels of concentration have been witnessed in the past 20-30 years within certain sectors, for example, the development of multiple retail outlets and restaurant chains. The small size of most professional business service firms in the UK is illustrated by the fact that in 1990, 83 per cent of all market research companies employed 12 or less professional staff, and for management consultancy firms the figure was 77 per cent (Bryson, Keeble and Wood, 1993, p.121).

As noted earlier, some service activities are able to benefit from economies of scale and scope, and it is in these areas that more sophisticated organisational forms are likely to occur. As firms evolve from their entrepreneurial beginnings they tend first, to increase in size from their original narrow area of chosen product market operations. At this stage some specialisation of the management task becomes necessary and leads to the adoption of a unitary or functional form (U-form) of organisation in which specialised functional divisions are set up controlled by a chief executive (Figure 4.1a). So long as the firm remains relatively undiversified this basic form of organisation, although becoming more complex, remains adequate. However, many firms find that they are unable to maintain their objectives for expansion, or capitalise on new opportunities without adding to their original operations new activities which extend the firm into new markets.

With diversification the task of management becomes more complex, resulting in the need for structural adaptation. As a firm expands there is a cumulative loss of control with its associated efficiency loss and an impaired capacity to take strategic decisions because of the proliferation of sub-goals which are not profit oriented. The inefficiencies of the U-form enterprise, as the size, diversity and complexity of

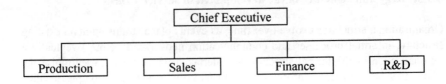

(a) Unitary Form

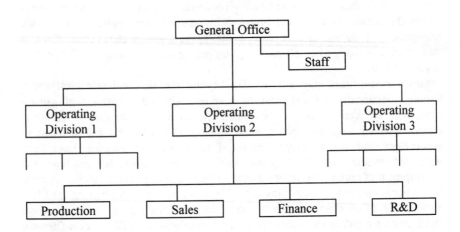

(b) Multi-division Form

Figure 4.1 Organisational structures

the firm increases, leads to the adoption of a multidivisional form (M-form). Here in place of the functional divisions of the U-form enterprise there are operating divisions which report back to a general office. The key operating responsibilities then tend to fall to the chief executives of the operating divisions, which are usually quasi-autonomous, measurable profit centres. The peak coordinator has the nature of a general office, assisted by an elite staff, which is concerned with formulating strategy (Figure 4.1b). If however, diversification is into very closely related areas then the U-form organisational structure may be sufficient.

Williamson (1975) argues that as firms grow and vertical integration is extended, transaction diseconomies are incurred and the advantages naturally deriving from internal organisation become impaired. These effects will occur for firms of a given organisational form, and will be ameliorated or reversed if the organisational form is adaptive. Williamson argues that diversified firms possessing an M-form structure should, ceteris paribus, enjoy a superior profit performance to those multi-product firms which retained functional holding company or undeveloped divisional structures.

In addition to the organisational forms outlined above Williamson (1975, pp.152-4) identifies a number of other forms[3] including the holding company (H-form), this is the divisionalised enterprise in which the requisite internal control apparatus has not been provided. The divisions are often affiliated with the parent company through a subsidiary relationship. This structure appears to be of particular importance among large business service firms with a fairly recent, though rapid, history of internationalisation.

A further organisational form which should be noted is the matrix system which attempts to obtain the benefits of both the U-form and M-form organisation by employing more that one organisational stratum. The key feature of the matrix organisation is the existence of a dual rather than a single chain of command. Davis and Lawrence (1977) argue that the matrix organisation maximises profits for companies that: must manage more than one key dimension of activity that can strongly affect the firms performance; and, face a heavy load of information processing. The matrix organisation is especially promising where scale economies in production must be reconciled with fragmented and diverse product markets. A matrix form may in a sense operate within a multidivisional structure. Whether it can be clearly distinguished from the M-form organisation with inter divisional coordination devices is open to argument (Caves, 1980). The matrix structure is of particular relevance to certain service sectors, particularly those like business services, which deliver a variety of services to the same customer and are involved in the manipulation of large quantities of information.

Chandler (1962) in his pioneering study of the evolution of the American corporation, demonstrated a clear historical connection between the firm's internal structure and the scope of its activities. He showed that for each stage of market development there appeared to be an appropriate basic structure, indicating a link between a firm's structure and the strategy it pursued. Chandler (1962) traced the spread of the M-form firm from its beginnings in the early 1920s through case studies of Du Pont, General Motors, Standard Oil, and Sears. Since the Second World War, this form has been widely adopted in the US, and from the late 1960s in Europe also. It is interesting to note that the M-form structure was adopted by Sears, a marketing firm, in the same manner as among the firms in other sectors.

Wrigley (1970) building on Chandler's work, found that the extent of firm diversification was not random, but was related to the company's core skills, that is, its basic product technology or market knowledge. Subsequent studies by Rumelt (1974) in the US, Channon (1973, 1978) in the UK, Dyas and Thanheiser (1976) in France and Germany, and Pavan (1972) in Italy, have revealed national variations but have tended to confirm Chandler's strategy - structure association.

Channon (1978), in his study of the 100 largest UK service industry corporations, found that the M-form was virtually unknown in the UK service industries in 1950. The principal organisational forms found among service firms at that time were functional and holding company systems. Most single business firms, and a substantial number of dominant business concerns, were managed with a functional structure. During the 1960s, Channon noted that the pace of product, and to a lesser extent geographical, diversification increased. In line with this diversification an increasing number of firms adopted a M-form organisation. Channon found that by 1974 37 per cent of the service firms studied had adopted this structure. As international activity increased it necessitated the addition of separate management activities leading to the adoption of more complex structures.

In addition to the functional, holding and M-forms, Channon (1978) found a relative frequent appearance of the critical function structure. In one respect a common critical function was observed as emerging in both service and manufacturing firms, namely the central treasury management function in MNEs. Channon (1978, p.20) defines the critical functional form as follows:

> In this organisational form the structure was subdivided into a series of geographic or product based operating units which were semi profit accountable. However, one or more critical functions were fully centralised and outside the responsibility of the operating units making full profit accountability unrealistic.

Channon (1978) concludes that the service industries revealed a clear relationship between strategy and structure with a gradual tendency towards both product and geographic diversification over time as the original business of the firm matured. The normal pattern of product diversification was a gradual movement from the single business firm to the development of related diversification. A substantial number of service corporations, however, had developed as conglomerates largely as a result of acquisition programmes.

This pattern of organisational development has more recently been identified in the organisation of British building societies (Gentle et al., 1991). The diversification in the building society sector, brought about by deregulation in the financial sector, has led to the adoption of M-form structures, however, computer based technology is being used to produce additional flexibility at all levels of the corporate hierarchy. This recent case of the adoption of the M-form structure is in contrast to the reorganisation and restructuring in the manufacturing sector which has been characterised by flexible specialisation and a vertical disintegrate form of organisation. This case highlights the fact that it is important not to generalise from the models of organisational change developed in selected manufacturing industries to service industries.

Enderwick (1989) argues that there are likely to be significant differences in both the structure and strategy between the service sector firm and their manufacturing counterpart. These differences are further accentuated when comparing international service firms with international manufacturing firms. In contrast to this view Morris and Johnston (1987) argue that the evidence for a difference in organisational forms between service and manufacturing firms is weak. In many service organisations the single most important reason for behaving differently from manufacturing firms is the interrelationship between production and consumption. In some cases, customers actually participate in the production of the service itself, and in many others they are present in person. Although in operational management terms the service customer may be processed in a similar way to information or materials. Production is likely to be carried out in a more dispersed way than in manufacturing, although, this does not necessarily imply the dispersal of other functional management parts of the organisation.

It is important to note that the separation of the service sector firm from the manufacturing sector enterprise is somewhat removed from reality. It is quite common to find a firm active in both sectors. In fact every manufacturing firm is involved in the provision of services, although, this may be the internal provision of services required in the process of manufacturing. However, firms exist which simultaneously produce both goods and services for the open market. For example BAT, a manufacturer of tobacco products, diversified into insurance in 1984 by acquiring Eagle Star. Other firms have become service providers through a process of externalisation (Howells and Green, 1986; Elfring and Baven, 1994). Indeed, it is also possible that service firms diversify into manufacturing. For example, Grand Metropolitan, a giant international service conglomerate, includes food and drink manufacturing companies among its operations. It is essential that when identifying the general differences between service and manufacturing sector firms, the overlap and links between the two sectors are recognised.

Some differences between service and manufacturing organisations may be accounted for by the nature of the product, for example, product standardisation may be less prevalent in services. Standardisation is clearly possible in certain areas, for example, fast food restaurants, however, many service activities are highly customised. Management consultancy services, for example, are depend upon the consumers specific requirements which will vary from customer to customer. As a result, it is possible to assume that those services where standardisation is limited or totally impossible will find economies of scale less significant in determining the firm's strategy and structure. In addition to this the immobility of many services implies that concentration of production and dependence on mass distribution is not a viable growth strategy for much of the sector. Economies of scale, however, are of significance to a number of capital intensive service industries such as transportation and communication. Also large size in banking and financial sectors bestows the advantages of risk spreading and arbitrage.

Horizontal integration may be pursued by the service firm in an attempt to gain economies of scale in the use of communications networks and central office specialisations. Although these economies will be limited due to the customised nature of many services. Vertically integrated service organisations are likely to be less apparent as long production runs in order to gain economies of scale are not viable in most service sectors.

Although some of the worlds largest firms are engaged in service provision, for example, the major banks, and telecommunication service providers, on the whole service firms tend to be smaller and display greater product specialisation than their manufacturing counterparts. Low barriers to entry, in terms of capital requirements, facilitate new service firm creation to a much greater degree than in the manufacturing sector. Production economies appear to be less important to service firms and this is reflected in low levels of concentration in many sectors.

It is widely accepted that the service firms may benefit from economies of scope (Enderwick, 1989; Dunning, 1993b), which exist where it is less costly to combine two or more product lines in one firm than to produce them separately. While apparent in areas such as retailing, banking and brokerage services they are becoming increasingly important in a number of business service sectors.

It is likely that the areas into which service firms diversify will be closely related to the original production area and utilise the firm's core skills. Indeed, diversification may be influenced by the desire to satisfy client needs or to exploit client banks by offering an increased range of services to existing clients. As in the manufacturing sector diversification will be influenced by synergy (Kay, 1984). Attempts to diversify more widely have failed, for example, the advertising company Saatchi and Saatchi's diversification into management consulting, and also the diversification of a number of banks and building societies into the estate agency sector. Where diversification is into very closely related areas then the use of a divisionalised structure along product lines may be unnecessary. Indeed other organisational forms may be more appropriate such as the matrix organisation. The extent and content of links between the various services being provided will dictate the appropriate form of internal organisation.

Kay (1984) emphasises the importance of environment as a factor determining strategy and so structure. In this respect it is important to note the significance of regulation in the service sector compared to in the manufacturing sector. The regulatory environment will no doubt have an impact on the strategy of service firms. For example, in the UK restrictions on the concentration of ownership in the media will influence the expansion decision of media firms, perhaps causing them to expand internationally rather than domestically, or alternatively to diversify into other sectors. Other environmental factors which will influence a firm's strategy include the level of competition, opportunities for innovation in service provision together with the general economic and political climate.

Another external element which may influence the strategic decisions of service sector firms is technological development. Of particular importance to information intensive services are the developments in ICTs, which are of greatest value where information can be standardised. Given the largely unique nature of many services such standardisation is limited. Perhaps the main benefit of ICTs is in terms of improving the productivity in the production of customised services by increasing the speed with which information is collected and compiled. Quinn and Paquette (1990), however, argue that well managed service technologies can simultaneously deliver both lowest cost outputs and maximum personalisation and customisation for customers. They go on to say that:

> ... enterprises generally obtain strategic advantage not through traditional economies of scale, but through *focusing on the smallest activity or cost unit* that can be efficiently measured and replicated - and then *cloning and mixing these units* across as wide a geographical and applications range as possible (1990, p.67).

Examples of the smallest replicable unit include: for accountants, audit check procedures, inventory control processes, or tax preparation documents; for lawyers, prepackaged documents, paragraphs, phrases, court opinions, or case briefings.

The use of ICT may be an important source of competitive advantage for information intensive service firms, and may well influence the strategies they pursue, and consequently their structures. Quinn and Paquette (1990) suggest that new service technologies are stimulating the development of new organisational structures in all sectors of the economy. In relation to service enterprises they identify three emerging structures. Firstly, the 'inverted pyramid' where all systems and support staff in the company 'work for' the frontline person to deliver the company's full capabilities at the moment of customer contact, an example is the Toronto Dominion Bank. Secondly, the 'infinitely flat' organisation where there are virtually no limits to the reporting span that a service organisation can make effective. Shearson American Express, Merrill Lynch and Federal Express are examples of this structure. Thirdly, the 'spider's web' organisation where the highly dispersed nodes of service operations or customer contact must interact frequently, an example is that of Arthur Andersen and Company. This third structure is of particular relevance for professional and business service companies, particularly those with a wide geographical spread. In certain circumstances, the individual nodes in the spider's web may need to operate in a highly coordinated manner to achieve strategic advantage for a specific purpose. In such a situation, companies with traditional organisational structures must resort to complex matrix organisations which allow the project leader to obtain resources, as needed, from an otherwise decentralised network.

Since the service sector consists of such a heterogeneous group of activities it is perhaps necessary to draw distinctions between its various parts. Different service activities may give rise to different organisational forms. Indeed, Sasser, Wyckoff and Olsen (1978) propose a distinction between those service firms serving mass market customers, such as retailing, banking and catering, and what they call 'professional service organisations', such as lawyers, consultants and doctors. They

81

use this dichotomy to illustrate key features of structure and systems. For example, they regard the professional service organisation's structure to be a flat unstructured hierarchy with loose subordinate-superior relationships with broad discretion at all levels, whilst the consumer service organisation's structure is a rigid pyramidal hierarchy with standard operating procedures and close top-down control.

To find completely different organisational forms in the service sector is unlikely, although slight variations may be identified. What is of interest, however, is the frequency of the occurrence of the various forms and the pattern of organisational development and adaptation followed by service sector firms. It is here that it may be possible to observe differences between service firms and their counterparts in the manufacturing sector.

4.4 The organisation of international service firms

International expansion adds an additional dimension to be taken into account in the design of a firm's organisational structure. Teece (1983) has extended Williamson's (1975) markets and hierarchies approach explicitly to the multinational firm. Transaction cost analysis can be seen as complementary to internalisation theory, which similarly has its origins in the work of Coase (1937). As noted in Chapter 3, internalisation theory is accepted as a key element explaining the existence of the MNE, and it also provides valuable insights into their organisational structures. Internalisation may be particularly important to MNEs in order to gain the benefits of international transfer pricing and vertical integration, and to improve quality control.

Clearly the transaction cost approach and internalisation theory are closely related, and at times they are used interchangeably (for example, Hennart, 1991), however, it is important to note that despite the substantial convergence there are differences in emphasis. Williamson (1975) forwards hierarchy as a means of reducing costs arising from market transactions, whereas internalisation theory emphasises an alternative to hierarchy as the means of resolving the problems of monitoring individuals within the organisation and reducing governance costs. Foreign subsidiary managers may have better knowledge of local conditions, thus it may be difficult to use hierarchical direction to remove discretion in decision-making. Buckley and Casson (1976, 1985) argue that, the internal organisation of the MNE is an approximation to a perfect market whereby the firm's internal processes are designed to transmit shadow prices to the key decision makers, which optimise the firm's overall profits. Hennart (1986) suggests that the incentives given by the internal market are more powerful and less costly than hierarchical control, which will only be used when price signals are inappropriate.

The MNE can therefore be seen as a device for reducing transaction costs by buying or creating complementary assets in different nations and integrating their generation within a single unit of control. This is the internal market for intermediate goods and services (Buckley, 1992). In this way, individual managers within the firm have decentralised decision making powers such that control over the intermediate product actually changes hands as the product moves between plant, although ownership of the product does not (Casson, 1981). Rugman (1981) argues that internalisation is undertaken in order to impose centralisation. However, as Buckley (1983,1992) notes, the internalisation approach implies not only a decentralised organisation, but decentralised decision-making based on central determination of goals and distribution of rewards.

Internalisation theory has been criticised as tautological: firms exist where they minimise transaction costs. This has led to it being described as a "concept in search of a theory" (Buckley, 1983, p.42). With transaction costs being central to internalisation theory there are the attendant definitional and measurement problems. Despite the differences between the markets and hierarchies and internalisation frameworks they are complementary in the sense that they share the view that organisations economise on transaction costs.

It has been shown (Casson, 1985; Teece, 1983; Buckley, 1987) that the incidence of transaction costs is particularly high in vertically integrated process industries, knowledge-intense industries, quality assurance dependent products and communication-intense industries. Given the knowledge and communication intensive nature of many services, together with the importance of quality assurance, one might expect internalisation to be of particular significance to service firms. The high incidence of transaction costs in market transactions for services must be taken into account when considering the organisational development of service MNEs.

It is also important to note that for some service MNEs subsidiaries may be regarded as transaction specific assets (idiosyncratic investments), they are in effect assets created to facilitate the international transaction of the service. Such subsidiaries may be required because of the non-tradability of a service, or because trade is only feasible in conjunction with an overseas presence. Trade facilitated by an overseas presence may be of the traditional type or may be intra-firm trade where a foreign market is supplied with a service largely produced elsewhere.

The transaction cost approach has been applied to the firm's choice of foreign market entry mode (Anderson and Gatignon, 1986). Erramilli and Rao (1993) investigated this choice for service firms using a modified transaction cost approach. They consider idiosyncratic services which they define as characterised by "high levels of professional skills, specialized-knowhow and customization" (p.23). The production of idiosyncratic services is characterised by high asset specificity, necessitating, as it does, non-trivial transaction specific physical and human investments in the value-added chain. Transaction cost analysis predicts that a firm's desire for shared control modes diminishes with increased asset specificity. However, Erramilli and Rao (1993) argue that this analysis is unduly restrictive since the relationship between asset specificity and entry mode choice is moderated by numerous factors which either raise the cost of integration or diminish the firm's ability to establish full-control modes. These factors include capital intensity, cultural distance between home and host countries, host country risk, the inseparability of production and consumption in services and firm size.

This exploration of idiosyncratic services is a useful contribution to the literature on the internationalisation of service firms. However, Erramilli and Rao's (1993) focus on asset specificity as the main source of market failure and transaction costs, thereby reduces all other influences to non transaction cost factors. This analysis takes, then, a rather narrow conceptualisation of transaction costs. Despite this, it does illustrate the value of transaction cost analysis as a method of explaining the nature of internationalisation among service firms.

4.5 Strategy and structure in the development of international service firms

Firms which expand over time eventually find further growth limited by the size of their domestic market. There are two choices in terms of strategy, which will enable the firm to overcome such a restriction these are either to expand internationally, thus extending the firm's market beyond national boundaries, or to expand the products and/or services which the firm offers in the domestic market, that is to diversify. These two choices can be regarded as alternatives (Wolf, 1977; Caves, 1982; Buckley, 1985; Ansoff, 1987). The strategy selected will depend upon industry and firm specific factors. If the firm can benefit from economies of scale then the extension of its market through internationalisation would be the preferred choice. On the other hand, if there are economies of scope to be gained through diversification then this strategy will be favoured.

Internationalisation will be used by service firms to extend their market. In some cases it may be a defensive measure, in order to retain clients which have expanded into overseas markets. Indeed much of the initial internationalisation in banking services was of this type (Yannopoulos, 1983). Esperanca (1992) actually found evidence of service firms following clients into countries where the domestic market was too small to break even. The objective being to preserve a good relationship with the client and avoid the client switching to a rival firm already established in that market. Internationalisation may also be a positive aggressive strategy rather than purely defensive. Particularly where a service firm has some competitive advantage, or where internationalisation may be facilitated at little additional cost. Erramilli and Rao (1990) distinguish between client following (CF) and market seeking (MS) entry strategies. They argue that CF strategies are more likely to be associated with 100 per cent equity ownership than joint venture or some form of contractual arrangement, and that firms pursing MS strategies are more likely to conclude cooperative alliances than those adopting CF strategies.

A number of studies (Johanson and Wiedersheim-Paul, 1975; Stopford and Wells, 1972; Aharoni, 1966; Behrman, 1969; inter alia) have found that the internationalisation of the manufacturing firm occurs in an evolutionary manner.

This view is not without its critics (Hood and Young, 1983; Hedlund and Kverneland, 1984), Turnbull (1987), for example, refutes this evolutionary approach, having failed to find any evidence of it in a study of the internationalisation of a number of British manufacturing firms. It is questionable whether service firms become international in an evolutionary manner. From the exploration of the internationalisation of services (Chapter 2) it is commonly accepted that the majority of services are non-tradable and that internationalisation requires the establishment of an overseas presence. Given this view service firms would progress rapidly from a national firm to an international firm without a period of exporting services. However, to class all services as non-tradable is misleading. Indeed, all services can be exported if the service is provided to a foreign client in the domestic market. Further to this, many information intensive services, including professional and business services, can be embodied in a tangible form, such as a report or computer disk, and exported in the traditional manner. Exports can also occur 'over-the-wire' and through personnel travelling to the client's location.

The level of exports, when this form of market servicing is possible, necessary to give rise to the consideration of the establishment of an overseas production facility is likely to be much lower for many service sector firms than for firms in the manufacturing sector. This is because the capital costs involved in the establishment of a production facility for many service firms are very much lower than for most firms in the manufacturing sector. For example, all that is required for a business service firm to set up an overseas production facility is an office and staff, whereas in the manufacturing sector costly plant and equipment will also be required. Also the office equipment utilised by business service firms will be non-specific and therefore relatively cheap. Staff, however, will be highly skilled and costly as they may be sector specific, although this is counter balance by the high mobility of professional staff.

The necessity of expanding abroad in order to supply an overseas market, due to the inability to export services, will lead many service firms to expand overseas at an earlier point in their life compared to firms in the manufacturing sector, where internationalisation begins with exports and is followed later by the establishment of an overseas subsidiary. Expanding overseas at such an early point in the firms life may lead to a variety of overseas market arrangements, since finance may not be available for a wholly owned subsidiary. However, these days with the changing economic environment and increasing hostility to wholly owned subsidiaries, there is greater use of other methods of international expansion by manufacturing firms. In addition, factors such as cultural distance and the nature of the service to be provided will influence the selection of a particular foreign market entry mode.

The small size of service MNEs is likely to be related to their relative immaturity. In industries such as retailing the degree of multinationality is widely considered to be low (White, 1984). Moreover, Enderwick (1989, p.32) notes that 62.9 per cent

85

of service MNEs have affiliates in only one country compared with 39.8 per cent in the case of manufacturing MNEs.

Methods of overseas expansion which minimise costs and risks may well be important. Service firms may set up a reciprocal arrangement with a firm in the overseas market or participate in a joint venture. Through this type of arrangement the firm can gain experience and knowledge of the foreign market. By doing so the risks and uncertainty involved can be reduced. As the firm becomes more committed to the overseas market the firm may choose to increase its ownership share in the overseas presence. This may indeed be required if as commitment increases intangible assets are shared, increased ownership will facilitate greater control over the foreign presence and thus ensure the protection of intangible assets. There is clearly a tendency for the use of majority owned subsidiaries to increase as the firm develops and this may well be related to the increase in commitment to, knowledge and experience of, foreign markets (Esperanca, 1992). Although, Erramilli (1991) found that service firms demand high-control modes of foreign market presences in the early and late stages of their international evolution.

The limited use of exporting by service industries suggests other areas where experiences will diverge from those of firms in the manufacturing sector. There is likely to be a much lower degree of locational substitutability between 'source' and 'host' nation facilities for service MNEs. Internationalisation may be purely in order to deliver the service to an overseas market, services being largely non-tradable in the traditional sense. So service production may occur in the home country but be delivered via a foreign subsidiary, that is, through intra-firm trade. Nonetheless, there is as yet little in the way of a complex system of international production among service firms. Although, new ICTs and organisational techniques may change this in time.

The comparatively late takeoff of service sector FDI suggests that acquisition may be a preferred form of entry for many firms. Analysis of inward investment in the US suggests that acquisition is a widely adopted strategy for service MNEs (Belli, 1981) allowing both more rapid entry and the achievement of a critical mass which may be considerable in industries characterised by multiple outlets. Furthermore, one would expect to observe considerable variety in the forms of overseas representation adopted by service MNEs (Enderwick, 1989). This is despite their preference for wholly owned subsidiaries (Dunning, 1989; Erramilli and Rao, 1993).

Where information assets need to be protected then full ownership of subsidiaries will be preferred, however, where this is not possible due to local regulation or lack of finance then franchising and licensing may provide an acceptable alternative. Dunning and McQueen (1982) commenting on the international hotel industry note that where contracts can be used to protect knowledge, licensing and franchising are acceptable. The extent to which knowledge is codifiable will influence the degree to which licensing and franchising will be an agreeable method of internationalisation. Esperanca (1992) notes that the importance given to the protection of intangible assets such as image and reputation, and thus the desire to maintain full control of a subsidiary, varies according to significance of global customers relative to local customers.

The structure adopted by a MNE depends upon a number of factors including the age, experience and success of the enterprise, the nature of its operations and its degree of product and geographical diversity. The problems of organising a MNE have to be considered in the context of various tensions in the firm and external pressures on it. The conventional evolutionary approach (Stopford and Wells, 1972; Channon and Jalland, 1979) has suggested an export sales organisation followed by autonomous subsidiary stage, then an international division approach which is commonly adopted in the early stages of development when there are several overseas subsidiaries. The international division is simply added on to the existing divisional structure. If the firm continues to expand the need arises for an organisational form which can integrate both the domestic and international operations of the firm. There are two possible options: firstly, to organise the firm on a global product basis; and secondly, to organise the firm's operations on a worldwide geographical basis. Each of these two global organisational forms solves one set of problems partly at the expense of another. For such reasons some of the large MNEs have begun to adopt sophisticated global matrix structures which contain elements of both product and area structures.

The view that a firm can only pursue a global strategy through the adoption of an M-form framework (Stopford and Wells, 1972), is an unnecessarily rigid approach. Brooke (1984) sees the organisation as a result of continuing conflicts to which the firm seeks a resolution. This leads to a dynamic view of organisational structure as an evolving, interim solution. At any point in time there will be pressures on head office towards greater centralisation and towards greater autonomy for the subsidiary; similarly these conflicting pressures will operate on the subsidiary (Brooke, 1986). Consequently, external pressures will be moderated, directed and influenced by power struggles within the firm. The resolution of these pressures depends upon the particular situation of the firm. Of great importance are: industry specific factors, regional specific factors, nation specific factors, and factors specific to the firm itself (Buckley and Casson, 1976; Brooke, 1986).

The dynamic nature of international service firms has been documented by Channon (1978) in a study of the impact of an international strategy on the organisation of a sample of service firms. He found that low levels of international activity (10 per cent or less of sales from international operations) tended to be the only condition under which the functional structure was workable. As international activity increased, of necessity, it required the addition of separate management activities leading to the adoption of a more complex structure. High levels of overseas activity (40 per cent or more of sales from international operations) were usually managed with a divisional or holding company structure. Overseas holding companies tended to be of the mother-daughter variety, where subsidiaries were allowed substantial autonomy subject to a personalised system of control. The divisional structures tended to be of relatively recent origin, and in most cases had not progressed beyond an international division stage which in turn was usually divided geographically. Where further subdivision had occurred, overseas activities were usually grouped into area based divisions rather than worldwide product or other alternative systems.

The relationship between international activity and diversification reveals that high levels of overseas activity usually go hand in hand with high product diversity, almost all the high international activity companies examined by Channon (1978) were diversified, related, or conglomerate business companies. Furthermore, it was found that deliberate overseas expansion strategies were most common among the medium international activity (between 10 and 40 per cent of sales from international operations) firms which were engaged in building and construction, hotels and leisure, and banking and finance services. These businesses, which had usually begun to diversify domestically, had concurrently, or shortly after, also started to expand their principal activities overseas. This strategy had been pursued usually with great speed, with investments being concentrated in the developed regions of Western Europe and North America or other high growth countries.

More recent research (Quinn and Paquette, 1990) has identified a variety of new organisational forms among service firms including those which are international in scope. These organisational developments are occurring in all sectors. Some firms are now moving towards a globally integrated network structure in which, according to Bartlett and Ghoshal (1989, p.89):

> ... increasingly specialized units worldwide ... [are] ... linked into an integrated network of operations that ... [enables] ... them to achieve their multidimensional strategic objectives of efficiency, responsiveness, and innovation ... The strength of this configuration springs from its fundamental characteristics: dispersion, specialization, and interdependence.

There is undoubtedly a tendency for some MNEs to move away from a hierarchical organisational structure in which there is a clear vertical division of control, to a flatter, more complex and flexible, networked structure. This does not necessarily imply a loosening of control or coordination.

Hedlund and Rolander (1990) argue that the organisational structure and mode of control in highly international MNEs is shifting towards a model which they call heterarchy. This entails a geographical diffusion of core strategic activities and coordinating roles, a break with the notion of one uniform hierarchy of decisions as well as organisational positions, and an increased focus on normative control mechanisms. It is probable that service firms which become highly international will adopt such a structure.

There are a wide variety of organisational forms used in the internationalisation of service firms. Internationalisation in some sectors may be via an international network of independent but associated firms, an example, is the form of some of the large international accountancy firms which operate on a federation type basis each branch being owned by local partners however all being linked into an international service network. Mayere and Vinot (1993) note in their study of intellectual services that firms within such networks have common objectives and shared organisational and operating principles.

It is important to note that new ICTs are increasing the scope for the internationalisation of services and provide an infrastructure through which information intensive services can be exported. Many information intensive services can be internationalised at little additional cost, with the use of information assets in a large international market giving rise to economies of scale. Services which are knowledge intensive, requiring large amounts of data collection and processing, can take advantage of truly international production due to advances in telecommunications technologies. For example, the labour intensive activity of data entry can be located in less developed countries where labour has the requisite skills but is much cheaper than in the developed countries. The pursuit of international production in this manner will have implications for the organisation of service MNEs. An increase in the scope for international production among service firms is likely to necessitate more integrated organisational structures with greater capacity for overseeing and coordinating activities over a wide geographical span.

4.6 Conclusion

From the above it would appear that organisational theory developed primarily for manufacturing sector firms is just as relevant to service firms. As Jones and Ricks (1989) argue, in order to facilitate organisational effectiveness, the key issues are similar whatever the industry orientation. What is needed is a responsive, flexible business providing added value where customers genuinely request it.

It is, however, apparent that the service firms may be faced with circumstances influencing the path of organisational development which differ from those faced by manufacturing firms. For example, many services cannot be exported, consequently, a service firm may have to establish an overseas presence if it is to provide services across national borders. Another example is the relatively low significance of economies of scale in many service sectors compared to the manufacturing sector, the results of this reveal themselves in the size of service firms and hence their organisational structure. Service firms also face environmental differences such as higher levels of regulation.

Even within the service sector the pressures which influence organisational design will vary, hence the difficulty of drawing general conclusions about service firms.

Moreover, it is important to recognise the rapid change in organisational structures in all sectors. As Dicken (1992, p.222) notes:

> The ways in which the production chain is organized, and the boundary between which functions are internalized within a firm and which are externalized and performed as a division of labour between firms, is extremely fluid. ... there are signs of *increasingly flexible* forms of organizational relationship in the global economy.

Structure should be consistent with strategy, and since strategy tends to change over time, organisational structure will be modified in line with such change. Economic theory views efficiency as the primary determinant of organisational structure, though clearly there are additional factors to take into account. In the context of the service firm the problem of measuring efficiency must be highlighted, dependent as it is on the ability to measure the quantity and quality of output. In many service sectors such a task is fraught with difficulties. It is then, more appropriate to refer to effective, rather than efficient organisations. Generally, the most strategically appropriate structure will often not be adopted due to the intervention of variables such as national political requirements, internal political power alignments, personal values and legal, fiscal and cultural constraints. It is also essential to recognise the wider role of the firm, as Hodgson notes (1988, p.208):

> The nature of the firm is not simply a minimizer of transaction costs, but a kind of protective enclave from the potentially volatile and sometimes destructive, ravaging speculation of a competitive market.

In a rapidly changing environment a firm's objectives must extend beyond short term profit maximisation to long term survival. This is the case for firms in all sectors of the economy, although more so for those in dynamic areas where the application of new ICTs and organisational techniques are changing the nature, modes of production and delivery of both goods and services. The ability to adapt and change in response to new market, technological and social forces, would seem to be of paramount importance to the competitiveness and survival of today's firms.

The organisational structure adopted by international service firms will be influenced by a wide variety of factors. The use of a range of organisational forms has been identified from the multidivisional structure to newer and innovative network structures. Clearly, the organisational form of a service firm evolves over time, and will be specific to the firm's output, stage of development, mode of expansion and environment. Through a focus on business service firms this study will provide a detailed exploration of the interaction of the forces which mould the international organisation of firms in this sector.

90

Understanding the evolution of international organisational structures within the service sector, together with an appreciation of trade and FDI in the sector, will enable the development of a framework within which the internationalisation of services can be fully explained. It is now time to draw together the findings of this chapter with those of Chapter 3 and in doing so provide a synthesis of the theories in the search for a comprehensive understanding of the internationalisation of services.

Notes

1   Asset specificity refers to the degree to which an asset is transaction specific. Transaction specific assets are non-redeployable physical and human investments that are specialised to a task. They are idiosyncratic investments.

2   Adverse selection (hidden information) refers to a situation when one party in a potential transaction is better informed about a relevant variable in the transaction than the other party. It is an ex ante information problem. Moral hazard (hidden action) refers to action which parties in a transaction may take after they have agreed to execute the transaction. It is an ex post information problem. See, for example, Ricketts (1994) for a detailed explanation.

3   These forms include the mixed form which is a divisionalised enterprise in which some divisions are essentially of the holding company variety, others M-form, and still others under close supervision of the general management. Two types of M-form organisation are distinguished: type D1, which denotes a highly integrated M-form enterprise, possibly with differentiated but otherwise common final products; and type D2, which denotes the M-form enterprise with diversified final products or services. The transitional multidivisional and the corrupt multidivisional forms are also identified.

5 The international business service firm: the evolution of an internationalisation framework

5.1 Introduction

The central aim of this research is to develop a framework within which the internationalisation of business services can be explained. The objective is to reach beyond exploration, and, drawing on the literature reviewed in the last three chapters, develop a model which has predictive qualities. The purpose of this chapter is to propose various elements which influence the process of service internationalisation. From these elements a framework will be constructed which will be subjected to empirical testing within the context of the international activities of UK business service firms. In Chapter 10 the framework developed here will be assessed and adapted in the light of the research findings. A model developed for business services cannot be applied to all service sectors, however, where possible generally applicable factors will be highlighted, thus shedding light upon the internationalisation of services in general.

When exploring the internationalisation of business services there are a number of questions which have to be addressed. Firstly, it is necessary to consider why internationalisation occurs? Secondly, how does this internationalisation occur? Thirdly, what factors influence the organisational structure of international firms? When addressing these questions it is necessary to consider whether such internationalisation and organisational structures can be conceptualised in terms of the existing theories of international trade and investment, and organisational theory. Each of these questions will be considered in turn.

5.2 Why does internationalisation occur?

In order to expand in size firms must seek out new markets, either through geographical or product/service diversification. Geographical expansion ultimately leads to internationalisation as the domestic market becomes increasingly saturated. Firms will then, initially tend to extend their geographical reach in the national market prior to international expansion. However, in some cases firms will become internationally active prior to any extension of national coverage. This is particularly the case for those business service firms located in capital cities (O'Farrell and Wood, 1993). In such locations service firms are more likely to have internationally oriented clients which will encourage international rather inter-regional expansion. Within the UK, business service firms located in or near to London are likely to become international prior to extending their national coverage, whereas those firms located in peripheral regions will tend to expand nationally at first and internationally later.

The influence of multinational clients on the internationalisation of service firms has been recognised and empirically confirmed (Dunning, 1989; Erramilli and Rao, 1990; Esperanca, 1992). It is argued here that there is a strong link between the internationalisation of business service firms and the importance to them of multinational clients. In the decision to become internationally active the actions of some large multinational clients may be crucial. However, once the business service firm has expanded overseas then its international activity will be determined by a more complex strategy than simply following clients into foreign markets. As firms become increasingly international their dependence on a small number of very large multinational clients decreases. As the business service firm becomes more established internationally then national firms in overseas markets will become an important source of revenue. Indeed, at this stage the service firms may actually encourage national clients to become international. The nature of a firm's clients, that is, whether they are MNEs will undoubtedly be a factor influencing the internationalisation of business service firms.

A strategy of internationalisation followed by a firm will be influenced by a variety of factors including general economic conditions and trends both within national and international markets. On the whole, firms in all sectors are becoming more globally oriented and as such they require their producer service suppliers to provide services on a worldwide basis. In addition to this, there is the general ongoing activity of restructuring of production within the manufacturing sector, with firms concentrating their efforts on core activities whilst buying in peripheral intermediate goods and services rather than producing them in-house. This process of externalisation is of particular significance to the growth of business services firms (Martinelli, 1991; Perry, 1992), which can achieve economies of scale and scope when providing services on a large scale, and, can in many cases supply services to clients at a lower cost and higher quality than it would be possible for them to achieve in-house. Substantial economies of scale can, however, only be achieved if a firm supplies a large market, hence the need for internationalisation among business services.

New ICTs have also been important in enabling business service firms to achieve economies of scale and scope. Business services are information intensive and thus lend themselves to the application of computer and telecommunications technologies which enable the rapid collection, analysis and communication of information. Such technologies are also influencing the level and manner of internationalisation among business service firms. Improved ICTs are facilitating the evolution of more complex yet flexible international organisational structure in all sectors of the economy. Furthermore, information intensive services can increasingly be exported over telecommunication networks. Given the potential of ICT as an enabler of internationalisation, it could be expected that international business service firms make greater use of ICT and derive higher levels of competitive advantage from their use of ICT when compared to national firms.

It is also necessary to think of internationalisation in terms of the exploitation of a country's absolute or comparative advantage, the firms of certain countries are able to provide services at a lower cost and/or high quality due to a national comparative advantage (Chapter 3). Internationalisation enables this advantage to be extended beyond national borders, thereby increasing global welfare. Trade in business services can be viewed as the exploitation of a country's absolute or comparative advantage, whereas the overseas expansion of firms might be viewed as the exploitation of a firm's competitive advantage, or ownership advantages. In some cases overseas expansion may occur as a result of the desire to exploit a locational advantage, for example, excellent market opportunities and low levels of competition in the emerging market economies of Eastern Europe or South East Asia. Thus it is possible to consider the internationalisation of business services within the context of the accepted theory of international trade and investment.

5.3 How does internationalisation occur?

It is widely accepted that the internationalisation of the firm occurs in an evolutionary manner, with the firm passing through distinct stages. As noted in the previous chapter a number of studies have confirmed this pattern of development among manufacturing firms. Although there are other studies which refute this pattern of international expansion (Chapter 4). Given then that the evolutionary approach to internationalisation is of questionable value when exploring the internationalisation of manufacturing firms, is it of any use when exploring business service firm internationalisation?

From the exploration of the internationalisation of services (Chapter 2), it is commonly accepted that the majority of services are non-tradable, in the traditional sense, they are what Boddewyn et al. (1986) refer to as 'location-bound'. For such services internationalisation requires the establishment of an overseas presence, and so, producers progress rapidly from a national to an international firm without a period of exportation. Sharma and Johanson's (1987) study of technical consultancy firms confirmed this pattern of rapid internationalisation among service firms.

However, to class all services as non-tradable is misleading. Indeed, all services (apart from those such as social services which may be provided solely to national citizens within their home country) can be exported if the service is provided to a foreign client in the domestic market, such exports may be referred to as *domestically located service exports*. Services may be provided to the overseas client, in for example the form of a report or computer disk, here exportation occurs in the traditional sense in the form of what can be called *embodied service exports*. Personnel travelling may facilitate what can be called *transhuman exports*, and finally, business services can be exported through telecommunication networks in the form of what can be termed *wired exports*.

It is argued here that business service firms follow an evolutionary path towards internationalisation, as firms grow in size and domestic geographical spread they become international. Internationalisation initially takes the form of exports. Although it is generally recognised that there are difficulties in terms of exporting services these can be easily overcome if the client travels to the provider or vice versa. Although, when it is the provider travelling across borders the transaction involves the temporary cross border movement of factors of production, namely personnel. Trade frequently arises when overseas customers enter the domestic market, seeking the services available there. For example, the foreign earnings of UK law firms overwhelmingly accrue to the activity of solicitors and barristers in the City of London where they carry out an essential back up function to all the main financial service industries (Sowels, 1989).

Exports then play a crucial role in the internationalisation of business service firms. It is through serving overseas clients in the domestic market together with serving domestic clients in overseas markets through personnel travelling and other forms of exporting that such firms get their first taste of internationalisation. It is interesting to speculate upon the relative importance of the various types of exportation available to business service firms. Since face-to-face contact is necessary in the delivery, if not production, of many services it can be argued that forms of exportation which incorporate such contact are those which are likely to be used most frequently. Exports of services embodied in goods or exported over-the-wire will be less significant than those which involve the movement of the client to the location of the producer, or the movement of personnel to the client's location. With advances in ICTs embodied service exports and wired exports may become closer substitutes with other forms of service exports and therefore used more widely. Non-client contact exports undoubtedly play an important supportive and to some extent a facilitating role for other forms of export and internationalisation through other means. Such trade is often likely to be intra-firm, rather than direct trade, and is an important element influencing the international organisation of business service firms. Foreign direct investment occurs in certain circumstances to facilitate intra-firm trade; trade which cannot occur in the market for a variety of reasons and must therefore be internalised within the firm. Overseas presences in some cases may then be regarded as transaction specific since their sole purpose is to facilitate trade.

Factors which inhibit direct trade in business services, or make such trade high risk, include the need for client producer contact, the simultaneous provision and consumption of a service, the need for cultural sensitivity and local knowledge, regulatory requirements, the desire to protect reputation and intangible assets together with the necessity of absolute confidentiality. These factors encourage the internalisation of trade within the organisation of the international service firm.

As export clients become more important the firm may choose to set up a presence in the overseas market for which most of the exports are directed. Business service firms follow their clients into overseas markets at least in the early stages of internationalisation. Later as they become more international then entering a market may be seen as a means of attracting new clients as the firm competes internationally with a small number of highly international firms. Once a firm enters the international arena it is necessary to build up an international network of offices in order to attract and retain clients. Once such a network is established this can be seen as an ownership advantage and therefore a source of competitive advantage. Such a network can be regarded as a barrier to new entrants into the market, moreover, there are opportunities to achieve economies of scale and scope in its use.

The manner in which business service firms become international will vary considerably from firm to firm. In particular, the age of the firm and the period in which it first embarked upon a strategy of international expansion will be important factors. The internationalisation of business service firms is not new, some of the large accountancy firms, for example, have been active internationally since the turn of the century. This early internationalisation being closely linked to the international activities of clients and carried out in a gradual and incremental manner. However, with the growth of business services in the past 25 years there has also been a wave of rapid internationalisation. In the 1980s this second phase of internationalisation was clearly visible as firms competed with one another to establish global networks of companies to service their ever increasingly international clients. This competition has led to a higher degree of market concentration within business service sectors at an international level. It would seem that internationalisation among business service firms has in recent times followed the pattern of oligopolistic reaction predicted by Knickerbocker (1973) in relation to the multinationalisation of manufacturing firms: business service firms have followed one another into markets. It is argues here then that it is possible to distinguish two phases in the internationalisation of business services. The first phase is one of gradual internationalisation through the establishment of overseas subsidiaries, whilst in the second phase rapid internationalisation is sought through mergers and acquisitions. The second phase reflects the rapid internationalisation of economic activity in all sectors as firms search for ever greater economies of scale.

Internationalisation through acquisitions and mergers is of particular importance to firms which are latecomers to the international market. As a result it is a common method of international expansion in the computer services sector. Such a method of internationalisation is also visible among latecomers to the international market in other business service sectors. It is then possible to determine two distinct paths followed by international firms on their way to internationalisation.

It is likely that the larger the firm domestically and the wider its domestic geographical spread the more international it will be. Also, as noted earlier, firms located in capital cities are likely to enter into international markets earlier than those located in other areas. The age of the firm will also determine the level of internationalisation to some extent, however, age is not such a good predictor of internationalisation. Business service firms are able to grow rapidly, an ability witnessed in the 1980s. Rapid growth is possible with the use of mergers and takeovers. In addition, since some service firms have low asset levels, organic expansion can also be achieved relatively cheaply. The capital required to set up an additional office is low, particularly since offices and the equipment necessary to allow them to function can be obtained through leasing arrangements. Such assets are non-specific hence the ability to obtain them easily and at relatively low cost. The most important asset for a business service firm is its staff; again these can be obtained and trained relatively cheaply since employees are paid on a monthly basis and even if salaries are high, to attract quality, the initial cost of obtaining the appropriate personnel is relatively low in terms of start up costs. Indeed, it is possible to attract high quality staff at a relatively low cost by offering share options and performance related benefits. Staff may be regarded as sector specific, though not necessarily firm specific. Firm specific staff may exist when the reputation of the firm is dependent upon the presence of a particular member or group of staff, in these circumstances there is the possibility of staff acting in an opportunistic manner. Consequently, the firm's organisational structure must take into account this possibility, with mechanisms to tie key staff to the company with, for example, favourable remuneration packages, good promotion prospects and high quality staff support systems.

There have been a number of cases of business service firms growing from small beginnings to huge firms in periods as little as 10 to 20 years, for example, Saatchi and Saatchi Plc. (now known as Cordiant Plc.) and WPP Plc. within the advertising sector. Some firms have been innovative in the way in which they have financed takeovers, using methods such as reverse buy outs. Many advertising and computer service firms have made use of the stock market to gain access to the funds required to finance expansion and acquisition activity. It is important to remember that even the very large business service firms are fairly modest in size, in terms of assets and turnover, when compared to large manufacturing firms.

The international market for business services is becoming increasingly concentrated. In contrast to this domestic markets consist of a large number of small firms. Although, large firms do dominate the domestic market, there is a buoyant element of small firms and start ups which present competition, particularly in terms of the servicing of small local, regional and national clients which have no need of an international network. The large number of small firms results from the low level of barriers to entry into the business service sector at a national scale. Some small firms are on contract to larger firms in the same sector, whilst others may be linked to an international network being a wholly or majority owned subsidiary of a large international firm. There is a polarisation in the business service market between the large firms which supply primarily large and multinational clients and the small firms which generally supply small national and local clients.

A crucial barrier to entry at the international level is access to a worldwide network of offices. A wide international coverage is an important source of competitive advantage for an international business service firm. Access to a large client base may also prove to be an important source of competitive advantage as well as being a barrier to new firms entering the market. As the international market becomes increasingly concentrated it is difficult for firms to expand organically in order to establish such a network. For the small firm the most effective strategy is to either be acquired by a larger and international firm or to merge with other local and national firms in overseas markets in order to establish an international network rapidly. This to some extent explains why the second phase of internationalisation among business service firms has been characterised by mergers and takeovers.

New entrants to the international market are then possible. For the computer service sector entry is also possible from firms which already have international networks and choose to diversify into the sector because of the excellent growth opportunities. So firms such as, end users, hardware manufacturers and telecommunication providers are moving into the sector at an international level. Despite the high level of concentration in the market for business services there is still a higher level of competition than can be found in many manufacturing sectors. The evidence suggests though, that the levels of concentration are set to increase as firms expand in search of economies of scale and scope. Technological developments may, however, provide opportunities for new innovative firms to enter the international market.

The larger the firms size then the more international it is likely to be. Internationalisation begins with exports and progresses to the establishment of an overseas presence, either through FDI, joint venture, or contractual arrangement with an overseas firm. The establishment of an overseas presence may be accompanied by trade, but initially trade is likely to be intra-firm trade, that is trade in intermediate services. Business service firms then, follow an evolutionary path towards internationalisation, however, it is important to note that firms may progress gradually or rapidly through this process. In recent years rapid international expansion appears to have been the norm with firms establishing overseas presences through mergers and acquisitions.

5.4 What factors influence the organisational structure of international service firms?

When exploring the internationalisation of the business services sector certain organisational structures emerge. Internationalisation overwhelmingly occurs through the establishment of an overseas presence. Direct trade does occur, however, whereas for a manufacturing firm this may develop over some time before an overseas market presence is established, overseas expansion occurs earlier in the internationalisation process for the business service firm. It is possible to explore internationalisation in terms of overseas market commitment (Johanson and Vahlne, 1977), where establishing an overseas presence requires higher levels of such commitment than exporting. However, if the cost of overseas expansion is compared between a business service and manufacturing firms it can be seen that for the business service firm the costs are much smaller. Thus the level of market commitment required by the business service firm to warrant the establishment of an overseas presence is less than that required for a manufacturing firm. Further to this, there is the difficulty incurred by service firms in terms of sustaining direct trade. Various types of overseas presences are utilised by service firms although a clear preference for wholly owned subsidiaries has been identified (Dunning, 1989; Erramilli and Rao, 1993).

Although, direct trade does occur in the business services sector, internationalisation is overwhelmingly achieved through the establishment of an overseas presence. Consequently, the internationalisation of the business service firm must be explored within the context of the theory of the MNE. It is possible to view the internationalisation of business service firms in terms of the exploitation of some ownership or firm specific advantage, or indeed, in terms of locational advantages relate to the availability of cheap labour, market opportunities or other factor. However, the intention here is to focus upon a particular element of the theory of the MNE. The framework which will be elaborated upon here will utilise internalisation theory, which has been forwarded as a general theory of the MNE, and incorporates within it the elements of ownership and locational advantages. This theory has been selected because it not only sheds light on why MNEs arise but it is also of value in terms of explaining the organisational form of multinational firms.

Most internationalisation in the business services sector is market oriented, that is, its objective is to service existing clients and seek out new clients. Although this is changing in some sectors, particularly computer services where the internationalisation of production is becoming apparent with resource oriented overseas expansion to take advantage of the availability of, for example, cheap skilled labour. A number of Asian and East Asian countries are proving to be low cost locations at which to produce software and databases. This research will confirm the dominance of market oriented overseas expansion in the business service sector, whilst seeking to highlight the potential for resource oriented expansion and the internationalisation of production within the sector.

The internationalisation of the business service firm through the use of FDI can be seen in terms of the internalisation of service trade transactions. As noted earlier, direct trade in services is difficult although possible. If international clients are to be retained and nurtured it is necessary to internalise these trade transactions within the boundaries of the firm. Thus the firm must physically expand into overseas markets. Services can be produced wholly in the local market, or they can be produced from intermediary services supplied through intra-firm trade from the parent firm, or other part of the organisation. To these intermediary services are added the element of personal delivery and customisation to the local market conditions. Indeed, the flow of intermediary services may be two way, with excess capacity in one location being used to the benefit of another location, or knowledge gained in one location being used elsewhere in the servicing of the same client or others.

An overseas presence facilitates investment related trade in addition to intra-firm trade. Intra-firm trade is of particular importance in the early life of a subsidiary when it may act as a point of delivery for a service largely produced elsewhere. Intra-firm trade then in the business services sector is not necessarily related to a complex process of international production as it often is in the manufacturing sector.

It would appear that direct service trade transactions occur in the initial phase of internationalisation, that is, when a firm is providing services to overseas clients in the domestic market and overseas through travelling personnel and services embodied in reports, and so on. Direct exports may also be possible when the firm has a highly developed relationship with its clients which enabled transactions to occur at times without personal contact. So the nature of international transactions will vary with the nature of the relationship with clients. When a firm is working closely with the client's parent company on an international project, which affects all the company's subsidiaries then there may be a higher level of trade transactions. While the provision of services to the parent company will be delivered through a locationally proximate presence, services may be delivered to subsidiary companies through direct trade. Indeed, when a business service firm works closely with a client it is possible to conceive of services being provided internationally through the client's own international network. For example, a report provided for head office may be distributed throughout the company through the client firm's own intra-firm trade mechanism. Business service firms may then use their client's internal structure to deliver services across international borders. At times it may be difficult to determine the boundaries between the client and the

100

service supplier as their organisations may become closely intertwined as they work together on a particular project. It is quite common for the personnel of business service firms to work within client organisations.

By and large the majority of business services are provided through an overseas presence, thereby eliminating the risks involved in direct trade transactions. So it is possible to see the strategy of internalising not as a method of reducing the cost of carrying out transactions but as a means of reducing the risks associated with such transactions in the open market. Foreign direct investment actually facilitates the international transaction of business services. There are significant imperfections in the international markets for business services which can be overcome through internalising the transactions within the firm.

It has been recognised that internalisation is of particular importance as a motive for FDI for firms involved in information intensive production, or involved with the production of intangible assets (Buckley and Casson, 1976; inter alia). The motivation being to protect such assets. For business service firms the protection of the quality of service and of goodwill are of particular importance, and account for the preferred use of FDI rather than licensing or other such arrangement. Dunning (1989) identifies two main reasons for integration for most kinds of information intensive business service and professional firms. Firstly, much of the proprietary knowledge and information is tacit, expensive to produce, complex and idiosyncratic, but easy to replicate. Secondly, there are substantial synergetic advantages to be gained from geographical diversification of production activities which can best be accomplished within MNE hierarchies (Chapter 3).

Transaction cost economics (Williamson, 1975,1980) can be used to explain the existence of the firm and why economic activity is organised through hierarchical structures rather that through the market mechanism (Chapter 4). It is important to note that when this theory is extended to the international market, in the form of internalisation theory (Buckley and Casson, 1976; Rugman, 1981; inter alia), that internalisation may not be as closely related to the development of hierarchical structures (Buckley, 1983,1988). Indeed, in a MNE the parent firm may have inadequate information to make decision for overseas subsidiaries, hence such subsidiaries may have a great deal of local autonomy. This may be particularly the case in the business services sector where local knowledge is vital to the success of the subsidiary. It is then argued here that international business service firms will give their overseas subsidiaries a high level of local autonomy.

It has been recognised that internationalisation among service firms is accompanied by diversification (Channon, 1978; Enderwick, 1989), this would also appears to be the case for business service firms. It is argued here then that internationalisation and diversification occur together among business service firms. However, the degree of product diversification is variable. Diversification enables the exploitation of client bases and international networks. So whereas in the manufacturing sector it is possible to identify a trend of firms returning to their core activity and divesting themselves of other secondary activities, in the business

101

services sector the trend is in the opposite direction. Firms are diversifying in order to gain economies of scale and scope. The direction of diversification is influenced by the opportunities for synergy and tend therefore, to be into closely related areas. That is, into services that can be offered to existing clients through the use of cross referral, and which will use the firms present skills and knowledge. Once an international network has been established, economies of scope can be gained in its use, since it is possible to deliver a number of services through such a network.

5.5 A framework for the internationalisation of service firms

To develop a framework within which to understand the internationalisation of services it is necessary to draw together the various elements considered in this chapter. Such a framework is presented in Figure 5.1. The model highlights a number of factors all of which have some influence upon the process and nature of service internationalisation. These factors are divided into those which are internal to the firm, and can to some extent be influenced by the firm itself, and those which are external to the firm and therefore largely beyond the scope of the firm's control. Clearly these various factors influence the nature of internationalisation, indeed, they may even interact and counteract one another. For example, the tradability of the service may be seen as internal to the firm since it is the firm which selects the output to be produced, and yet tradability may be influenced by external factors such as developments in ICTs. Equally, the firm's strategic choice between supplying a niche market or market growth will be influenced by the competitive environment, and the level of diversification may be influenced by the regulatory environment. The factors influencing internationalisation will vary from country to country, and hence service firms may pursue alternative market servicing strategies in different overseas markets. Indeed, firms may use a variety of methods within one overseas market. In particular, trade and the establishment of an overseas presence are not mutually exclusive. The framework illustrates the diversity of modes of internationalisation which may be adopted by a service firm. Trade, trade in conjunction with an overseas presence, and an overseas presence, are the three main forms of internationalisation, however, for each of these there are a number of subgroups. Through empirical research it will be possible to establish which factor have a dominant influence on the internationalisation of business services under various circumstances. It is likely that the weight of the influences will vary from firm to firm and from sector to sector.

There is no doubt that the theory of international transactions developed in relation to the extractive and manufacturing sectors is of value to the understanding of the internationalisation of the service sector, and in particular, business services. It is clear that trade theories are less relevant, apart from in the early stages of internationalisation. The theory of the MNE is of prime importance, especially

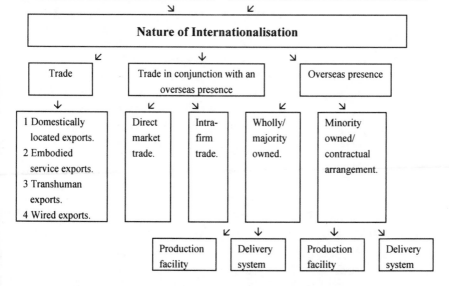

Internal Influences	External Influences
Nature of service: tradability; information intensity; economies of scale and scope in production and distribution.	National absolute and comparative advantages.
Age, size and international experience of the service firm.	Impact of ICT on tradability of services and organisation of international service firm.
Strategic choice between niche market and growth.	Competitive environment.
Level of diversification.	Regulatory environment.
Domestic location/ locational spread.	General economic and political environment.
Funds available for international expansion.	Scope for mergers and acquisitions.
Cost of establishing overseas presence - scope for organic international expansion.	Locational advantages available in overseas market.
Level of sophistication of relations with clients.	Cultural proximity of overseas market.
Pressure to internalise market transactions.	Client needs.

Nature of Internationalisation

Trade

Trade in conjunction with an overseas presence

Overseas presence

1 Domestically located exports.
2 Embodied service exports.
3 Transhuman exports.
4 Wired exports.

Direct market trade.

Intra-firm trade.

Wholly/ majority owned.

Minority owned/ contractual arrangement.

Production facility

Delivery system

Production facility

Delivery system

Figure 5.1 The internationalisation of service firms: a framework

internalisation theory. Furthermore, the significance of intra-firm trade is stressed as a means of providing services across national borders.

The end of this chapter completes, for the time being, the preoccupation with theoretical matters. Attention will return to these issues in Chapter 10 where the framework presented here will be assessed and elaborated upon in the light of the empirical research findings. In the intervening chapters attention is predominantly focused on empirical issues and the analysis of primary and secondary data. In the chapter that follows an overview of the three business service sub-sectors selected for in-dept study will be provided. This will set the context against which the postal survey, and analysis of data gathered, can be meaningfully discussed.

6 Internationalisation of business services: an overview of advertising, accountancy and computer services

6.1 Introduction

The internationalisation of the business services sector has already been considered at a general level in Chapter 2. The purpose here is to set the context for the analysis of the survey and case study results by providing a detailed examination of the internationalisation of the three sub-sectors selected as the central focus of this research: advertising; accountancy; and, computer services.

A review of each of the sub-sectors will be provided, which will begin with the consideration of definitions and related issues, followed by a brief historical setting. Levels of competition and concentration will be assessed at the level of the UK and international market. The manner in which internationalisation occurs within the sub-sector will be examined, as will the degree of internationalisation and diversification. The organisational development of firms within the sub-sectors will be explored and common organisational forms identified. The impact of the regulatory environment together with developments, including technological innovations, will also be assessed. Similarities and differences between the three sub-sectors will be highlighted in the concluding section.

6.2 Internationalisation of advertising services

Advertising services and their origins

Advertising is a tool of communication, it is a way of delivering a message from one party to another. It is used by individuals, corporations and governments as a means of communicating information. Advertising for commercial purposes, that is, for the sale of goods and services by firms, is the most significant type. The role of advertising as a means of increasing, or indeed decreasing, competition has attracted much attention (Kaldor, 1950; Doyle, 1968; Schmalansee, 1972; inter alia), however, the purpose here is not one of assessing the economic merits of advertising. Rather it is the provider of advertising services which is the central focus of this section. Attention will be addressed to the development and internationalisation of the advertising agency.

A number of detailed histories of advertising have been produced (Nevett, 1982; Elliott, 1962; Turner, 1952) which trace the origins of the advertising agency to the 1820s. It was not, however, until the 1880s that advertising agencies really came into their own, with the growth of mass consumption goods, the development of brand names, and the establishment of popular newspapers which gained much of their revenue from advertising (Fraser, 1981). Originally media brokers, which sold advertising space for newspapers and magazines in return for commission, as their links with, and loyalty to advertisers developed, advertising agencies became buyers of space, the creator of advertising, and adviser as to where advertising should appear so as to reach the maximum number of potential buyers most economically. Advertising was initially retained within the advertisers organisation, however, as advertising became more complex, advertisers increasingly turned to advertising agencies. This process of evolution began in earnest in the 1920s. Many of today's agencies were founded between the 1910s and 1930s, indeed some like JWT go back even further, originating in 1864 (Sinclair, 1987).

Rapid advances in advertising services were made after the Second World War, with the development of new marketing concepts in the US which spread throughout the world. The greatest period of advertising growth in history stretched from 1946 to 1960 (UNCTC, 1979). Advertising agencies grew in line with the demand for advertising services, which resulted largely from increases in the production of consumer goods, together with rising levels of concentration and competition in such markets. Instrumental in the growth of advertising were several innovations in communications, such as, the introduction of television and transistorised radios.

By the 1960s most large advertising agencies were considered to be 'full service' agencies offering many of the following services to their clients: market analysis; behavioural research into consumer buying habits; pre-testing and post-testing of advertisements; media effectiveness; public relations; packaging research and design; brand name research and advice; and, pricing advice. Some agencies diversified into related fields, such as motion pictures and community antenna systems (Foote, Cone and Belding), while others invested in unrelated fields such as insurance (JWT), and ice-cream factories (Doyle, Dane Bernbach) (UNCTC, 1979, p.3). The 1960s was also a period of great transnational expansion of the agencies and this trend continued into the 1970s and 1980s. Such expansion has been encouraged by the high growth of advertising expenditure in markets other than the US.

106

The world advertising market defined as expenditure in the major media, newspapers, magazines, television, radio, cinema, and outdoor, is estimated by Zenith Media Worldwide (Cordiant 1995 p.14) to have been worth US $240,800 million in 1994. The US is the largest world market with 37 per cent of the total, followed by Europe with 30 per cent, Asia Pacific with 22 per cent, Latin America with 7 per cent and the rest of the world having 4 per cent of the market. World advertising expenditure grew rapidly during the 1980s. In 1982 total expenditure across the three major regions amounted to US $90,914 million by 1992 this had more than doubled to $205,773 million representing a compound annual growth rate of 8.6 per cent. This growth slowed in the early 1990s, between 1990 and 1992 US expenditure fell slightly whilst the European market grew by 3.5 per cent per annum and Asia Pacific grew by 5.5 per cent per annum. The economic slow down has been exacerbated by the dramatic growth in the supply of media available during the 1980s. Technological change has given rise to the proliferation of magazines, as publishing cost fall, and also to the increased number of commercial TV channels with the growing importance of satellite and cable TV.

The vast majority of advertising expenditure derives from the developed countries, most of which have experienced growth in their advertising expenditure as a percentage of GDP in recent years (The Advertising Association, 1994, p.245). Advertising expenditure is linked to economic activity, so as countries develop and grow it can be expected that advertising expenditure will increase. Although the world economy is currently recovering from a period of recession and restructuring, there is great potential for economic growth with the opening up of the Eastern bloc, together with the rise of East Asian economies including China. Many of these emerging markets have little advertising experience, thus there are opportunities for established international advertising agencies to extend their reach into these territories.

There were some 9,340 advertising and market research businesses in the UK in 1993 with a total turnover of £9,322 million (Business Monitor SDA29 1995). Examining the top 30 UK advertising agencies in 1994 (Table 6.1) it can be seen that the top 5 agencies account for 35.6 per cent of the total billings earned by these top 30 agencies. The level of market concentration appears to be fairly modest, however, many of the agencies belong to groups and when exploring the market share of the top 5 UK groups for 1993 (Table 6.2) it can be seen that they account for over 69 per cent of the billings of the top 15 groups. The market is then dominated by a small number of large groups.

Advertising is relatively fragmented on a global scale, with acquisition strategies being utilised to build worldwide market share. The market share of the top 10 advertising agencies worldwide increased from approximately 46 per cent in 1983 to just under 55 per cent in 1993 (WPP Group Plc 1993 p.42). The merger activity of the 1980s resulted in the development of major international advertising agency

107

Table 6.1
The top 30 UK advertising agencies in 1994

Rank 1994	Agency	Billings* £ millions
1	Saatchi & Saatchi	295.59
2	Abbott Mead Vickers BBDO	246.03
3	J.Walter Thompson	243.00
4	Ogilvy & Mather	238.91
5	BMP DDB Needham	194.06
6	D'Arcy Masius Benton & Bowles	188.84
7	McCann-Erickson London	165.60
8	Bates Dorland	164.95
9	Lowe Howard-Spink	157.44
10	Grey London	157.33
11	Publicis	131.29
12	Leo Burnett	113.86
13	Euro RSCG Wnek Gosper	113.82
14	Bartle Bogle Hegarty	110.82
15	WCRS	105.75
16	Still Price Lintas	103.90
17	TBWA	83.99
18	Young & Rubicam	72.45
19	Collett Dickenson Pearce	61.45
20	GGT	60.97
21	DFSD Bozell	58.26
22	Bainsfair Sharkey Trott	54.11
23	Foote Cone & Belding	43.95
24	CME KHBB	41.36
25	Howell Henry Chaldecott Lury	39.92
26	Kevin Morely Group	39.30
27	Barker & Ralston	36.67
28	McCann-Erikson Manchester	35.26
29	BDH	32.77
30	Butler Lutos Sutton & Wilkinson	32.42

* Register-MEAL figures: all media and other activities.

Source: Compiled from The Campaign Report, 24th. February 1995.

Table 6.2

The top UK advertising agency groups in 1993

Rank 1993	Group	Billings* £ million
1	WPP	2,155
2	Interpublic	955
3	Saatchi and Saatchi	896
4	Omnicom	816
5	Euro RSCG	550
6	Grey Communications Group	404
7	DMB&B Holdings	385
8	Abbott Mead Vickers	342
9	MMS	327
10	Young and Rubicam Group	295
11	Gold Greenlees Trott	201
12	BDDP	130
13	WMGO Group	108
14	DFSD Bozell Group	98
15	ARC Group	95

* Declared billings.

Source: Compiled from The Campaign Report, 25th. Feb. 1994.

groups like Saatchi and Saatchi, Omnicom and WPP Group. Though this type of international expansion is not a new phenomenon, beginning as it did with the formation of Interpublic in the 1960s. This merger activity has to some extent been spurred on by small agencies which, not wishing to lose their clients to a larger more international agency, agree to yield ownership to such an organisation. The small firms remain relatively intact within a larger group, yet have a greater base of operations and information on which to draw.

Three distinctive groups of agencies can be identified. Firstly, those with global compatibilities and resources. This group consists of a few select firms which undeniably possess the ability to provide services worldwide. In addition, this group includes firms that are very large in their own right but lack integral components, that is, they are able to handle the 'mega' accounts but lack standing in some overseas countries. These firms will usually engage in contractual arrangements with foreign agencies for advertising in particular countries. The second group is composed of small advertising firms that usually have a regional base, that is, those with national and regional capabilities and resources. The third group consists of small local advertising firms. It is the first group that is the most visible, attracting as it does large multinational clients. With over 20 per cent of all advertising now being purchased by conglomerates, these firms enjoy a large market share and engage in strong competition (Kaynak, 1989).

The world's top 30 advertising organisations are listed in Table 6.3. A global network is a feature of all of the top agencies, with the exception of the Japanese companies. Top agencies seek to satisfy all of the advertising needs of their clients including providing services in their overseas markets. Top agencies are represented in over 50 countries and many service clients in 20 or more countries. For example, Ogilvy and Mather has a presence in 58 countries and service 26 clients in more than 10 countries, whilst, McCann Erickson has a presence in 85 countries and services 40 clients in more than 10 countries (WPP Group Plc., 1993, p.42).

As international agencies grow in size the problem of client conflict can raise problems for future expansion. Since the relationship between advertisers and their agencies is a close one, in which competitive strategies and product developments are considered, advertisers insist that their agency do not simultaneously work for their competitors. To alleviate this problem, large advertising agencies have found that continued expansion is dependent upon the formation of an advertising group which incorporates a number of advertising networks that operate independently and are therefore able to work for competing clients. For example, WPP Plc. includes Ogilvy and Mather, and JWT, whilst, Interpublic includes Lintas and McCann Erickson, and Omnicom includes BBDO and DDB Needham.

Overseas agencies have made little impact on the Japanese market because of cultural and economic obstacles. Indigenous agencies have been able to expand on the basis of domestic domination. Dentsu and Hakuhodo collectively accounted for 42 per cent of all Japanese agency billings in 1987 (James Capel, 1989, p.87). The dominance of the larger agencies is made possible by the lack of concern in Japan about client conflicts. At the same time Japanese agencies have not expanded successfully overseas. It is widely recognised that Japanese exporters and MNEs prefer to use local agencies to service their international advertising needs. Despite this a number of Japanese agencies have developed links with US and European advertising groups.[1] Although the international activity of the large Japanese agencies is insignificant when compared to that of other top world agencies, they do have great potential for international expansion, particularly in those countries which attract Japanese manufacturing direct investment.

The internationalisation of advertising agencies began early. For example, JWT, originating in the US, opened its first overseas office in London in 1899. The process began in earnest in the 1920s as US agencies followed their clients into overseas markets. In 1927, for instance, McCann Erickson opened offices in Paris, London and Berlin at the request of its principal client Standard Oil of New Jersey (UNCTC, 1979). This early period of internationalisation gained speed after 1945

Table 6.3
The world's top 30 advertising organisations in 1994

Rank 1994	Agency	Billings $ million
1	WPP Group	20,025
2	Omnicom Group	16,059
3	Interpublic Group of Companies	14,866
4	Dentsu Inc.	12,326
5	Cordiant	11,355
6	Young & Rubicam	7,990
7	Euro RSCG	6,116
8	Hakuhodo Inc.	5,767
9	Grey Advertising	5,428
10	D'Arcy Masius Benton & Bowles	5,339
11	True North Communications (FCB)	5,141
12	Leo Burnett Co.	4,592
13	Publicis Communications	3,602
14	Bozell, Jacobs, Kenyon & Eckhardt	2,530
15	Tokyu Agency	1,629
16	BDDP Group	1,622
17	Asatsu Inc.	1,531
18	Daiko Advertising	1,444
19	Dai-Ichi Kikaku	1,078
20	Ketchum Communications	1,052
21	Dentsu, Young & Rubicam Partnerships	1,040
22	Yomiko Advertising	986
23	Gold Greenlees Trott	931
24	I&S Corp	902
25	N W Ayer & Partners	874
26	TMP Worldwide	847
27	Asahi Advertising	668
28	Gage Marketing Group	638
29	Cheil Communications	593
30	Man Nen Sha	584

Source: Compiled from Advertising Age, 10th. April 1995.

and can be seen as demand driven, with agencies following their clients at a time when account alignment was important. Advertising agencies would even operate loss making offices in some countries in order to serve clients and prevent a rival obtaining an account. Thus the internationalisation of advertising agencies has followed the internationalisation of manufacturing industry (Weinstein, 1973). Mattelart (1979) refers to this early period of internationalisation as the 'imperialist phase'. Such expansion still occurs though is less frequent these days (for example, the case of Saatchi and Saatchi following Proctor and Gamble into Brazil). Whilst the overseas expansion of agencies and producers was linked, the rapid expansion of both was not always coordinated, for example, one MNE was reported to be working with 1,200 separate agencies (Lanigan, 1984).

By the 1960s most of the major MNEs had selected an agency so it was hard for agencies to find unaligned advertisers, this lead to what Mattelart (1979) calls the 'nationalisation phase' of expansion. Which was characterised by overseas expansion through the partial acquisition of foreign agencies, motivated by a desire to lower the profile of the agency in a time of economic patriotism, whilst providing access to local markets. Now that expansion was often in the Far East or Latin America, away from culturally similar regions, working with local agencies became a practical advantage.

The globalisation of production since the Second World War has given rise to global markets and the idea of global marketing. A major proponent of this view is Theodore Levitt (1983,1986) who argues that the world is becoming a common market place in which people, no matter where they live, desire the same products and lifestyles. New ICTs, low cost travel, and education, are encouraging these developments which have certain implications for international marketing.

In the past MNEs have tried to cater for specific markets adapting their products accordingly, increasingly though, in a bid to reduce costs and increase competitiveness firms have been developing globally standardised products with a uniform brand image. With the move towards world brands multinationals are centralising their advertising decisions and reducing the number of agencies they use worldwide. According to Kaynak (1989) only 21 per cent of multinationals are now running centrally organised advertising campaigns but 41 per cent are in transition. Campaigns to produce world brands are not necessarily identical around the world, but they are similar from market to market and in most cases create economies of scale worldwide. The success of a number of global brands (for example, Coca Cola and Sony) and the handling of brands on a global scale by a single advertising agency (for example, British Airways by Saatchi and Saatchi in the 1980s) have created a renewed interest in global products and advertising agencies (Rosen et al., 1988).

Despite the popularity of the idea of standardised advertising empirical evidence indicates that the use of globally standardised advertising campaigns is somewhat limited (Hite and Fraser, 1988).[2] The influences which determine how far a MNE standardises its advertising are related to the type of product/service produced, the

112

character of the local market and, in particular, the structure and skills of the company concerned (Harris, 1984).

Wind and Douglas (1986) argue that the latest developments in ICTs and networks, as well as the growing integration of markets, certainly needs a global perspective in the planning of strategy, but such a perspective does not necessarily imply that it must be based on the commercialisation of standardised products and brands throughout the world. Indeed, the evidence suggests that although global advertising campaigns may be possible, the successful application of such strategies may be limited. Although the ability to standardise advertising across market segments worldwide is becoming increasingly possible. New ICTs offers the ability to segment audiences together with providing a wider range of media.

In search of the ability to service MNEs in all their markets, advertising agencies have been engaged in an eager pursuit of subsidiaries, affiliates and partnerships abroad. In host countries the agencies do not concentrate solely on the overseas clients but they are their most important source of income. Peebles and Ryan (1984) highlight the point that an important consideration for MNE when selecting an overseas agency is evidence of its ability to communicate to the local consumer as indicated by their local client base. Perry (1990, p.41) in a survey of New Zealand agencies found that MNE accounts generate around two thirds of the income of most overseas agencies. In contrast local agencies rarely had more than one fifth of their income from overseas owned MNEs. This evidence highlights the importance of MNE clients to the international advertising agency and lends support to the view that international expansion is driven by a desire to service multinational clients.

Internationalisation of advertising firms

Advertising services may be provided across borders in a number of ways. Some agency business is conducted in the home market for foreign clients and thus is regarded as an export in the traditional sense and recorded as such in the balance of payments statistics. For example, advertising and market research services provided to non-residents in the UK in 1994 totalled £101 million (CSO Pink Book, 1995, Table 3.7).

Exporting in the traditional sense of the service being embodied within a tangible form and being moved across borders is of little significance, (for example, a filmed advertisement could be exported). Although exports of this type are increasingly possible with the use of new ICTs, there is as yet little empirical evidence of exporting occurring in this way. Where such transfers do occur it is likely to be in conjunction with the movement of personnel and capital. That is, such trade is likely to be intra-firm trade. This type of export is illustrated by Kaynak (1989) when referring to Backer and Spielvogel's Miller beer account in Britain after the agency had been acquired by Saatchi and Saatchi:

113

The British advertisements are now handled by a distribution subsidiary of Saatchi & Saatchi, though the actual promotion is developed in the United States (p.188).

Trade in the traditional sense, however, is limited because of the need for personal contact, together with market and cultural knowledge. Though intra-firm trade does occur and is likely to increase as the ability of technology to facilitate such trade develops. As reported by Campaign (1993), advertisements are already being transmitted over the wire via high speed ISDN (Integrated Systems Digital Network) lines in the UK. As such facilities become more common, transmitting advertisements around the world will increasingly be just a question of pressing a button. Although, copyright and industry standards are areas which have yet to be considered. Furthermore, there is the issue of the regulation of transborder data flows. New ICTs can also enable staff to draw on the experience of personnel in other national offices without the need to travel to those offices. The US agency Chiat Day is heavily involved in the use of new ICT, for example, using video conferences to allow their New York and Boston offices to work closely together (The Business, 1995). There is no reason why such activities cannot be extended to the international level.

The internationalisation of advertising service firms has most frequently taken the form of setting up a presence in an overseas market. This may be achieved in a variety of ways from setting up a greenfield office to acquisition, merger or joint venture. Anderson (1984, p.91) identified three main methods of overseas expansion used by what he terms transnational advertising agencies (TNAAs):

> *Branch agency* - in which the overseas office is a local office or subsidiary of the parent TNAA. The branch may have been started from scratch, or it may have been an existing agency that the TNAA bought out.
>
> *Affiliate* - in which the parent TNAA has a substantial, but not 100 per cent, control of the overseas agency. The parent TNAA might have a majority or a minority interest in a 'joint venture' with indigenous interests.
>
> *Associate* - in which the parent TNAA is loosely or tightly connected to a local advertising agency, but has no official equity. This form can vary considerably from a very informal gentleman's agreement in which the two parties agree to assist one another when the need arises to a more formal agreement in which the TNAA, for a fee, actually manages the agency under a management contract or technical assistance agreement.

There are advantages and disadvantages for all these various modes of entry into foreign markets. Firstly, opening a local office allows the greatest level of control

114

over the form and size of the overseas office, however, it can be costly since the payback period is delayed until the new office has generated sufficient clients to make it profitable. Secondly, acquiring full or partial interest in an existing agency, may offer financial and administrative control over an on going operation with well trained staff and an existing client bank. It may however be difficult to achieve total control over an agency that has previously established operating procedures. Where the agency is entering a culturally different market partial ownership may be an advantage in terms of access to market knowledge and reduced risk. As regards joint ventures, it is interesting to note that there is a tendency for these arrangements to develop into full ownership (Weinstein, 1974). The formation of a holding company, owning agencies in a number of countries is a further alternative method of overseas expansion which is increasingly common. Also alliances between the large companies though joint ventures are gaining popularity.

The mode of entry depends on a number of factors which according to UNCTC (1979, pp.16-17) can be listed as follows:

1   Time of entry: Weinstein (1974, p.34) estimated that before 1950, 90 per cent of the cases of expansion studied involved whole ownership. While after 1950 only 36 per cent of the cases studied involved full ownership and 56 per cent involved partial ownership.
2   Financial strength and the size of the purchasing agency: large agencies with sufficient capital tend to choose 100 per cent or at least majority ownership strategy.
3   Type of national regulation, as some countries prohibit full or majority ownership.
4   Agencies which have more or less the same clients as the agency that is to be purchased, may opt for minority ownership while those that do not may have to opt for majority ownership in order to achieve the same degree of market access.
5   Apart from national regulations, foreign advertising firms may encounter general hostility and resistance to foreign acquisitions of domestic firms.

It is clear then that an international advertising agency may use a variety of different market entry modes, the choice of which will depend not only on the resources available for international expansion, but also on the characteristics of the market to be entered.

Organisational structure of advertising firms

The organisational structure of an advertising agency will depend on a number of factors including its size, the range and type of services it provides and the requirements of its clients. Since the market is dominated by large and medium sized firms attention will be focused on the organisation of such firms.

The agency may operate on a departmental basis, with the departments including: account service; market research; copy; art media; production; traffic; and, public relations. The account service department consists of account executives, each of whom works with one or more client on a regular basis. The account executive maintains client contact, that is, s/he is the person who provides the liaison between the various departments of the agency and the advertising manager of the client company. All the departments of the agency work together towards a common goal of satisfying a client's requirements. In recent years many of the larger agencies have favoured a matrix type organisation. Under this arrangement a creative group is formed by copywriters, artists, television producers and media buyers, all working as a team under a creative group head and responsible to an account executive who is the liaison between the agency and the client.

Agencies which are internationally active have added dimensions to their organisational design. Firstly, they are large but such agencies cannot specialise by product type of advertising due to the problem of client conflict. As a result, all agencies tend to be generalists, and consequently advertisers are free to move their business to other agencies. To counter this agencies try to be distinctive by offering unique services such as, research techniques, market consulting services, special management assistance to clients, specialisation in the targeting of consumer groups and so on.

Similarity between agencies and the non competing account rule leads to a high turnover of clients. According to the American Association of Advertising Agencies, 7.2 years is the average period for advertisers to be with one agency, there are some much longer relationships, such as JWT's with, Unilever for 85 years, Kodak for 56 years, and Ford for 44 years, but these tend to be the exception. The loss of a single client may lead to a substantial drop in revenue, while the limitation of holding directly competing accounts restricts expansion. A further element of vulnerability relates to the loss of key staff who can take clients with them to a competing agency.

Where long term relationships exist with clients they are not usually exclusive. Firms will use a range of agencies for various geographical regions or products. This is partly due to the divisional structure of large companies which provide autonomy to divisional managers. Also it is unlikely that an agency will not have an account conflict in some area. Finally advertisers retain a number of agencies so that the threat of account loss can be effective.

A consequence of the above factors is that as an agency expands in size and level of internationalisation the holding group structure offers advantages, bringing together as it does a number of advertising agency networks. It is a structure which allows expansion that would otherwise be frustrated by account conflicts. As the scale of individual advertisers has grown through a process of concentration the vulnerability of agencies to the loss of one account has increased. By retaining the separate identities of agencies, and maintaining competition between them the holding group can control a larger client base. The impact of the loss of one client

116

is reduced, and greater financial resources are available to the parent organisation. Moreover, conflicting clients can be passed on to separate agencies in the group.

The holding group can also provide a greater range of services, the firm can diversify into areas which show higher levels of growth. A further benefit derives from the ability to centralise media buying, which enables the negotiation of discounts from media vendors and therefore higher profits for the firm. There is also the increase in productivity derived form the computerisation of the media buying activity. Such centralisation of media buying also gives the agencies a counterweight to the increase in the concentration which has occurred in some sectors of the media. Although there is the problem of account conflict with some advertisers declining to be involved in such centralised media buying (for example, Nestlé).

Regulation of the advertising sector

The types of regulation encountered by advertising firms vary from country to country. Self regulation is important in many countries, however, UNCTC (1979 p.41) identified a trend towards government regulation. Peebles and Ryan (1984) argue that advertising is becoming one of the most highly regulated business practices in the world. They identify restrictions in the following areas:

1 The type of products that may be advertised.
2 The content or creative approach that may be employed in advertising.
3 The media that advertisers are permitted to employ.
4 The amount of advertising that a single advertiser may employ in total or in a specific medium.
5 The use of advertising materials prepared outside the country.
6 The use of local versus international advertising agencies.
7 The specific taxes that may be levied against advertising.

Boddewyn (1981) identifies a number of issues of concern to various countries and regions including: advertising to children in Canada, Scandinavia and US; use of foreign language materials in France, Mexico and Quebec Province; and sexism in advertising in Canada, Netherlands, Scandinavia, UK and US. The International Advertising Association regard Germany, UK, France, US, Canada, Australia, Sweden, Austria, Belgium, Argentina, Mexico, Italy, Finland and Denmark to be the most restrictive countries.

Regulation has implications for the internationalisation of the advertising sector, for example it would be difficult to use the same advertisement worldwide not merely because cultural differences would impinge on its effectiveness in diverse markets, but also because countries may restrict the use of advertisements produced overseas. Restrictions on the foreign ownership of advertising agencies may restrict the access of international agencies to some markets. Differences in regulation between countries can then act as a barrier to the achievement of economies of scale and internationalisation.

Within the European Union, the regulation of advertising is in the process of being harmonised, however, a single system of regulation throughout the Union has yet to be achieved. The difficulties encountered give an indication of what would be faced in any attempt to harmonise regulation on a global basis.

Developments in the advertising sector

In recent years, advertising agencies have been expanding globally to serve an increasing number of clients with worldwide needs. They have also been diversifying into related areas to offer a wider range of services to their clients. The international expansion of advertising agencies was initially demand driven as note earlier, however, it is becoming supply driven as agencies seek to expand their international market share in an increasingly competitive sector. Competition intensified in the 1970s with the general economic decline. It was during this period that the emphasis in agencies shifted from overwhelming concern and attention to creativity to a more balanced concern with creativity and business capability (Farbey, 1979).

Diversification is not a new idea but it has been pursued aggressively in the 1980s, particularly by UK agencies, largely through acquisition or start ups of separately branded companies which are known, or have become known, for their individual expertise. Acquisition strategies have been possible by UK firms because of a good relationship between them and the financial markets in the 1980s, with a number of UK agencies being floated on the stock market. Innovative methods of financing takeovers have also been used to good effect such as the reverse buy out. Diversification has been stimulated by a number of factors. Firstly, the saturation of the advertising market in the developed markets, especially the US, has encouraged agencies to extend themselves not only into other geographically separated markets but also into other closely related services where growth rates outstrip those of the advertising market. As the marketing process is becoming more sophisticated, direct marketing and other forms of communication are increasing in size, being as they are, complementary to major media advertising. Zenith (Saatchi and Saatchi Plc., 1993) estimate that in 1992 $27,298 million was spent on direct mail and $27,453 million on sales promotion/miscellaneous media in the US market. The US market experienced growth between 1982 and 1992 in direct mail at a compound annual rate of 9.6 per cent and in sales promotion of 7.9 per cent.

The second factor stimulating diversification is that clients, especially small and medium sized enterprises, are interested in an 'integrated offer', or a one-stop-shop. Thirdly, agency groups may promote the cross-referral of business amongst its subsidiaries. James Capel (1989) argue that this 'Octopus' principle can help to promote the longevity of a client relationship, as well as winning a greater

118

proportion of the marketing budget, so long as the quality of work is uniform across all subsidiaries. Finally, diversification has been stimulated by the search for economies of scale and scope in relation to the use of global networks. Examples of this diversification trend are: Saatchi and Saatchi which diversified from being concerned solely with advertising in 1983 to being in 10 separate marketing services and 7 management service disciplines in 1987; and, WPP Group which was operational in 15 marketing service categories in 1989. However, since the late 1980s some companies, having over extended their reach have consolidated their holdings, disposing of some of their less central activities.

For a prolonged period agencies were relatively affluent with a stable economic framework. Agencies used to receive 15 per cent commission on advertising placed as remuneration for their work, however, these days much work is carried out on a fee basis or a mixture of fees and commission. The reasons for this include: prevailing higher media costs in some countries; governmental regulation; and, specialised services performed by full-service agencies that base their service costs on fees rather than on standard commission (Advertising Age, 1979, p.51). A poll of advertising agencies in the UK by James Capel (1989, p.42) confirmed that the fee element had increased between 1986-1987 and 1987-1988 from 22.5 per cent to 29.8 per cent. A similar trend is apparent among US agencies between 1986 and 1992 (WPP Group Plc., 1993, p.42). James Capel (1989) also reported that the 15 per cent level for commission based revenue has been variable for some time, with lower commission rates fairly usual for retail and some financial services clients, due to the reduced creative, repetitive, press-concentrated nature of the business. There have also been developments in performance related remuneration in the US,[3] which may become more widespread in the future.

The prosperity of the advertising sector is related to the general economic climate. Although, advertising expenditure may be relatively unaffected by periods of mild recession, since firms will maintain or even increase their advertising expenditure in order to stimulate demand. Mild recessions also tend to have a larger impact on the capital goods industries where advertising expenditure is less significant when compared to that for the consumer goods industries. Recessions which have a strong impact on consumer goods markets will affect the level of advertising expenditure, for example, the period of recession in the early 1990s resulted in a decline in advertising expenditure. Given that globally economic growth is set to continue with, rapid economic growth anticipated in the Far East and Eastern Europe in the longer term, together with the further liberalisation of international trade with the conclusion of the GATT Uruguay Round, it can be expected that advertising expenditure will continue to rise. In addition, new types of advertising are growing in size such as the use of advertising to promote corporate image.

The advertising services market is highly concentrated at the international level, firms are organised on a network basis either in the form of a holding group or more loosely in an alliance between major firms. This concentration is likely to continue, although at a local level competition is strong with numerous small agencies, which often carry out work on a contractual basis for the larger firms.

Technological change is influencing the advertising sector in a number of ways. Firstly, there is the impact on the production of advertisements. Secondly, in the distribution of advertisements with the explosion in the availability, and specialisation of the media, giving opportunities for market segmentation, though reducing the availability of media which can reach mass audiences. Computer analysis of audiences is allowing more accurate targeting of advertising. The growth in the use of video has reduced the effectiveness of television advertising and has encouraged advertisers to use alternative methods of product promotion such as sponsorship. Also the increasing popularity of the Internet raises further advertising opportunities. Finally, there is the increasing use of technology to transfer advertising intermediate services between parts of the advertising organisation and even across international borders. New ICTs have the potential to revolutionise the production and distribution of advertising as well as the organisational structure of advertising service firms.

6.3 Internationalisation of accountancy services

Accountancy services and their origins

Accountancy services may be defined as those services provided by an accountant, namely, the maintenance and audit of business accounts and the preparation of consultant reports in tax and finance (Collins Dictionary, 1986). A number of detailed histories of the sector have been produced (Jones, 1981; Richards, 1981; Winsbury, 1977; Margerison, 1980). It is useful for the purposes of this study to highlight the most important points in the historical development of the accountancy profession.

Jones (1981) traces the existence of accountants in the UK back to the 1770s. The evolution of the profession derives largely from the growth in both size and complexity of commercial activity, brought about by the Industrial Revolution. As businesses expanded the need for outside investment increased and with it the need for more sophisticated book keeping. The growth of the railways was of particular significance as Parliament granted them the right to raise vast sums of money by the sale of shares to the public, but there were few safeguards against the fraudulent use of shareholder's money. These problems acted as a trigger for the development of the accountant's 'watchdog' function.

In 1835 the Great Western Railways Act required that half yearly financial statements be laid before the shareholders at a general meeting. Further to this the 1844 Joint Stock Companies Act required companies to file audited accounts with the Registrar of Companies, and to make the books available to one of the shareholders, so that he might act as 'auditor'. The actual form of the balance sheet was specified in the Companies Clause Consolidation Act which was passed in 1845.

In the mid nineteenth century the principle role of accountants was as liquidators and receivers involved in the winding up of business.[4] However, insolvency business evaporated over night with the 1883 Bankruptcy Act which established the office of Official Receiver. This proved a crisis for the profession, but it was rescued by the growth in auditing. Apart from the compulsory audit of railway companies, auditing was still largely voluntary in the second half of the nineteenth century. The rise of auditing closely followed the rapid growth of joint-stock companies after the 1862 Companies Act, which prohibited partnerships of more than 20 people. The requirement for a compulsory audit was extended to the banks in 1879, and to all public companies in 1900 (1900 Company Act). The 1948 Company Act required such audits to be conducted by qualified auditors, and that companies file fuller accounts, including consolidated group accounts, while the audit was now made a statutory requirement for private as well as public companies.

In order to safeguard professional standards, the first Institute of Accountants was established in Scotland in 1854, with the English Institute being set up in 1870. The expansion of accountancy can be seen from the increased membership of the Institute of Chartered Accountants in England and Wales (ICAEW) from an original total of 587 in 1880 to 13,332 in 1945, and to more than 100,000 members by 1993 (Margerison, 1980; Chamberlain, 1993).

Over time the role of accountants has expand in line with the increasing complexity of economic activity. The services offered by accountancy firms today extend beyond accountancy and auditing and include insolvency work, tax consultancy, management and information technology consultancy and investment services, among others.

International market for accountancy services

According to Lafferty Business Research (The Accountant, May 1992) the world market for the top 10 firms (whose aggregate fees represent 87 per cent of total worldwide fees for the 27 associations represented by the World Chapter) in 1991 was $32,743 million, with North America and Europe accounting for 43.1 per cent and 42.2 per cent respectively of this total. Average growth of fees for the top 10 firms was 13.4 per cent on a global basis, although this varies from 4.3 per cent in the US to 16.3 per cent in the UK, and to 31 per cent in Switzerland (The Accountant, May 1992). The demand for accountancy services, being linked, as it is, to the level of economic activity, is concentrated in the developed countries.

The supply of accountancy services is concentrated in the hands of a small number of large firms. The trend appears to be towards further concentration with a number of mega mergers in the late 1980s reducing the Big Eight to the Big Six accountancy firms. This process of concentration within the accountancy sector began in the late nineteenth century and reflects the increasing levels of concentration among client firms. Table 6.4 shows the world's top firms between 1990 and 1991.

The post war period has seen a steady growth in the number of accountancy practices, due principally to an increase in the number of small firms. Throughout the period, mergers have been occurring frequently. In the UK the repeal of the '20 partners maximum' law in 1967 accelerated the merger movement as did the Institutes ruling that no client should contribute more than 15 per cent of the firm's gross fee income. Firms initiating mergers or takeovers may hope to gain operational or territorial advantages by taking over firms either with strong regional presences or a specialisation which they lack. The fundamental reason for the merger movement in accountancy has remained the merger of clients.

The effect of the merger movement has been to squeeze out the medium sized accountancy practices. The number of such firms fell by a factor of four in the period 1968-1978 (Briston, 1979). Indeed, the number of firms with any listed companies as audit clients fell from 1,422 to 511 in the 30 years from 1948-1978, mirroring the reduction in the number of listed clients available (Briston, 1979). There now exists a clear polarisation in the profession. The vast majority of accountancy firms are small concerns with only a handful of partners. These firms function on a local basis providing a service to small clients. For example in the UK in 1993 there were some 17,392 accountancy firms (Business Monitor SDA29, 1995). At the other end of the spectrum are the large internationally active firms, collectively known as the Big Six, which have over 300 partners in the UK and more than 2,000 partners worldwide. These firms operate on both a national and international basis and their clients consist mainly of large firms, often MNEs which require international services. The large practices have grown by capturing an increasing share of the market in large company audits. Thus the 8 largest firms held 24 per cent of the UK listed company audits in 1948 and this share increased to 51 per cent by 1979 (Briston, 1979), by 1993 the top 8 firms accounted for 69.3 per cent of the UK audit fees market (ICC Group, quoted in Accountancy Age, 20.5.1993). Details of the size and activities of the top 20 UK accountancy firms in 1994 are given in Table 6.5.

The intensification of competition among international accounting firms together with the stagnation in the demand for auditing services has resulted in a general reduction of audit fees as a percentage of a client's sales or assets during the period 1984-1990 (International Accounting and Auditing Trends by Centre for International Financial Analysis and Research 1991, quoted in The Accountant, Jan. 1992). This has encouraged diversification, although, auditing and accounting remain the major activities of the large firms. They have been obliged to extend the range of their services in order to achieve continued growth. The diversification which has taken place since the 1960s brings into question whether accountancy is the correct title for firms whose activities may include, among other things, auditing, accounting, executive head hunting, merger making, tax, IT and management consulting, financial planning and public relations.

Table 6.4
The world's largest accountancy firms 1990-1

Rank	Name	Fee income (US$)
1	KPMG	5,400
2	Ernst & Young	5,006
3	DRT	4,200
4	Arthur Andersen	4,200
5	Coopers & Lybrand	4,100
6	Price Waterhouse	2,881
7	BDO Binder	1,005
8	Grant Thornton	875
9	Horwarth	720
10	Moores Rowland	639
11	DRMP	542

Source: Compiled from the International Accounting Bulletin, various issues (1990-1).

The process of internationalisation began early for accountancy firms. Leyshon, Daniel and Thrift (1987a) identify two distinct historical periods of internationalisation among UK accountancy firms. The 'Early' period which began in the 1890s and lasted until 1939 and the 'Late' period which began in 1945. During the early period the impetus came entirely from the UK as City based accounting firms followed the movement of manufacturing capital into overseas markets. International expansion was then at first client led. Touche Ross, Price Waterhouse and Deloitte and Haskins Sells opened their first overseas offices before the end of the 1900 (Richards 1981; Deloitte, Plender, Griffiths & Co., 1958). The development of the overseas office network of these firms preceded the opening of their regional UK offices as they aligned themselves with the movement of British industrial capital into overseas markets. The period up to 1939 saw a steady increase in the overseas representation of those accounting firms that had embarked upon early internationalisation (Leyshon et al., 1987a).

The later stage has involved a more structured build up of multinational activities through the formation of international partnerships. These have been predominately between Anglo-American firms, although more recently associations on an international level have been formed between leading European partnerships, which for example has led to the creation of major groups like KPMG and BDO. The earliest merger between a leading US and UK practice was that of Peats of London with Marwick Mitchell of New York in 1911 (Wise, 1981). Prior to 1939

Table 6.5

Top 20 UK accountancy firms in 1994

	Fee income 1994 (£mil)	Auditing/ accounting %	Tax %	Management advisory services %	Insolvency %	Corporate finance %	Other %	Number of offices	Number of partners	Total staff
Coopers & Lybrand	560.0	42.9	21.5	22.4	13.2	-	-	36	677	9,397
KPMG Peat Marwick	497.6	40.2	21.8	14.2	9.7	14.1	-	41	594	8,816
Arthur Andersen	433.3	18.9	15.7	-	7.2	-	58.2	10	270	5,365
Ernst & Young	388.4	43.2	28.3	18.1	10.4	-	-	27	392	6,583
Price Waterhouse	384.6	41.3	27.9	21.7	9.1	-	-	26	415	6,245
Touch Ross	342.5	39.4	24.1	20.3	11.5	4.7	12.5	26	354	5,656
Grant Thornton	107.0	34.9	29.0	-	23.6	-	12.5	52	200	2,434
BDO Binder Hamlyn	106.5	60.0	29.0	4.0	7.0	-	-	28	216	2,309
Pannell Kerr Forster	79.7	46.4	24.0	6.1	15.7	-	7.8	36	174	1,877
Stoy Hayward	78.0	47.8	20.6	11.5	20.1	-	-	23	172	1,750
Kidsons Impey	55.7	53.0	25.0	7.0	15.0	-	-	36	153	1,302
Clark Whitehill	53.6	65.6	25.6	2.1	2.6	3.0	1.1	63	217	1,637
Moore Stephens	40.0	n.a.	n.a.	n.a.	n.a.	n.a.	n.a.	47	134	1,111
Robson Rhodes	36.6	33.0	29.0	5.0	22.0	11.0	-	9	73	708
Neville Russell	33.2	60.7	25.5	5.3	8.5	-	-	20	87	783
Moores Rowland	30.9	51.5	29.6	10.5	5.8	-	2.6	16	89	602
Baker Tilly	28.5	61.4	26.3	3.9	8.4	-	-	16	71	604
Smith & Williamson	27.0	n.a.	n.a.	n.a.	n.a.	n.a.	n.a.	4	61	n.a.
Haines Watts	20.3	n.a.	n.a.	n.a.	n.a.	n.a.	n.a.	20	46	449
Saffery Champness	16.3	60.7	25.8	-	-	-	13.5	9	40	360

n.a. not available.

Source: Compiled from The Accountant, August 1994.

representational links between firms in the two countries were common, however, it was not until after 1945 that these international contracts were extensively strengthened by a series of mergers that created new Anglo-American firms.

The increasing multiplant multinational tendency of large firms and the requirement for them to produce consolidated accounts based on returns from each of their operating units acted as a further encouragement for accounting firms to extend their international office networks. More recent international expansion and consolidation has been supply driven as accountancy firms compete for market share in both regional markets, such as Europe, and globally. A number of the recent mergers have resulted from firms seeking to strengthen and extend their international coverage.

Internationalisation of accountancy firms

As with other business services, accountancy services may be transacted internationally in a number of ways, however, the establishment of an overseas presence is the usual manner of servicing foreign markets. The industry's international operations are organised as more or less loose collections of largely autonomous partnerships; reflecting this organisational form, they are partnerships of partnerships, expansion overseas being carried out by merger. The transnational accounting companies (TNAC) created in this manner include national firms operating either under their own name or those of their parent companies. The national firms are owned and managed by citizens of the country in which they are located, but are linked to TNACs. Centralised activities consist mostly of setting operating standards, offering training, referring clients and, increasingly, providing a common data-service infrastructure, especially regarding the application of software. Accounting firms vary principally according to the extent to which they integrate and control the management of their global operations. In some cases, profits are shared, in others, the parent corporations merely receive fees for services rendered. Other arrangements include: the representation of an international organisation in certain markets by independent firms, and the temporary assignment of personnel for specific projects in countries in which a firm has no permanent base. Along with those prevailing forms of organisation, accounting companies also use foreign affiliates in which they have an equity stake.

Bavishi and Wyman (1983, p.27), identify seven major types of organisational arrangements used by accountancy firms which can be listed as follows:

1. International Name:
    - where an auditing firm uses its international name to practise in a foreign country. These are some times referred to as 'world firms'.
2. Combined Name:

- where auditing firms combine their international names with names of local firms which are fully affiliated with the international firm.

3. Local Name:
- where an international firm uses a local firm's name and the local firm is fully affiliated with the international firm.

4. Association:
- where an international name is used mainly for coordination purposes among member firms, with the local name being used exclusively for the local practice. Also referred to as a federation.

5. Correspondent:
- where an international firm is represented exclusively by a local auditing firm. The local auditing firm will have clients other than those referred to it by the affiliated international firm.

6. Multiple Affiliations:
- where a local firm represents several international firms. Although the total in this category is not significant on a regional or global basis, it may be significant for certain countries.

7. Two+ Names:
- where an international firm operates under two or more local firms' names.

These arrangements vary essentially according to the relationship between the 'international firm' and the 'local' practice. The categories are not mutually exclusive since firms may operate under more than one organisational arrangement depending on the regulatory and other circumstances prevailing in the country concerned. However, the 'International Name' and the 'Association' forms are fairly independent of one another. One form tends to dominate, for example, Price Waterhouse and Arthur Andersen prefer the international name, whereas BDO and Grant Thornton International favour the association.

The 'International Name' organisational structure signifies those firms that operate a 'World Firm'. The World Firm is a central controlling body that plans and integrates the firm's flow of international services. Each national firm uses a common name, thus ensuring that the worldwide operations of the international firm are closely identified with one another. Until relatively recently this had been the preferred mode of operation of the large firms but attempts at cross border litigation has encouraged some firms to lower their transnational profile. The uniform transnational name is primarily used by accountants to help promote their international identity and status to clients (Cairns Lafferty and Mantel, 1984).

The 'Association' is the second most important organisational structure operated by international accountancy firms and signifies those partnerships that operate within federated networks of national firms. Such groups operate without a common practice name. The largest and most successful example of the federated organisation is Klynven Main Goerdler (KMG) which came into operation in 1979 through the amalgamation of leading national firms outside the Big Six, it has since merged with Peat Marwick to form KPMG.

KPMG is the only firm among Big Six to operate the federated structure. The original formation of KMG, and BDO another federated conglomerate, were essentially defensive measures designed to counteract the international dominance of the Anglo-American firms. Primarily European in origin, they provide member national practices with the means to offer clients a global geographical coverage. However, the strength and lengthy history of several of the individual firms within the federation mitigate against the adoption of a uniform name within each country of operation (Cairns Lafferty and Mantle, 1984) and so the worldwide integration of the firms is not as clear as with those partnerships that operate as World Firms.

Several countries maintain anti-monopolistic legislative barriers (Cairns Lafferty and Mantle, 1984) to preserve the independence of national accountancy firms (for example, France). In such instances those firms that operate as a World Firm are forced to enter into a different relationship with the national partnership. The usual practice is for the national partnership to retain its local name but to be nevertheless fully integrated at the international level. Thus one international organisational structure is not exclusive to another.

Organisational structure of accountancy firms

Accountancy firms are organised on a partnership basis. The partners are required to invest a certain amount of capital, in return they share in the firm's profits or losses, as they have unlimited liability status. The archetypal structure of the professional firm is one containing three professional levels. In the accountancy firm these are referred to as staff accountant, manager and partner. These three levels form a hierarchical structure.

Like most professional service companies accountancy firms have few fixed assets, they only require capital to fund accounts receivable and other working capital items. Consequently, the vast majority of revenues are disbursed in the form of salaries, bonuses and net profits.

Given the extent to which diversification has occurred within the large accountancy firms, it is not surprising that their internal structures are under growing pressure. To date firms have implemented variations of three structural prototypes:

1 The functional structure, where employees are grouped according to their speciality and project assignments typically occur within a division.

127

Reporting relationships are vertical, with clear lines of authority specified and clear distinctions between the levels in the hierarchy.

2 The project management structure, this is a more dynamic structure in which staff from various areas might be combined into a relatively permanent project team. Personnel report to their project manager rather than to only a senior person in their own functional division, this reduces the hierarchy and puts greater emphasis upon lateral communication.

3 The matrix design, which combines the benefits of the first two structures without their shortcomings. Here employees are assigned to both a functional division and a project group.

Gordon, Corsini and Fetters (1985) suggest an alternative structure to those described above. They argue that an integrated structure would be of most benefit to firms in the currently changing environment. This structure has the characteristics of a matrix design, including flexibility, adaptability and decentralised decision making, combined with an emphasis on client needs, product development and product marketing. An integrated structure goes beyond a matrix in its flexible grouping of employees and its strong market driven orientation. Similarly, Quinn and Paquette (1990) identify what they call a spider's web structure being used by Arthur Andersen and Company (Chapter 4) in which various dispersed elements in the organisation interact frequently to provide the client with the highest level of service.

If the large accountancy firms are to continue to prosper it is essential that they adapt their internal structure to the changing market demands. At present such is the diversification without integration that the traditional areas differ substantially from the consultancy areas, which have a totally different culture. Greater integration would be of immense benefit to accountancy firms, in particular, it would increase the cross referral of business as well as enabling client needs to be more fully satisfied. At present, though, the conflict is such that some firms run their management advisory services as separate, but wholly owned, companies.

In the long run, the internal structures of accountancy firms will inevitably change. Such change may be towards greater integration or alternatively, as firms become more diversified they may disintegrate with divisions being hived off leaving the accountancy functions. Pressure for this type of change is brought about by the argument that the undertaking of audit work along side management advisory services within a single firm has the potential to create certain conflicts of interest. Auditing requires that accountants perform a public role in line with the ethics of a professional code. They serve to protect investors by reporting to the users of financial statements upon the performance of management. For this auditors need to display integrity and independence from management. As advisers, the accountants however must also act directly on behalf of management, by whom the usefulness of their work will be assessed. Renewed impetus has been given to this debate by the failure in recent years of a number of large companies, such as, BCCI and Polly Peck.

International activity adds a further dimension to the organisational design of accountancy firms, the various organisational forms at an international level have been considered in the previous section. There are broadly two types of international structure the World Firm or International Name and the Federal or Association structure, often referred to as a Network. The national organisational structure may vary between countries in response to varying environmental factors, for instance, in some countries the scope of activities of accountancy firms is limited to auditing, thus preventing diversification into areas such as management consultancy. In France, for example, accountants cannot offer insolvency services or tax advice, except in very limited circumstances (European Commission, 1994).

As Reynolds (1993) notes:

> ... whereas international companies are legally part of the same organisation in most cases, accountancy partnerships are separate and distinct entities in each country. The international partnerships are agreements to co-operate, to adopt the same logo, utilise a common business approach, endorse a unitary audit manual and agreement to be checked out by the international firm. The real test for the key elements of the premier international firm is to hold together a network of top-grade national firms which share common approaches and objectives. The rapid collapse of the Deloitte international network shows how fragile these structures can be (p.77).

Regulation of the accountancy sector

The regulatory environment will influence the choice of international organisational structure. Accountancy firms face general restrictions such as those on international payments, restrictions on the mobility of personnel, impediments to technology and information transfers, and 'buy national' practices, together with more specific restrictions such as professional certification difficulties, differences in national standards, scope of practice limitations, restrictions on the use of international names, among others (Hegarty, 1994).

Noyelle and Dutka (1988) conclude that it would seem that most countries are fairly liberal in granting foreign auditors the right to practise as residents, permission being based on partial or total equivalency for diploma and work experience acquired abroad. It seems that restrictions in accounting come mostly in the form of restricting the right of establishment, be it the number and size of the offices that a firm can open or the scope of activity that they can carry out. Scope of activity is seen as a particular important issue in mature markets, where accountants see diversification as the primary means to expand their businesses.

129

While it may be true that a number of European countries have attempted to restrict the scope of business of some of the largest multinational accounting firms, such restriction has been difficult to implement because the national affiliates of these firms are typically set up as local partnerships or locally owned corporations. Furthermore, many European countries traditionally seem to have been far less restrictive than the US in allowing accountants to offer a wide range of professional services, including not only tax and management consulting but also legal counsel. This is the case at least in Belgium, Switzerland, and Germany.

Developments in the accountancy sector

Developments within the field of ICT have had a major impact upon the accountancy sector (Barras and Swann, 1984). In particular ICT has enabled: an increase in productivity, reducing the cost of providing existing services; the quality of services to be improved; and, accountants to increase the range of services to meet client demands. Initially, computer technology was used to aid the firms' own internal operations. The use of computers in the provision of client services by accountancy firms was stimulated by the increased use of computers by clients. The first function to be computerised was the audit during the 1960s: other functions have more recently been automated. Perhaps the most significant development in computer related services has been the provision of management advisory services on the selection and implementation of computer systems. As ICT becomes more sophisticated and costs fall this will further influence the development of accountancy firms.

Another development has been the increasing number of litigation cases against accountancy firms, which are increasingly being used as guarantors of the successful operation of financial systems. Evermore frequently, the failure of a public company will stimulate groups with vested interests to take out a damages claim against the auditor. The dramatic growth in this activity is demonstrated by the fact that claims remaining open against the UK's Big Six accountancy firms rose from less than 10 in 1982/3 to well over 600 in 1992/3 (Trapp, 1994). For the Big Six firms the annual cost of insurance and settlements in Britain alone amounts to approximately 8 per cent of their local fee income, in the US it is more like 12 per cent (The Economist, 7.10.95, p.135). A number of possible strategies could be implemented to resolve this problem, such as limiting the level of damages in any liability claim against one party. Alternatively, accountancy firms could become limited liability companies, this would protect the individual partners' personal finances and property, but, the firm could still fail under the weight of large claims. KPMG is currently pursuing this strategy having announced that from 1996 it will incorporate its auditing business as a limited liability company, other companies will no doubt follow this lead. Essentially, though, this problem requires new legislation resulting from a government re-evaluation of the role of auditors. The Institute of Chartered Accountants is currently lobbying the British government to change section 310 of the 1985 Companies Act, which at present makes auditors the only providers of professional services unable to limit their liability through agreements with their clients; this echoes similar lobbying activity in the US (Trapp, 1994). At present, it is not the job of the auditor to seek out fraudulent activities, their task is to ascertain whether the company's accounts are 'true and fair'. The auditor's role may be extended in the future to include the identification of fraudulent practices (Reynolds, 1993).

A further development in the accountancy sector has been the introduction of advertising which was first allowed in the UK in 1984. Individually some firms are spending upwards of £750,000 per annum, even so such advertising expenditure makes up less than 1 per cent of financial advertising as a whole (The Accountant, April 1988). The aim of accountancy firms is to build up a brand image, although the impact of advertising is questionable. Wright, Watkin and Chiplin (1986), for instance, argue that accounting firms would be better disposed if they made use of personal contacts with business advisers and ensure that the quality of service provided to existing users are maximised, as these approaches are likely to be more potent in generating new business than advertising can ever be.

Growth in the demand for accountancy services is likely to continue for a number of reasons. The demand for accountancy services is inextricably linked to developments in the global economy, and despite the recent economic slow down, economic growth is set to continue. One element stimulating such growth is the recent Uruguay GATT agreement, further developments in regional trading blocs which have the effect of opening up trade between groups of countries will further stimulate growth. Also, there is the establishment of new market economies in former Communist countries, since such countries may have shortages in accountancy skills there is great potential for the expansion of the large international firms into such states. Indeed, a number of the large firms are involved in the privatisation of industries in Eastern Europe. The role of accountancy firms in the public sector may also increase as greater emphasis is put on the efficient management of activities in this sector. Growing concern for the environment is likely to increase the demand for the services of accountancy firms to provide environmental audits of the activities of enterprises.

Increasing pressure on costs may lead to further diversification. This may result in changes in the structure of accountancy firms to become public limited companies, which would permit them to raise capital on the stock market and thereby enable them to increase the range of their activities, in particular, to extend activities further in the area of corporate finance. However, the incorporation of the accountancy firms gives rise to the problem of conflicting interests. If shares in the firms are freely bought and sold a company could acquire a major share holding, could the accountancy firm then audit this company? Would there not be a conflict of interest? Proponents of incorporating argue that the majority of the shares would be retained by the partners thus preventing such a problem arising.

However, recent trends indicate a desire among accountancy firms to return to specialised areas. Mr Sharman, senior partner of KPMG in Britain, describes his firm's strengths as auditing, accountancy, tax and corporate finance (The Economist, 1.4.95., p.100). Increasingly the top companies are promoting themselves as experts in certain industrial sectors. For example, Coopers and Lybrand claim to be world class in advising telecommunications, insurance and pharmaceutical industries on strategic and financial management, whereas Price Waterhouse focuses on banking, insurance and the oil and gas industries. Clearly, the accountancy sector is subject to a variety of pressures which may, in time, result in the emergence of new organisational structures, whether these will reflect a diversity of interests or a more focused approach has yet to be seen.

6.4 Internationalisation of computer services

Computer services and their origins

Computer services encompass a wide variety of activities which can be broadly placed into four categories: software; processing; consultancy; and, recruitment and training. Some computer service firms go beyond these areas being also involved in hardware maintenance and provision, telecommunication services, and increasingly firms are becoming multi media.[5]

The development of the computer in the twentieth century and the rapidly rising importance of ICTs has brought about the need for various services to facilitate the optimum use and operation of such technologies. Thus the growth of the computer services industry is crucially dependent on the rise of the computer. As such the sector has a relatively brief history beginning in the 1960s. At this time computers were prohibitively expensive for many small and medium sized firms, with computer facilities only being available to them through the computer bureau. These were organisations which sold computer time, enabling the sharing of computer facilities. Many of these bureaux offered additional services based on standard software including payrolls and accounting, while others specialised in providing services to specific vertical markets and industries, such as banking, construction and insurance.

In addition, some large firms unable to fully utilise their computers, offered their services to other firms. Eventually, some of these computer departments were externalised to produce separate computer service firms such as Centre File Ltd. (derived from, and still wholly owned by, the National Westminster Bank Plc.), and Compower Ltd. (derived from British Coal).

Many computer services are provided within large firms by internal departments. It is important to distinguish between internal and external supply. Since here the focus is on computer service firms the emphasis is on external supply. By examining only external supply the extent of computer services will, however, be underestimated as too will the level of internationalisation, since intra-firm trade in computer services by non computer service firms will not be included in the analysis.

The 1970s saw the rapidly rising importance of independently supplied services to the computer user. Initially, computer services were supplied by the computer manufacturers, however, major developments in the independent supplier market were stimulated in 1969 by the decision of the largest hardware manufacturer - IBM - to separately price application programmes from it data processing equipment (that is, to practise unbundling) (OECD, 1989, p.15). This gave computer service firms the opportunity to compete in the software market. Because of the convergence between computer and telecommunication technologies, computer services suppliers have begun to offer some services on a network basis, commonly labelled value added network services (VANS). VANS are largely perceived as an evolution of time-sharing, an activity which has declined in importance. On the wave of the above mentioned technological evolution hardware manufacturers are moving into systems integration and networking, and they are providing a number of additional functions (for example, databases) previously mainly supplied by independents (OECD, 1989).

International market for computer services

The computer services market is relatively easy to enter on a small scale, this is illustrated by the rapid growth in the number of computer service businesses in the UK from 33,219 in 1989 to 39,185 in 1993 (Business Monitor SDA29, 1995). However, barriers do exist which hamper growth in the size of computer service firms, these include the ability of managerial staff and the availability of investment funds. For small niche companies and start ups the logical evolution path seems increasingly one of being acquired. The fact that in 1993 there were some 661 acquisitions in the UK sector (Business Monitor SDA29, 1995) would appear to indicate that many firms are pursuing just such a strategy.

Large software developers grow by extending their line of offerings and absorbing pioneering breakthroughs. The easiest way to expand is via acquisitions, and one of the reasons for this is probably the growing inter-connections between various kinds of computers. Other factors stimulating acquisitions have been the number of companies active in less attractive industries; the need for firms active in the hardware and telecommunications field to raise their returns by adding more information service value; growing interest from foreign buyers; and the intensifying competitive pressures felt by small privately held firms (OECD, 1989).

As Howells (1989) notes the computer service sector appears to be evolving into a dual economy, with a number of major global operations emerging in world markets, while below them a buoyant new and small firm sector operates in specialised niche markets. It is however important to note that some of the small companies are the subsidiaries of major groups. Groups such as Sema Plc. have a

133

number of separate specialist subsidiary businesses offering various types of services, including consultancy, facilities management, training and applications development. The number of actual groups in the services market is therefore much less than that implied by the number of businesses.

The UK market for computer services was worth approximately £5.8 billion in 1995 (Key Note, 1995, p.4). The level of market concentration, which has been increasing in recent years, is illustrated in Table 6.6, with the top 14 companies in the UK accounting for 45.6 per cent of the market. According to the Computing Services Association (CSA) member billings in 1992 were £4,959 billion, of these 15 per cent were derived from overseas sales. Furthermore, 25 per cent of CSA members are owned by non British parents, whilst 45 per cent are owned by larger groups and 55 per cent are independent companies (CSA, 1994).

Computer services are a part of the Information Technology (IT) market which, according to MACE (1992, p.45), has increased in value at a world level from $284 billion in 1986 to $558 billion in 1991 and is expected to reach $1,079 billion in 1996. The share of computer services and software has increased from 27 per cent in 1986 to 38 per cent in 1991 and is expected to reach 38.5 per cent by 1996. The centre of growth for the IT industry has shifted towards the software and services sectors and away from the hardware sectors. The US is the largest IT market with 47.8 per cent in 1991 followed by Europe with 27.9 per cent and Japan with 14.3 per cent leaving the rest of the world with a share of only 10 per cent (MACE, 1992, p.46). The focus here is upon computer services and Table 6.7 shows the world's top 10 firms which between them supply some 71 per cent of the market.

The software, computer and computerised information services industry has always been competitive, but historically it has exhibited a relatively low level of international trade relative to the size of domestic markets, due to language barriers and small size of the competing firms. This situation is now changing. In software, the balance of activity is shifting away from custom towards package programmes and international standards for software engineering are emerging. Information service providers are also extending their marketing activities and providing access commands and summary abstracts in several languages. Internationalisation is also increasing as MNEs adopt corporate strategies which use the same software programmes and the same service providers in all countries (OECD, 1989).

Internationalisation of computer service firms

As in other industries, the internationalisation of computer services occurs through direct exports, licensing and foreign subsidiaries. However, in this sector problems arise as a result of its specific characteristics and development process. It is necessary to emphasise that the values that show domestic and/or worldwide revenues include an unknown quantity of imports. In many cases, country based firms adapt and/or translate imported software or simply commercialise software

134

Table 6.6
The UK's largest computer services suppliers 1994 (% of total value billings)

Company	% of total billings
ICL UK	6.9
IBM UK Ltd	5.5
EDS-UK Ltd	4.7
Andersen Consulting	4.2
Sema Group PLC	3.4
Hoskyns Group PLC	3.0
ACT Group PLC	2.9
Syntegra Ltd	2.7
Olivetti UK Ltd	2.6
AT&T Istel Ltd	2.6
Digital UK	2.0
McDonnell Information Systems Ltd	1.7
Logica	1.7
Easams	1.7
Others	54.4
Total	100.0

Source: Key Note (Computer Services, 1995, p.14).

imports. It is also not known to what extent software provided by foreign subsidiaries is imported and eventually reproduced in the required quantity; to what extent it is adapted and/or translated; and how much of its value is originally developed in the country. Consequently, the output actually produced in a country is unknown (OECD, 1989). However, in recent years the UK's computer service sectors foreign earnings have been reported by the Central Statistics Office showing an increase in value from £619 million in 1992 to £894 million in 1994 (CSO Pink Book, 1995).

Computer services may be exported in a number of forms, for example, a report, advising on the selection of hardware, in the form of disks containing training material or 'over the wire'. As computer and telecommunications technologies converge this type of 'over-the-wire' service is likely to increase in importance. Direct exporting is the most obvious source of international trade, but there is also substantial cross border trade within international companies, that is, intra-firm trade. For example, Logica companies worldwide derive around 10 per cent of their revenue from exporting directly to foreign customers, but an additional 5 per cent

Table 6.7

The world's top computer services firms 1993 (revenue in $ Millions)

Rank	Company	1993
1	IBM	9,711.0
2	EDS	8,507.3
3	Andersen Consulting	2,588.7
4	CSC	2,502.0
5	ADP	2,339.2
6	TRW	1,900.0
7	Digital	1,875.0
8	Unisys	1,593.1
9	First Data	1,500.0
10	AT&T	1,235.0

Source: Compiled from Datamation, June 15th. 1994, p.54.

from cross border trade with sister companies in other countries (Rowlands, 1993, p.17).

Internationalisation may also occur through the establishment of an overseas presence, through FDI. 'Greenfield' FDI by computer service companies has not generally produced large international groups. Foreign start ups have often proved costly and time consuming, and although there are countless examples of successful one-country start-ups, few have succeeded internationally. Relatively low entry barriers to the industry enable local entrepreneurs to set up their own companies which provide ongoing concerns available for takeover by companies with international ambitions. Cross border mergers and acquisitions have been important methods of internationalisation, indeed, they have proved a faster and generally more effective route to building overseas networks than investment in greenfield start-ups. Further to this type of internationalisation, substantial service activities have been built on to the international businesses of major computer hardware suppliers, telecommunication suppliers and accountancy practices.

Subcontracting is a well developed route to internationalisation in computing services. IBM, for example has been subcontracting software product development over a very wide geographical area for at least the last decade. Interestingly this work has often been executed through IBM intermediaries in the country of supply and developers have had little or no contact with their end clients. In this sense internationalisation is taking the form of the internationalisation of production. Software developers in advanced and high cost western economies are experiencing increased competition from less developed nations. Indian software companies have pioneered this trend. Their exports are reported to be growing at over 40 per cent annually and they are aiming at $1 billion of software export revenues in 1995 (Rowland, 1993, p.18). China and other developing Asian countries are also supplying technically competent development resources at remarkably low cost. In Europe, well educated professionals from the former Communist countries will make an increasing impact on Western European computer services.

Although US suppliers dominate software product supply globally, associated services are frequently provided by local distributors. International licensing is thus an important alternative to direct investment or international trade for the development of services connected with particular products or proprietary methodologies and is an important source of growth for the industry globally.

Joint ventures between independent service providers in different countries have had some success as a route to international development in this industry. Links with computer suppliers are common and links with customers to address particular vertical markets internationally are becoming important in some sectors. International inter-firm agreements have become popular recently, even between close competitors. They can be of clear value in reducing R&D and marketing costs for the partners involved. Collaborative European R&D under ESPRIT and EUREKA programmes has had prominence for some years. International consortia are also a standard vehicle for pursuing international business in which national return has to be matched to national contribution.

Various factors, including the following, will lead to steadily increasing internationalisation in computing services businesses:

1 Customers are restructuring internationally. Some of these customers will wish their computing service requirements to be met by service providers which can offer wide geographic coverage.

2 In Europe, current directives require public procurement to be open to competition across the community. There is an increasing requirement from the European Commission to link national systems and develop EU wide systems.

3 The knowledge required to provide systems integration services can be developed and deployed most effectively outside the country of origin by the larger international companies.

4 Effective integrators will need to develop and exploit an international network of alliances and distributorships to bring product-based solutions to their customers.

Although such factors mean that international activity will be increasingly important, the significant advantages of cultural and physical proximity to clients will ensure that domestic (but not necessarily domestically owned) computing services industries thrive in developed and developing countries. Truly international computer service businesses will have a strong domestic presence in several key economic areas. These domestic operations will derive value from the larger groups to which they belong and have distinct capabilities which they can contribute to them. The kinds of benefit which can accrue in international service firms cover intangibles, such as common ways of working or methodological approaches, shared market image, through to shared value chain activities in, for example, R&D, product procurement, training, sales and marketing. The value of the intangibles often exceeds that of the tangibles. International computing services businesses will tend to structure activities with a fair degree of local control within a common approach to the way in which business is conducted.

Organisational structure of computer service firms

The organisational structure of the computer service firm will depend on a number of factors including its size, the range and type of services provided and the requirements of its clients. Since it is relatively easy to enter the market on a small scale there are many small firms which are organised on the basis of simple hierarchical structures. This study is concerned with those firms involved in the international market and as such is therefore concerned with larger computer service firms or those which are a part of a larger group.

Computer services encompass a variety of activities as noted earlier, ranging from maintenance to training. As a computer service firm evolves its range of activities is likely to increase, and as a result, the larger firms are organised on a multidivisional basis, each division being concerned with one distinct area of activity. As a firm becomes international, perhaps through setting up a subsidiary or through the acquisition of an overseas company, the firm develops an international division. Fully internationalised computer service firms may be organised around either product or geographic markets. In addition to these two international organisational structures, Gentle and Howells (1994), in a study of the European computer service industry, identify a 'centres of excellence' organisational strategy. Here centres of excellence are developed which draw on the expertise of particular offices, and on the skills of the countries in which they are located. For example, financial expertise is concentrated in London, telecommunications in Paris, and so on. Such expertise can be used to give competitive advantage in the provision of global services.

When considering the international structure of computer service firms it is important to note a number of features common among such firms. Firstly, as noted earlier, a number of successful computer service companies originate from the computer departments of large firms through a process of externalisation. Some of these firms have remained linked to the source firm through ownership. For example, Centre-File Ltd., which is a wholly owned subsidiary of the National Westminster Bank Plc., provides computer related products and services to a wide range of commercial industrial and professional organisations, including the

National Westminster Group which accounts for just over half of the firm's business (Centre-File, 1993). In some cases ownership has not been retained but has passed to large international computer service groups, for example, Unilever Computer Services Ltd. which was acquired by EDS (Electronic Data Services). It is interesting to note that EDS itself was purchased by General Motors in 1984, although, it is due to become independent in 1996 giving it scope to link up with a major telecommunications supplier.

A second feature influencing the development of computer service firms is the fact that the sector is enjoying a relatively rapid rate of growth. Datamation (1995, p.65), for example, reported a 15 per cent rate of revenue growth in the US. from IT services in 1994. As a result many firms have been diversifying into the sector, in particular, hardware manufacturers, the large end users, accountancy firms, management consultants and telecommunication providers. As a consequence, of this diversification, together with the process of externalisation, it is possible to find computer service firms forming part of groups involved in both related and unrelated activities.

Internationalisation is increasingly occurring through the establishment and extension of large global groups, mainly US owned, which expand overseas through the takeover of national firms. These firms are integrated into an international network of firms able to offer global coverage to MNEs. For example, EDS has pursued such a policy building up it international network through acquisition, a recent example being the acquisition of SD-Scicon Plc., a UK company. When examining the top computer service providers for 1993 (Table 6.7) the dominance of US firms can clearly be seen.

The IT market is a dynamic one, which has been growing and developing rapidly, within this the computer services market has been evolving quickly. If companies are to expand to satisfy market and client needs the easiest way is to takeover existing firms. This is facilitated by the large number of firms available for takeover. As noted earlier, entry into the market is achieved relatively easily, however, expansion is made difficult by lack of management expertise and funding, so the easiest way to expand is to be acquired. Through the process of acquisition and mergers it is possible to build up an international network of firms in a relatively short period of time. In order to survive firms must either identify a niche market upon which to concentrate, or alternatively ally themselves with one of the large global groups.

Regulation of the computer services sector

The barriers to internationalisation of the computer services sector are those which exist in most sectors: market access; national treatment; non-discrimination; and transparency. Howells (1989) identifies proper access to distribution channels (including telecommunication networks) to be of particular importance to computer services, together with the need for reasonable tariffication rates on telecommunication networks; and, the unrestricted transfer of personnel to service overseas markets.

The computer service sector is covered by a number of national laws and regulations which may aim, inter alia, to guarantee intellectual property, investment in information bases, and to define the role of the State with regard to the circulation of information. Legislation also exists which deals with information, for instance, that which governs the processing of data and its transportation. Unlike most other service sectors, industry observers believe that the computer service sector is generally under-regulated, particularly in relation to the legal protection of intellectual property rights. In other areas regulation covering computer services are embryonic or ill defined, which in turn creates problems of 'transparency' particularly for foreign companies (Howells, 1989). Associated with the need for more regulation in key areas covering computer services, there is also the growing recognition for the need of harmonisation in the field of national legal environments. It is felt that harmonisation will help minimise the impact of non-trade related regulations such as personal privacy issues. There is also great dependence on the regulatory environment that exists for telecommunication services.

The issue of intellectual property rights is seen as of prime importance in computer service trade. Indeed, it is seen as an essential precursor to trade in computer services, which are costly to create but can be reproduced easily and cheaply. Many smaller firms may not bother to enter into international service transactions if such rights are not in place. Progress on the international protection of computer programmes and data bases was achieved by the Uruguay Round of GATT negotiations under the agreement on trade related aspects of intellectual property rights. However, the effectiveness of such protection is yet to be seen. Other trade issues relate to economic dominance and market structure and the role of the developing countries' interests in the trade debates (Howells, 1989).

Developments in the computer services sector

Massive restructuring is taking place in the worldwide IT industry because of the combined effects of the move to open systems and the decreasing cost of hardware. Hardware is becoming a commodity, sold down to a price, while software is increasingly being used as the differentiator in the supply of IT systems. Dataquest (Datamation, 1995, p.65) estimate that IT services including maintenance, outsourcing, and consultancy now represent 34 per cent of all IT spending. Expenditure is moving from those who supply the technology towards those who can apply the technology. The hardware manufacturers are restructuring their organisations to take advantage of the growth in software and services and to compensate them for their declining revenues form hardware products. Many of the leading manufacturers have restructured their organisations to form separate computer service subsidiaries or are buying computer services companies to ensure they are positioned correctly to exploit the expected growth in computer services (Eyeions, 1993). Along with the movement of hardware manufacturers into the service sector there is the increasing blurring of the distinction between service and hardware providers. This is likely to continue and indeed intensify.

An important problem in the software sector is that of piracy. The world's leading software houses estimate that unauthorised copying of their programmes costs them around £3 billion a year throughout Europe. They believe that unless it can be stopped it will grow at an annual rate of 10 per cent per annum. In the UK the Federation Against Software Theft estimates that illegal copying costs the software industry £300 million in 1989, double the figure in 1985 (Key Note, 1992). Such problems underline the need to develop a firm regulatory framework for the sector at an international level.

The market for computer services is set to continue its growth, indeed a Key Note report (1995, p.5) predicts that the market will grow by 74.8 per cent in value terms between 1995-2000, with major growth coming from facilities management, systems integration and consultancy. As the use of, and dependence upon ICTs, in the developed economies continues to grow so too will the need for computer services. Innovations such as virtual reality are expanding the potential applications of ICT in an increasingly multi-media market. Computer service firms must adapt to the emerging market, and, given its dynamic nature, those firms which are able to maintain a high level of flexibility will no doubt be better positioned to exploit the opportunities which arise.

6.5 Conclusion

The sub-sectors explored above display certain common characteristics. They all, for example, demonstrate the dynamism and growth which is a feature of the business services sector as a whole. The three sectors are all involved in the processing of information and hence developments in ICTs have major implications for the manner in which their services are produced and distributed. Indeed, new ICTs are giving rise to the development of new services in all the sectors studied. A high degree of internationalisation is evident in the three sectors and the application of new ICTs has implications for the manner of in which international transactions are conducted together with the organisational structure of international service firms in these sectors.

At a national level there is a clear polarisation between many small firms servicing local and niche markets and a small number of large firms servicing national and international markets. Although on a small scale there are few barriers to entry in all three sectors, at a large scale, in particular at the international level, barriers to entry do exist. The level of concentration at the international level has been rising in all three sectors as companies have sought to extend their international coverage.

141

Client relations are important to all three sectors, with the provision of services being highly dependent upon client producer contact. The desire to satisfy client needs has been crucial to the early international development of firms in these sectors. Furthermore, diversification has in some circumstances been stimulated by the aspiration to cater for an extending range of client demands. Diversification has also arisen out of the search for opportunities for growth, particularly in the mature sectors like accountancy, where the core markets have little scope for significant expansion.

Regulation has an impact on all three sectors, although the nature and level of control does vary. Clearly, though, regulation does influence the level and nature of international activity in the sectors studied. The harmonisation of regulation on an international scale would no doubt lead to greater scope for economies of scale in the production of business services, and therefore lower costs to clients. The General Agreement on Trade in Services provides the first step towards the liberalisation of trade in services. Whether it will have any major impact on the international market for business services remains to be seen, however, the fact that services are clearly on the trade liberalisation agenda is significant.

All three sectors studied make an important contributing to the smooth operation of economic activity. Since economic growth is set to continue as the world economy recovers from the recession of the early 1990s, and the benefits of the Uruguay GATT agreement come to fruition, all business service sectors will both benefit from and contribute to such growth. Moreover, there are also the opportunities which arise from the economic developments in East Asia and the Eastern European economies.

As shown the three sectors studies are similar in many ways, however, there are also important differences. In particular, the various sectors are at different stages of development. Accountancy being the oldest activity, and this being reflected in the relative maturity and slow growth in the audit market. In contrast, computer services is a relatively new sector and one which is experiencing rapid growth. Furthermore, differences also occur in the manner in which new ICT developments affect each sector. Such developments are crucial to the computer service sector dependent as it is on computer and communications technologies. Similarly, all three sectors face specific regulatory challenges and developments.

Through the exploration of the main three sub-sectors in this chapter the background has now been provided against which the survey and case study results can be meaningfully analysed. The survey sample includes not only firms from the advertising, accountancy and computer services sectors, but also firms from the management consultancy, public relations and market research sectors. Attention will return to the three main sub-sectors in Chapter 9 where case studies from each sector will be considered. The next two chapters are concerned with the operation of the postal survey, and the analysis of the data generated.

142

Notes

1   For example, Dentsu formed a joint pacific network with Young and
     Rubicam in 1983 (West, 1988), and in 1987 these two agencies together
     with the French group Eurocom came together to create a world scale
     advertising agency, HDM (Mattelart, 1991). In addition, Hakuhodo has a
     joint venture relationship with McCann Erickson and Tokyu Agency has
     developed the Toyku Agency International which is 24 per cent owned by
     DMB&B, whilst Daiko has a joint venture relationship with Grey
     Advertising.

2   In a survey of 418 of the Fortune 500 business firms conducting
     international trade, Hite and Fraser (1988) found that of those firms
     advertising internationally (two thirds of the population) 9 per cent relied
     solely on standardised advertising, 54 per cent used a combination of
     centrally and locally created advertising, while 37 per cent utilised solely
     localised advertising. Where advertising is adapted to the local market, this
     invariably involves the use of an agency located in that market.

3   For instance, RJR Nabisco gives 20 per cent bonus for outstanding and 10
     per cent for very good advertising, average and poor work receives an
     undisclosed fixed commission rate which is probably slightly below the 15
     per cent level (James Capel, 1989).

4   The 1848 Winding Up Act made the appointment of a public accountant as
     official manager a virtual necessity, while the subsequent 1862 Companies
     Act, which created the role of Official Liquidators, led to the insolvency
     work becoming the main source of revenue for accountants.

5   For a detailed overview of the variety of activities in which computer
     services providers are engaged see the Computing Services Association
     Handbook (1993) where members services/products are listed.

143

7 The UK business services sector: survey framework

7.1 Introduction

The purpose of this chapter is to clarify the research objectives and to prepare the way for a useful discussion of the results generated from the analysis of data gathered through the postal survey. The research aims and hypotheses to be tested will be reviewed. This will be followed by an in-depth examination of the postal survey which proved a significant tool for the collection of primary data. A further section will consider the characteristics of the sample of business service firms surveyed. Firstly, though it is necessary to explain the focus upon the UK business services sector, and to provide a brief review of the UK sector.

7.2 The UK business services sector

The selection of business services as the focus of this research has already been considered (Chapter 2), however it is now necessary to account for the choice of the UK business services sector. This book is concerned with the process of internationalisation and the organisational forms used by international business service providers. In order to study the process of internationalisation it is necessary to examine the development of individual firms within a particular market environment. Internationalisation is then being explored from a national base, and, in the context of this research that national base is the UK. A number of factors influenced this choice, firstly, many sections of the UK's business services sector are highly competitive and already display a high degree of internationalisation. Secondly, limited research resources were a significant factor determining the national base from which internationalisation could be explored. It

144

Table 7.1

Numbers employed in the business services sector 1985 and 1994 (1000's)

	Division	Dec. 1985	Dec. 1994
Business services	83	999.9	1653.4
Activities auxiliary to banking and finance	831	25.5	53.2
Activity auxiliary to insurance	832	79.1	99.8
House and estate agents	834	85.8	98.6
Legal services	835	n.a.	212.2
Accountants, auditors and tax experts	836	n.a.	164.0
Professional and technical services nes	837	202.5	205.3
Advertising	838	40.8	46.2
Computer services	8394	66.3	165.0
Business services nes	8395	195.9	581.6
Central offices not allocable elsewhere	8396	40.6	27.5

n.a. not available.

nes not elsewhere specified.

Source: Complied from Employment Gazette (July 1986, and July 1995).

is useful at this point to provide a brief overview of business service sector activity in the UK in order to set the context for the research.

The UK business services sector, as defined by the 1980 Standard Industrial Classification (SIC) (Division 83), covers a set of specialised and varied activities which at the end of 1994 employed almost 8 per cent of the nation's workforce (Employment Gazette, July 1995). The activities which make up the business services sector are listed in Table 7.1 together with the numbers employed in December 1985 and 1994. It can be seen that employment in the sector has increased from 999.9 thousand in 1985 to 1,653.4 thousand in 1994, an increase of 653.5 thousand or over 65 per cent on the 1985 figure (Employment Gazette, July 1986 & 1995).

As Rajan (1987) notes, despite their diversity, business services do have two common features. Firstly, all of them are amenable to self-employment because of their low start up costs or their high value added. Secondly, every one of them created new jobs in the 1980s in a way that no other similarly varied industrial group has. In a special feature on the service sector the Employment Gazette

(1989) confirmed this view, the survey found that the fastest level of employment growth over the decade to 1987 was within the business services sector where the numbers of employees had increased by 78.2 per cent. The survey also found that the level of self-employed doubled to 302 thousand in the decade from 1977 within Division 8, which includes business services. Furthermore, business services enjoyed an annual average growth rate of output between 1978 and 1987 of 8.4 per cent the largest in Division 8, and indeed throughout the service sector. Over the same period business services experienced an average annual growth rate in productivity of 2 per cent.

It is clear then that the business services sector makes up a significant, expanding, and dynamic sector within the British economy. Indeed, business services are important producer services and as such have an impact upon the competitiveness of all areas of economic activity in Britain.

The geographical distribution of business service sector employment compared to that of employment in general and service sector employment is illustrated in Table 7.2. Business services are more heavily concentrated in the South East with 47.76 per cent of employment in this area compared to 31.99 per cent of all employment and 34.98 per cent of all service sector employment.

The employment levels in the three sub-sectors of the business services sector which provide the central focus of this study are shown in Table 7.3. In December 1990 the three sectors accounted for 24.1 per cent of the business services sector employment, this figure fell to 22.69 per cent by December 1994. It is interesting to note that despite this overall decline, computer services sector employment grew in both absolute and percentage terms during this period. The recession of the early 1990s clearly hit certain business services sectors harder than others, however as the British economy recovers the level of employment in the business services sector in general can be expected to increase.

Information on UK international service transactions is limited, however, some insight can be gained from the information provided in Chapter 2. From Table 2.5 it is clear that the UK is among the top exporters and importers of services. Also, the significance of FDI in the service sector, and more specifically, the subgroup 'other services' which includes business services has been illustrated (Table 2.6). A more detailed view of trade transactions can be gained from an examination the UK balance of payments statistics (CSO Pink Book, 1995) which show that services enjoy a positive balance on the current account. The most significant contribution to this balance was from financial and other services which has increased its positive balance from £5,803 million in 1984 to £11,243 million in 1994 (CSO Pink Book, 1995: Table 3.1). The financial and other services category is of most interest to this study because they include business services.

Two main factors are apparent from the crude statistics in Table 7.4 on overseas earnings of a number of Britain's business services. First, when compared to other branches of the service sector, the foreign contribution of these activities is marginal. In 1991 overseas revenues amounted to £706 million, up from £232

Table 7.2

Geographical distribution of employment March 1995: a comparison between the distribution of all employment, service sector employment and business services sector employment

	Percentage of all employment	Percentage of service employment	Business service sector employment (1000's)	Business service sector employment as % of total
Northern Ireland	2.62	2.63	21	1.26
Scotland	9.00	8.93	110	6.58
Wales	4.47	4.23	47	2.81
North	5.03	4.72	47	2.81
North West	10.52	10.28	140	8.37
Yorkshire & Humberside	8.44	8.04	97	5.80
East Midlands	7.08	6.20	78	4.66
West Midlands	9.29	8.27	145	8.67
South West	7.84	8.08	127	7.59
East Anglia	3.70	3.66	62	3.71
All South East	31.99	34.98	799	47.76
Greater London	14.45	16.77	463	27.67
Great Britain	97.38	97.37	1651	98.69
UK	100	100	1673	100

Source: Complied from Employment Gazette (August 1995).

million in 1984. Second, though the relative contribution is limited, it is growing steadily.

The most consistent performance was achieved by management and economic consultancy. Its aggregate earnings expanded from an estimated £48 million in 1984 to £238 million in 1994, achieving a small nominal rise in almost every year, with a significant rise between 1993 and 1994. By comparison, advertising revenues fluctuated slightly, suffering a decline in 1989 and again in 1993. Nevertheless, overall nominal performance was positive, with earning rising from £64 million in 1984 to £101 million by 1994. The legal profession showed a significant level of growth in foreign earnings over the period from £120 million in 1984 to £502 million in 1994. This growth is related to the expansion of work brought about with the deregulation of the financial markets in the UK in the 1980s. Most of these foreign earnings relate to services carried out in the UK for overseas clients. The figures for computer services, only available since 1992,

147

Table 7.3

Employment in selected business service sub-sectors 1985-1994 as a percentage of employment in the business services sector

	Dec. 1985 % (1000's)	Dec. 1990 % (1000's)	Dec. 1994 % (1000's)
Advertising	4.08 (40.8)	3.36 (51.9)	2.79 (46.2)
Accountants, auditors and tax experts	n.a.	11.01 (170.2)	9.92 (164.0)
Computer services	6.63 (66.3)	9.73 (150.4)	9.98 (165.0)

n.a. not available.

Source: Compiled from Employment Gazette, (July 1986, May 1992, and July 1995).

Table 7.4

Foreign earnings in selected business services (Million £)

	1984	1985	1986	1987	1988	1989	1990	1991	1992	1993	1994
Management and economic consultancy	48	53	54	59	67	122	166	166	164	157	238
Computer services	..	..	..	..	..	..	..	..	619	790	894
Legal profession	120	155	190	241	300	350	395	425	473	466	502
Advertising and market research	64	77	78	98	95	85	90	115	167	106	101
Total	232	285	322	398	462	557	651	706	1423	1519	1735

Source: Compiled from CSO Pink Book 1995 (Table 3.7).

148

indicate an important and rapidly expanding contribution to foreign earning from this sector up from £619 million in 1992 to £894 million in 1994.

From the information on international trade in services it would appear that the UK has a competitive advantage in the international market for services in general, it is difficult to extend this statement to business service due to the lack of statistical evidence however, given the growing importance of this sector domestically it is highly likely that the UK enjoys a competitive advantage in the supply of such services. This view is confirmed by Porter (1990) who estimated, on the basis of extensive research, the pattern of national competitive advantage in international service industries for a number of countries. As can be seen from Table 7.5, Porter estimates that the UK has a leading position in advertising and a position in a variety of other business service activities. It would appear that the UK is second only to the US in having the strongest competitive advantage in the provision of business services. Indeed, the UK's strength in the provision of business services in Europe is indicated by the fact that UK business service enterprises represent about 21 per cent of the total European Union (EU) business services sector, whilst employment in the UK sector accounts for 31 per cent of all persons employed in this sector in the EU (EUROSTAT, 1994, p.194).

The UK's competitive advantage in the provision of business services derives from a number of sources. Firstly, services domestically and in particular business services, have become important in the UK ahead of many other countries, this has given the UK together with countries like the US a competitive advantage in the provision of such services. Secondly, the nature of the workforce in terms of high educational standards provides the UK with the necessary factor inputs to produce services competitively. Thirdly, the application of ICT, and lastly the regulatory environment and deregulation in many areas, are important factor contributing to the competitiveness of UK services. The service sector is generally highly regulated, reducing competition. In the UK examples of deregulation include the telecommunications market and financial sector in the late 1980s. All of these things give UK business service firms some advantage.

7.3 Research aims and hypotheses

The review of literature concerning the internationalisation of services provides a background against which to explore and understand the internationalisation of the business services sector. The central aim of the research is to provide a framework within which to understand the manner in which internationalisation in the business services sector occurs. Having reviewed the literature on the internationalisation of services in general, and business services specifically, it was possible to draw a number of conclusions regarding the manner in which business service firms become international and the factors which influence the level of internationalisation. It was on the basis of such conclusions that the framework

Table 7.5
Estimated patterns of national competitive advantage in international business service industries

Industry	Denmark	Germany	Italy	Japan	Korea	Sweden	Switzerland	UK	US
General business									
Accounting								X	XX
Legal services								X	XX
Advertising								XX	XX
Public relations								X	X
Management consulting		X					X	X	XX
Engineering/architectural[a]	X	X	X	X	X	X		X	XX
Construction			X		X		X	X	XX
Construction research								X	X
Design services			XX						
Temporary help							X		XX
Industrial laundry/ apparel supply	X							X	XX
Industrial cleaning (facilities, tools, equipment)						X			X
Security services						X	X	X	X
Building maintenance services	X						X	X	
Equipment maintenance and repair						X			
Wage support and management									XX
Information									
Information processing									XX
Custom software[b]								X	XX
Information/data								X	XX

XX leading position.
X position.
a National positions in engineering tend to be in different types of projects.
b France also had a significant position in custom software.

Source: Complied from Porter (1990).

150

considered in Chapter 5 was developed. A number of hypotheses were generated based upon the findings of the review of both theoretical and empirical literature, these are listed below.

Hypotheses

H1: Internationalisation among business service firms is accompanied by diversification.

Channon (1978) in a study of a number of UK service companies found that internationalisation was accompanied by diversification. This first hypothesis seeks to test this finding in relation to business service firms. Preliminary research indicates that many large and international business service firms are diversified to some degree. It is argued that business service firms diversify in order to gain economies of scale and scope in the use of their core skills and international networks (Dunning, 1989; Enderwick, 1989).

H2: International firms will seek to use cross referrals and provide a number of services to each client.

This second hypothesis is clearly related to the first, if international business service firms are diversified then they will seek to obtain as much business as possible from each client through the use of cross referral. Clearly a number of business firms do pursue such a strategy and seek to provide a one-stop-shop where clients can obtain many of their business service needs. Moreover, by providing a greater number of services to a client the business service firm is able to solicit a higher level of client loyalty. It becomes increasingly difficult for clients to turn to competing suppliers since they have invested a great deal in their relationship with their original supplier.

H3: Business service firms go through a evolutionary approach to internationalisation.

Hypothesis three derives from the proposition forwarded in Chapter 5, that the stages or evolutionary approach to internationalisation (Johanson and Wiedersheim-Paul, 1975; Stopford and Wells, 1972; inter alia) evident among manufacturing firms is relevant to the internationalisation of business service firms. This is contrary to the commonly held view that since services are non-tradable internationalisation must occur rapidly through the establishment of an overseas presence with no export only stage.

H4: Internationalisation is more common among firms which are part of a larger group or which are public limited companies.

151

For a strategy of internationalisation to be pursued a firm must have access to the resources required for overseas expansion. Hence those firms which have access to such resources either from a parent company or from the ability to raise financial support through share floatations are more likely to realise their international ambitions. It is therefore reasonable to conclude that those firms which are Plcs or part of a larger group will more often have international interests than those firms which have less access to financial support.

> H5: Overseas presences are frequently used merely as a means of delivering the service to clients.

This hypothesis seeks to test the proposition that an overseas presence may often be regarded as transaction specific in the sense that its whole purpose is to facilitate trade in services, that is intra-firm trade. It is clear that in some cases exports may only be possible in conjunction with an overseas presence, whether that presence is required to actually facilitate the transaction or whether it is necessary to provide backup services to clients.

> H6: Exports 'over the wire' and embodied in goods are limited despite the availability of ICTs which enable the embodiment of information intensive services into goods and exports across telecommunication networks.

This hypothesis seeks to test the proposition developed in Chapter 5 that business service exports embodied in goods or exported 'over the wire' will be less significant than those which involve the movement of the client to the location of the producer, or the movement of personnel to the client's location. This relates to the view that face-to-face contact is necessary in the delivery, if not production, of many services, particularly business services. Even though new ICTs are making the export of services embodied in goods or 'over the wire' easier in a practical sense, these methods of exportation are imperfect substitutes for exports involving face-to-face contact, and therefore will not be the dominant methods of exportation. Such exports provide an important supportive role to other forms of export but are of limited use on their own. The need for a local presence encourages the establishment of a permanent office in the overseas market.

> H7: Client relations are of great importance and limit the extent to which exports without personal contact can be used.

This hypothesis follows on from hypothesis 6. As noted in Chapter 5 a number of factors inhibit direct trade without personal contact in business services, these include: the need for client producer contact; the simultaneous provision and consumption of a service; the need for cultural sensitivity and local knowledge;

regulatory requirements; the desire to protect reputation and other intangible assets; together with the need for absolute confidentiality.

> H8: ICT is given greater importance as a source of competitive advantage by firms which are internationally active.

Large international business service firms derive a competitive advantage from their extensive networks from which they can draw resources. The application of ICTs enables a firm to maximise the benefits from such widely dispersed resources. ICTs are also an important tool which promotes the efficient operation of complex organisational structures. The more widely dispersed a business service firm is the greater the significance of ICT. Intra-firm trade in intangible assets such as knowledge and skills is facilitate by ICT. Firms derive competitive advantage from the use of ICTs since they allow a complex yet flexible organisation of resources which can be used to maximum effect to satisfy the needs of individual clients (Quinn and Paquette, 1990). As a firm becomes larger and increasingly international ICT will become more important as a source of competitive advantage.

> H9: International firms are more involved in merger and acquisition activity to build up international networks.

The importance to international business service firms of their international networks has been identified in the literature. To compete internationally firms must be able to offer clients a service in many geographically dispersed locations. As client firms become increasingly global, business services firms must follow suit. Mergers and acquisitions enable business service firms to achieve greater international coverage rapidly. As identified in Chapter 5, this method of expansion has been popular since the 1970s among well established firms which in the past made greater use of setting up facilities from scratch, and also among the younger firms wishing to establish international networks rapidly in order to compete effectively with the older and more established firms. It can be expected then that international firms will be more involved in merger and acquisition activity. National firms tend to be small and compete in local or niche markets where wide geographical coverage is not a significant source of competitive advantage.

> H10: International firms will regard international coverage to be an important source of competitive advantage.

For large and international business service firms multinational clients are important. Companies will seek to provide their clients with services in all of their overseas locations. Thus international coverage will be an important source of competitive advantage for international business service firms. Indeed lack of international coverage can act as a significant barrier to entry for firms wishing to provide services at an international level. Firms wishing to expand in recent years have found that they must establish an international network rapidly through mergers, acquisitions and contractual arrangements if they are to compete effectively with those which already have an established international network.

H11: The nature of a firm's clients will influence the level of internationalisation.

The influence of multinational clients on the internationalisation of service firms has been widely recognised (Yannopoulos, 1983; Dunning, 1989; Erramilli and Rao, 1990; Esperanca, 1992). Hypothesis 11 seeks to test this relationship among UK business service firms.

H12: Firms located in the South of the UK and those with a wide domestic geographical spread are likely to be international in scope.

As noted in Chapter 5, geographical expansion ultimately leads to internationalisation as the domestic market becomes saturated. Firms usually expand national coverage prior to internationalisation. However, in some cases business service firms located in capital cities will become internationally active before extending their national coverage (O'Farrell and Wood, 1993). Thus it can be expected that firms with either a wide geographical spread nationally or located in the South of the UK, that is, close to a major centre of agglomeration - London, will be more international in scope than other firms.

H13: Firms prefer to have majority ownership in their overseas subsidiaries.

The preference highlighted in this hypothesis has been identified among service firms generally (Dunning, 1989; Erramilli and Rao, 1993). For business service firms ownership is necessary to protect intangible assets such as brand names, reputation, firm specific methodologies and so on. Majority ownership facilitates the level of control required to protect such assets, it is however, important to note that such control is not necessarily centralised among business service firm organisations.

H14: Internationally active companies give their subsidiaries a higher level of autonomy compared to national firms.

This is particularly the case among business service firms where local knowledge concerning culture, business practices, and regulatory conditions, for example, is vital to the success of a subsidiary. A parent company located in another country

154

will not have the necessary information and will therefore have to give the local presence a high degree of autonomy.

H15: Business service sector overseas investment is market-oriented as opposed to resource-oriented.

Most business service firms expand overseas in order to service existing or potential clients in the overseas market. International expansion is largely market-oriented, although, it is clear that the potential for resource oriented expansion is increasing with technological developments.

The hypotheses outlined here were subjected to empirical testing through the analysis of data collected with the use of a postal questionnaire. The remainder of this chapter gives a detailed review of the administration of the postal survey, together with the characteristics of the sample of business service firms examined.

7.4 Framework of the postal questionnaire[1]

The survey sample was selected from the three main business services sub-sectors, advertising, accountancy and computer services, together with three additional though related sub-sectors, management consultancy, public relations and market research. These additional sub-sectors were included in the postal survey for a number of reasons. Firstly, as illustrated in the previous chapter, these sectors are not only closely related to the main three sub-sectors, but, in many cases firms in the advertising, accountancy and computer services sectors are often also involved in the provision of management consulting, public relations and market research services. Secondly, through the inclusion of these sub-sectors the relevance of the survey was extended, and the sample surveyed provided a more useful and representative cross section of the UK business services sector. Given resource restrictions the survey was targeted at the large firms. Since internationalisation is generally associated with the larger firms it was important to ensure that a significant portion of the samples surveyed were of a certain size. Hence the samples were weighted towards firms which ranked among the top 30 of their particular sector, in terms of fee income, turnover or billings. With the prevalence of small firms in the sector, a totally random sample of such a small size would undoubtedly have thrown up only a small number of firms with international activity. As noted earlier, the business services sector is one with low barriers to entry and amenable to the self employed because of the low start up costs and high value-added, hence the large number of small firms in the sector.

The top firms in each sub-sector were identified from the trade press and directories, such as, Campaign (24.2.89);The Accountant (June 1989; February 1987); Hollis Press and Public Relations Annual (1989); and, CSA Official Reference Book (1989). Having selected the top 30 firms for each sub-sector the remainder of the samples were selected at random from a population drawn from the various trade directories.

A pilot survey[2] was held in March 1990 in order to ascertain the viability of the questionnaire. It was administered by a personal interviewer in order to identify problems and clarify questions for the respondent. The pilot survey proved valuable in terms of increasing the clarity of the questionnaire and in removing ambiguities. As a consequence, the questionnaire was significantly redesigned prior to the launch of the main postal survey.

The questionnaire was sent out to 1019 companies within a two week period in May 1990. After a period of almost six weeks a follow up letter with a further copy of the questionnaire was sent out to those firms which had not yet responded. By September 1990 when the survey was closed 409 responses had been received giving a total response rate of 40.1 per cent. Of these 81 constituted nil returns covering firms which:

1   Did not wish to participate in the questionnaire for reasons of confidentiality.
2   Those that did not feel it was relevant as they had no international activity.
3   Those which had a policy of not responding to questionnaires.
4   Those which did not have the time or relevant information to be able to provide valid responses.
5   Firms which were no longer in business.

A number of the firms not wishing to participate in the survey did provide useful information in the form of company reports or details of their international activities. This information has been incorporated into the research findings wherever possible. The usable returns amounted to 328 a response rate of 32.2 per cent. Table 7.6 gives a breakdown of the response rates for the various sub-sectors. The lowest response rate of 30.4 per cent was obtained from advertising firms whilst the highest response rate of 39.5 per cent was obtained from the market research firms. 74.8 per cent of the questionnaires were completed by senior decision-makers in the firms, the remainder being completed by assistants to senior decision-makers or senior members of particular departments. A similar pattern was found for each of the sub-sectors.

7.5 Characteristics of the sample

The location of the respondents reflected the geographical distribution of the total sample surveyed. Since, wherever possible, questionnaires were sent to head office locations it was found, as expected, that the majority of respondents were from the South.[3] Of the 328 cases 74.1 per cent were located in the South of England. A

156

Table 7.6
UK business service sub-sectors surveyed and response rates

Sector (SIC 1980)	Number surveyed	Responses Total	Usable	% Responses Total	Usable
Advertising (8380)	289	99	88	34.2	30.4
Accountancy (8360)	203	78	62	38.4	30.5
Computer services (8394)	205	84	68	40.9	33.2
Management consultants (8395/1)	196	88	61	44.9	31.1
Public relations (8393/2)	50	22	19	44.0	38.0
Market research (8395/2)	76	38	30	50.0	39.5
Total	1019	409	328	40.1	32.2

Source: Postal survey.

further 10.8 per cent were located in the Midlands and 11.7 per cent in the North. 2.5 per cent were located in Scotland whilst only 0.6 per cent in Wales and 0.3 per cent in Northern Ireland. This pattern of distribution was reflected in the sub-sectors with all having more than 73 per cent located in the South apart from accountancy firms where the figure was 57.4 per cent. Market research firms displayed the highest level of location in the South with 86.7 per cent. As noted earlier, when examining Table 7.2, there is a high concentration of business service employment, in the South East, and indeed in the South, greater than for services employment and employment in general. The pattern of the sample's location reflects this and the fact that business service firms are attracted to major centres of agglomeration, in particular, to London.

The age of the firms varied considerably, with the oldest having been established in 1821. In all 6.2 per cent of the firms were established by the turn of the century. The distribution of the dates of establishment are shown in Table 7.7. It can be seen

Table 7.7
Date of establishment

Date of establishment	Number of firms	Percentage
Before 1850	4	1.3
1851-1900	15	4.9
1901-1950	31	10.1
1951-1960	14	4.6
1961-1970	49	16.0
1971-1980	89	29.1
1981-1990	104	34.0
	N=306	

Source: Postal survey.

that the majority (over 60 per cent) of business service firms surveyed were established after 1970. This reflects the growing importance of business services over the past 20-30 years, with their supply being provided by separate and distinctive organisations. Indeed, 34 per cent of the firms surveyed were established between 1981 and 1990 a fact which highlights the youthful age profile of the sample. Manufacturing firms have externalised service provision and business services firms have expanded in their own right. Computer services firms provide a particularly good example of this growth. With regard to sub-sectors in all cases apart from accountancy firms the majority of firms were established after 1970. The accountancy sector consisted of a higher proportion of older firms than other sectors. There were no public relations or market research firms established before 1900. Although there were a number of computer service firms established in the nineteenth century, the present companies originate from firms whose core business has migrated to computer services, for example, Anderson Consulting which used to be primarily an accountancy firm but is now a major supplier of computer services. 90.5 per cent of computer service firms and 100 per cent of the public relations firms were established after 1960 compared to 79.1 per cent of the whole sample illustrating the recent development of these sub-sectors.

The employment levels in the UK and overseas for all the firms surveyed are provided in Table 7.8. It can be seen that 48.3 per cent of all the firms had UK employment levels of more than 50 people, whilst only 16.2 per cent had overseas employment levels of over 50 people, indeed 75.1 per cent of the firms had no overseas employment.

158

Table 7.8
UK and overseas employment for business service firms 1989

Numbers employed	UK %	Overseas %
0-10	12.2	75.1
11-20	12.9	4.9
21-50	26.4	3.7
51-100	17.3	2.4
101-200	15.1	2.0
200-500	7.5	2.0
501-1000	3.1	1.6
1001-2500	2.8	2.9
2500+	2.5	5.3
	N=318	N=215

Source: Postal survey.

Table 7.9
UK and overseas turnover for business service firms 1989

Turnover	UK %	Overseas %
<0.25	12.3	64.2
0.25-0.5	6.3	5.7
>0.5-1	6.3	5.7
>1-5	30.9	6.6
>5-10	18.3	3.1
>10-25	11.0	2.2
>25-50	4.7	2.6
>50-100	4.3	1.7
100+	6.0	8.3
	N=301	N=229

Source: Postal survey.

Table 7.10
Company type

Company Type	Number	Percentage
Sole proprietorship	20	6.1
Partnership	57	17.4
Limited company	112	34.1
Public limited company	34	10.4
Wholly owned subsidiary	88	26.8
Majority owned subsidiary	12	3.7
Associate company	3	0.9
Other	2	0.6
Total	328	100.0

Source: Postal survey.

The distribution of firms among the various levels of employment varied slightly between sector. For example, market research and public relations sectors did not have any firms with employment levels above 500, and accountancy and computer services accounted for the majority of firms with over 1,000 employees. Computer services displayed a larger proportion of firms with employees of 100 or more, 70.7 per cent compared to 31 per cent for the total group. Among accountancy firms there appeared to be a polarisation between firms with low levels of overseas employment and a small number with high levels of overseas employment.

Turnover varied substantially between the firms surveyed. The most frequent figure for the whole group was between £1-5 million (Table 7.9), but for advertising and computer services the same figure was between £5-10 million. For accountancy firms the figure was between 0 and less than £0.25 million with between £1-5 million being a close second. This would appear to reflect the prevalence of small firms in the accountancy sector, and the polarisation between them and the small number of very large firms. Similarly, this polarisation was reflected in the levels of overseas turnover.

The company type is shown in Table 7.10, the largest group were limited companies, followed by wholly owned subsidiaries. Limited companies were the most popular company type in the advertising sector accounting for 53.4 per cent of firms, in the management consultancy sector with 47.5 per cent of firms and in the market research sector with 36.7 per cent of firms. Partnerships were most important in the accountancy sector making up 74.2 per cent of the firms. For the computer services and public relations sectors wholly owned subsidiaries were the

160

largest groups with 42.6 per cent and 36.8 per cent of firms respectively. Limited companies were the second most important type for computer services and public relations sectors with 26.5 per cent and 31.6 per cent of firms respectively. Computer services had the highest level of Plcs with 25 per cent compared to 10.4 per cent for the whole group. The importance of wholly owned subsidiaries may derive from the development of the computer services and public relations firms out of the departments of other firms, that is, through externalisation with ownership remaining intact.

7.6 Conclusion

This chapter has provided an outline of the survey framework utilised in this study. Attention has been given to the construction and administration of the postal questionnaire and the characteristics of the sample of business service firms surveyed. The postal survey constitutes a crucial element in the overall research design since the data it generated facilitated the empirical testing of the hypotheses listed earlier in this chapter.

The characteristics of the sample, outlined in the previous section, indicates that the group of firms surveyed provide an accurate reflection of the wider population of firms in the business services sector. For example, the concentration of activity in the South of the UK, the high proportion of young firms in the sample, the dominance of small firms measured both in terms of turnover and employment levels, are all features of the business services sector as a whole. In addition, the sample reflects the polarisation of activities within the sector between a large number of small firms and a small number of large firms. The rapid growth of the sector in general, and of some relatively young firms, in particular, during the 1980s is also evident in the survey sample.

Differences between sub-sectors are also visible in the sample surveyed, for example, the company type varies with advertising firms generally being limited companies whilst accountancy firms are most often partnerships. The differences which exist highlight the fact that the business services sector does not consist of a homogenous group of activities, important differences exist even between a group of closely related sub-sectors.

The detailed consideration of the postal survey and sample characteristics provided in this chapter prepares the way for Chapter 8 in which the findings of the analysis of the data generated are examined in detail. Given that the survey sample provides a fair reflection of the business services sector as a whole, the results reported can be extrapolated to the wider population of business service firms.

Notes

1   Additional consideration of the research techniques employed is provided in Appendix 1. Copies of the questionnaire used in this study can be obtained from the author.

2   The following firms participated in the pilot survey: Dewe Rogerson Ltd, Valin Pollen Ltd., Austin Knight Ltd, Rex Stewart Newcastle, BIS, and Robson Rhodes.

3   For the purpose of the postal survey the eleven standard regions of the UK as defined by the CSO (Regional Trends 1995 p.9), were condensed into six regions these being: the South, which consists of the South East, the South West and East Anglia; the Midlands, which consists of the East Midlands and the West Midlands; the North, which consists of the North, the North West, and Humberside and Yorkshire; Scotland; Wales; and, Northern Ireland.

8 The internationalisation of the UK business services sector: survey results

8.1 Introduction

The purpose of this chapter is to present the results of an in-depth analysis of the primary data gathered through the postal survey of UK business services sector firms conducted in 1990.[1] The hypotheses, generated from the review of literature, and set out in Chapter 7, will be tested using the survey data. During this analysis sub-sectors will only be considered in terms of the extent to which they diverge from the total group. The three main sub-sectors will be examined further in Chapter 9 where case studies of individual firms will be presented.

This chapter is divided into sections according to the hypotheses to be tested. Each section will assess the evidence in relation to one or more hypothesis. In the concluding section the research findings will be briefly summarised and their contribution to the understanding of the internationalisation of business service firms evaluated.

8.2 Diversification and internationalisation

A generally accepted view in the literature on the internationalisation of services is that firms which become international are often diversified (Channon, 1978; Dunning, 1989; Enderwick, 1989; UNCTC, 1990; inter alia). It is argued that diversification enables a service sector firm to gain economies of scale and scope in the use of its international network of offices, staff and communications facilities. The maximum level of business can be obtained from each client via the use of cross referral. The research attempts to establish whether this is the case for business service sector firms by testing hypothesis 1: *'internationalisation among business service firms is accompanied by diversification'*.

163

Respondents were asked to list the services and/or products which they offered to clients together with the percentage of revenue gained from each activity. For the purpose of analysis services were grouped according to the six sub-sectors surveyed together with other categories of services/products defined at the four digit level, consistent with the UK's 1980 SIC.[2] The information on services/products provided together with that on the level of overseas turnover was used to establish whether a link existed between the number of services offered and internationalisation. There appeared to be a general move towards diversification among the firms surveyed between the years 1980 and 1989, with Table 8.1 indicating the number of services provided by the firms in the two years. Thus only 27.4 per cent of the firms offered two or more services in 1980, however by 1989 this figure had grown to 39.5 per cent. This movement towards greater diversification was apparent in all sub-sectors. Although, the computer services and market research sectors were the least diversified with over 77 per cent of firms offering only one service in 1989. If we look at the same figures but for firms with an overseas turnover in 1989 (Table 8.2) it would appear that such firms are more diversified than the whole group. In 1980, for example, 28.1 per cent of such firms delivered two or more services and in 1989 this figure was 43.7 per cent. From this analysis it would appear that there may well be a connection between internationalisation and diversification, with firms which have an overseas turnover having a higher level of diversification.

Measuring diversification by counting the number of services offered may, however, suggest a higher level of diversification than is the actual case, for example, a firm may offer four services but 95 per cent of its revenue may derive from only one activity. Thus it is necessary to have some measure of the degree of diversification. To provide such a measure the firms were categorised into the following groups adapted from Channon's (1978) study of the services industries: *single business* - where 95 per cent or more of the firms revenue is derived from one area; *dominant business* - where 70 per cent or more, but not more than 94 per cent, of the firms revenue is derived from one area; and *related business* - where no one business area accounts for more than 70 per cent of the total revenue. Since it was found that all cases of diversification were into related areas there was no need for a category to measure diversification into unrelated businesses. Thus in the sample surveyed there were no conglomerate type companies, or what might be called truly diversified companies. It is important to note here that the level of analysis is that of the responding firm, so although respondents did not appear to be highly diversified, many formed a part of a larger more diversified group of companies.

Using the above categories it was found that in 1989, 64.6 per cent of the sample were single business firms, 16.2 per cent dominant businesses and 19.2 per cent related businesses. In 1980 the figures were, 65.8 per cent single business, 12.4 per cent dominant business and 21.8 per cent related business, which indicates that there has been no major shift towards diversification over the ten year period. On a sub-sector basis for 1989, advertising firms appear to be the most diversified with only 55.7 per cent of the sample being single business firms and 29.5 per cent being

Table 8.1

Number of services provided by all firms

Number	1980		1989	
of services	No. Firms	% of total	No. Firms	% of total
1	143	72.6	194	60.4
2	36	18.3	72	22.4
3	17	8.6	45	14.0
4	1	0.5	10	3.1
	N=197		N=321	

Source: Postal survey.

Table 8.2

Number of services provided by firms with an overseas turnover

Number	1980		1989	
of services	No. Firms	% of total	No. Firms	% of total
1	41	71.9	53	56.4
2	7	12.3	23	24.5
3	9	15.8	15	16.0
4	0	0.0	3	3.2
	N=57		N=94	

Source: Postal survey.

related business firms. Management consultancy firms also showed a higher than average level of diversification with 58.1 per cent being single business firms. Market research and computer service firms appeared to be the least diversified with 73.3 per cent and 77.9 per cent single business firms respectively.

To test the significance of the association between internationalisation and the level of diversification the Chi-square test of independence was used. The results revealed that there was no significant association between the number of services provided and whether the firm was international, that is, whether it had an overseas turnover (Table 8.3). Looking at the business services sub-sectors similar results were found for all groups apart from the accountancy firms sample (Table 8.4). Here, the Chi-square test shows that there is a statistically significant association between whether an accountancy firm has an overseas turnover and the number of services provided. How can these results be explained?

Among accountancy firms diversification has tended to be into related, yet

165

Table 8.3
Business services firms: diversification by overseas turnover

Services provided	Overseas turnover		Total	χ^2	Significance level
	0	>0			
1	85	53	138		
				1.33	0.249
2 or more	46	41	87		n.s.
Total	131	94	225		

Zero expected frequencies < 5.
n.s. not significant.

Source: Postal survey.

Table 8.4
Accountancy firms: diversification by overseas turnover

Services provided	Overseas turnover		Total	χ^2	Significance level
	0	>0			
1	24	2	26		
				7.33	0.0068
2 or more	10	9	19		significant
Total	34	11	45		

1 of 4 cells with expected frequencies < 5.
Yates correction applied.

Source: Postal survey.

distinctly different, areas in the sense that the main activities into which such firms have diversified are management consultancy and information technology consultancy operations. Whereas, in other sub-sectors firms have diversified into more closely related areas. The full service advertising agency, for example, provide a range of services from media buying to brand development. However, such firms do not always regard themselves to be diversified and this raises the issue

166

of what is actually meant by the term diversification? Diversification is defined here as extending the firms range of service into another of the sub-sectors surveyed, or indeed, into any other activity at the four digit level of the UK SIC. As far a the survey sample was concerned it was found that firms when diversified had generally spread into closely related areas, to the extent that the activities in many cases fall under one business service category at the SIC four digit level. Respondents may not perceive their firms to be diversified and indeed this perception may well be correct if we use the above definition. A number of well publicised diversifications in the sector into less closely related areas occurred in the 1980s (for example, Saatchi and Saatchi's diversification into management consultancy), however, these have not always proved successful, and indeed, would appear to be the exception rather than the rule. Thus, when it is suggested that for service firms internationalisation and diversification go hand in hand, it is important to note that in the business services sector such diversification tends to be limited to closely related areas. This evidence confirms Enderwick's (1992) view of the scope of diversification in service firms generally.

Furthermore, some of the large internationally diversified service companies, especially in the advertising sector, operate a loose organisational structure. Such companies may be diversified but individual firms, or operating units, within the wide parent group company structure have relatively low levels of diversification. The survey was sent to a number of companies which were a part of a larger parent group, that is, to subsidiaries of larger and perhaps more diversified groups. In some cases the range of diversification of parent group companies reached beyond services into the manufacturing sector.

If we look at accountancy firms we can see that the nature of diversification is into other distinctive categories of business services, a fact which may explain the research findings. It is in the accountancy sector, which after all is one of the most established and has the longest history of internationalisation, that the relationship between diversification and internationalisation is most apparent.

The survey evidence suggests then, that the link between diversification and internationalisation is not a statistically significant one, at least not in all-sub sectors. Hypothesis 1 would appear to have some validity in the case of accountancy firms, however in other sub-sectors the relationship is not as clear. Since there is no strong association between diversification and internationalisation, it is interesting to explore other factors which may influence the level of diversification.

A motive which is thought to stimulate diversification in some service sectors is the ability to cross refer clients from one part of the firm to another to obtain the maximum level of business from each client, in doing so firms can achieve economies of scope in the use of their organisational and information networks (Dunning, 1989; Enderwick, 1989; UNCTC, 1990; Normann, 1991). Hypothesis 2 seeks to test this view in relation to business service firms by arguing that 'international firms will seek to use cross referrals and provide a number of services to each client'. To gain an indication of the extent to which firms provide a

167

number of services[3] to their clients respondents were asked to give the percentage of clients to which they delivered one, two, and three or more services, the results are summarised in Table 8.5. It can be seen that 36.9 per cent of the sample delivered one service to 76-100 per cent of their clients, 49.6 per cent supplied over 50 per cent of their clients with one service. Whereas 10.3 per cent delivered two services to between 76-100 per cent of their clients, 17.4 per cent supplied over 50 per cent of their clients with two services. Finally, 14.2 per cent delivered three or more services to 76-100 per cent of their clients, 18.1 per cent supplying over 50 per cent of their clients with three or more services. This evidence suggests that providing more than one service to a client is a common practice.

Among the firms with an overseas turnover in 1989 there did appear to be a greater proportion which delivered more than one service to their clients (Table 8.6). For example, 37.8 per cent of this group had no clients accepting three or more services compared to 43.3 per cent for the whole group, and 29.3 per cent of this group delivered one service only to 76-100 per cent of their clients compared to 36.9 per cent for the whole group.

When firms are part of a larger parent group (that is, if they have subsidiaries or are a subsidiary of another firm), the practice of referring clients to other parts of the group appears to be particularly common. The questionnaire asked companies which formed a part of a group, whether, if the needs of their clients could not be adequately serviced, they would refer them on to other companies within the group. Of the 122 respondents 80.3 per cent (98) said 'yes' with the remaining 19.7 per cent (24) saying 'no', the figures for firms with an overseas turnover in 1989 were 82.9 per cent (79) saying 'yes' and 17.1 per cent (16) saying 'no'. A similar response was found when examining the individual sub-sectors. It would appear then that the practice of cross referral is slightly more common among firms which have an overseas turnover.

The evidence does then support hypothesis 2, however, the practice of cross referral is not confined to international firms. Although, cross referral may be more important among the large diversified groups of companies. Evidence from the survey reveals that the degree of diversification at the level of the individual firm is relatively low, hence the value of cross referral can be expected to be low at the firm level. However, among groups of companies with diverse activities, cross referral is an important and useful tool for increasing market share.

Exploring firm age and the level of diversification Table 8.7 shows that the firms which were established before 1981 displayed a movement towards greater diversification between 1980 and 1989. Further exploration of the level of diversification revealed that the older the firm the more diversified it appeared to be, a higher proportion of the older firms offered a wider range of services than the younger firms. For example, of the firms established in or before 1950 only 55 per cent offered one service in 1989, this compared to firms established after 1950 where 61.4 per cent offered one service only in 1989.

The survey results also suggest that the level of diversification does increase with

168

Table 8.5
Number of firms delivering numbers of services to clients

Percentage of clients	1 service	2 services	3 or more services
0	44 (17.5)	79 (31.2)	110 (43.3)
1-10	32 (12.7)	37 (14.6)	46 (18.1)
11-25	22 (8.7)	51 (20.2)	31 (12.2)
26-50	29 (11.5)	42 (16.6)	21 (8.3)
51-75	32 (12.7)	18 (7.1)	10 (3.9)
76-100	93 (36.9)	26 (10.3)	36 (14.2)
	N = 252	N = 253	N = 254

(% in parenthesis).

Source: Postal survey.

Table 8.6
Number of firms with an overseas turnover in 1989 delivering numbers of services to clients

Percentage of clients	1 service	2 services	3 or more services
0	11 (14.7)	19 (25.7)	28 (37.8)
1-10	10 (13.3)	5 (6.8)	15 (20.3)
11-25	8 (10.7)	18 (24.3)	12 (16.2)
26-50	13 (17.3)	17 (23.0)	8 (10.8)
51-75	11 (14.7)	6 (8.1)	3 (4.1)
76-100	22 (29.3)	9 (12.2)	8 (10.8)
	N = 75	N = 74	N = 74

(% in parenthesis).

Source: Postal survey.

the size of turnover. For example, 53.8 per cent of firms with UK turnover of more than £5 million in 1989 provided one service only, whereas 45.5 per cent of firms with UK turnovers of over £25 million provided one service only, these figures compare to 60.4 per cent of all firms in the sample providing one service only.

To explore further the link between both the age and size of the firm with the level

Table 8.7
Number of services provided by firms established before 1981

Number of services	1980		1989	
	Number of firms	% of total	Number of firms	% of total
1	130	73.9	115	58.4
2	31	17.6	45	22.8
3	15	8.5	32	16.2
4	0	0.0	5	2.5
	N = 176		N = 197	

Source: Postal survey.

of diversification, a number of correlation coefficients were calculated. Firstly, UK turnover was correlated with both the range of services offered and the measure of relative diversification considered earlier, the resulting coefficients were very weak and not statistically significant. Similar results were obtained when the date of establishment was correlated with the same two measures of diversification. This further analysis indicated that the relationship between the business service firm's age or size and diversification is not a linear one.

Diversification allows firms to utilise their resources and gain economies of scale and scope, however, it would appear that this is as relevant to domestic firms as it is to international firms. Indeed, diversification can be seen as an alternative to internationalisation (Wolf, 1977; Buckley, 1985; Caves, 1982). Rather than attempting to expand the number of clients in one sector of the market it is possible to extend the number of services delivered to existing clients.

Companies which had been involved in diversification were asked to rate a number of factors in terms of their importance in the decision to diversify. The results are shown in Table 8.8, a similar pattern of responses was found when looking at the firms which declared an overseas turnover, with factors given the same level of priority in terms of the extremely important category. It can be seen that client needs appears to be the most significant factor influencing the decisions to diversify, with 61.9 per cent of firms rating this as extremely important. The opportunity for market growth was also ranked highly with half rating this as extremely important, whilst 24.7 per cent rated the competitive advantage of offering a range of services as being extremely important and 19.4 per cent moves into a more profitable area as extremely important. Only 13.2 per cent ranked the opportunity for cross referral of clients as being extremely important.

Looking at these responses it is clear that a number of areas are important in the

Table 8.8
Factors influencing diversification

	Extremely important %	Very important %	Important %	Of little importance %	Totally un-important %
Client needs (N=215)	61.9	20.0	11.6	1.4	5.1
Opportunity for market growth (N=218)	50.0	30.3	12.4	4.6	2.8
Competitive pressure in main area of business (N=210)	11.0	19.0	27.1	31.4	11.4
Opportunities for cross referral of clients (N=205)	13.2	25.9	33.2	18.0	9.8
New economic conditions (N=203)	6.9	17.2	30.0	27.6	18.2
New legal requirements (N=202)	8.9	8.9	14.4	15.8	52.0
Diversification into more profitable services (N=206)	19.4	27.7	28.2	15.0	9.7
By product of acquisition or merger activity (N=190)	7.4	10.5	17.4	17.4	47.4
Opportunity to utilise the complementary skills of staff (N=204)	9.3	21.6	38.7	19.6	10.8

Table 8.8 Continued.

	Extremely important %	Very important %	Important %	Of little importance %	Totally un-important %
Competitive advantage of offering a range of services (N=198)	24.7	40.4	24.7	6.1	4.0
Other (N=9)	66.7	22.2	0.0	0.3	0.0

Source: Postal survey.

decision to diversify, but client needs together with the opportunity for market growth appear to be given the greatest importance. This highlights the role of clients in influencing diversification, to a large extent diversification may be viewed as demand driven, although, the importance of opportunities for market growth suggest supply driven forces are also influential, with the search for growth and increased profitability being significant.

The saturation of core markets is recognised as a factor influencing diversification (Ansoff, 1987). This may be the case in the business services sector, for example, accountancy firms have increasingly been moving into the computer services sector where rates of growth are much higher than those in the audit market. This view, however, would seem to be at odds with the response of 31.4 per cent rating competitive pressure in main area of business as of little importance in terms of a motivation for diversification, although as noted earlier diversification into more profitable services is given a higher rating. These results suggest that although core markets are not saturated they do offer less scope for profitability and future growth.

It is often argued that diversification occurs among service sector firms so that they may take advantage of economies of scale and scope. In an attempt to identify the importance of economies of scale and scope respondents were asked to rate the opportunity to utilise the complementary skills of staff in the decision to diversify, only 9.3 per cent firms rated this as extremely important. This would indicate that economies of scale and scope in the use of staff skills are not the main factor motivating diversification, although they may well be a consequence of such diversification.

When examining the individual sectors some important differences were revealed. Firstly, for both the public relations and market research sectors a higher percentage of the firms ranked the opportunity for market growth as being extremely important,

172

60 per cent and 62.5 per cent respectively, compared to the whole group where the greatest number ranked client needs as being extremely important. Secondly, new legal conditions appeared to be of greater importance to the accountancy sector compared to the others as a factor influencing the diversification decision, with 19.4 per cent of the accountancy firms rating this as extremely important. Thirdly, the opportunity for cross referral of clients appeared to be of greater importance to both the accountancy and public relations sectors, where 22.2 per cent and 33.3 per cent respectively, of firms ranked this as being extremely important. Finally, public relations, market research and management consultancy firms gave the opportunity to utilise complementary skills greater weight in the decision to diversify, with 13.3 per cent, 20 per cent and 24.2 per cent respectively ranked this as being an extremely important factor motivating diversification.

The evidence presented in this section raises major doubt on the views which are generally accepted in the literature concerning the internationalisation of service sector firms (Channon, 1978; Dunning, 1989; Enderwick, 1989; UNCTC, 1990). Firstly, there is a failure to find a strong link between internationalisation and diversification, apart from in the accountancy sector where a statistically significant association was found. Elsewhere diversification tends to be into such closely related areas that it is questionable whether the term diversification is appropriate. The role of cross referral is also less certain than that proposed in the literature, it is clearly a factor influencing diversification among all firms whether international or not. However, it is apparent that there are other factors which are by far of greater importance for the majority of firms, in particular, client needs and the opportunity for market growth. The evidence fails also to show a strong link between firm size and age, with the level of diversification. Economies of scale and scope are an often quoted reason for diversification however, this measured in terms of the opportunity to utilise the complementary skills of staff, again is only extremely important in the decision to diversify for a small number of firms. It is then questionable whether the process of internationalisation and diversification are as closely linked among business service sector firms as they may be in other parts of the service sector.

8.3 An evolutionary approach to internationalisation?

The view that firms progress through various stages on the way to internationalisation is well established (Aharoni, 1966; Stopford and Well, 1972; Johanson and Wiedersheim-Paul, 1975; inter alia). Hypothesis 3 argues that *'business service sector firms go through an evolutionary approach to internationalisation'*. If this is the case, we might expect to see a relationship between the age of the business service firm and the level of its overseas turnover; we might also expect to see a relationship between the UK turnover and overseas turnover. These relationships were explored by an examination of the correlation coefficients between the variables concerned.

173

When firm age (indicated by the date of establishment), and the level of UK turnover were correlated, a negative relationship was found. The older the firm (that is, the lower the date of establishment) the higher the level of UK turnover. The results of the correlation of the date of establishment with a number of variables are given in Table 8.9. Although the correlation coefficients reported do not appear to be strong, the two tailed significance test shows that the linear association between the variables are statistically significant. The correlation coefficients between the level of UK turnover in 1989 and employment, overseas employment and turnover in the same year are higher and statistically significant; indicating a positive and stronger linear association between UK size and the level of internationalisation compared to that between age and level of internationalisation (Table 8.10). The rapid growth in number of business services firms over the past 25 years may account for the weaker correlation between date of establishment and internationalisation. A number of firms have grown rapidly and become international in only a short period of time primarily through a process of mergers and takeovers. Indeed, as noted in Chapter 7, the sample surveyed displayed a relatively youthful age profile reflecting the rapid growth of business service firms in the past 10-20 years.

In addition to the examination of size and age as factors influencing the level of internationalisation, it is also worth looking at the company type which also provides an indication of the stage of development of the firm. Hypothesis 4 argues that *'internationalisation is more common among firms which are part of a larger group or which are public limited companies (Plcs)'*, evidence form the survey confirmed this. Firms which were Plcs or the wholly-owned subsidiaries of other companies displayed higher mean values for UK and overseas employment and turnover in 1980 and 1989. Plcs having higher mean values than wholly-owned subsidiaries in general. This confirms the view that Plcs are bigger and more international than other company types. Wholly-owned companies following close behind. This no doubt is related to the ability to raise finance for expansion, Plcs and wholly-owned subsidiaries may have better access to funds compared to other company types. An exception to this pattern is found among accountancy firms where the predominant company type is the partnership and this is the case whether the firm is international or not.

The evidence supports the view that an evolutionary process of internationalisation occurs within business service sector firms. This result is contrary to Turnbull's (1987) findings in the manufacturing sector. Unfortunately though, no specific insight into the various stages through which a firm may pass can be elicited from this. However, the results confirm what is expected in that the older the firm is, or the large it is, in terms of UK turnover, the more international it is likely to be, that is, the higher its overseas turnover will be. Also, the more developed the company structure the higher the level of internationalisation.

When examining the evolutionary path towards internationalisation among manufacturing firms it is common to find that firms began their ventures abroad

174

Table 8.9
Age and size, domestic and international: correlation coefficients

Date of establishment with:	Correlation coefficient
UK employment 1989	-0.3628 (299) P=0.000
Overseas employment 1989	-0.2244 (229) P=0.000
UK turnover 1989	-0.2311 (284) P=0.000
Overseas turnover 1989	-0.2226 (216) P=0.000

Coefficient/(cases)/ 2 tailed significance.

Source: Postal survey.

Table 8.10
UK size and internationalisation: correlation coefficients

UK turnover in 1989 with:	Correlation coefficient
UK employment in 1989	0.5985 (230) P=0.000
Overseas employment in 1989	0.5905 (230) P=0.000
Overseas turnover in 1989	0.5838 (226) P=0.000

Coefficient/(cases)/ 2 tailed significance.

Source: Postal survey.

175

initially through exportation (Johanson and Wiedersheim-Paul, 1975). It has, however, been argued that this option is not available to service sector firms because of the non tradability of many service activities. Further to this, it has been suggested that some service exports are only possible if the firm has a presence in the overseas market which can act as a delivery system. For service sector firms then internationalisation is thought to occurs through the single step of setting up an overseas subsidiary, rather than gradually through the build up of exports in the initial phase, and later with the establishment of an overseas presence. Although this may be the case in many instances, the survey evidence suggests that an evolutionary process certainly does occur among firms in the business services sector.

Firstly, of the 141 firms who attributed a portion of their overseas revenue to exports, 36 firms attributed all of their overseas revenue to exports (that is, 25.5 per cent). Exploring these 36 firms more closely it was found that they appeared to be smaller in size (in terms of both UK employment and turnover) compared with the group as a whole, and compared with the group which declared an overseas turnover in 1989. These 'export only' firms also had smaller levels of overseas turnover generally, which suggests that they are in the early stages of internationalisation. Given that the firms which declare that all of their overseas revenue derives from exports are small and have only low levels of overseas revenue then this would seem to support the view that business service firms go through an evolutionary process towards internationalisation. Exportation as a stage en route to full internationalisation cannot be overlooked in the case of service firms. Exportation does occur, although the period during which a service firm uses exports only to service foreign markets may be less prolonged than is the case for manufacturing firms.

Secondly, business service firms are certainly able to export service prior to setting up a permanent presences in an overseas market, and indeed evidence from the postal survey confirms that they do. When asked whether they export to countries in which they do not have a presence, of a total sample of 256 firms, 154 (60.2 per cent) said 'yes' whilst 103 (39.8 per cent) said 'no'. This confirms that business service firms are able to export services independent of a permanent presence in the export market. This, to some extent undermines the commonly held view that service firms can only export to markets in which they have a permanent physical presence, that is, an overseas outlet.

The questionnaire asked firms if, when an overseas presence is necessary to provide services to overseas clients, such a presence would initially be used merely as a delivery system for services largely produced elsewhere. Of 162 firms responding to this question 43.8 per cent (71) said 'yes' whilst 56.2 per cent (91) said 'no'. This lends supports the view embodied in hypothesis 5 that *overseas presences are frequently used merely as a means of delivering services to clients'*. Overseas presences are in some cases established in order to facilitate 'exports' from the domestic market. They may then be regarded as transaction specific assets

176

which facilitate the flow of intra-firm trade in services (Chapter 4). However, it is important to note that in the majority of cases overseas presences are established as more than just a delivery system, and are actively involved in the production and provision of services to the market.

Looking at the sub-sectors the results vary, only 26.7 per cent of accountancy firms say that a presence is merely a delivery system, and the figures for market research and public relations sectors are 10 per cent and 22.2 per cent respectively saying 'yes'. These figures are substantially lower than for the group as a whole and suggest that in these sectors presences are less likely to be set up merely as a delivery system. These results then reflect certain characteristics of the particular sub-sectors. The regulation of accountancy firms, for example, often require practising accountants to obtain local qualifications. Thus if personnel are located in an overseas market they must possess the ability to produce services locally. For the market research and public relations firms the need for market knowledge is extremely important and may account for the low levels of use of an overseas presence as a delivery system.

The evidence suggests that business service firms are active in the export market. However, as noted in Chapter 2, service sector exports may occur in a variety of ways. Respondents were asked a set of questions relating to the nature of their exports, the results are presented in Table 8.11. The most popular ways in which business services are exported are through supplying services to overseas clients in the domestic market and through personnel travelling abroad to supply the services in an overseas market.

A similar pattern was found among all the sub-sectors, although a few discrepancies between them are worth noting. Only the advertising and computer service sectors had any firms which claimed that exports were always carried out via the export of services embodied in a tangible product, 7.2 per cent and 3.6 per cent respectively. Whilst 90.9 per cent of accountancy firms said that they never exported in this manner. This type of export also seemed to be of little importance to market research, public relations and management consultancy firms. Travelling personnel appeared to be of particular importance to management consultancy firms with 21.8 per cent always, and 34.5 per cent often, exporting in this way. No public relations firms always exported through personnel travelling, although 42.9 per cent said they often used this form of exportation. Again this area appeared to be less important to accountancy firms with 54.5 per cent saying they never exported through personnel travelling. A similar pattern for domestic production for overseas clients was found among all sectors.

With regard to exports via a telecommunications network, 10.9 per cent of computer services firms said always compared to 3.4 per cent for the whole group. This greater use of a telecommunications network as a medium of export may be accounted for in terms of the nature of computer services, some of which, for example software, can be easily transmitted 'over the wire'. It is clear though that computer service firms use a variety of methods of exportation. As one might expect

177

Table 8.11

Table 8.11

How services are exported

	Embodied in a tangible product %	Travelling personnel %	Domestic provision for overseas client %	Delivery via telecommunications network %
Always	2.7	10.7	4.9	3.4
Often	9.5	20.6	26.2	10.7
Sometimes	13.0	20.2	33.1	15.3
Occasionally	25.2	18.3	19.8	22.2
Never	49.6	30.2	16.0	48.3
	(N=262)	(N=262)	(N=263)	(N=261)

Source: Postal survey.

Table 8.12

How services are exported by export only firms

	Embodied in a tangible product %	Travelling personnel %	Domestic provision for overseas client %	Delivery via telecommunications network %
Always	5.7	25.0	5.6	0.0
Often	14.3	36.1	30.6	8.6
Sometimes	22.9	13.9	38.9	14.3
Occasionally	17.1	11.1	11.1	28.6
Never	40.0	13.9	13.9	48.6
	(N=35)	(N=36)	(N=36)	(N=35)

Source: Postal survey.

export only firms made greater use of all methods of exporting, apart from delivery via a telecommunications network (Table 8.12). In particular much greater use was made of travelling personnel with 25 per cent of these firms always using this method compared with 10.7 per cent for the whole sample.

It is interesting to investigate the relationship between the level of overseas turnover and the various methods of exportation. As firms become increasingly

Table 8.13

Overseas turnover and methods of exportation: correlation coefficients

Overseas turnover 1989 with the importance of exports:	Correlation coefficient
Embodied in a tangible product:	-0.2133 (182) P=0.0038
Through travelling personnel:	-0.3909 (181) P=0.0000
Domestic provision for overseas client:	-0.2169 (183) P=0.0032
Delivered via a telecommunications network:	-0.2605 (180) P=0.0004

Coefficient/(cases)/ 2 tailed significance.

Source: Postal survey.

international, do their exports give way to overseas production? The overseas turnover for the year 1989 was correlated with the data giving the importance of various types of exports, the results are shown in Table 8.13. Weak negative correlation coefficients were found indicating a weak linear association between overseas turnover and the importance of the various types of exportation. However, all the results appear to be statistically significant when the 2 tailed test of significance is applied. These results would suggest that the higher the level of overseas turnover the greater the importance given to all methods of exportation. The strongest correlation being with personnel travelling. In order to examine this further the sample was divided into those firms which had an overseas turnover of £5 million or less and those which had an overseas turnover of more than £5 million, the results highlighted some interesting differences. For those firms with an overseas turnover of less than £5 million the correlation coefficients were stronger in most cases, the exception being domestic provision which was weaker and not statistically significant (Table 8.14.). Thus for firms with a lower overseas turnover the linear association between overseas turnover and the importance of various types of export is stronger in most cases than for the total group. For firms with overseas turnovers of more than £5 million the same correlation coefficients were

179

Table 8.14

Overseas turnover and methods of exportation for firms with an overseas turnover of £5 million or less: correlation coefficients

Overseas turnover 1989 with the importance of exports:	Correlation coefficient
Embodied in a tangible product:	-0.2888 (145) P=0.0004
Through travelling personnel:	-0.4785 (145) P=0.0000
Domestic provision for overseas client:	-0.1712 (147) P=0.0381
Delivered via a telecommunications network:	-0.2732 (144) P=0.0009

Coefficient/(cases)/ 2 tailed significance.

Source: Postal survey.

weaker and not statistically significant. These results suggest that as internationalisation proceeds, firms choose an increasing variety of mechanisms through which to trade. However, beyond a certain level of overseas turnover this weak linear association deteriorates. This highlights the importance of more direct forms of exports in the early stages of internationalisation among business service firms.

The evidence would seem to support hypothesis 6 which argues that *'exports "over the wire" and embodied in goods are limited despite the availability of ICTs which enable the embodiment of information intensive services into goods, and exports across telecommunication networks'*. Although 48.3 per cent of the whole group say they never use telecommunications as a method of export this leaves 51.7 per cent which do use this method at some time. It is clear then, that exports of this sort do occur, and will no doubt increase as ICTs become more integrated into the process of service provision. A factor which may inhibit the rapid growth in the use of ICT in the exportation of business services is the lack of standardisation apparent in much business service activity. So although ICT may become more important in areas where output can be standardised (for example access to data banks) where

180

Table 8.15
Factors as a source of competitive advantage

	Extremely important %	Very important %	Important %	Of little importance %	Totally un-important %
Quality of staff (N=318)	78.6	13.5	2.2	0.3	5.3
Use of ICT (N=309)	19.1	46.9	31.7	12.6	8.7
Use of knowledge (N=319)	50.8	31.3	12.2	1.6	4.1
Location (N=311)	7.1	15.1	42.8	23.5	11.6
Quality control (N=311)	34.7	34.1	21.9	5.1	4.2
Client relations (N=317)	73.8	15.1	4.4	2.5	4.1
Range of services (N=308)	14.9	30.2	38.6	11.7	4.5
Good will/ Reputation (N=318)	53.8	28.0	11.9	2.8	3.5
International coverage (N=311)	11.9	19.6	18.0	20.9	29.6
Cost (N=313)	10.2	17.3	47.3	19.2	6.1
Other (N=14)	64.3	14.3	0.0	14.3	7.1

Source: Postal survey.

there is less scope for such standardisation, ICT will have a more limited role. However, this role might still be significant as a means of supporting other types of exports, such as, through personnel travelling. The element of personal contact with clients is of particular importance in many business service activities and client relations ranks high as a source of competitive advantage (Table 8.15). Evidence

181

from the survey would therefore, seem to provide some support for hypothesis 7, which argues that *'client relations are of great importance and limit the extent to which exports without personal contact can be used'*.

The increasing importance of ICTs may, however, be in the form of intra-firm trade, intermediate service may be provided 'over the wire' as an input into the final service which is created by personnel located in the overseas market. Skilled personnel can in a sense become the 'modem' through which the information is communicated to the client, being tailored to their specific needs in the final delivery process. Indeed, as proposed in hypothesis 8, *'ICT is given greater importance as a source of competitive advantage by firms which are internationally active'* with 22.7 per cent of firms declaring an overseas turnover in 1989 rating ICT as extremely important compared to 19.1 per cent of the whole group. As well as ICTs being important to business service firms as means of facilitating the supply of services across national borders, the role of ICTs in promoting the efficient management and organisation of resources on an international basis should be recognised. As Quinn and Paquette (1990) note ICTs enable a complex yet flexible organisation of resources which can be used to maximum effect to satisfy the needs of individual clients (Chapter 4).

Undoubtedly, some service firms become international through overseas investment, initially, perhaps, as a by product of merger or intentionally through mergers or takeovers in order to establish an international network rapidly. The 1980s saw a period in which business service firms sought to establish international networks quickly, partly in a bid to catch up with the older firms in the sector and partly in anticipation of the changing market environment with the completion of the Single European Market in 1992. Indeed, a number of respondents specifically mentioned the building and consolidation of European networks to be a factor motivating cross border merger and acquisition activity.

Firms were asked whether they had been involved in merger and/or acquisition activity during the past five to ten years. The results obtained are shown in Table 8.16. It can be seen that there was almost an equal split between firms which had and those which had not been involved in such activity. Looking at firms established before 1981 a greater percentage had been involved in merger and acquisition activity, and those firms with an overseas turnover displayed an even greater involvement. Thus the older the firm or if the firm has an overseas turnover the more likely it is to have been be involved in merger and acquisition activity. The evidence then supports hypothesis 9, which argues that *'international firms will be more involved in merger and acquisition activity to build up their international networks'*. These results may highlight the importance of establishing networks rapidly particularly in international markets, indeed those firms with an overseas turnover give a higher than average rating to international coverage as a source of competitive advantage (Table 8.15.) thus supporting hypothesis 10, which states that *'international firms will regard international coverage to be an important source of competitive advantage'*.

182

Table 8.16
Merger and acquisition activity in the past 5-10 years

	All firms		Firms established by 1980		Firms with an overseas turnover in 1989	
	No. Firms	% Firms	No. Firms	% Firms	No. Firms	% Firms
Yes	160	49.4	107	53.5	61	64.9
No	164	50.6	93	46.5	33	35.1
	N=324		N=200		N=94	

Source: Postal Survey.

Table 8.17
Purpose of merger and acquisition activity

	All firms		Firms with an overseas turnover in 1989	
	No. Firms	% Firms	No. Firms	% Firms
Geographical expansion	68	43.3	36	53.7
Diversification	89	56.7	31	46.3
	N=157		N=67	

A small number of firms ranked both geographical expansion and diversification as important.

Source: Postal Survey.

Those firms which had been involved in merger and acquisition activity were asked which was most important in terms of motivating such activity, geographical expansion or diversification (Table 8.17). For the firms with an overseas turnover geographical expansion proved to be the most important motive whereas, for the whole group diversification appeared to be more important.

Computer services and public relations firms appeared to be more involved in merger and acquisition activity with 64.7 per cent and 68.4 per cent respectively of these firms having been involved in such action. On a sectoral basis diversification appeared to be more important as a motivation for merger and acquisition activity for advertising firms, computer services, management consultancy, market research, and public relations firms, but for accountancy firms geographical expansion appeared to be more important.

The results reported in this section provide fresh insights in to the internationalisation of service sector firms. The evidence considered here supports the view that business service sector firms do progress through an evolutionary approach to internationalisation, with exports playing an important role in this process, in the same way that they do in the internationalisation of manufacturing firms (Johanson and Weidersheim-Paul, 1975; inter alia). This finding is in sharp contrast to the results of Sharma and Johanson's (1987) study of the internationalisation of technical consultancy firms.

The first step en route to internationalisation for business service firms is most likely to be the delivery of services to overseas clients in the domestic market, this would then be followed by personnel travelling into overseas markets. Client needs may require a firm to set up an overseas office, at first to service existing clients. This may be achieved by taking over a firm in the overseas market or by setting up a presence from scratch. This would then lead on to the growth in overseas clients as the overseas office attract new business. As the firm becomes international it faces competition from other international firms and is therefore forced to extent its international coverage in order to compete with such firms. The establishment of an international network becomes important and may be achieved via the establishment of greenfield sites or through mergers and takeovers. Given the importance of local knowledge together with regulatory requirements in this sector, setting up a subsidiary from scratch is perhaps less likely than in other service sectors.

The importance of international coverage to a firm's competitive position is illustrated. Furthermore, the survey evidence confirms that business service firms have been actively extending their networks through mergers and acquisitions throughout the 1980s, providing support for the findings of Chapter 6. The research also sheds light on the role of ICTs in the internationalisation of business service firms, indicating that, although they may have a small role in facilitating independent trade, they have a significant part in terms of intra-firm trade and as a promoter of the efficient management of an international organisation.

8.4 International clients - international business service firms?

It is often argued that service MNEs are drawn into international activity by their clients. An often quoted example, is the case of multinational banks which appeared to follow their clients into overseas markets (Yannopoulos, 1983). To explore whether this is the case for business service firms respondents were asked to estimate the percentage of their revenue gained from national companies, MNEs, government and other sources. The results are shown in Tables 8.18 and 8.19. Firms with overseas revenue are more likely to have MNEs as clients, for example, 23.2 per cent of all firms have no MNE clients, whereas for firms with an overseas

184

Table 8.18
Source of revenue: all firms

Percentage	Government	National companies	MNEs	Other
0	150 (51.0)	52 (17.9)	67 (23.2)	166 (57.4)
1-10	82 (27.9)	31 (10.7)	36 (12.5)	38 (13.1)
11-25	26 (8.8)	44 (15.2)	45 (15.6)	18 (6.2)
26-50	22 (7.5)	80 (27.6)	69 (23.9)	13 (4.5)
51-75	11 (3.7)	49 (16.9)	37 (12.8)	7 (2.4)
76-100	3 (1.0)	34 (11.7)	35 (12.1)	47 (16.3)
	N=294	N=290	N=289	N=289

(% in parenthesis).

Source: Postal survey.

Table 8.19
Source of revenue: firms with an overseas turnover

Percentage	Government	National companies	MNEs	Other
0	28 (32.6)	9 (10.8)	3 (3.6)	57 (68.7)
1-10	36 (41.9)	10 (12.0)	7 (8.4)	14 (16.9)
11-25	7 (8.1)	18 (21.7)	15 (18.1)	4 (4.8)
26-50	11 (12.8)	25 (30.1)	30 (36.1)	4 (4.8)
51-75	4 (4.7)	16 (19.3)	12 (14.5)	1 (1.2)
76-100	0 (0.0)	5 (6 .0)	16 (19.3)	3 (3.6)
	N=86	N=83	N=83	N=83

(% in parenthesis).

Source: Postal survey.

revenue only 3.6 per cent have no MNEs as clients. Of the firms with overseas revenue 69.9 per cent derive over 25 per cent of their revenue from MNEs compared to 48.8 per cent of the total group of firms. Firms which have overseas revenue derive a greater proportion of revenue from the government, 67.4 per cent as compared to 49 per cent for the whole group, gain some revenue from the government. Is there a connection between internationalisation and revenue from

Table 8.20
Revenue from MNEs and overseas turnover

Overseas turnover	Revenue from MNEs						Total	χ^2	Signific -ance
	0	1-10%	11-25%	26-50%	51-75%	76-100%			
0	43	20	14	21	11	10	119		
>0	3	7	15	30	12	16	83	38.91227	0.0000
Total	46	27	29	51	23	26	202		

Zero expected frequencies > 5.

Source: Postal survey.

the government? It may be that the government prefers to use well established and large companies, which would also be more international.

The Chi-square test was used to measure the strength of association between the level of revenue from MNEs and whether a firm had an overseas turnover. The results (Table 8.20) indicate that there is a statistically significant association, which implies that there is a link between the level of revenue from MNEs and internationalisation. This finding supports hypothesis 11 which argues that *'the nature of a firm's clients will influence the level of internationalisation'*. The more revenue gained from multinational clients the more likely the firm is to be international. This also lends support for the generally accepted view that service firms become international in order to supply their multinational clients (Dunning, 1989; Erramilli and Rao, 1990; Esperanca, 1992; Leyshon et al., 1987a, 1987b; Yannopoulos, 1983; Weinstein, 1979; inter alia).

To some extent the findings reflect the polarisation of the business service market between, on the one hand, a small number of large companies which provide services to large mainly MNEs, and a large number of small companies which provide services to small indigenous companies. This polarisation is evident in all of the three sub-sectors selected as the central focus of this study and was clearly illustrated in Chapter 6. There are few barriers to entry in all the sub-sectors on a small scale, and there is sufficient demand for the services of small companies in these areas. However, firms attempting to enter the market on a larger scale face significant barriers to entry, including access to an international network and adequate management skills, among others.

8.5 Location and internationalisation

Hypothesis 12 argues that '*firms located in the South of the UK and those with a wide domestic geographical spread are likely to be international in scope'*. Of the firms which declared an overseas turnover in 1989, that is, 95 cases in all, 85.3 per cent were located in the South,[4] 5.3 per cent in the Midlands, and, 9.5 per cent in the North. Overall 74.1 per cent of the total sample were located in the South, so does it seem that being located in the South is more common among firms with an overseas turnover? The Chi-square test was used to test the significance of this association. Location was defined as either the South or elsewhere and internationalisation was defined in terms of a range of levels of overseas turnover in 1989. The results (Table 8.21) reveal that there is a statistically significant association between location and the level of internationalisation. Those firms located in the South are more likely to have a higher level of overseas turnover.

The degree of domestic geographical spread and internationalisation was explored in the same way (Table 8.22). These results suggest that there is a statistically significant association between the extent of a domestic geographical spread and internationalisation. That is if a firm has a wide domestic geographical spread it is more likely to have an overseas turnover than a firm which does not have a wide domestic geographical spread.

It is clear then that a firm's location and domestic geographical spread appear to be closely linked with internationalisation. As firms expand in size they at first increase their share of local markets, later reaching out to a wider national market and eventually to an international market. It would seem that this is also the case among business service sector firms since those with a wide domestic geographical spread are more likely to be international. It is also clear though that those firms located in the South are more likely to be international in scope and this may be explained in terms of the South being a head office location for many firms, including foreign companies, supporting the view of O'Farrell and Wood (1993). As a consequence, business service firms located in the South are more likely to attract international clients at an earlier stage in their domestic development.

8.6 Ownership and autonomy of overseas establishments

It has been suggested that service sector multinationals, just as those in the manufacturing sector, will prefer to have a majority share in the ownership of overseas presences (Dunning, 1989; Erramilli and Rao, 1993). The survey found a range of types of 'overseas presences' including: wholly owned subsidiaries; majority owned subsidiaries; associate companies; joint ventures; franchise and licensing arrangements; together with others types of presences such as reciprocal agreements between firms. It is important to note that many firms used a variety of different types of presence. This pattern was evident among all subgroups, although

Table 8.21
Location by internationalisation

Overseas turnover 1989	Location		Total	χ^2	Significance
	South	Elsewhere			
0	159	71	230		
up to £0.5mil.	20	6	26		
> £0.5mil. to £10 mil.	30	4	34	11.76566	0.0082
> £10mil+	31	3	34		
Total	240	84	324		

Zero expected frequencies < 5.

Source: Postal survey.

Table 8.22
Domestic geographical spread and internationalisation

Overseas turnover	Domestic geographical spread - number of locations:			Total	χ^2	Significance
	1	2-3	4-6			
0	98	24	7	129		
>0	46	26	20	92	19.46819	0.0001
Total	144	50	27	221		

Zero expected frequencies < 5.
Firms which failed to indicate any offices were excluded from the analysis.

Source: Postal survey.

in a number of sectors certain presences seemed to be clearly preferred. For the computer services sector wholly owned subsidiaries were by far the most common, whereas among accountancy firms other presences were the most important category.

Respondents were asked to list the number of majority owned presences and all other presences for various geographical regions for the years 1980 and 1989. The results reveal that there has been a marked increase in the number of other presences compared to majority-owned presences, which included wholly owned presence (Table 8.23). This would seem to refute hypothesis 13 which argues that *'firms prefer to have majority ownership of their overseas subsidiaries'*. Although the evidence shows that other presences are more prevalent than majority owned presences this does not necessarily reflect the preference of the firms. It may be that there are factors which prevent majority ownership, such as the availability of funds or the regulatory environment in an overseas market.

Exploring further the relationship between overseas turnover and the number and type of overseas presences the level of overseas turnover was correlated with the number of majority owned presences and the number of other presences (Table 8.24). Low, but statistically significant, correlation coefficients were found, the linear association between overseas turnover and the number of majority presence being almost twice as strong as that between overseas turnover and the number of other presences. These results lend support to the view that as firms become increasingly international they are more likely to set up majority owned subsidiaries in foreign markets (Erramilli, 1991).

The relationship between overseas turnover and the geographical spread of overseas presences was also explored through an examination of correlation coefficients (Table 8.25). Low but statistically significant correlation coefficients were found, with the linear association between overseas turnover and the geographical spread of majority presences being stronger than that between overseas turnover and the spread of other presences. This would seem to support the view that as firms become increasingly international there is a preference towards majority owned presences in a wider range of geographical locations.

It is important to note that firms will no doubt have a variety of different ownership positions depending on the stage of development within different foreign market. So in a well established market the presence may be wholly owned whereas in a market only recently entered the presence may be a joint venture or franchise agreement. Local market characteristics will also influence the nature of the presence.

The use of non-majority owned modes of foreign market entry by business service firms may be accounted for by the relatively small size of such firms compared to manufacturing firms at the point at which they decide to enter an overseas market. It may well be that funds are not available to purchase a going concern or set up a facility from scratch. Moreover, given the importance of client relations to service firms a good knowledge of the overseas environment is required and this is best obtained by using local staff. If a takeover is not an available option, then it may be necessary to set up a joint venture with a firm already established in the market. Also, if firms want to establish an international network rapidly then linking up with similar firms in overseas markets may be the best solution.

The pattern of ownership of overseas presences may reflect the immaturity of international business service firms. Much of the literature on the evolution of

Table 8.23
Number of types of overseas presences

| | 1980 | | 1989 | |
Number	Majority ownership presences %	Other presences %	Majority ownership presences %	Other presences %
0	90.2	89.3	81.1	69.5
1	4.6	2.4	3.7	4.0
2 or more	5.2	8.2	15.2	26.5
	N=328	N=328	N=328	N=328

Source: Postal survey.

Table 8.24
Overseas turnover and the number of different types of overseas presences: correlation coefficients

Overseas turnover in 1989 with number of:	Correlation coefficient
Majority presences in 1989	0.4298 (229) P=0.000
Other presences in 1989	0.2320 (229) P=0.004

Coefficient/ (cases)/ 2 tailed significance.

Source: Postal survey.

MNEs suggest that many firms begin their ventures into overseas expansion through the use of presences, such as joint venture and licensing agreements. This gives the benefit of local market knowledge and reduces the capital required, and the element of risk. As time passes and the level of uncertainty and risk falls, much of the literature suggests that firms will establish a wholly-owned subsidiary, if this is permitted by local regulations. In addition, over time firms become more committed to their overseas presences, which may involve the sharing of intangible assets, increasing the need for full ownership in order to protect and control the use of such

Table 8.25
Overseas turnover and the international geographical spread of overseas presences: correlation coefficients

Overseas turnover in 1989 with the geographical spread of:	Correlation coefficient
Majority presences in 1989	0.5576 (229) P=0.000
Other presences in 1989	0.3854 (229) P=0.000

Coefficient/ (cases)/ 2 tailed significance.

Source: Postal survey.

assets (Welch and Luostarinen, 1988; Esperanca, 1992). This appears to be what is happening in the business services sector. Establishing a presence other than through majority ownership reduces risk. In the future these presences may become majority-owned. There has also been a rapid increase in the internationalisation of these business services sectors. Joint ventures may not only be the safest way to enter a market, but also the cheapest allowing fast expansion. Finally, the sector is heavily regulated and this must not be overlooked as a factor influencing the nature of an overseas presence.

The ratings given to various factors influencing the form of ownership which an overseas presence may take are shown in Table 8.26. The availability of a suitable company for a joint venture ranks highly with 27 per cent of the firms rating this as extremely important, the desire to maintain control through majority ownership is also ranked highly with 25.5 per cent rating this as extremely important. Furthermore, initial familiarity with the country concerned is ranked highly as is the availability of a suitably priced firm for takeover. Similar results were found for each sub-sector, although a number of differences are worth noting. Among advertising firms 33.3 per cent rated the availability of a suitably priced firm to takeover as extremely important, whilst 45.5 per cent of accountancy firms ranked this factor as extremely important with other factors being given little importance. Among computer service firms 29 per cent rated the desire to maintain control as extremely important and 28.6 per cent initial familiarity with the country concerned as extremely important. The desire for control and the opportunity for setting up from scratch ranked highly among management consulting firms with 33.3 per cent

Table 8.26
Factors determining the form of ownership which an overseas presence takes

	Extremely important %	Very important %	Important %	Of little importance %	Totally un-important %
Availability of fund for 100% ownership (N=108)	18.5	12.0	23.1	21.3	25.0
Availability of suitably prices firm to takeover (N=106)	20.8	16.0	24.5	14.2	24.5
Opportunity for setting up from scratch (N=107)	15.9	15.0	21.5	17.8	29.9
Availability of a suitable company for joint venture (N=111)	27.0	26.1	23.4	10.8	12.6
Legal restraints upon % ownership by foreign firms (N=105)	9.5	12.4	20.0	26.7	31.4
Initial familiarity with the country concerned (N=108)	22.2	31.5	27.8	8.3	10.2
Desire to maintain control through majority ownership (N=110)	25.5	21.8	19.1	16.4	17.3
Other (N=12)	66.7	16.7	0.0	8.3	8.3

Source: Postal survey.

192

rating both these factors as extremely important. The opportunity for setting up from scratch was also highly rated among market research firms with 30 per cent rating this as extremely important. Finally among public relations firms the availability of a suitable company for joint venture was ranked most highly with 44.4 per cent rating this as extremely important.

Hypothesis 14 argues that *'international active companies give their subsidiaries a higher level of autonomy compared to national firms'*. This was explored in the survey by looking at the levels of capital expenditure permitted without consent from the parent firm. Of the 100 cases which were subsidiaries of other firms, 51 per cent reported that their capital expenditure was limited to less than £10 thousand without the consent of the parent company. A further 26 per cent reported levels of expenditure of between £10-50 thousand without the consent of the parent firm, 13 per cent between £50-250 thousand without parent firm consent, and 10 per cent expenditure of more than £250 thousand without parent firm consent. Of the 67 cases which responded to the question about the level of expenditure they allowed their subsidiaries to make without their consent 77.6 per cent said less than £10 thousand, 17.9 per cent said between £10-50 thousand, 3 per cent £50-250 thousand and 1.5 per cent said over £250 thousand. Those firms which responded to the question, appeared to keep a firm control over their subsidiaries. The above evidence would seem to suggest that control and decision making, among the companies which either have or are subsidiaries, is primarily centralised in this sector.

Computer service firms and market research firms appear to have higher than average levels of autonomy from their parent companies measured by the level of expenditure they can make without the parent firm's consent. This may be because the firms are in unrelated business areas to the parent company and hence greater autonomy is necessary. In the computer services sector, for example, many of the firms which are wholly owned subsidiaries have developed out of the computer departments of large firms and been externalised, but with ownership retained (e.g. Centre-file Ltd.).

When exploring these figures for firms with an overseas turnover it was found that the levels of autonomy given to firms which were subsidiaries was higher, for example, only 30.6 per cent of the firms (36 firms in all) were limited to less than £10 thousand of capital expenditure without the consent of the parent firm, a further 33.3 per cent to £10-50 thousand, 22.2 per cent to £50-250 thousand and 13.9 per cent to over £250 thousand. For those firms with subsidiaries (42 in all), they limited the expenditure of their subsidiaries, as follows: 66.7 per cent limited to £10 thousand; 26.2 per cent to between £10-50 thousand; 4.8 per cent to £50-250 thousand; and, 2.4 per cent to more than £250 thousand. The evidence would appears to support hypothesis 14, since international firms do appear to have greater autonomy from their parent firms, and those firms which are parents do give more autonomy to their subsidiaries. This is likely to be the case for international firms because of the possible communication problems together with the fact that the

193

subsidiary will have more information and be able to make a better judgement as to whether an investment should proceed. This may be more important in the case of business services, where local market knowledge may be essential. The immaturity of international business service firms resulting in a general lack of experience in overseas markets may also be a factor contributing to the higher level of autonomy given to subsidiaries. However, it must be recognised that the level of capital expenditure permitted by a parent company may be an imperfect measurement of the level of autonomy given to a subsidiary.

The survey evidence reveals that the ownership pattern of overseas presences does not conform to that suggested in the literature (Dunning, 1989; Erramilli and Rao, 1993). However, a number of reasons have been suggested which might explain these differences, in particular, the immaturity of many international business services firms. It is suggested here that as business service firms develop majority owned presences become more important. In terms of the level of autonomy given to subsidiaries, the results appear to support the accepted view (Buckley and Casson, 1976; 1985) that international firms give greater autonomy to their subsidiaries.

8.7 Business service sector FDI: market-oriented or resource-oriented?

The findings of the survey support hypothesis 15: *'business service sector overseas investment is market-oriented as opposed to resource-oriented'*. The importance attached to various factors influencing the location of an overseas presence is shown in Table 8.27. It is clear that the overseas presences of the firms in the sample are primarily market-oriented rather than resource-oriented, for example greater importance is attached to client location, market opportunities, and potential opportunities than to the availability of skilled labour and the productivity and cost of labour. These findings were reflected at a sub-sector level with only a few variations. It is useful to note that both the management consulting firms and the public relations firms ranked the availability of skilled labour more highly with 27.3 per cent of firms in both sectors rating this as extremely important. Despite these variations, the evidence supports the view that there is, at present, little in the way of an international division of labour in the production of the business services studied.

Market-oriented overseas expansion is not the only manner in which service firms may develop internationally. In some, for example, information services and computer software services, there is an international division of labour whereby firms locate labour intensive activities in countries where labour is relatively cheap, though educated, compared to the industrialised countries (Lakha, 1994). There is perhaps a need to develop a model of international production for such service firms. One might expect these types of services to be relatively well developed in highly competitive markets where price is very important. For business services

194

Table 8.27
Factors which determine the location of an overseas presence

	Extremely important %	Very important %	Important %	Of little importance %	Totally un-important %
Location of client (N=151)	43.7	24.5	16.6	5.3	9.9
Present market opportunities (N=148)	43.2	35.1	10.8	4.1	6.8
Potential market opportunities (N=149)	41.6	32.2	16.8	4.7	4.7
Availability of skilled labour (N=143)	17.5	19.6	30.1	15.4	17.5
Productivity and cost of labour (N=138)	5.8	8.0	31.9	27.5	26.8
Knowledge of the country (N=138)	19.6	26.8	29.7	12.3	11.6
Other (N=9)	66.7	22.2	0.0	0.0	11.1

Source: Postal survey.

quality and customisation of service provision are of great importance. Price competition is undoubtedly important in the mass markets for standardised services, however the companies surveyed did not place great importance on the cost of their services as a source of competitive advantage (Table 8.15). The scope then for resource-oriented overseas expansion in the business services sector is as yet limited.

8.9 Conclusion

This chapter has provided an analysis of the activities of a sample of UK business services firms surveyed in 1990. The results have proved useful in terms of providing evidence to support the framework developed in Chapter 5. Many of the hypotheses, derived from this framework, were found to be valid, although, in some cases support for them was inconclusive. Having explored the research findings in detail above it is now worth summarising them briefly and examining their value in terms of providing an understanding of the internationalisation of UK business service firms. A number of important insights into the internationalisation process have been gained.

Firstly, it its clear that many business services firms which are international in scope are also diversified, however, it has been found that such diversification tends to be into very closely related activities. In addition, the main motivation for such diversification appears to be the desire to satisfy client needs and opportunities for market growth. Although the achievement of economies of scale and scope, as well as the opportunity to cross refer clients from one service to another, may be outcomes of diversification the survey suggests that these are not the main motivation behind such activity. Just as the process of internationalisation appears to be demand driven among business service firms, diversification can also be viewed as demand driven.

The evidence considered above indicates that the internationalisation of business service firms occurs in an evolutionary manner, with the export of services playing an important role in this process. Clearly, if trade is important among business services there is a need to reassess its role in the internationalisation of other service sectors. Trade no doubt plays a role in the internationalisation of many service activities, particularly those, which like business services, are information intensive in their nature.

It has been found that for some business service firms overseas presences are merely a vehicle through which services, produced elsewhere, are delivered to clients. Such overseas presences can be regarded as transaction specific assets and their existence indicate that a flow of intra-firm trade in finished services between the home and overseas location occurs. Intra-firm trade may also occur in intermediate service inputs. However, since the survey evidence confirms the market-oriented nature of FDI in the business services sector, such intra-firm trade does not indicate a complex system of international production which would be characterised by resource-oriented FDI.

Despite evidence that trade in business services does occur, as expected the use of ICTs as a means through which services are exported appears, as yet, to be underdeveloped. Information intensive services are those most able to take advantage of ICTs within the process of internationalisation. It is, nevertheless, apparent that the need for client contact and the maintenance of good client relations limits the use of ICTs as a means of direct exportation. It is quite likely though that

196

ICTs are used extensively in intra-firm transactions. Indeed, firms with international interests do give greater weight to the use of ICTs as a source of competitive advantage. This is no doubt related to the use of ICTs not only in intra-firm trade, but also as a means through which complex geographically disperses activities can be most effectively managed.

Those firms which were international in scope regarded their international coverage to be an important source of competitive advantage. The survey provides evidence of merger and acquisition activity throughout the 1980s as firms sought to develop their international networks. The need to establish international coverage is related to the fact that international business service firms depend heavily for revenue upon clients which are multinational in scope. Such clients prefer to employ a business service firm which can supply services to all of their international operations. Indeed, the survey findings do confirm the importance of multinational clients to international business service firms.

A higher level of internationalisation was found among firms with a wide national geographical spread and those located in the South. This confirms the view that business service firms which are located in, or near, major centres of agglomeration are likely to become international in scope at an earlier stage in their development than firms which are located in peripheral areas. In major capital cities business service firms are more likely to come into contact with internationally active clients, which will encourage them to become international in scope.

The survey results illustrate that business service firms use a wide variety of foreign market entry modes, from wholly owned subsidiaries to franchise contracts and reciprocal arrangements. However, the evidence does suggest that as firms become increasingly international there is a tendency for the majority owned presence to become a more important method through which foreign markets are serviced. The range of market entry modes in use by business service firms can to some extent be explained by the need for rapid internationalisation. As firms become more established internationally they may seek to exert greater control over their international network by increasing the level of ownership. Having said this, it is evident that although the ownership of subsidiaries may increase, they still have a higher level of autonomy than the subsidiaries of national firms. Such autonomy can be explained by the local presence having greater knowledge regarding local cultural and regulatory environments, a factor which is of particular importance in the business services sector.

Many of the findings reported in this chapter confirm previous research in the service sector as being equally relevant to the internationalisation of business services. Nonetheless, a number of findings question accepted views, indicating that it may not be possible to draw general conclusions regarding the internationalisation of the service sector, and indeed that it may be necessary to reassess the internationalisation of services generally. Trade is clearly important in the internationalisation of business services and it is likely to be so in other service activities, particularly those which are information intensive in nature.

The findings reported here make a significant contribution to the understanding of the internationalisation of business service firms. There is a clear indication that the general view of the internationalisation of services may not be appropriate for all sub-sectors. Indeed, it is important to note that there are significant differences between the business service sub-sectors surveyed here. The presence of such differences requires that the individual sub-sectors are given specific attention. Any framework developed for business services must take into account the variations between sub-sectors. In addition, it is necessary to substantiate the survey results with further research on a sub-sectoral basis. The limitations of the postal survey from which the above results derive, must be recognised. As a consequence, further consideration will be given to the three main sub-sectors selected for study. The following chapter will present case studies of individual firms, two from each of the three sub-sectors. In this way detail can be given to the broad overview of business service internationalisation provided here.

Notes

1   Appendix 1 provides technical details of the data analysis undertaken from which the findings reported in this chapter are derived.

2   As noted in Chapter 2 there is a lack of consistency between classification systems in terms of defining categories of business services. The UK SIC for example includes market research, public relations and management consultants at the same four digit level (8395), whereas under the ISIC and NACE classification systems these services fall within different groups.

3   The meaning of a distinct service in this particular part of the analysis was left to the perceptions of respondents, these results must therefore be considered with this in mind.

4   See note 3 Chapter 7.

9 Multinational structures and strategies in the business services sector

9.1 Introduction

The importance of exports in the internationalisation of business service firms was illustrated in the previous chapter. However, it was found that those firms which depended solely upon exports for their overseas revenue were relatively small in size measured in terms of domestic turnover. As business service firms expand they tend to use a variety of modes of foreign market servicing, with the establishment of a permanent presence in overseas markets becoming the preferred method of internationalisation. As noted in Chapter 4, business service firms may be able to establish an overseas presence at a relatively low cost, and consequently, such firms may engage in FDI at an early stage in their international development. Furthermore, independent exports may give rise to risks and uncertainties which can be eliminated when such transactions are internalised with in the boundaries of the firm.

As a result, the internationalisation of business service firms generally takes the form of an extension of the organisation across national borders. The survey found evidence of a wide variety of types of overseas presences utilised by business service firms ranging from wholly owned subsidiaries to licensing and reciprocal arrangements. The nature of cross border activity varies from sector to sector and indeed from firm to firm. The survey findings reported in Chapter 8 provide general information regarding the internationalisation of the business services sector. To investigate the evolution of organisational forms within the sector it is necessary to examine individual firms in detail. The international organisational forms frequently used among the three main sub-sectors were identified in Chapter 6, and it is clear that these forms are evolving rapidly. The objective here is not only to explain the selection of organisational structure, but also to identify the factors which influence this choice. An appreciation of the determinants will

199

incorporate a dynamic element into the discussion of organisational choice, since the influence of such factors will vary over time.

Each case study will consider the development of the firm concerned and attempt to identify the factors which have influenced its international development. By presenting an in-depth analysis of two firms from each of the three sub-sectors a useful cross section of the business services sector will be explored. The case studies presented in this chapter will not only provide support for the findings of the postal survey reported in Chapter 8, but will also provide additional insights into the internationalisation of business services at the level of the individual firm.

Each sector will be considered in turn, with a brief discussion of the organisational trends, followed by an examination of two firms from each sector, selected to highlight different organisational approaches. The firms have been chosen from those active in the UK, though they are not necessarily wholly UK owned. When examining each firm factors internal and external to the firm will be considered as influences on organisational design. Following the case studies from each sector, successful structures and strategies for internationalisation will be highlighted. Having explored all three sub-sectors an evaluation of the structures and strategies adopted by UK business service firms will be presented.

9.2 Advertising firms

Among advertising firms the dominant multinational organisational structure is that of the holding group. As an agency expands the problem of client conflict may arise. In order to overcome this an agency will set up or acquire a separate network which has its own distinctive character and a 'brand' name of its own. The networks then operate autonomously and independently of each other with a holding company being established to control both networks. In this way services can be provided to clients who may be in competition with one another without the issue of client conflict arising.

It is possible to find various company types in this sector, including partnerships, private limited companies and public companies. The larger firms which are international in scope are generally limited or public limited companies. During the 1980s an increasing number of the larger agencies became public after witnessing Saatchi and Saatchi's successful use of the London Stock Exchange to fund expansion.

The companies selected for study here are Cordiant Plc. and Gold Greenlees Trott Plc.. The first is selected for its size and rapid growth, whilst the second is smaller but following a similar though more measured path of expansion.

200

Cordiant is a public limited company listed on the London, New York and Tokyo Stock Markets, the company was established in 1970 by Charles and Maurice Saatchi and was, until 1995, known as Saatchi and Saatchi Plc.[1] Over a sixteen year period the Saatchi and Saatchi agency grew from one small office in London to the world's largest advertising company. This phenomenal growth and success has attracted much media attention, with numerous articles being devoted to the Saatchi and Saatchi story, indeed even a number of books (for example: Kleinman, 1989; Fallon, 1988). In addition, the work of the agency for the Conservative party during the 1979 election campaign, undoubtedly drew attention to the Group, providing it with favourable publicity and linking its fortunes with those of the Conservative government.

Through the 1970s and 1980s Saatchi and Saatchi's growth was primarily fuelled by mergers and acquisitions. The first significant step being the merger with Compton Partners in 1975 to form a publicly quoted company. This merger gave Saatchi and Saatchi the accounts of a number of 'blue chip' clients, including Procter and Gamble. Moreover, the merger provided access to the London Stock Exchange and the means of raising the funds needed for further expansion. At the time advertising agencies were not regarded as a good investment, however, Saatchi and Saatchi impressed the Stock Market with its steady growth.

As well as having access to the funds for expansion, Saatchi and Saatchi also took advantage of new financial techniques, in particular the procedure known as 'earn-out'. Under this mechanism the firm being acquired is paid off in two instalments: the first payment is made in cash, raised through fresh share issues; the second represents a stake in the performance of the firm acquired, since it depends on the profits over the next two or three years. This method gives the former owner an incentive to work with the Saatchi organisation and shifts some of the burden of conflict-related lost billings to the seller. An important factor in the success of this expansion strategy has been the ability to hold on to key people at the agency acquired. The bases of this ability are the high degree of independence given to executives, the profit-dependent deferred pay off, and the Saatchi name (Michell, 1988).

As a consequence of this acquisition strategy by 1979 Saatchi and Saatchi became the largest UK agency and in 1981 it was the largest European agency group. In 1982 Saatchi and Saatchi became a worldwide agency network with the acquisition of Compton Communications in the US.

During the 1980s the Group embarked upon a strategy of diversification with the aim of transforming itself into 'a global superstore of services' providing all the business services a client might need under one roof. This diversification was stimulated by the desire to obtain growth through cross referral and efficiency gains through economies of scale and scope and the exploitation of synergy. As Burger (1988, p.32) put it:

The Saatchis' ideal conglomerate would combine the advertising skills of Saatchi and Saatchi, the consulting prowess of a McKinsey & Co., the accounting acumen of an Arthur Andersen and the financial clout of a Goldman Sachs.

Considering the relationship between member firms in 1987 Maurice Saatchi noted that:

Member firms are distinctive by industry-recognised excellence in their particular service line, while the bond of association with Saatchi enables each one to benefit from the proven track record of the others. The success of each firm, in turn, enhances the reputation of the Group. This mutually beneficial relationship provides an engine for internal growth by creating opportunities for synergy among the member firms (Annual Report and Accounts, 1987, p.8).

Diversification into consultancy occurred in 1984 with the acquisition of the Hay Group, and the following year saw the development of marketing services with the acquisition of Rowland a public relations company, Siegel & Gale a design company, and Howard Marlboro a sales promotion company. By 1988 Saatchi and Saatchi claimed that 213 clients were working across 3 or more of its service lines (Annual Report, 1988, p.9). It also claimed that a fifth of all its new business came from cross referral (Kleinman, 1989).

In 1986 Saatchi and Saatchi underwent a major expansion in advertising with the acquisition of Dancer Fitzgerald Sample, Backer & Spielvogel and Ted Bates Worldwide. Becoming, as a result, the largest agency group in the world. Saatchi and Saatchi attempted to fulfil its ambitions of entering the financial services sector in 1987 by launching a takeover bid against the Midland bank, the fourth largest bank in the UK at the time. Following the failure of this bid, approaches were made to Hill Samuel, the merchant bank, but these also came to nothing. This flirtation with the financial sector was not only unsuccessful but also damaging to the Group's image among institutional investors. In the following year Saatchi and Saatchi renounced its ambition to move into financial services stating that it would concentrate on establishing each of its existing communications and consulting services as the market leader in every country (Harris, 1988).

A major reorganisation of the Group's advertising interests took place in 1987 with 19 units being merged into two global networks: Saatchi and Saatchi Advertising Worldwide (SSAW) and Backer Spielvogel Bates Worldwide (BSBW). By 1988 the Company was established as a communications and consulting group, becoming the world's tenth largest consulting firm. Furthermore, Zenith, a centralised media buying unit, was formed to capitalise on the concentration of media buying capacity within the Group.

202

The 1989 results showed the first year without growth since the company was founded. With profits significantly down on previous years Saatchi and Saatchi announced its intention to part with its consultancy activities and refocus on its core business. In 1990, the consultancy branch - the Hay Group - was acquired by its management and since then the Company has continued to dispose of other non-core activities.

The grand strategy of becoming a global superstore of services abandoned, Saatchi and Saatchi returned to the business it knew best - advertising. The failure of this diversification strategy revealed that the economies of scale and scope together with the benefits of cross referral and synergy were insufficient to sustain the Group's wide interests. Indeed, with such diversification comes the danger that firms within the Group which do not maintain high standards can have a detrimental impact on the reputation of the Company as a whole.

Since 1988 Saatchi and Saatchi has experienced difficulties and has been unable to recapture the growth and profitability achieved through the 1970s and the largest part of the 1980s. However, the company remains a major advertising group being ranked third in the UK in 1993 and fifth in the world in 1994 (Chapter 6). At the end of 1994 the company employed some 10,913 people worldwide: 1,803 in the UK; 3,863 in the US; 2,697 in the rest of Europe; and 2,550 in the rest of the world. Turnover[2] in the same year amounted to £3,906.2 million, revenue[3] amounted to £775.4 million: 14.7 per cent from UK; 40.5 per cent from US; 26.3 per cent from the rest of Europe; and 18.5 per cent from the rest of the world (Cordiant Plc., 1995a, pp.42,46 & 66). The US is the dominant market with Europe close behind. Although the rest of the world is a less significant source of revenue, at the moment Saatchi and Saatchi are extending their presence in Asia Pacific in an effort to benefit from the rapid economic growth being experienced in parts of this region.

In 1991 a wide spread restructuring of management and operations was undertaken designed to focus management's attention on their core area of expertise and to allow them to concentrate on serving their clients. Five principles were laid down which will guided Saatchi and Saatchi's action: financial discipline; responsibility and accountability; focus and expertise; performance and incentives; organic growth (Annual Report and Accounts 1992, p.10).

By 1993 Saatchi and Saatchi consisted of three advertising networks: SSAW; BSBW; and Campbell Mithun Esty. The latter being drawn together in 1992 from the two independent units of Campbell Mithun Esty of North America and KHBB of the UK. In addition to the advertising networks there are also companies in the direct marketing and public relations sectors these are Kobs & Draft Worldwide and Rowland Worldwide respectively. Finally, there is Zenith Worldwide a media buying organisation and a number of independent companies in the UK and US. The Company's organisational structure is shown in Figure 9.1. Something in the order of 85 per cent of the firm's turnover derives from its advertising networks, which operate autonomously and in competition with one another.

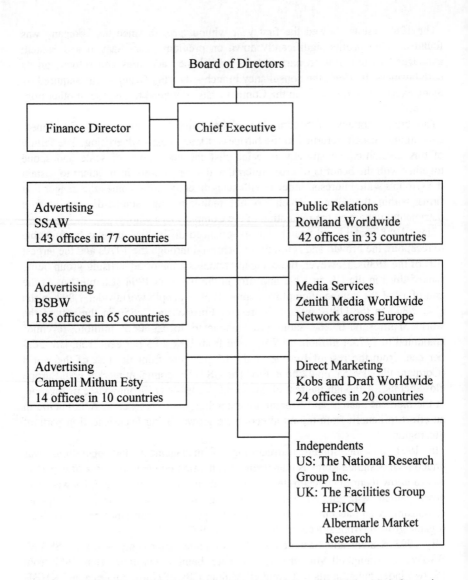

Source: Adapted from Saatchi and Saatchi Annual Report 1992 with information from 1993 Annual Report.

Figure 9.1 Cordiant Plc. organisational structure

It is clear that Saatchi and Saatchi's international expansion was primarily through acquisitions in the 1980s. Their policy was one of acquiring fast growing and or profitable agencies and control them as profit centres through stringent financial controls (Michell, 1988). This policy was extremely successful with earnings per share having increased by an average of 36 per cent between 1975 and 1987 (Annual Report and Accounts, 1987).

The corporate role performed by the Saatchi and Saatchi Group is very similar to that provided by any conglomerate. The holding company interacts with each agency setting financial objectives and evaluating the subsidiaries results bi-weekly. The system appears to be carefully structured so that problems cannot be hidden within aggregate results (Alter, 1987). Additionally, the prestige of the Saatchi name is a bonus in new business development and also in the hiring of creative staff.

After many years of rapid international expansion Saatchi and Saatchi is now in a period of consolidation. It can no longer raise capital on the financial markets to the same extent that it could in the early and mid 1980s. Consequently, since 1989 the emphasis has been on organic growth rather than acquisitions. Although these are still important when the acquired firm can strengthen the Company's position in a particular market. Recent expansion in East Asian and the Eastern European countries have been achieved by the setting up of new offices, rather than acquisitions. This can partly be explained in terms of the Company's new policy, but also, the fact that there is a lack of indigenous advertising expertise in these countries. International expansion is undoubtedly stimulated by competitive pressures together with the desire for continued growth.

In terms of the nature of overseas presences it is clear that Saatchi and Saatchi maintains a variety of ownership modes, in 1993 of a total of 220 overseas presences 101 were owned by the company with the remaining 119 being affiliated offices (Annual Report and Accounts, 1993, pp.8-9). Affiliate offices dominated in South America and other developing countries reflecting perhaps a higher level of risk together with local cultural and regulatory environments. Advanced industrial markets were primarily served by wholly owned subsidiaries.

It is clear that Saatchi and Saatchi has a number of ownership specific advantages which include its reputation for creativity, with a track record of awards in this area which expands each year. Furthermore, there is the Saatchi name, which can be regarded as a brand name. As also can the Bates Worldwide name which was adopted by the BSBW network in 1994 as a global brand name.

International coverage and size are undoubtedly of advantage when serving multinational clients. The Saatchi Group puts great emphasis on the ability to provide services to MNEs, and this is evident in the appointment of worldwide account directors in 1991. The Annual Report for that year stated, with reference to SSAW, that:

The network is committed to serving clients on a worldwide basis and has created 12 worldwide account directors. These executives will play a key role in providing clients with the seamless global service they are increasingly seeking and in driving that process with precision, clarity and force. They are expected to raise further the quality of service for their clients, with particular focus on maintaining the standard of their multinational advertising at world class levels (Annual Report 1991, p.13).

The Group is also renowned for its promotion of global advertising campaigns, which it has successfully undertaken for a number of clients, including for example British Airways in the 1980s (Leslie, 1995).

In recent years the Group has been increasing its investment in information technology to improve the quality and efficiency of services. There is also the desire to be at the forefront of new developments which give rise to new forms of advertising. For example, the Interactive Advertising Group has been established to help clients benefit from the emergence of new media technologies, in addition the Hudson Street Partners, a separate unit, has been set up to help clients experiment with 'infomercials', home shopping channels, computer on-line services and other new forms of 'interactive' media. Finally, in 1993 video conferencing facilities were introduced in the US for client/agency meetings, and these are being expanded through the Group (Annual Report 1993 p.16).

Although, the Saatchi name is clearly an ownership advantage in particular for the SSAW network, the fact that the holding group and one of the networks share a name does present difficulties for the other networks. As discussed in Chapter 6, client conflicts can be a major problem in the expansion of an advertising agency, thus beyond a certain size it is necessary to set up a separate network with its own distinctive character, in the case of Saatchi and Saatchi this is the Bates Worldwide network. However since the holding company retains the Saatchi name this taints the independence of Bates Worldwide, itself a global brand with a reputation for quality and creativity. This problem was addressed in March 1995 with the Saatchi and Saatchi holding group changing its name to Cordiant Plc. (Cordiant Plc. 1995a).

This change of name came at a time of major disruption for the Group. Following shareholders dissatisfaction with Maurice Saatchi in the position of Chairman he was asked to step down on 16th. December 1994. Shortly after Maurice Saatchi left the Group (Charles Saatchi having resigned from the group the previous year) followed by a number of senior staff who have join him in the establishment of a new agency - 'M & C Saatchi'. As a result of the debacle a number of Cordiant's important clients have withdrawn or put under review their advertising accounts with the Group. Maurice Saatchi has since forged global links with Publicis which will support his new agency with logistical and technical services, media strategy, planning and buying. This will enable the new agency to draw upon an

206

international network of 7,000 people, working from 180 offices in 56 countries (May, 1995). The new agency has already won a number of accounts from the Cordiant Group.

It is still early days since the departure of the Saatchi brothers from the company they founded twenty five years ago. The newly named Cordiant Group has to steer a steady course if it is to avoid disintegration and demise in the years ahead. It presents an interesting case for those studying service sector firms since it is a example of a firm losing significant assets in the form of key members of staff, however, surely a Group of this size can withstand the loss of a small number of such staff. There is also the issue of the protection of intellectual property, and the need to preventing the new agency from poaching clients. The Group is currently involved in an number of legal actions to protect its interests in the UK and US. Financial performance since the departure of Maurice Saatchi has been hit by the loss of major clients, and as a result, the Company undertook a financial restructuring programme at the end of 1995 with rights issue valued at an estimated £126.6 million (Cordiant Plc., 1995b). The Cordiant Group has then been hit rather hard by recent events, time will tell whether it succeeds in overcoming its present difficulties.

Gold Greenlees Trott Plc.

Gold Greenlees Trott (GGT) was established in 1980 and became a public company in 1986. By 1994 it had a turnover of £298 million and employed 891 people (Report and Accounts 1994, pp.3 & 41). Following steady growth since its inception, together with access to the Stock Market, by 1987 the Company was in a position to put into place a strategy of diversification into non-media related marketing services. As a result in July of that year the Company acquired the Option One Group a firm involved in sales promotion, direct marketing and sponsorship. In the October GGT became a partner in the COBA strategic consultancy group, and in February of 1988 it acquired RM Communications an audio visual communications firm (Report and Accounts, 1988).

This diversification would enable the Group to offer clients a broader range of services, and thus allow the organisation to capitalise on a traditional strength of winning additional business from existing clients. Only a year after its acquisition Option One shared five major clients with GGT Advertising. The diversification was clearly motivated by the desire to win additional business from clients through cross referral.

In May 1988 GGT made its first step towards internationalisation with the acquisition of Babbit & Reiman, an Atlanta based advertising agency. This was the first step in GGT's plan to build a significant North American network based upon regional centres of excellence. The motivation for such international expansion was clearly to enhance the agency's ability to serve clients on both sides of the Atlantic. In the Company's 1988 Report and Accounts the intention to continue to seek acquisitions where they will help to serve the increasingly sophisticated needs of clients was clearly signalled. "Our aim is to build the most highly regarded international marketing service group" (p.6). However such expansion would not be at the expense of creativity:

> We will aggressively pursue the very highest standards in thinking, creativity and execution believing that this will provide us with our strongest competitive edge in a sector which seems totally preoccupied with the pursuit of volume for its own sake (p.6).

The whole strategy of the Company would seem to be determined by the needs of their clients. The importance of the quality of staff is a major influence on the acquisition strategy with GGT placing management, skills, high standards of intelligence and professionalism together with strong organic growth potential ahead of size as factors influencing the choice of prospective acquisitions.

The Group has continued to grow gradually through acquisitions. For example, in 1988 Bowden Dyble Hayes and Partners (BDH) based in Manchester was acquired. This further strengthened the Group's advertising position in the UK. As well as enabling the Group to handle conflicting business (James Capel, 1988). Following the international expansion and diversification in the late 1980s by 1992 the Group's profits came in equal amounts form the UK and US, whilst advertising accounted for 80 per cent of profits and marketing for 20 per cent (Report and Accounts, 1992).

By the early 1990s GGT was ready for its next stage of international development. The Group's ability to help clients develop their business had been inhibited by the lack of a sufficiently convincing European Network. As a result in June of 1993 GGT announced the creation of a joint venture with GGK, a privately owned European network, which would provide GGT with an important platform for future growth in Continental Europe. GGT Plc. and GGK signed a Network Operating Agreement which enable the two companies to operate as one network called GGK/GGT Worldwide. This network has offices in 24 countries, being represented through the GGK agencies in every major West European market including the most significant of the emerging Eastern European markets, and by the GGT agencies in the UK and the US. The Company claims that:

> This agreement will allow us to service our clients' advertising needs in these important markets, and will, we believe, remove one of the most significant barriers to the continuing growth of our business from major international advertisers.
>
> It will also provide a base from which to grow internationally our marketing services businesses, in sales promotion, direct marketing and sponsorship, all of which are becoming progressively more

208

involved in cross-border transactions (Report and Accounts, 1993, p.20).

GGK is a partner which shares many aspects of GGT's culture. It is also experienced in the running of international business for clients like IBM. The relationship between the two companies developed further in 1994 when GGT took over the GGK European network which was facing financial difficulties.

GGT plans to be more flexible than many of its competitors. It recognises that not all clients' needs are the same, and so will be designing systems which are flexible enough to accommodate this. The Company is organised on a holding group basis, Figure 9.2 shows GGT Plc's organisational structure. It is only recently that a worldwide network has been established and the level of integration into this network attained by the various companies within the Group would appear to be low, however, this will no doubt change as the firm develops. GGT's expansion strategy has continued with for example merger negotiation with Young and Rubicam early in 1994. These, however, fell through after client clashes proved insoluble (The Campaign Report, Feb. 24th 1995).

In 1993 GGT was the eleventh largest agency group in the UK and in 1994 the twenty-third largest advertising organisation in the world (Chapter 6). Compared to companies like WPP Plc. and Cordiant Plc., GGT is small, however, it has successfully established an international network and is well placed to build upon this. Clearly GGT views internationalisation as a source of competitive advantage, and is keen to increase its ability to service international clients. The Company is pursuing a strategy of steady expansion which may in time lead it into a major merger.

Multinational structures and strategies among advertising firms

There are many similarities between the structures and strategies of the two advertising firms considered above. Cordiant is older and more developed than GGT and this is reflected in a more complex organisational structure. Both companies operate on a holding group basis, although, Cordiant is structured around a number of international networks, each network being an integrated organisation within itself. The adoption of the holding group structure is clearly influenced by the issue of client conflict.

Cordiant has evolved rapidly from the accumulation of firms acquired and gradually integrated into specific networks within the Group. GGT being a less developed organisation has yet to fully integrate the various subsidiary firms within the Group. GGT is still in the process of establishing its first clearly united international network, and so far has operated a structure wholly based on subsidiary companies. The GGT network consists of 'independent' firms in the UK, US and Europe, each having its own identity. The first step towards the development of a worldwide network came with the joint venture with the GGK

209

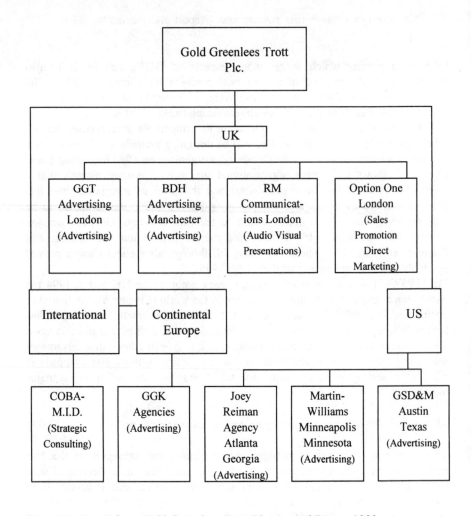

Source: Adapted from Gold Greenlees Trott Plc. Annual Report 1993.

Figure 9.2 Gold Greenlees Trott Plc. organisational structure

European network. The evolution of GGT's organisational structure looks set to follow the pattern of the larger groups like Cordiant. Given its recent merger talks with Young and Rubicam, GGT appears to be keen to develop a second network following the trend set by the larger firms. It is possible that there may be a spate of mergers among groups of GGT's size as they position themselves to compete with the larger advertising groups. What distinguishes GGT from Cordiant in its expansion strategy is its willingness to use joint ventures on a major scale. The adoption of this method of expansion may reflect the caution required of firms in the difficult economic climate of the early 1990s together with the desire to avoid the financial burdens to which large scale acquisitions give rise.

GGT has expanded primarily through obtaining hundred percent ownership of subsidiaries whilst Cordiant has many wholly owned subsidiaries and even more affiliated offices. Complete ownership would appear to be important in this sector though not essential. Firm specific methodologies and brand names may be important intangible assets that require protection within the boundaries of the firm, particularly to ensure the reputation of the firm. However, there is one asset which is crucial to the success of advertising firms and this is the creativity of its staff. The retention of such staff is important, and involves high rewards and promotion as means of aligning their interests with those of the firm and thereby reducing damaging opportunistic behaviour (Chapter 4). There is, though, no means by which staff can be prevented form departing. By creating teams of creative staff their skills can be spread and more securely embedded in the firm.

Growth through internationalisation would appear to be the objective of both companies. The motivation for such internationalisation is related to client needs and the desire for steady growth. In the early stages of internationalisation client needs would appear to be of great importance as for example in the case of GGT, such expansion can be regarded as demand driven. This provides support for Weinstein's (1973) view that the internationalisation of advertising has followed that of manufacturing firms. As the firm becomes increasingly international then the motive is not only to satisfy existing clients but also to capture new clients, internationalisation develops a momentum of its own, as in the case of Cordiant where expansion is supply driven.

Both firms are diversified into closely related areas, Cordiant refers to itself as a communications services group, and provides advertising, public relations, direct marketing and media services. GGT calls itself an international marketing service group and provides advertising, audio visual presentations, sales promotion, direct marketing and strategic consultancy services. Diversification is into closely related areas. GGT has not attempted the more wide ranging diversification strategy followed by Cordiant in the early 1980s, before it returned to its core activities in the late 1980s.

GGT diversified prior to international expansion, with the motive being to benefit from the cross referral of clients. Cordiant was also motivated by the opportunities for cross referral of clients together with economies of scale and scope. This contrasts with the findings from the survey where client needs and the opportunity for market growth appeared to be the major factors stimulating diversification. Clearly diversification is an important means of increasing business opportunities although internationalisation would appear to be an even more effective way of expanding business. Indeed, internationalisation would appear to be essential to the retention of clients which are increasingly becoming international themselves.

If an advertising agency can offer services in a number of countries they are well positioned to win the business of international advertisers. However, having an overseas presence is not sufficient alone. That presence must be able to deliver a high quality service. Although the idea of global advertising received a lot of attention in the 1980s (Levitt, 1983,1986; Rosen et al., 1988) the reality of cultural differences and regulatory requirements in many cases prevents the use of global campaigns (Chapter 6). It is therefore essential that overseas subsidiaries are able themselves to provide a high quality service to international clients.

The two advertising groups studies both put great emphasis on the quality of their staff, and in particular their creativity. A reputation for creativity is an important competitive weapon among such firms. There is also the desire to present a distinctive service to clients, so for example, GGT talks of its 'entrepreneurial culture', whilst Cordiant places great emphasis on creativity and also uses firm specific methodological approaches. The Bates Worldwide network, for example, is known for its technique of developing a 'Unique Selling Proposition' for products. Image and reputation are highly important to these firms.

International coverage and the ability to offer clients a range of services are also of great importance. Both firms are seeking to attract international advertisers. Cordiant is attempting to increase the quality of its service offered to international clients with the appointment of international account directors. This firm is also investing in new ICTs with the aim of gaining a competitive edge in the newly evolving interactive media. Both Cordiant and GGT are pursuing broadly similar strategies and their structures reflect this with the organisational development of GGT corresponding to that of Cordiant's in the early 1980s.

9.3 Accountancy firms

In the accountancy sector there are two main types of multinational organisational structures. The first is the 'International Name' or the 'World Firm' and the second, is the 'Federal' or 'Network' structure. Mergers between firms with these different structures have led to hybrids. The timing of internationalisation appears to be an important influence upon the type of structure adopted. The international name is the structure adopted by those firms with a fairly long history of internationalisation. Whilst those which are relatively new to the international market have evolved through the establishment of international networks of well established national firms. Firms with an international name structure have evolved gradually with the firm seeking out appropriate partnerships in particular countries over time, with those national partnerships developing in their own right as part of an international group. In some cases the international firm has established partnerships in overseas markets, starting them from scratch perhaps in order to service a particular client's needs in that market.

For firms with the federal or network structure, internationalisation has been a much more hurried affair. The federal structure represents the formation of an international coalition between national firms which already have success and a reputation in their own domestic market. Such national firms have faced the dilemma of either becoming international in scope or risk losing clients to the larger international accountancy firms. It is therefore not surprising that many large national firms have sought rapid internationalisation by joining an international network of firms. In doing so they gain the ability to offer international services, thus retaining clients that would otherwise have looked elsewhere for the satisfaction of their accountancy requirements. Moreover, they gaining new clients specifically because of their newly acquired ability to offer international services. At the same time firms in a network are able to maintain a degree of independence, in particular they are able to retain their domestic name.

It is also important to note that the nature of a presence in an overseas market will be influenced by local regulation, such that most firms display a variety of different types of presences, despite having a clear preference for a particular organisational form. The partnership structure which is currently found among accountancy firm results partly from local regulation. Furthermore, since the key asset of accountancy firms is its staff, the partnership structure would seem to be most appropriate, as it gives all key members of staff a vested interest in the success of the firm. Pressures resulting from a spate of litigation cases against accountancy firms may lead to the adoption of limited, or even public limited company status in the future. Such a change would permit firms to raise capital which would improve their role as merger and acquisition advisers, giving them the ability to compete with the merchant banks in this area of business.

The companies selected for study here are Price Waterhouse and BDO Binder Hamlyn. The former is selected as an example of an international name, whilst the latter is as an example of the looser federal structure.

Price Waterhouse

Price Waterhouse was founded in London in 1849. It has since grown, through organic developments, takeovers and mergers, to the extent that in the period 1992-3 Price Waterhouse was ranked as the sixth largest accountancy firm in the world with a fee income of US $3,887 million and growth rate of 3.4 per cent per annum (PW Facts & Figures 1992-3, quoting International Accountancy Bulletin). In the same period Price Waterhouse had 448 offices located in 117 countries throughout the world.

The US, where the first overseas office was opened in New York in 1890 (Allen and McDermott, 1993), is the largest source of income for Price Waterhouse, followed closely by Europe. Areas such as South East Asia and South America are at present less significant although they are experiencing high growth rates and demonstrate the potential to become major sources of income in the future (PW Facts & Figures 1992-3).

Price Waterhouse, as with the vast majority of accountancy firms, is organised on a partnership basis. However, unlike small partnerships which might be organised on a peer group, or simple hierarchy basis, Price Waterhouse, having some 48,781 staff (PW Facts & Figures 1992-3) and well over 2,000 partners, has a complex organisational structure. Ownership however, generally remains with the partners of each individual practice.

Looking firstly at the national level, Figure 9.3 shows the structure laid out in the 1986-7 Annual Review (p.24). Each national firm is represented by their senior partner in the organisation of the World Firm which is a non-practising corporation that does not conduct or supervise client engagements. The corporation assists the Price Waterhouse firms in the continuing advancement of their individual practices (PW Facts & Figures 1993-4). The organisation of the World Firm is illustrated in Figure 9.4. In addition to the elements outlined, there are a number of World Firm advisory groups and panels covering matters such as: continuing education and human resources; the development of worldwide tax; management consulting and insolvency services; technical standards; audit research and methods; and, quality control. There has been an international organisation coordinating activities since 1945.

Since the mid 1980s there has been an increasing emphasis on the development on a regional basis of the practices in the Americas, Asia/Pacific, and Europe/Africa. For example, in October 1987 (Annual Review 1987-88, p.1) the partners in the UK and in Continental Europe approved, by an overwhelming vote, proposals for a combination of the UK and Continental European Firms. Although legal and professional requirements preclude any question of a merger of the separate firms or the creation of a single firm, the relationship is like that of the members of the group of companies, with a Dutch BV company carrying out a coordinating function similar to that of a group holding company. The aim of the combination being to set and follow common policies and objectives, to share expertise, much of which is highly specialised, and to fund joint investment programmes. The extension of this cooperation in the form of the European Firm was motivated by the need for greater integration in order to seize the opportunities presented by the formation of the Single European Market in 1992.

The various regional and international arrangements have a common overriding aim, that is, to strengthen the cohesiveness and worldwide availability of Price Waterhouse services of the highest quality to both multinational and national clients. The changes in the structure of Price Waterhouse have largely been determined by client needs. As clients require an integrated service throughout

214

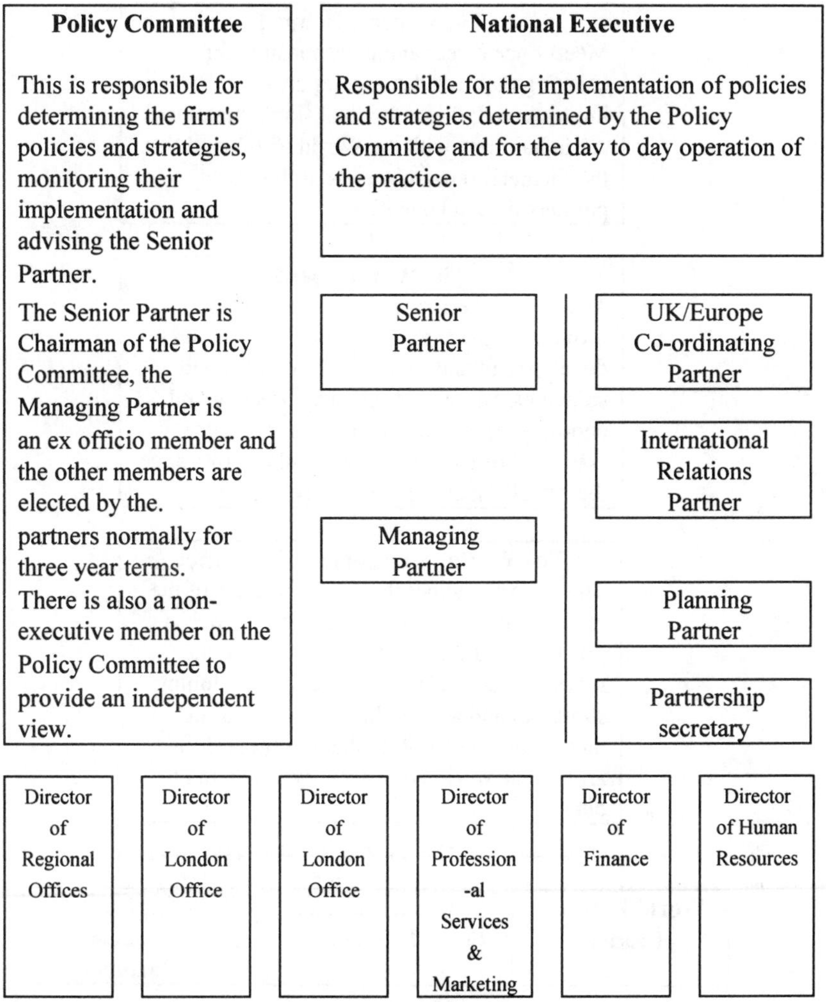

Policy Committee	National Executive	
This is responsible for determining the firm's policies and strategies, monitoring their implementation and advising the Senior Partner.	Responsible for the implementation of policies and strategies determined by the Policy Committee and for the day to day operation of the practice.	
The Senior Partner is Chairman of the Policy Committee, the Managing Partner is an ex officio member and the other members are elected by the. partners normally for three year terms.	Senior Partner	UK/Europe Co-ordinating Partner
		International Relations Partner
	Managing Partner	
There is also a non-executive member on the Policy Committee to provide an independent view.		Planning Partner
		Partnership secretary

Director of Regional Offices	Director of London Office	Director of London Office	Director of Profession-al Services & Marketing	Director of Finance	Director of Human Resources

Source: Adapted from Price Waterhouse 1986-7 Annual Review.

Figure 9.3 Price Waterhouse UK national structure

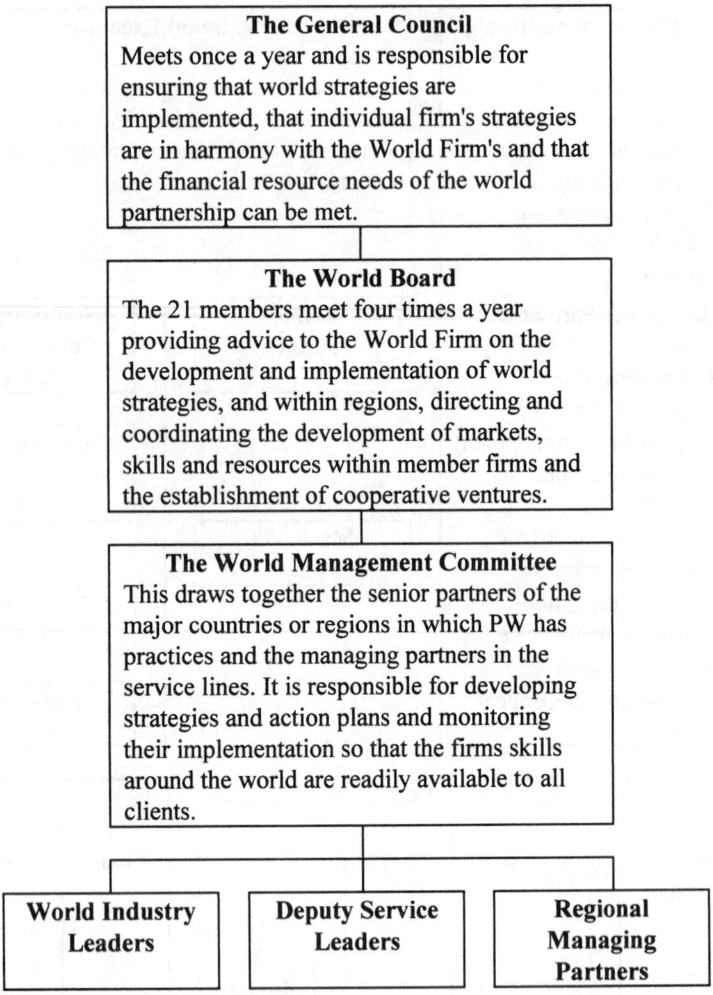

```
┌─────────────────────────────────────────────┐
│              The General Council              │
│  Meets once a year and is responsible for     │
│  ensuring that world strategies are           │
│  implemented, that individual firm's strategies│
│  are in harmony with the World Firm's and that │
│  the financial resource needs of the world     │
│  partnership can be met.                       │
└─────────────────────────────────────────────┘
┌─────────────────────────────────────────────┐
│                The World Board                 │
│  The 21 members meet four times a year         │
│  providing advice to the World Firm on the     │
│  development and implementation of world       │
│  strategies, and within regions, directing and │
│  coordinating the development of markets,       │
│  skills and resources within member firms and  │
│  the establishment of cooperative ventures.    │
└─────────────────────────────────────────────┘
┌─────────────────────────────────────────────┐
│         The World Management Committee          │
│  This draws together the senior partners of the │
│  major countries or regions in which PW has     │
│  practices and the managing partners in the     │
│  service lines. It is responsible for developing│
│  strategies and action plans and monitoring     │
│  their implementation so that the firms skills  │
│  around the world are readily available to all  │
│  clients.                                       │
└─────────────────────────────────────────────┘
```

World Industry Leaders	Deputy Service Leaders	Regional Managing Partners

Source: Compiled from Price Waterhouse Annual Reviews (1985- 6 & 1987-8).

Figure 9.4 The worldwide Price Waterhouse organisation

Europe, Price Waterhouse has pursued a policy of greater integration within Europe. Indeed, increasingly firms are looking for global service providers and in response Price Waterhouse is pursuing global integration within its own organisation. For example in his initial address when becoming Chairman of the World Firm in September 1988 (Annual review 1987-8, p.24), Joseph Connor explained Price Waterhouse's worldwide strategy as follows:

> Our overriding objective is to ensure that no matter what office around the world our clients may visit or call upon, they will have immediate access to the collective expertise, experience and technology of the Price Waterhouse organisation. That goes for all clients - local businesses, national companies, multinational companies, international joint ventures and partnerships, clients with industry-specific requirements, and the public sector.

The desire to service clients to the highest standard has been a fundamental factor motivating the international expansion of Price Waterhouse:

> Throughout its entire 144 year history, PW's guiding principle has been to provide outstanding service to clients - whatever their industry, their size, or their location. This client service philosophy is practised by individual PW firms and supported through world-level initiatives (PW Facts & Figures 1992-3, p.3).

There is no doubt that a driving force behind global integration has been the needs of Price Waterhouse's multinational clients, it can then be seen as a demand driven strategy. The World Firm promotes business relationships with global clients, including offering a world Transfer Pricing Service.

Given that the member firms of Price Waterhouse Worldwide are all separate autonomous firms, the question arises as to what form does internationalisation and integration take? The essential elements of membership of the Price Waterhouse World Firm are interdependence, mutual support, a sharing of policies and objectives and a close cooperation in the conduct of professional business through the integration of services to clients. These various elements are achieved through a variety of means. Initiatives which aim to integrate activities at an international and regional level include standard methodological approaches to various types of work. The Audit Guidance Service, for example, was introduced in the 1987-8 audit season and is designed to ensure consistency of approach and the highest quality of audit work by Price Waterhouse offices throughout the world. Also, there is the System Management Methodology, an approach developed for undertaking all types of IT consultancy work, which is used to market IT services by demonstrating a structured approach to systems development work, and to ensure that work is conducted to a consistently high standard.

217

Other initiatives developed by the World Firm include the establishment in the period 1985-6 in California's Silicon Valley of the Price Waterhouse Technology Centre to monitor developments in IT and provide information on technology issues important to Price Waterhouse firms and their clients. Price Waterhouse is committed to using technology to increase efficiency, effectiveness and quality. Technology is certainly important in terms of enabling the sharing of knowledge through, for example, joint data bases. The use of technology is also of importance in terms of enabling the firm to operate consistently on an international scale.

The World Firm has initiated a major effort to promote the development of industry specific skills and services throughout the world. Territorially the World Firm has given a high priority to the development of the practices in Japan and Germany in recent years. Increasingly attention is being given to East European countries and South East Asia, in particular China.

Price Waterhouse invests in the development of new methodologies and other initiatives designed to ensure that they remain responsive to the competitive pressures upon them, and sensitive to the stringent demands stemming from new legislation. It is in this way that Price Waterhouse aims to provide a differentiated audit service together with an increasingly wide range of skills which address the needs of all their clients. A recent methodological development has resulted in the pilot testing of the 'Audit of the Future'.

A standard methodology is one source of integration, another important element relates to the role of staff. Firstly, in the sense that it is they who use the standard methodologies, and secondly, in the sense that they are able to share their expertise and skills on a global basis through secondments to other national firms. The World Firm plays an important role in coordinating the many exchanges of partners and staff between national firms. Such exchanges are important to widen staff experience and increase their ability to serve international clients. Staff are also seconded into industry and the public sector where they are able to gain insight into the operations of clients thereby enabling them to better understand the needs of such clients and others.

Staff play a crucial role in determining the cost and efficiency of the service provided since, for example, over half of the UK firm's outgoings are accounted for by staff salaries and benefits (Annual Review 1985-6). As a result Price Waterhouse puts great emphasis on the need to recruit, develop and retain the very best people. There is, for example, a unified training programme for the staff in Audit and Business Advisory Services (ABS) throughout Europe. In 1990 Price Waterhouse declared it intention to invest in a new Management Development Centre for the European Firm where staff will not only develop their skills but will also meet colleagues from all parts of the firm. It is hoped that this will promote the transfer of knowledge and technology and reinforce common business values enhancing synergy. It is through training programmes and the exchange of staff between firms that it is possible to achieve and maintain the high standard of quality, efficiency and effectiveness on a global basis.

Having explored the international structure of the firm and how policies and strategies are unified globally it is now worth exploring the way in which Price Waterhouse extends its international coverage. Unlike other top accountancy firms, such as Ernst Young and KPMG, it has not been involved in any major worldwide mergers - nor the resulting problems of merging different cultures. Price Waterhouse has entered into discussions with other major firms, for example with Deloitte Haskins & Sells in 1984 and with Arthur Andersen Worldwide in the period 1988-9. Such discussions explored the advantages to clients and staff but on both occasions they were terminated.

Price Waterhouse has developed both nationally and internationally through a strategy of investing for organic growth, supplemented where appropriate by strategic mergers to build up strength in certain key territories. For example, in the period 1989-90 Price Waterhouse merged with Seier Petersen in Denmark, whilst in the period 1988-9 it merged with Befec, a leading French accounting firm, thereby creating the largest auditing practice in France and making the Paris office the third largest in the world after London and New York. In the same period Price Waterhouse merged with Revisuisse in Switzerland and acquired Plant Location International, which specialises in feasibility and location studies in Belgium. Scandinavian operations were strengthened by a merger in Denmark with management consultants IKO Gruppen AS; a cooperation agreement with Kihlman Oy and the acquisition of the tax consultancy of Pallonen and Salonen in Finland; and the merger with the audit and tax practice of Ollen Falths in Sweden. In the UK Price Waterhouse acquired CASCO; a specialist property consultancy. As a result of this activity Price Waterhouse greatly improved its position in these countries and strengthened the overall European Network.

Additionally, Price Waterhouse is extending into new territories through the setting up of new offices with a nucleus of partners and staff drawn from elsewhere in their practices. The first task being to recruit the best national people available and then to train them to Price Waterhouse standards, to guarantee the firm's long term capabilities to provide high quality services. This type of strategy is currently visible in the expansion into Eastern Europe. By 1990 offices had been established in Budapest, Berlin, Moscow, Prague and Warsaw (Annual Review 1989-90). Price Waterhouse aims to maintain 100 per cent ownership of such operations so that clients are assured of receiving the consistently high standard of professional advice and support associated with the firm everywhere in the world.

The development of Price Waterhouse has increasingly become associated with mergers as the pace of globalisation advances. However, in markets such as Eastern Europe and parts of South East Asia, where there is less likelihood of finding a suitable firm to merge with, setting up from scratch remains the prevalent strategy.

Price Waterhouse uses its name throughout the world providing a signal to clients and potential clients of the quality they can expect to receive from its firms. Even in Japan, where other top firms are known by their local name, Price Waterhouse is known as 'Price Waterhouse Japan'. The firm's name can be regarded as an asset shared by the member firms. The World Firm might be viewed as a means of internalising this brand name, together with other intangible assets such as standardised methodologies and training. The World Firm is able to police the use of such intangible assets. The Price Waterhouse name is synonymous with quality. It is only through control by the World Firm that such quality can be maintained across all international activities.

Further to being internationalised, Price Waterhouse like all of the top accountancy firms is diversified having three main areas of activity: audit and business services; tax consultancy; and, management consultancy. These areas accounted for approximately 50 per cent, 24 per cent and 19 per cent respectively of worldwide fee income in 1993 (PW Facts & Figures 1992-3). Diversification has been motivated by the search for growth together with the desire to cater for client needs.

Regulation influences the structure of the Price Waterhouse firm in the sense that some national firms have limitations set upon their areas of activity. Also, where only locally qualified accountants are permitted to practise then the expansion strategy of sending a nucleus of partners to a country is not feasible. In some respects then regulation may be responsible for some of the merger activity.

It is clear that the strongest motive for internationalisation has been to satisfy client needs. As clients become increasingly global then their accounting requirements also become global in dimension. In order to adequately service clients Price Waterhouse must have a globally integrated network, without which it would lose clients to other large firms which have such a facility. For Price Waterhouse then the choice was continued global expansion, and indeed quicken the pace, or risk losing clients. With this line of reasoning it is clear that the level of global coverage is of vital importance to Price Waterhouse's competitive position. The rate at which the firm has been expanding internationally can be seen from Table 9.1.

BDO Binder Hamlyn

The origins of BDO Binder Hamlyn in the UK can be found in the establishment of Binder, Hamlyn & Co in 1918 (Accountancy, Feb. 1989). The firm in its present form is the result of a number of mergers through the years, including the formation in 1963 of a loosely knit international group called Binder Seidman International known as BSI. This was the first post war exposure to international work. Between the wars the UK firm had offices in Berlin, Prague and Vienna, but none of these reopened after the war. The original members of BSI were Binder Hamlyn in the UK, Seidman and Seidman in the US, Deutsche Warentreuland in Germany, and other leading firms in Canada, Holland and Belgium. These were later joined by firms in Denmark, France, Italy, Norway and Switzerland (Shirley-Bevan, 1979, p.26).

Table 9.1
Price Waterhouse worldwide network locations 1985 -1993

Year	Number of countries	Number of offices
1985	94	359
1986	99	381
1987	100	400
1988	100	412
1989	103	420
1990	111	451
1991	110	458
1992	113	453
1993	117	448

Source: PW Worldwide Facts & Figures 1992-3 p.11, and; Price Waterhouse
Annual Reviews various issues 1984-90.

Between 1963 and 1971 BSI fulfilled its limited defensive purpose. There was
very little referred work except between the US and Canada. In 1971 domestic
developments, in particular, merger activity, overrode international alliances, as a
result a number of firms left the Group. It became clear that the loosely knit
structure of BSI had become inappropriate in the changed environment.
Consequently, in 1973 Binder Dijker Otte (BDO) an international group of
accounting firms, was formed, consisting of Binder Hamlyn, UK; Dijker en
Doornbos, Netherlands and Belgium; and Deutsche Warentreuland, Germany,
whose managing partner was Hans Heinrich Otte (Accountancy, Feb. 1989).
In 1979 Michael Shirley-Bevan, managing partner of Binder Hamlyn described
BDO as follows (1979, pp.26-7):

> It is a truly European partnership of 12 partners, being four partners
> from each founder firm acting as nominees for their remaining
> domestic partners. Because as yet there is no such thing as an EEC
> partnership, the mechanics have been to form identical partnerships
> of the same four partners from each firm in London, Amsterdam and
> Hamburg. In each of the three countries BDO is authorised to sign
> accounts under the same rules as apply to the domestic partner firms.
> In other countries where we have formed BDO firms in association
> with local partners, those firms are normally only used for referred
> work and the name is controlled by the founder partner firms.

221

Each of the three partner firms shares equally in the cost of substantial development expenditure in opening new offices, technical standards, review, and so on, but make their own profits or losses on referred work. There is no head office of BDO ..... Our present philosophy is that the management committee and the technical standards committee consist of the managing partners and senior partners in the domestic firms and they get on with the job.

With its origins in Western Europe and the early links with North America, BDO has now clearly established itself as one of the leading international accounting organisations on the world stage. In 1991 total worldwide fee income amounted to US $1,080 million, in this year there were 445 office in 63 countries with a total staff of 15,772 of which 1,723 were partners (Annual Report, 1991, p.18). By 1993 BDO Binder had more than 480 offices in 65 countries, and cross-border work both into and out of the UK continued to grow (Annual Review, 1993, p.3). Europe generates just over 50 per cent of the total combined fees of the international network (Annual Report, 1991).

The international organisation is referred to as a 'network' rather than a 'firm'. Each national firm retains its own identity, so for example, in the UK the firm was until 1994 BDO Binder Hamlyn, in the US it is BDO Seidman and in the Netherlands BDO Camps Obers. There are a number of reasons for the retention of national names. Firstly, there is the familiarity of the name in local markets, and secondly, and more importantly the fact that many of the firms have long histories and well established reputations in their domestic markets and are unwilling to forego such an important trade mark in return for one which is relatively youthful and less well known in the domestic market. There is also the fact that firms join and leave the network according to their own requirements, thus it is essential for them to retain a separate domestic identity, for example, BDO Reads joined in 1990 in Guernsey, in place of the previous member firm Carnaby's. BDO Reads was previously a member of Spicer & Oppenheim and is the leading firm in Guernsey (Annual Review, 1991).

The main advantage of membership of the international network is the international coverage which it provides. National firms are able to refer clients to overseas firms secure in the knowledge that they will be offered a high quality service. National firms also benefit from receiving referrals from other national firms and, in addition, national firms attract more domestic business because of their international capacity.

All overseas offices are fundamentally indigenous to the country in which they are located. They are staffed with local people with knowledge of their country's laws and business customs and with a network of useful contacts in the business and professional communities. Consistency in standards and working methods is vital to clients. Every office uses common manuals and parallel methods of approach and presentation. Client service teams are made up of national professional staff,

222

supported as necessary by colleagues on secondment from offices abroad. Partners and staff regularly attend international training courses to keep abreast of worldwide developments (Binder Hamlyn Chartered Accountants, p. 15).

In 1993 BDO Binder Hamlyn had 2,228 staff including partners working from 24 offices located throughout the UK with an annual fee income of £108.5 million (Annual Review, 1993). The UK firm is focused on four groups of clients, that is, on four distinct markets: business; not for profit organisations; private clients; and, the public sector. Private clients form a significant market for the UK firm, accounting for nearly 15 per cent of fee income. Figure 9.5 shows the organisational structure of the UK firm in 1991, it can be seen that a range of services are offered.

The UK firm enjoys positive benefits from membership of BDO. The reassurance of having its clients affairs secured overseas is important but also significant are referrals which contributed £3.6 million to UK fee income in 1988 (Annual Review, 1989). The international firm is an essential support to the corporate practice and to the reputation of the UK firm. Because of BDO's relative strength and credibility, the UK firm has been able to retain its larger clients who have been well served by the worldwide network (Annual Review, 1989).

The international organisation is illustrated in Figure 9.6. The BDO committees are supported by task forces covering training, marketing and the Single European Market. (Annual Report, 1991, p.8). At the beginning of 1991 the International Business Committee was established. Its primary purpose is to focus on the development and delivery of BDO services round the world, not from BDO's perspective, but from the perspective of their international clients (Annual Report, 1991, p.8).

It is claimed in BDO Binder's 1991 Annual Report (back of front cover) that:

> Its special skills lie in applying local knowledge, experience and grasp of the international context to provide an integrated global service. In BDO, common operating and quality procedures are not a constraint on innovation and independence of thought but the starting point. It is a vigorous organisation committed to total service.

BDO's reputation derives from consistently offering fast, imaginative and objective advice. BDO takes pride in its clients' success and its relationship with them. It is a personal relationship which combines the benefits of professional knowledge, integrity and an entrepreneurial approach, with an understanding of a client's business and an ability to communicate. This ensures the highest quality objective professional service tailored to meet the individual needs of all clients whether they be governments, MNEs, national businesses or private individuals.

BDO consolidated its international client base in 1991. The volume of international work referred around the network continued to grow at a level of 13 per cent in that year (Annual Report, 1991). In this period the network was

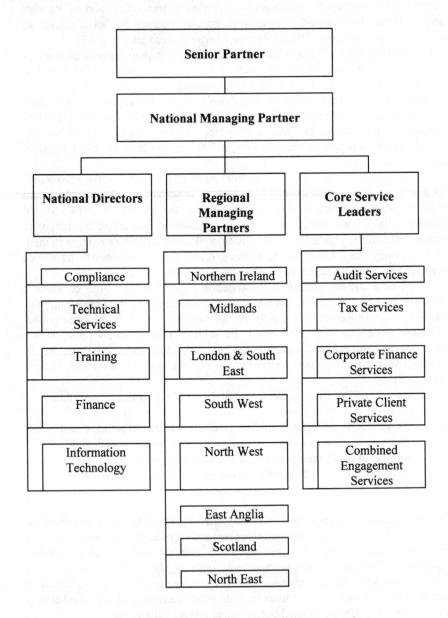

Source: Adapted from BDO Binder Hamlyn Annual Review 1991 p.16.

Figure 9.5 BDO Binder Hamlyn national structure

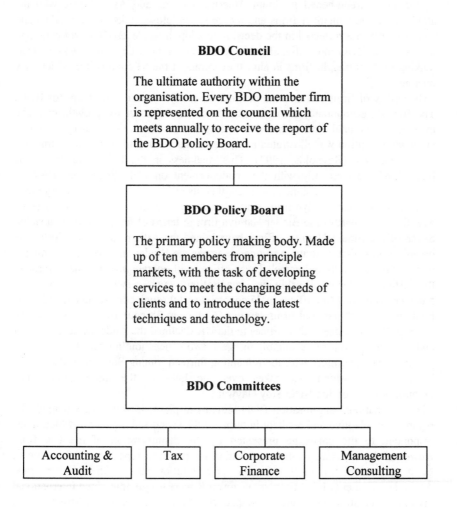

BDO Council

The ultimate authority within the organisation. Every BDO member firm is represented on the council which meets annually to receive the report of the BDO Policy Board.

BDO Policy Board

The primary policy making body. Made up of ten members from principle markets, with the task of developing services to meet the changing needs of clients and to introduce the latest techniques and technology.

BDO Committees

| Accounting & Audit | Tax | Corporate Finance | Management Consulting |

Source: Compiled from Annual Report 1991 BDO Binder p.8 & p.19, Annual Review 1992.

Figure 9.6 BDO international organisation

significantly strengthened in South America, Canada and Asia Pacific with the admission of new member firms and mergers. The closer links between BDO and member firms are reflected in the decision to adopt a single 'BDO' worldwide logo in 1994. The BDO international network is firmly established with member firms ranking in the top eight firms in almost everyone of the 63 countries in which they operate.

The ability of firms to leave the network so easily is a major problem for BDO. The Big Six accountancy firms, constantly on the look out for growth, can take over just a national firm rather that attempting an international merger. BDO's vulnerable position was illustrated a few years ago when Dijker, a Dutch firm, left to join Deloitte (Reynolds, 1993). This weakness in the federal structure was highlighted most recently with the announcement on 26th. September 1994 by Arthur Andersen that, in a move to strengthen its UK position, it was to merge with parts of the Binder Hamlyn firm. Since then Arthur Andersen has effectively taken over the major part of the Binder Hamlyn firm in terms of fee generating capacity. Seven of the Binder Hamlyn offices have joined the Arthur Andersen Worldwide organisation whilst continuing to operate under the Binder Hamlyn name which is to be retained as a 'brand name'. These offices will operate internationally through the Arthur Andersen Worldwide organisation which services clients through member firms with 360 offices in 75 countries and through correspondent and other relationships with national firms serving 46 cities in 38 countries (Binder Hamlyn 1995, p.20). Seventeen other offices in the UK declined the Andersen merger offer and have sought out more suitable mergers, two offices joining Touche Ross, two joining Grant Thornton, with the remaining thirteen joining Stoy Hayward (Kelly, 27.9.94, p.12) which also takes over the links to the international BDO organisation, becoming BDO Stoy Hayward.

The international organisation BDO remains in place, in some ways it might be regarded as adaptive and resilient in terms of the speed and manner in which it has responded to the challenge presented by the disintegration of the UK firm. However, the structure of the organisation is open to a repetition of this type of event. A fact which reduces the scope for integration between the member firms. As the larger international firms move towards increasingly integrated international organisational structures there is a danger that firms within a federal structure will lag behind in this area, and of course, they will increasingly become targets for the larger firms looking to take over the most attractive firms within such networks.

Multinational structures and strategies among accountancy firms

The accountancy firms examined above illustrate the two main alternative international organisational structures: the international name or world firm; and the federal or network structure. Despite the differences which exist between these two structures there are many similarities.

226

For both firms studied the strategy of internationalisation has been influenced by client needs and competitive pressures, however the structure that this has brought about varies according to the timing of internationalisation. In terms of the ownership structures of the two accountancy firms examined here, they are the same. Ownership remains in the hands of the partners of individual firms within the group. So given that there is no central ownership how are these groups held together? Self interest is an important element, each individual firm benefits from its association with the group. This benefit results from the ability to offer international services, and, particularly in the international name structure, the brand image created and maintained by the group. Both firms have international boards which are responsible for the development of group wide strategies, although for Price Waterhouse the international organisation is more complex reflecting the greater cohesion and age of the international organisation.

The accountancy firm's brand image is an intangible asset which requires protection. This gives rise to a number of initiatives designed to harmonise and enhance the quality of service provision. These include training programmes, and common methodological approaches embodied in, for example, audit manuals used worldwide. This type of activity is visible in both the cases of Price Waterhouse and BDO, however, it is clear that such initiatives are more highly developed in the case of the former.

For the federal structure the need to develop an international image is vital and can be seen in the case of BDO with the recent adoption of the 'BDO' logo. This desire to establish a united name among the federal style groups is also important because with national firms retaining their own names it is very easy for them to leave the group. The federal structure is therefore vulnerable to approaches from the larger firms which may simply wish to select the more attractive parts of the group for a merger, as the recent Arthur Andersen merger with parts of the Binder Hamlyn firm so clearly illustrates.

Internationalisation occurs primarily through the establishment of a presence in an overseas market. However, for both firms staff may join another national firm on secondment for a year or so, with the aim of broadening their experience. Such practices are common among the top accountancy firms (Beaverstock, 1990, 1991). Also staff may work overseas on the development of particular projects, for example, setting up a presence in East European countries. Internationalisation through the movement of personnel, however, would appear to be small, though important in terms of increasing the cohesiveness of the whole firm, spreading best practice, and stimulating synergy.

Both firms are keen to take advantage of new technological developments as a means of improving service quality and efficiency of provision. Price Waterhouse is by nature of its size more able to invest in this area.

Regulation of the sector has influenced the way in which the firms have developed. Both Price Waterhouse and BDO offer a range of services, a strategy founded on client needs and the search for growth and cross referrals. However, in some countries regulation restricts the activities of accountancy firms to auditing (e.g. France). Furthermore, the requirement that accountants hold local qualifications is common and may therefore necessitate the presence of indigenous people in a local partnership (Chapter 6).

Finally, both firms examined look set to continue their international expansion. It is clear that they are not always able to expand in their preferred manner and as a result both firms make use of a variety of different types of overseas presences including the correspondent firms: local firms which act on behalf of other accountancy firms but which remain independent from a group.

9.4 Computer service firms

A variety of multinational organisational structures are apparent in the computer services sector. Many companies are the subsidiaries of a holding group whose main activity is in a different sector. This, as noted in Chapter 6, is a results of a number of computer service firms deriving from the externalisation of computer service departments. In addition, firms in other sectors, in particular computer hardware, telecommunications and accountancy sectors have set up computer service firms in order to benefit from the relatively high levels of growth in the sector. Many different company types exist from the sole proprietor and partnership through to the public limited company and the wholly owned subsidiaries. US and Japanese ownership is dominant among the larger firms in the international market.

The companies selected for study here are Sema Group Plc. and Logica Plc., the reason for their selection has largely been determined by their nationality, Logica being a UK based firm whilst the Sema Group results from the merger of a UK and French company and regards itself very much as a European firm. Although there are other UK firms to choose from the need to examine firms with an international network did give rise to a somewhat limited choice.

Sema Group Plc.

Sema Group originates from the merger in June 1988 of the UK's CAP Group Plc. with Sema Metra of France. The original UK company, CAP, was founded in 1962 and became a public company in July 1985. In 1986 it acquired Yarrow Plc., in 1987 the business services of LRT, Data Networks Plc. and Baddeley Associates, and in 1988 Principia Mechanica (CSA, 1989). The merger with Sema Metra in 1988 saw the creation of a pan-European Group of some 6,500 employees with a turnover exceeding £250 million. Sema Group is a European company listed in both the London and Paris Stock Exchanges. In its 1993 Annual Report it describes itself as follows:

228

Sema Group is an Information Technology company with 8,200 employees in 60 European and Far East locations and a turnover in excess of £500 million. The main trades of Sema Group are systems integration including consulting, outsourcing and products. Our main clients operate in the fields of Defence, Energy, Banking, Transport, Industry, Telecommunications and Government (Annual Report, 1993, p.2).

Sema Group has three intrinsically linked business areas: systems integration, which in 1993 represented 73 per cent of its turnover and includes a strong element of consulting (12 per cent); facilities management, which is the management of all or part of a client's information systems, accounting for 20 per cent of turnover; and, standard software products, which can be used as a basis for bespoke solutions, accounting for 7 per cent of turnover in 1993 (Annual Report, 1993, p.8). Since 1988 Sema Group has focused its activities upon these three areas, disposing of its market research company, Sofres, in January 1992 (Annual Report, 1992). Moreover, there has been a significant growth in the importance of facilities management services with turnover generated from this area rising from 5 per cent in 1988 to 20 per cent by 1993 (Annual Report, 1988, 1993). The firm is not diversifies beyond the IT sector, however, clients are attracted from a variety of sectors, Table 9.2 shows a breakdown of turnover by market sector, revealing a particular strength in the defence market.

Sema Group was ranked 5th. among the top UK computer service suppliers in 1994 (Table 6.6). Although it does not feature among the top 10 international computer service firms (Table 6.7), on a European basis it is a major company being ranked 2nd. by turnover in 1991 (European Commission, 1994). The focus on the European market is an important element in Sema Group's business strategy:

> The formation of Sema Group was based on a clear vision of the type of technology company which would best meet the needs of the European market: based on strong geographical presence, regional centres of excellence, and a cooperative approach to customers and markets (Annual Report, 1990, p.5).

Although focused on Europe, Sema Group has proved itself capable of managing major international projects, and where necessary will team up with top quality partners and sub contractors.

The Group has successfully strengthened its position in Europe, for example in 1989 it acquired ADV/Orga AG in Germany, and in 1993 it acquired a 1,200 strong operation in Sweden. In 1993 99 per cent of turnover derived from Europe, the remaining 1 per cent came from South East Asia. The UK was the major source of turnover accounting for 42 per cent, with France accounting for 34 per cent,

Table 9.2
Turnover by market sector: Sema Group Plc. and Logica Plc.

Sector	Sema Group Plc. Percentage of turnover (1993)	Logica Plc. Percentage of turnover (1994)
Industry	10	7
Government & Public sector	12	12
Telecoms	5	10
Banking & finance	14	32
Energy & utilities	17	10
Commerce & services	6	-
Transport	10	9
Computing & Electronics	-	6
Space	-	5
Defence	26	9

Source: Compiled from Sema Group Annual Report 1993, p.9, and Logica Plc. Annual Report, 1994 p.2.

Germany 8 per cent, Spain 5 per cent, Benelux 5 per cent, and Sweden 5 per cent (Annual Report, 1993).

In the UK, Sema Group and BAeSEMA (a company jointly owned by Sema Group and British Aerospace) together employ 3,200 people and offer the complete range of services to all sectors of business and government. The UK is the centre of the Group's facilities management activities, and one of the Group's main strengths in the UK is its well established regional presence, with more than 20 regional offices (Annual Report, 1993).

In France, Sema Group's 2,000 staff specialise in consulting and systems integration for business and technical systems. The joint ventures TIBET and Sema Group Telecom specialise in stock exchange systems and civil telecommunications respectively. Sema Group's businesses in Sweden, acquired in October 1993, have a total of 1,200 staff, DAFA specialises in facilities management and marketing of on line information, whilst Sema Group Konsult covers consultancy and systems integration. In Spain, Sema Group is one of the country's leading software service companies with 700 staff concentrating mainly on the financial, commercial, telecoms and public sectors. In Germany, the group employs 400 staff mainly servicing the industrial and defence markets and a successful facilities management business was launched in 1993. The Group's 400 strong team in Benelux concentrates on three areas: management consultancy, systems integration and software products. The activities in South East Asia are developing from the bases of Singapore and Malaysia (Annual Report, 1993, p.9).

To serve increasingly global clients Sema Group recognises the need to attain critical mass through judicious growth both organic and acquisitive, and by partnerships with others. Sema Group's strategy for growth is to move into markets which have a logical connection with its existing base. The Group also forms alliances which strengthen its offerings to customers, teaming with 'best class partners'. Partnerships are also formed with customers, these involve the pooling of expertise to jointly develop kernel software, for example, as with Credit Agricole, or establishing a business to support clients wherever they require services, for example, the creation of the facilities management joint venture in South Africa to support BP (Annual Report, 1993, p.11).

Although Sema Group remains independent from hardware manufacturers, it does have working relationships with them, and has established strategic initiatives with a number including Bull, Digital, Hewlett-Packard, IBM and Sun. For example in 1992 Sema Group joined forces with IBM to pursue the development and marketing of its I-Linie product (Annual Report, 1992, p.7).

Sema Group's expertise in methodologies and tools developed over a number of years underpins its success. The Group's Common Technological Platforms, developed by the central R&D team, bring together best practice and experience from a large number of major technical and business software projects. Such expertise can be regarded as a firm specific advantage.

Great emphasis is placed on the quality of staff, and Sema Group provides various training programmes which are seen as a force for synergy and a means of disseminating the Group's quality policy. A Group wide training strategy brings together participants from all corners of the organisation on the same course. Staff are regarded as a major asset, and Sema Group seeks to recruit and develop expertise of the highest calibre. It is claimed that quality has established Sema Group as a European leader, and it is quality which will continue to reap dividends in the years ahead.

The Sema Group is also strongly committed to R&D, undertaking a wide variety of projects, mainly devoted to application packages, methods and tools, frequently in cooperation with other companies or with universities. Total expenditure on projects that were internally funded in 1993 was £14.6 million up from £ 13.2 million in 1992 (Annual Report, 1993, p.48). Research is also carried out in participation with other European industrial and software companies on major cooperative R&D projects. Involvement in such projects is essential as they deal with technological and economic developments of the future. In many instances Sema Group acts as a consortium leader, and is involved in projects such as Euro Method, Esprit II, Eureka Software Factory and Eureka Genelex (Annual Report, 1992, p.16).

Research and development together with the building of synergy are regarded to be crucial to the success of the Sema Group. The drive for synergy has led to the creation of a Transnational Strategic Business Unit devoted to telecommunications and bringing together all of the Group's activities in this area (Annual Report, 1992 p.7).

Sema Group's success depends on having an extremely sound technical base, combined with expertise in very diverse areas: consulting; software engineering; project management; and many other disciplines. The business strategy, focused on systems integration, and the formation of a number of well targeted alliances, has enabled the company to take full advantage of the changing market place.

The Group's firm specific assets are its staff, quality, expert methodological tools, and ability to be locationally close to clients. Such assets are largely intangible and difficult to protect giving rise to the need to internalise them. Sema Group would appear to be internalising such assets given the wholly owned nature of most of the company's overseas presences. The firm is loosely organised on a holding group basis, with policies from the centre concerning business strategy, quality, training and synergy. The organisational structure is shown in Figure 9.7, it can be seen that the firm is largely split into its French and UK interests, a legacy from the 1988 merger between the French and UK companies.

Sema Group is a multinational service company, although it is regionally focused with a strong presence in Europe. It is independent from hardware companies and indeed form companies in other sectors. There are, however, a number of large shareholders which included in 1993 a 40.23 per cent holding by Financiere Sema SA (a company jointly owned by Compagnie Financiere de Paribas SA [50.1 per cent] and France Telecom [49.9 per cent]) and a 27.9 per cent holding by CAP Gemini Sogeti. Sema Group has grown both organically and through mergers and acquisitions and appears to be set to continue this strategy. It is also involved in alliances with other companies both in the same and other sectors. It claims to be focused on niche markets, and this would appear to be a sensible strategy if the firm wishes to remain independent. However, with a number of firms having large shareholdings in the company, the future of the Sema Group may hold a merger with, or takeover by, a larger group.

Logica Plc.

Logica Plc. is a holding company, with its group activities being in the field of information technology. The company was established in 1969 and by 1980 employed approximately 500 people in the UK and a further 250 overseas. By 1994 the company employed 2,131 staff in the UK with a further 1,285 employed overseas (687 in Continental Europe; 411 in North America; and 187 in Asia Pacific), of these 29 were employed in associated undertakings (Annual Report, 1994, p.24). The company was ranked 13th. in the UK among the top computer

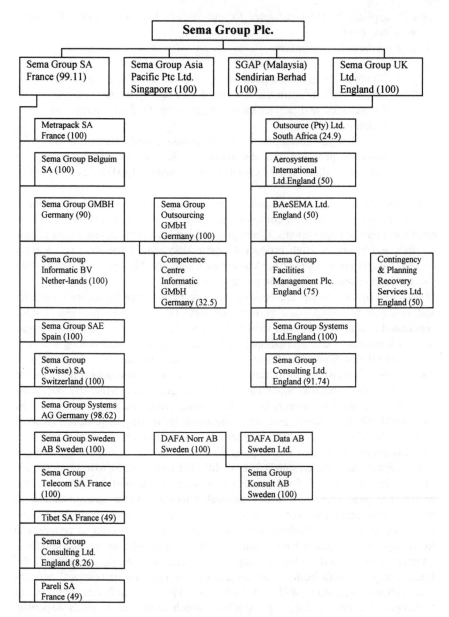

Figures in parenthesis are ownwership shares.
Source: Compiled from Sema Group's 1993 Annual Report.

Figure 9.7 Sema Group Plc. organisational structure

233

service suppliers in 1994 (Chapter 6) and 7th. in Europe in 1991 (European Commission, 1994).

Logica's principal activities are:

1　The marketing, design, production, integration and maintenance of custom built software and associated hardware systems.
2　Consultancy and project management in the field of information technology.
3　The design, development, implementation and marketing of software products and the re-usable elements of applications software, called systems kernels (Annual Report, 1994, p.22).

The company sees these three areas as reinforcing and interlinked, providing a source of strength. Technical consulting can lead to systems supply, and products often form part of total systems. Client projects can lead to the development of new services and products. Both product design and systems integration provide the first hand experience to strengthen consulting capability. Thus providing more than one service to clients is of great importance to Logica.

Many of Logica's clients are seeking strategic partnerships to ensure continuity and consistency in software systems support. For example, in 1990 Logica announced a joint venture with British Airways - Speedwing Logica, to capitalise on developments in the international air transport industry. Maintaining mutually beneficial relationships with clients is key to Logica's business development, as a result there is increased emphasis on developing account management initiatives at all levels of the company. Since its inception, Logica has consistently pursued a strategy of building an independent international group, both by establishing its own worldwide subsidiaries and, where desirable by making acquisitions (Annual Review, 1988, p.4). As well as internationalisation through the establishment of overseas presences, Logica also exports directly to foreign customers and engages in intra-firm trade between subsidiaries in different countries (Rowlands, 1993).

Logica has a clearly defined acquisition strategy to support its objectives, the principal targets being to broaden product offerings and to strengthen market position in selected geographical areas. This strategy was apparent in May 1994, when Logica acquired Precision Software Corporation, a provider of commercial loans systems to leading banks. This was the first significant acquisition for a number of years, and builds on Logica's strengths in banking and extends the breadth of Precision's business by the addition of Logica's international network and systems integration skills. In September 1994 the Software Division of Synercom Technology Inc. was acquired, which combines Logica's expertise, utility industry knowledge and international network with Synercom's advanced client/servicer systems for work management in utilities. In the Netherlands, Logica BV purchased Fray Data International, further strengthening that subsidiary. This

234

acquisition strategy based on strengthening international lines of business is to continue over the next few years (Annual Report, 1994).

In Italy, as part of a strategy to focus the business and improve its profitability, the associate company disposed of its activities in the health care sector. Elsewhere Logica has been active in extending its business, firstly, in Eastern Europe, and secondly, in the Middle East where a representative office was opened in September 1994 in Dubai (Annual Report, 1994). Thus the company has been concentrating on its core activities whilst extending its international coverage.

In the UK Logica appears to be organised along market activities (Figure 9.8) with the exception of Logica Cambridge Ltd. which is concerned with R&D and therefore relevant throughout the Groups activities. The break down of Logica's market by sector for 1994 is given in Table 9.2, it can be seen that work in the financial sector accounts for the largest share.

Between 1993 and 1994 Logica underwent a period of restructuring with new management and organisational structures being put in place together with a more focused approach to developing the business internationally. The aim being to improve profitability and to lay the foundations for a substantial increase in the revenue growth rate. Logica has been building on the existing strengths of the company. Establishing key corporate goals to maintain a clear sense of direction and purpose:

1 For our shareholders - to deliver superior financial performance in terms of growth in earnings per share and return on capital employed.
2 For our clients - to be an international leader in the provision of IT consultancy, systems integration, software and support to solve our customers' business challenges in our chosen markets.
3 For our staff - achievement of our customer and shareholder objectives both requires and enables us to employ and reward the best people in our industry and offer significant opportunities for career development. (Annual Report, 1994, p.4).

Logica has been focusing on core businesses, paying attention to detail and applying strong operational management. To provide the structure for growth administrative lines have been streamlined and operations restructured into three clearly delineated regions working to integrate worldwide strategies. In the UK management has been delayered and a divisional structure has been introduced instead of subsidiaries.

Some business such as government, defence and transport, remain primarily national businesses, whilst others offer the opportunity to leverage the international network. Logica has established international lines of business, focusing on markets (finance, telecommunications, energy and utilities and space) where the company has proven strengths and where products and services successful in one market can

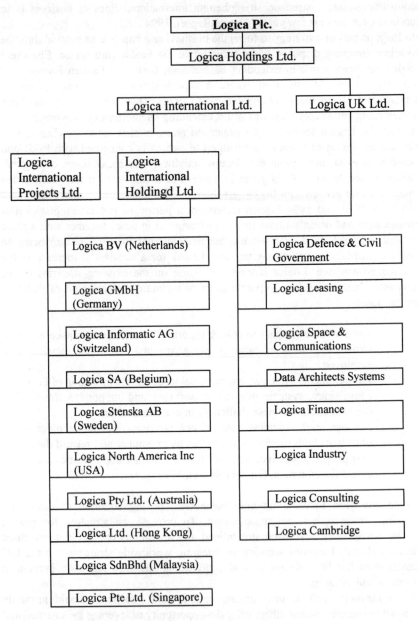

Source: Compiled from Logica Plc. Annual Reports.

Figure 9.8 Logica Plc. organisational structure

be sold throughout the network. International line of business managers have been appointed for these sectors. Their task is to determine strategy and global market position in their sector, build product and capability portfolios and ensure that the international network is able to sell and support solutions to customer's business needs. Furthermore, an international account manager was appointed in 1994 for Reuters Plc., which is served in five countries. Logica intends to appoint international account managers for other globally focused clients.

International coverage is seen by Logica to be an important factor differentiating them from other companies. In 1994 50 per cent of Logica's clients were located in the UK, with a further 27 per cent in Continental Europe, 13 per cent in North America and 10 per cent in Asia Pacific (Annual Report, 1994, p.3). The firm regards its international coverage as not only a market aid but also a real benefit to customers around the world. In 1992 the company claimed:

> Individual Logica companies, both small and large gain from the worldwide capability of the group. We get the right people in the right place at the right time, bringing scarce and specialised skills and expertise to our customers problems. Through the supply of our products and the people who develop and support them, we transfer industry specific technology between Logica's international operating companies (Annual Report, 1992, p.18).

Logica says that relationships with clients which are multinational often develop around the world, giving IBM as an example of such client relations.

Emphasis is put on Logica's ability to maintain client confidentiality, and where required it will practice exclusivity, that is, refrain from working with a client's competitor. There is also emphasis on the quality of staff with various training and recruitment policies aimed at obtaining and retaining quality people. In 1994 Logica continued to lead the field in quality by gaining corporate ISO9001 TICKIT quality registration for all the wholly owned businesses across Europe in addition to registration for the Hong Kong and Australian operations (Annual Report, 1994, p.5).

Logica is also involved in R&D, investing in new technology to secure increased benefits for customers and more effective delivery systems. In 1994 £5.7 million was spent on R&D compared to £4.6 million in 1993 (Annual Report, 1994, p.22).

The company highlighted a number of firm specific assets in 1992 (Annual Report, p.18):

> Our infrastructure includes our quality management system, our experienced team of commercial managers and the careful control of risk through ongoing review and scrutinising. Our tools include comprehensive on-line data bases for accessing staff skills. Other assets are product and kernels, often specialised to an industry or

237

application. These are trusted components which allow us to transfer experience cost effectively to new projects.

It would appear that the firm is able to gain economies of scale and/or scope in the use of such assets. The fact that Logica operates primarily through wholly owned subsidiaries may be interpreted as a reflection of the importance of internalising such intangible assets. There were only two associated undertakings in 1994, these being: firstly, Logicasiel SpA (Italy) which is owned 55 per cent by Data Management SpA and 45 per cent by Logica; and secondly, Speedwing Logica Limited (England) which is owned 51 per cent by British Airways and 49 per cent by Logica. In 1994 Logica also had partnership relationships with companies in Riyadh, Saudi Arabia, and Tokyo, Japan. In all Logica has 36 offices around the world, 6 in the UK, 12 in Continental Europe, 2 in the Middle East, 7 in Asia Pacific, and 9 in North America. Although Europe is the dominant source of activity at present, Logica is keen to extent its international coverage adding offices in New Zealand and the United Arab Emirates to its network in 1994 (Annual Report, 1994).

Further to the above mentioned assets Logica also regards its technical excellence and track record for reliability and performance to be formidable strengths. As well as its independence (Annual Report, 1994, p.8):

> Our independence ... makes us well placed to advise on the most appropriate combination of hardware, software, communications protocols and specialist applications to meet our client's needs. Few in our industry can make this claim.

With its largest shareholder having only a 3.75 per cent holding in 1994 and all of the shareholders with more than a 3 per cent interest being financial institutions, Logica's claim of independence is certainly legitimate. Whether Logica will be able to retain its independence in the future is questionable. However, it is clear that the strategy of expansion is designed to strengthen the present group without recourse to merger or falling prey to the acquisition strategies of the larger groups.

Multinational structures and strategies among computer service firms

The computer service firms considered above illustrate a number of important similarities. Both companies are organised on a holding group basis, and both are independent from larger corporate groups. This latter characteristic could be viewed as unusual within this sector which is dominated by firms which are a part of a much larger group in sectors such as electronics, computer hardware and telecommunications, among others.

Subsidiaries of the holding groups operate independently, although Logica has recently integrated its UK interests into a divisional structure, reflecting a move

238

towards a more highly integrated organisational design. As with most firms the organisational structures reflect the companies' histories, this is particularly the case for Sema Group where the structure is clearly divided between the UK and French interests reflecting it origins in the merger between the UK and French companies in 1988.

A range of services is offered by both companies, although these services are confined to the computer services sector, complementing one another and giving rise to cross referrals. Indeed, Sema Group has seen a consolidation of its activities in recent years, and Logica also has been focusing its activities on particular sectors.

Both companies are international in scope although Sema Group is centred on Europe with little business in the rest of the world. Logica has a wider international spread although it is smaller in terms of turnover when compared to Sema Group.

The two firms have expanded through organic growth, the setting up of new subsidiaries in overseas markets, and acquisition. Also, joint ventures and partnerships are used where appropriate, these may be established with clients, hardware manufacturers or other computer service firms. Both firms are experienced at working within international consortia set up for particular projects. Expansion occurs where it supports objectives, strengthens market position in selected geographical areas and broadens product offerings.

Great importance is place upon client needs, indeed Logica is active in developing client relations with account management initiatives. Logica is the more integrated of the two companies with a clear strategy of international integration, for example, it has established international lines of business. Sema Group in its own search for integration has developed the Transnational Strategic Business Unit in a quest for synergy in the area of telecommunications.

Both companies place great emphasis on the quality of their staff and training, together with the use of their own methodologies, processes and tools throughout the group. Ensuring a standardised high quality of service group wide is vital.

Research and development is important to both groups, being essential to the maintenance of competitiveness in this sector. High investment in this area may be one reason for the fact that most subsidiaries are wholly owned ensuring that intangible assets are internalised within the boundaries of the firm. Nevertheless, both companies do participate in partnerships and joint ventures to a lesser extent.

The competitive advantage of these firms rests with their reputation, track record, firm specific methodologies and international coverage. Logica further identifies it independence as a source of competitive advantage. The future strategies of these companies would seem to be further internationalisation for Logica, whilst Sema Group continues it focus upon the European market. Whether they will remain independent is questionable given the polarisation of the sector.

239

9.5 Multinational structures and strategies in the UK business services sector

The case studies detailed above provide a useful in-depth examination of the operations of business service firms from three distinctive sub-sectors. The evidence generated through these studies corroborate a number of the important findings of the postal survey. It is clear that diversification is a characteristic of the international business service firm. However, the case study evidence reinforces the survey findings that generally diversification is into closely related areas which utilise the firm's core skills. This provides further support for Enderwick's (1992) view of service sector diversification. In addition, the two computer service firms studied demonstrate a low level of diversification, focusing instead on diversification by market segment rather than by product/service. This coincides with the survey results which found the computer services sector to be one of the least diversified sub-sector among those studied. The experience of Cordiant during the late 1980s when diversifying into areas which reached beyond those utilising its core competencies is clearly a lesson for all business service firms to note when considering a diversification strategy.

The motivation behind the diversification strategy among the case study firms appeared to be the desire to increase revenues through market expansion and to cater for the needs of existing clients by providing a wider range of services. These findings confirm those of the survey where client needs appeared to be the most significant factor stimulating diversification followed closely by the opportunity for market growth. It is clear from the case study findings that both demand and supply side factors influence the level of service diversification.

In line with the survey findings some of the case study firms do appear to be actively pursuing a policy of obtaining as much business as possible from existing clients by offering them a wider range of services. The process of cross referring a client from one part of the firm to another would appear to occur between different service activities and geographically. Indeed, Cordiant's diversification strategy in the 1980s was specifically motivated by the opportunity to use cross referrals and thereby increase revenue, as well as achieving economies of scale and scope. In this particular case there was a failure to sustain the level of synergy necessary for successful diversification, resulting eventually to a return to the firm's core activities.

An exploration of the historical development of the case study firms indicates that the level of diversification tends to increase as the firms develop over time, this is clearly visible for the two advertising firms. It is, nevertheless, evident that firms may also divest themselves of certain activities over time, as in the case of Cordiant disposing of its management consultancy business. Such divestment was also evident among the computer service firms studied. The level of diversification is influenced by a variety of factors both internal and external to the firm, as such factors change over time so too will the level of diversification deemed appropriate by a particular firm.

All of the case study firms demonstrate an evolutionary pattern of development expanding in size and international scope over time. In relation to the process of internationalisation the firms studied used a variety of methods to service foreign markets. The establishment of an overseas presence appeared to be the most dominant method of supplying services across international borders, although there was evidence of other methods being utilised, in particular, the use of travelling personnel, as well as exports in a tangible form and 'over the wire'. All firms were clearly involved in the transfer of services internationally within the boundaries of the firm, that is, intra-firm trade. Such trade occurred through, for example, the introduction of common methodological approaches to business at an international level, in addition to the use of common data bases and the general sharing of skills and knowledge across national boundaries.

The nature of overseas presences utilised varied from wholly owned to associate companies and contractual agreements. As found in the survey results the computer service firms appeared to have a stronger preference for wholly owned subsidiaries, this results from the nature of the service they provide. Both computer service firms examined above invest heavily in R&D which gives rise to the development of intangible assets which can be easily replicated and disseminated, it is therefore essential to protect such assets by internalising them within the boundaries of the firm. As noted in Chapter 3, knowledge intensive assets are those which are most likely to give rise to the practice of internalisation (Caves, 1971; Buckley and Casson, 1976). This desire to internalise knowledge intensive assets, which include a range of ownership specific advantages from common methodological approaches to brand names and reputation, was visible among all of the business service firms studied. However, the extent to which internalisation occurred through ownership varied between sub-sectors.

Advertising firms used a variety of types of overseas presences, though wholly owned and majority owned appeared to dominate. An understanding of local culture and regulatory conditions is important for advertising firms, and this explains the use of affiliate companies to service some foreign markets. In the case of Cordiant it is clear that this type of presence is often established in less developed countries. There is a significant cultural distance between Cordiant's home market and those in developing countries, which consequently can be better served by local companies affiliated to the international group.

The accountancy firms studied demonstrated the international pattern of local ownership usual within this sector. The international organisation being created through the integration of separately owned national partnerships. Clearly, each sub-sector faces different influences which determine the nature of ownership at the international level. However, both among computer service and advertising firms there does appear to be a preference for wholly owned overseas subsidiaries supporting the view expressed by Dunning (1989).

All of the firms examined appear to be pursuing a strategy which utilises technology to increase the level of efficiency and also improve communications

241

throughout the group, as well as with clients. Technology is changing the manner in which services are produced and delivered. It is also creating new services and changing the nature of established services. So in advertising, for example, Cordiant is developing services in the field of interactive media, whilst in the accountancy sector Price Waterhouse has established a centre specifically concerned with technological developments.

The extension of international coverage was viewed as important by all the firms studied in-depth. Its importance in terms of retaining existing clients and gaining new clients was stressed by all firms. This then confirms the findings of the survey that FDI in the business services sector is market oriented rather than resource oriented. Overseas locations are determined by market opportunities rather than the availability of resources. Sema Group was alone among the companies studied in its adoption of a strategy of focusing primarily on the European market. All the companies have been involved in expanding their international networks in a variety of ways including mergers, acquisitions and organic expansion. Setting up new firms has been particularly important in the South East Asian and Eastern European markets where there is little in the way of firms available for takeover.

Multinational enterprises are an important source of revenue for the firms studied. Clients which operate on an international scale certainly influence the international activities of their business service suppliers. The desire to retain multinational clients is clearly a significant factor motivating the international expansion strategies of the case study firms, giving further support to the survey findings.

The importance of client contact and good client relations is clearly vital to all the firms studied. The provision of business services often requires close contact between the supplier and client, with the supplier having detailed knowledge of client's activities. The ability to ensure confidentiality and develop trust between the supplier and client is crucial. The nature of the business services studied here require close cooperation between the purchaser and the provider. In the computer service sector such cooperation is so important that in some circumstances the supplier will set up a strategic partnerships with a client in order to ensure continuity and consistency, an example is Logica's joint venture with British Airways forming Speedwing Logica in 1990. Indeed, business service firms will practice exclusivity in order to secure client business. This is evident among advertising firms, where the issue of client conflict is a significant factor influencing the nature of organisational expansion. However, such practices are also important in other business services, including computer services. Logica, for example, is willing to practice exclusivity when necessary.

All the case study firms appeared to operate on a fairly decentralised basis giving a high degree of autonomy to local presences. This is partly related to the nature of professional business services and the client contact that they necessitate. A high level of autonomy at the point of contact with the client is required. Local knowledge is of particular importance. Most of the firms are organised on a holding group basis, or similar form, at the international level. However, there does

242

appear to be a move towards more integrated structures in a number of the firms studied, for example, Logica has recently reorganised its domestic operations along divisional lines, whether this reorganisation will be extended to an international level has yet to be seen. Cordiant has also been involved in merging its various advertising agencies into a number of integrated networks. Price Waterhouse demonstrates a trend towards increased integration with the introduction of training centres and technology resources available to the World Firm with the aim of consolidating and improving standards of service throughout the company. Whether this increased integration will lead to the adoption of the M-form organisational structure by business service firms as Channon (1978) found among other service sectors remains to be seen. Clearly, there is a trend towards greater integration, but this may result in the adoption of new organisational forms with more flexible structures, perhaps along the lines of the spider's web structure used by Arthur Andersen (Quinn and Paquette, 1990). The application of new ICTs gives greater scope for the design of organisational structures which combine flexibility with efficiency (Chapter 4). Knowledge intensive services such as those studied here are among those most able to utilise ICTs successfully in the organisation of their diverse activities.

The case studies presented in this chapter have been particularly important as a means of exploring the organisational development of firms in the business services sector. The research demonstrates that there is a trend among some firms towards increased integration. However, there are specific problems for business service firms which favour decentralisation at an international level. The firms which will prove most successful will be those which can achieve the most appropriate balance between a centralised and decentralised international organisational structure.

9.6 Conclusion

In this chapter a number of business service firms have been explored in-depth. Similarities and differences between the multinational structures and strategies of two firms from each of the three main sub-sector have been considered. It is possible to explore the multinationalisation of these firms in terms of the theory of the MNE reviewed in Chapter 3. All the companies examined possess ownership specific advantages which they internalise through the development of multinational organisational structures. For advertising and computer service companies these structures largely consisted of wholly or majority owned overseas presences. The international accountancy firm provides an interesting case whereby ownership specific advantages are internalised within the boundaries of the firm, though ownership remains decentralised. The boundaries of the firms are in this case not synonymous with the boundaries of ownership.

The case studies reveal that the strategies pursued by the business service firms determine their organisational structures supporting the strategy - structure relationship found in other sectors (Chandler, 1962; Channon, 1973, 1978). Clearly, structure adapts over time, reflecting strategic decisions. Rapid international expansion among business service firms is later followed by integration and the adoption of more formal organisational structures. The common use of the holding company structure reflect certain characteristic of the sector, for example, the need for local autonomy, and also the rapid expansion of firms through mergers and acquisitions. The firms studied here are all competitive in their particular field. Each one appears to be successfully pursuing an expansionary policy. The evidence would suggest that they are adapting to their market environments and following competitive strategies. Organisational structures are evolving with a tendency towards higher levels of integration having been identified.

Having explored the multinational structures and strategies of business service firms through the examination of individual firms, it is now appropriate to proceed to the next chapter where the findings of the case study research and those derived from the survey of the UK business services sector will be drawn together for further analysis.

Notes

1   During this historical account of the development of Cordiant Plc. the company will be referred to by its former name of Saatchi and Saatchi Plc. up to the point at which the change in name occurred (i.e. 1995).

2   Turnover comprises amounts billed to clients, excluding sales taxes and intra-Group transactions.

3   Revenue represents the fees and commissions, excluding sales taxes, from services provided to clients.

10 A model for business service firm multinationalisation

10.1 Introduction

The objective of this research has been to explore the internationalisation of business services and in doing so to establish factors which influence the manner in which internationalisation occurs. The ultimate aim being to develop a framework within which to explain the multinationalisation of business service firms. An examination of the theoretical literature in the early chapters of this book enabled a model for the internationalisation of service firms to be tentatively proposed and forwarded for empirical testing. Having completed a detailed exploration of the internationalisation of the business services sector in the past three chapters, through the use of both primary and secondary sources, it is now possible to reconsider the aims and objectives of the research. The model developed in Chapter 5 will be elaborated upon in order to provide a framework to explain the multinational development of business service firms.

The following section will explore the extent to which business service firms progress through an evolutionary process towards full internationalisation. A conceptual framework will be presented which identifies the factors that influence the multinationalisation of the sector. This will be followed by an evaluation of the relevance of trade and FDI theory to an understanding of the internationalisation of business services. Given the importance of intra-firm trade within the sector an assessment of its role in the multinationalisation of the business service firm will be provided. Multinational organisational structures will be considered and a model presented to explain the level of centralisation within business service firm organisations. Finally these various elements will be drawn together to form a model for the multinational development of the business service firm.

10.2 An evolutionary approach to business service firm internationalisation

Business service firms which expand over time eventually find further growth limited by the size of the domestic market. There are two strategic choices which will enable the firm to overcome such a restriction on growth. These are either to expand internationally, thus extending the firm's market beyond national boundaries, or to diversify the range of products/services which the firm offers in the domestic market. These two choices can be regarded as alternatives (Wolf, 1977; Buckley, 1985; Caves, 1982), at least initially, although some firms may pursue both strategies in unison. The strategy selected will depend upon sector and firm specific factors. If the firm can benefit from economies of scale then the extension of its market through internationalisation would be the preferred choice. On the other hand, if there are economies of scope and the benefits of synergy to be gained through diversification then this strategy may be favoured. From the empirical research it is clear that the strategy adopted varies between firms, for example, GGT embarked on a path of diversification prior to internationalisation, whereas Cordiant became international before diversification occurred. It is also evident that business service firms tend to diversify into closely related areas, such that it is possible to question whether they are truly diversified. In addition, the survey failed to find substantive evidence to suggest that internationalisation and diversification occur simultaneously among business service firms, a finding which contrasts with evidence from other service sectors (Channon, 1978). Internationalisation would appear then to be the dominant strategic objective for many large business service firms seeking continued growth.

Can an evolutionary model of internationalisation, with firms passing through distinct stages such as those proposed by Johanson and Wiedersheim-Paul (1975, p.306) (Table 10.1), be of value when exploring the internationalisation of business service firms? From the exploration of the internationalisation of services in Chapter 2, it is commonly accepted that the majority of services are non-tradable, in the traditional sense, they are what Boddewyn et al. (1986) refer to as 'location-bound'. For such services internationalisation requires the establishment of an overseas presence, and so, producers progress rapidly from a national to an international firm without a period of exportation. A pattern of internationalisation confirmed by Sharma and Johanson (1987) in a study of technical consultancy firms.

However, as noted in Chapter 5, to class all services as non-tradable is misleading. Indeed, all services can be exported if the service is provided to a foreign client in the domestic market. Whether a business service firm is involved in exportation prior to establishing a presence overseas will depend largely on the characteristics of the service together with the nature of the firm's clients. If the firm provides services in the domestic market for foreign clients then clearly exportation does occur in the form of *domestically located service exports*. Services may be provided to the overseas client, in for example a letter or report, here exportation occurs in

Table 10.1
Stages in the internationalisation of the firm

Johanson and Wiedersheim-Paul Manufacturing firms	Roberts Business service firms
1 No regular export activity.	1 Provision of services to domestic clients only (no exports).
2 Export via independent representatives (agents).	2 Provision of services to foreign clients in the domestic market (domestically located exports).
3 Sale subsidiary.	3 Provision of services to foreign markets through embodied service exports, transhuman exports and wired exports.
4 Production/manufacturing.	4 Establishment of a presence through which to deliver a service largely produced in the domestic market.
	5 Establishment of service production facility in the overseas market.

the traditional sense in the form of *embodied service exports*. Personnel travelling may facilitate *transhuman exports,* and finally, business services can be exported through telecommunication networks in the form of *wired exports*.

The survey results (Chapter 8) provide evidence that business service firms do export in the above forms. Indeed, for some firms such exports are highly important. The survey findings, for example, identified a group of export only firms. So it is quite possible for business service firms to begin their internationalisation through exportation only. This is clearly in contrast to the view that services are non-tradable.

When exploring the internationalisation of business service firms a wide variety of methods of foreign market servicing were identified. Exports and FDI were important but firms also used joint ventures, franchise agreements, associate firms and reciprocal arrangements among other methods.

Independent exports are somewhat limited, and it is likely that if a firm has clients in a foreign market it will eventually set up a presence in order to adequately service

247

those clients. The level of exports necessary to give rise to the consideration of the establishment of an overseas production facility is likely to be much lower for business service sector firms than for firms in the manufacturing sector. As noted in Chapter 4, the costs involved in the establishment of a production facility for a business service firm are very much lower than for most firms in the manufacturing sector. All that is required for a business service firm to set up an overseas production facility is an office and the appropriate skilled labour, whereas in the manufacturing sector costly plant and equipment will also be required. Furthermore, the office equipment utilised by business service firms will generally be non-specific and therefore available in competitive markets. Skilled labour though, may be costly and sector specific. However, it is important to note the high mobility of skilled, especially professional labour, which can be transferred between locations and activities with ease. In the business services sector then setting up a presence will involve a lower capital investment compared to that required in the manufacturing sector. Consequently, the level of market commitment required for a business service firm to establish a presence in an overseas market can be expected to be less than that required for a manufacturing firm. Business service firms might then be expected to set up an overseas presence at an earlier stage in their development than manufacturing firms (Figure 10.1).

Despite the relatively lower cost for business service firms of setting up an overseas presence, it is important to note that many business service firms are smaller and have relatively lower turnovers at the point at which they consider internationalisation than their manufacturing counterparts. Thus cost may be a factor for small business service firms when deciding upon the method of overseas expansion. Additionally, if rapid internationalisation is sought then contractual arrangements might be used to build an overseas network quickly.

Methods of overseas expansion which minimise costs and risks may well be important. Business service firms may set up a reciprocal arrangement with a firm in the overseas market or participate in a joint venture. Through this type of arrangement the firm can gain experience and knowledge of the foreign market. By doing so, the risks and uncertainty involved in the process of internationalisation can be reduced. As the firm becomes more committed to an overseas market the firm may choose to increase its ownership share in the local presence. This may indeed be required, if as commitment increases intangible assets are shared. Increased ownership will facilitate greater control over the foreign presence and thus ensure the protection of intangible assets. This is particularly important where the knowledge assets being shared with overseas subsidiaries are non-codifiable, as is often the case in business service firms which deliver customised services to their clients. As the survey results indicate there is clearly a tendency for the use of majority owned subsidiaries to increase as the firm becomes more international, and this may well be related to the rise in commitment to and knowledge of foreign markets.

A firm may be at different stages of international development within different

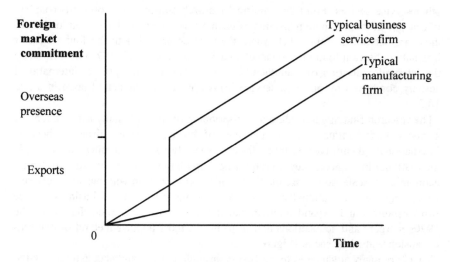

Figure 10.1 Internationalisation of business service firms

foreign markets or regions. This explains the use of a variety of types of overseas presence within one firm. There is also the need to take into account local regulation on the ownership of foreign subsidiaries together with sector specific regulation which may influence the nature of the market presence. As a firm's experience of foreign markets increases then there will be less risk and uncertainty when entering new markets. With increased internationalisation firms may establish overseas presences more rapidly, with less need for caution and with higher levels of market commitment from the beginning. Internationalisation can, then, develop a momentum of its own.

The evidence from both the survey and the case study findings support the view that business service firms do progress through an evolutionary path towards full internationalisation. Although the number of stages and the length of time spent in each one is variable. Indeed business service firms may miss stages, even becoming international in one step through a merger or acquisition. Not only can mergers and acquisitions enable a business service firm to enter a particular market rapidly but they also facilitate the speedy establishment of international networks. International capabilities can also be acquired rapidly through contractual arrangements, an example of this is the M & C Saatchi advertising agency's arrangement with Publicis (Chapter 9).

However, the main point which must be emphasised here is that it is possible for business service firms to progress through various stages en route to full internationalisation. Moreover, the stage of exporting only must be recognised within the process of business service firm internationalisation, and indeed among

249

other service sectors. From the empirical research considered in previous chapters five stages in the internationalisation of business service firms have been identified, these are set out in Table 10.1 where they are compared with the four stages of internationalisation found by Johanson and Wiedersheim-Paul (1975) in their study the internationalisation of manufacturing firms. The various types of international activity conducted by business service firms are further elaborated upon in Table 10.2.

The research findings indicate that the servicing of internationally active clients is a major factor influencing the decision of business service firms to become international themselves. Since firms generally are becoming increasingly international in scope as they search for new and larger markets in order to exploit economies of scale, so too are the firms which provide them with business services. As the pace of internationalisation quickens so the rate at which business service firms establish and expand international networks increases. Such that, since the 1970s mergers and acquisitions appear to be the most popular method of overseas expansion within the sector (Figure 10.2).

There are many advantages to expansion through mergers and acquisitions. Firstly, there is the speed with which the business service firm can establish an international network. Secondly, by taking over an existing firm a client bank and wealth of information concerning local market conditions, including culture specific knowledge (highly important in terms of ensuring good client relations) are acquired. Thirdly, by taking over profitable companies the business service firm avoids a period of loss making whilst a presence establishes itself in a new market. The acquired firm immediately contributes positively to the groups profits and performance. Fourthly, setting up a presence from scratch can be difficult, particularly in the developed world where the business services sector is well established and highly competitive, making it difficult for a new comer to gain a foothold in the market. It is therefore easier to enter such markets through the acquisition of a going concern.

It is only in markets where business services are underdeveloped, for example in the former Soviet Union, Eastern Europe and parts of South East Asia, that expansion through the setting up of greenfield operations occurs to any great extent. This can be explained by the lack of domestic expertise in these countries and thus the absence of suitable business service firms for takeover. Such expansion has been identified, in particular, among the accountancy and advertising case study firms.

The international markets for the business services studied are highly competitive with a tendency towards increasing concentration. The large international firms have been expanding rapidly throughout the 1980s and into the 1990s. Among the firms studied in-depth two types of rapid international expansion were visible. The first being when firms select overseas firms for takeover, the second type being where firms are drawn together from different countries to establish or indeed expand an international network through contractual arrangements or merger. Price Waterhouse, Cordiant and Logica are examples of the former with Sema Group and

250

Table 10.2
A classification of international activities conducted by business service firms

Exports: - Embodied services e.g. report, letter, video.

                         - Wired services e.g. telephone conversation, telecommunications data transfer.

                         - Domestically located service exports e.g. legal services provided to a foreign client in the home market.

                         - Transhuman exports e.g. personnel travelling to overseas market to advise foreign client, or present a report.

                         - Intra-firm exports e.g. services delivered from the home country to foreign clients via a local office in the overseas market.

Overseas Presence*   - Export delivery system.

                         - Service production facility - producing services for the local market and perhaps geographically proximate foreign markets.

                         - International production unit - e.g.: involved in collecting data on local markets to be used in other countries - management consultants, market research firms; or, data entry facility or computer programming unit taking advantage of lower labour costs in overseas market and exporting output back to the home country.

                         - Operations in conjunction with other firms, local or international, to provide services to a particular client e.g. consortia of firms often used in the computer services sector.

* These may include wholly or majority owned subsidiaries, joint ventures, franchise or licensing operations, partnerships, associate firms, reciprocal arrangements, together with other methods of local representation.

Note: A business service firm may be involved in any combination of the above within individual markets and between markets.

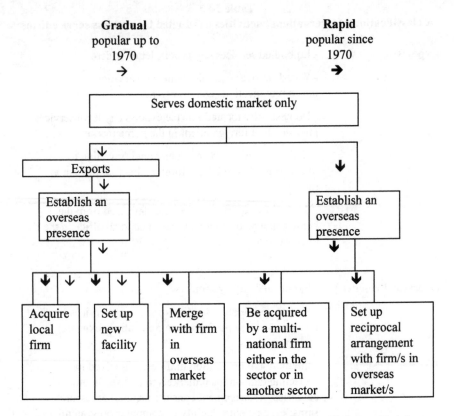

Gradual
popular up to
1970
→

Rapid
popular since
1970
→

Serves domestic market only

Exports

Establish an overseas presence

Establish an overseas presence

| Acquire local firm | Set up new facility | Merge with firm in overseas market | Be acquired by a multi-national firm either in the sector or in another sector | Set up reciprocal arrangement with firm/s in overseas market/s |

Figure 10.2 Paths of development in the evolution of a multinational business service firm

BDO being examples of the latter. Clearly firms may expand internationally through both mechanisms, as has been the case for GGT, though it is often the case that one form of expansion dominates.

Client needs appear to be the major motivation for internationalisation. Initial internationalisation can be said to be demand driven. The more international the firm becomes the more likely it is that further international expansion will be motivated by the desire to capture new clients, that is, it will be supply driven. As the markets become increasingly concentrated, competitive pressures influence the pattern and extent of international expansion. Seeking out new clients, retaining existing clients, and offering them greater scope, both geographically and in terms of the range of services offered, become important in the search for continued growth and maintaining the firm's competitive position relative to other highly international firms in the sector.

252

The survey results provide evidence of a link between the size of a firm's domestic turnover and its level of internationalisation measured in terms of overseas turnover. This adds weight to the view that firms progress through an evolutionary process towards internationalisation, expanding domestically at first and then becoming international. However, there are exceptions, small business service firms may have international interests. In particular, the location of the domestic firm may influence the speed and timing of foreign market entry together with the pattern of international development (O'Farrell and Wood, 1993). Those firms located in capital cities or in other major areas of agglomeration are more likely to come into contact with international clients at an earlier stage in their development compared to firms located in peripheral regions. Such contact with international clients may result in the firm expanding internationally prior to its domestic expansion as was the case for Price Waterhouse in the late nineteenth century when it opened an office in New York prior to its domestic expansion in the UK. The survey results provide further support for this view.

The evidence presented in the last two chapters strongly supports the argument that business service firms progress through various stages towards full internationalisation. However, the nature of the stages through which a business service firm may progress may differ from those stages manufacturing firms pass through. In addition, it is clear that not all business service firms progress through all of the stages mentioned above. However, it is evident that internationalisation does occur in a incremental manner for many business service firms.

It is possible to group the various factors which influence the internationalisation of business service firms into those which are external to the firm and those which are internal (Table 10.3). The internationalisation of business service firms can be viewed as a function of these various influences. As a firm increases its multinational scope then further factors will influence the degree of multinationalisation. For example, the firm may pursue an aggressive policy of expansion seeking out new clients, hence, the firm becomes supply driven rather than demand driven. The various influences interact over time and the significance of each varies with the level and stage of internationalisation. For example, risk and uncertainty may be highly important in the early stages of internationalisation, however, as the firm gains experience of the international environment the level of risk and uncertainty can be expected to diminish.

There is a wealth of diversity in the types of overseas presence used by business service firms, although a clear preference for majority owned subsidiaries as the firm becomes increasingly international is supported by the research findings. Furthermore, the importance of an export only stage is evident among business service firms contrary to the generally accepted view that services are non-tradable. Finally it must be noted that as in the manufacturing sector some business service firms do not develop their international capabilities gradually but rather become international rapidly through mergers, takeovers, or network agreements.

Table 10.3
Conceptual framework: factors influencing the development of multinational business service firms

External Factors: General economic climate.
Competitive environment.
Regulatory environment:
- sector specific;
- trade and investment.

Technology of service provision:
- communications;
- transport.

Client needs/demands.
Location specific advantages of overseas markets:
- client location.
- market opportunities.
- potential market opportunities.
- regulatory environment.

Cultural differences between markets.
Risk and uncertainty.

Internal Factors: Nature of service/s provided:
- tradability of service.
- frequency of provision.

Company strategy.
Resource availability.
Domestic location.
Company size.
Experience of international activity.
Knowledge of overseas market to be entered.
Firm specific advantages:
- reputation and quality.
- knowledge assets e.g. brand names.
- international coverage.
- economies of scale and scope.

Company's perception of risks and uncertainty.
Propensity to internalise transactions:
- level of knowledge specific assets used in service production.
- nature of service e.g. only tradable within the firm.

254

10.3 Explaining trade and FDI in business services

Business service firms become international in a variety of ways including through trade and FDI. Consequently, theoretical developments in these areas, reviewed in Chapter 3, are important to our understanding of business services sector internationalisation. The theory of comparative advantage in its extended form of the Heckscher-Ohlin-Samuelson model, remains the most widely accepted explanation of international trade. But how relevant is it to trade in business services? The importance of comparative advantage, based as it is upon factor abundance, can be applied to trade in business services between developed and developing countries. The business services studied here are knowledge intensive and require skilled labour to produce them. Thus countries which have a relative abundance in skilled labour will export business services to those countries which have a relative scarcity of skilled labour. Developing countries will then import business services from developed countries.

However, much trade in business services is between countries with similar factor endowments, that is between developed countries. Can the theory of comparative advantage, based as it is on differences in factor endowments, explain such trade? If the factors of production are extended to include knowledge intensive skilled labour, R&D capabilities, managerial and organisational skills, technology, among others, then the theory of comparative advantage may be a useful tool for explaining the pattern of trade in business services, with countries specialising according to their relative factor endowments. Such trade would comply with Linder's (1961) theory of overlapping demand, with countries exporting to each other similar but differentiated business services, specialising in the production of those varieties which incorporate the countries abundant factor most intensively.

Business services firms require specialised knowledge in order to cater for the specific needs of their clients. The services produced are generally differentiated rather than standardised and as Nusbaumer (1987b) argues trade in such differentiated knowledge intensive services is more likely to be determined by absolute advantage rather than comparative advantage. Where services can be standardised, in terms of their knowledge input and the identification of separate units, trade is more likely to be determined by the comparative advantage conferred by factor endowments. The scope for the standardisation of business services may increase over time as firms increasingly apply ICTs to their production and distribution. As Quinn and Paquette (1990) note, with the use of well managed service technologies it is possible to combine customisation with standardisation by focusing on the smallest service activity that can be efficiently measured and replicated (Chapter 4).

The theory of intra-industry trade (Grubel and Lloyd, 1975) which focuses on the role of non-competitive market structures, product differentiation and decreasing costs is of value to our understanding of business service trade. The search for economies of scale and scope have been forwarded as reasons for the

255

internationalisation of services including business services (Enderwick, 1989). Clearly market concentration is increasing in the sectors studied, especially within international markets. However, decreasing costs may be less relevant, in a direct sense, to business service firms compared to other service and manufacturing firms. The survey results indicate that cost is not perceived to be highly important as a source of competitive advantage by business service firms (Chapter 8). Of greater importance to competitive advantage are quality related issues such as the calibre of staff, client relations, goodwill and reputation together with the use of knowledge. Reduced production costs are not necessarily passed on to clients in the form of lower prices. Rather lower cost enable the firm to invest more heavily in resources which will satisfy client needs. Cost savings are invested with the aim of producing an innovative and higher quality service, and thereby enhancing the firm's competitive advantage and creating further barrier of entry for new firms.

Although, periods of economic decline, such as that experienced in the early 1990s, undoubtedly put increased pressure on companies to be price competitive. In addition, price is certainly a source of competitive advantage in the more mature sectors and those which are relatively well standardised, for example, in the audit market.

In some cases a domestic business service firm may obtain clients merely because of its location, for example a foreign firm may use a domestic business service firm because of its locational proximity to a subsidiary. Here then location may be seen as a source of competitive advantage. A country may have a locational comparative advantage if it is home to a major centre of agglomeration within a global region. Certain cities in the world are viewed as major players in particular markets, for example, London is the centre for insurance. Clearly, a firm providing insurance services in London will have a locational advantage over a firm located in, say, Newcastle upon Tyne or indeed New York. Comparative cost advantages which arise for firms located in centres of agglomeration, derive from the presence of sector specific infrastructures, including communications, the availability if skilled labour, the regulatory environment, and so on.

Trade theories have much to offer to our appreciation of international trade transactions in business services. However, it is important to distinguish between the comparative advantage of nations and the competitive advantages of individual firms (Porter, 1990). In some cases these may coincide, with the competitive advantage of a firm giving rise to an absolute or comparative advantage for its home country, or indeed, vice versa. However, it is essential to recognise the international mobility of labour and capital which allow firms with a competitive advantage to move overseas and exploit such advantages in other markets. Dissemination of competitive advantage through a global network of subsidiaries diminishes the extent of comparative advantage held by the originating country. It is also clear that a country's comparative advantage will change over time (Rybczynski, 1955) independently of the activities of national firms. Thus it is unwise for a firm to rely upon national comparative advantage as a source of competitive advantage in the longer term.

It is necessary to recognise the dynamic nature of business services and other information intensive services. The way in which they are produced and delivered is changing rapidly, challenging our understanding of them. The static nature of much trade theory gives rise to a crucial weakness in its ability to explain trade in business services. It is necessary therefore to develop and build upon the dynamic elements within trade theory.

The role of the client and that of travelling personnel should also be incorporate in any model of trade in business services. The role of services embodied in tangible forms is also important and perhaps these should be explored as vehicle for service trade just as ships are important to trade in goods. Or should these tangible forms be considered as factor of production? Clearly, if services are transmitted over-the-wire then countries with a highly developed telecommunications network would have a comparative advantage in the export of such services compared to those countries which have a poor telecommunications network. Those countries well endowed with skilled labour, particularly multilingual, might have an advantage in the export of services transacted through personnel travelling to clients. The technology of embodiment may be significant, that is, how services can be embodied in a tangible form, a country which is well endowed with such technology or the capacity to generate such technology may have an advantage in the exportation of services. For example, an abundance of computer programmers might give rise to a comparative advantage in the production of those business services embodied in computer terminals. In the US personal legal and employment services are now available through computer networks. As technology advances business services may be increasingly available in the same manner in the international market.

Business services hold great potential for internationalisation over-the-wire and so understanding such trade is important to our appreciation of the internationalisation of the sector. As telecommunications systems become more sophisticated, over-the-wire contact may increasingly replace face-to-face meetings. The establishment of video conferencing facilities by companies such as Cordiant and Chait Day are examples of such developments. Client contact however, for the time being, remains important and reduces the scope for independent trade. Indeed, the use of technology within the business service firm's organisation may actually enable client contact to be enhanced; inter-organisational communications may increasingly become mediated through telecommunication networks freeing resources which can be redirected towards enhancing client relations.

Trade in business services often requires a presence in the foreign market. The survey results demonstrate that many business service firms initially establish an overseas presence merely to act as a delivery system for services largely produced elsewhere. Hence this area of trade also requires exploration. Trade which is dependent on an overseas presence to complete final delivery must be regarded as intra-firm trade - to which further consideration will be given in the next section.

The limitations of trade theory must be recognised when used to explore the internationalisation of business services. Clearly trade does exist, however internationalisation through the extension of the business service organisation into an overseas market is the predominant method beyond an initial stage of exportation. When exploring the theory of the MNE (Chapter 3) it is clear that such theories do have relevance for the multinationalisation of service firms, including those in the business services sector.

Exploring business service multinational firms within the context of Dunning's (1981, 1993a, 1993b) eclectic paradigm it is clear that the various elements have explanatory value. Firstly, *ownership advantages* which are of particular importance to business service firms consist of, for example, the company's reputation, its client bank, a particular firm specific methodological approach to service provision, together with other firm specific knowledge assets including, brand names. The ability to process and disseminate information is also of particular importance to business service firms. As a firm expands its overseas network, international coverage may become an important firm specific advantage, as also might economies of scale and scope.

Secondly, *locational advantages* are also relevant to the business service firm. From the research findings it is clear that location for the majority of business service firms is determined by the market or potential market opportunities. Clients are a fundamental influence upon overseas subsidiary location, particularly in the early years of the firms multinationalisation. Foreign direct investment in the business service sector is primarily market-oriented and consequently influenced by the size and potential of the market together with the country's general stability. The regulatory environment within a market may prove of particular significance to some sectors if it gives rise to a location specific advantage. The tradability of a service will be an important factor determining the locational advantages of particular markets. Resource-oriented FDI does occur, and in such cases the location of a business service firm's subsidiary might be determined by, for example, the availability of low cost skilled labour. However, such investment is at present limited in this sector. Intra-firm trade does occur and thus some cross border production does take place, though there is as yet no complex system of international production. One of the most important resources in the sector is information which is highly mobile, a characteristic which diminishes the importance of location from a resource oriented perspective. The high mobility of professional labour has a similar impact.

Thirdly, *internalisation* is an important element in the multinationalisation of business service firms. As noted by Buckley and Casson (1976) and Caves (1971) internalisation is of particular importance for the protection of knowledge assets. Transactions in information are more cheaply and more easily conducted within the boundaries of the firm. Market transactions of information can be costly, since it can be easily replicated and disseminated. As noted earlier (Chapter 3) there are significant incentives to internalise the market for services. It is interesting to note, however, that internalisation of firm specific advantages may occur within business service organisations, in particular accountancy firms, without a unified ownership structure being established.

For some business service firms the establishment of an overseas presence may be necessary to facilitate trade, that is, intra-firm trade. Business services may be non-tradable in the traditional sense, or trade may carry a high risk, incurring substantial transaction costs. The quality of a service exported without adequate on site delivery may be low relative to one which can be personally delivered to a client. Unsupported trade may, as a result, damage a firm's reputation. If the business service firm has a highly developed and sophisticated relationship with a client then unsupported trade may be successful. On the whole, though, internalisation makes intra-firm trade possible and reduces the level of risk and transaction costs involved in international transactions, thereby protecting the firm's knowledge advantages. Internalisation will be given further consideration later in this chapter when the organisation of multinational business service firms is explored.

The research findings show that the internationalisation of business service firms occurs not only through trade and FDI but also through other forms of cross border activity including joint ventures, licensing and franchising agreements, and reciprocal arrangements. There is however, evidence of a preference for wholly owned subsidiaries, particularly as firms become increasingly international. Despite this any exploration of the multinationalisation of business service firms must look beyond the trade/FDI dichotomy. When defining business service MNEs the need for full ownership or indeed any ownership between parts of the organisation must be omitted. The UNCTC definition provided in Chapter 3 would seem to be the most appropriate, with its emphasis on groups of entities in two or more countries operating under a decision-making system which permits common coherent policies and strategy, and with these entities being linked by *'ownership or otherwise'*, with one or more of them being able to exert a *'significant influence'* over the activities of the others (UNCTC, 1984, p.2).

The variety of ownership structures found among the firms studied may be accounted for by the type of service produced together with the nature of the firms' ownership advantages, the regulatory environment and historical factors. This will be considered further when multinational organisations among business services firms are examined. At this stage it is worth looking at the connections between trade and FDI in terms of the role of intra-firm trade in the business services sector.

10.4 The role of intra-firm trade in the multinationalisation of business service firms

The importance of intra-firm trade in the manufacturing sector has been widely recognised (Helleiner and Lavergne, 1979; Casson, 1986; UNCTC, 1988; Gilroy, 1989; Julius, 1990; inter alia). The explanations of intra-firm trade relate to the

259

arguments surrounding the reasons for the existence of the firm (Chapter 4). Intra-firm trade is trade which is internalised within the boundaries of the firm.

The international production of manufactured goods gives rise to intra-firm trade in intermediate products and services. An international division of labour is established with labour intensive components being produced in countries which have an abundance of labour, whilst capital intensive components are produced in countries with an abundance of capital. It is possible to identify intra-firm trade within international business service firms. Intermediate services among business service firms are exported usually from head office to subsidiaries, but also between subsidiaries. Such services range from almost finished business services which merely require internal transacting to facilitate international trade, to services which are required in the production of a business service, that is, business service components. These components may include the use of common data banks, training services, knowledge assets, and the specialist skills of personnel. The extent of intra-firm trade in service components will depend on the similarity of markets and the extent to which business services or service components may be standardised between countries. Proximity of regulatory environments and cultural characteristics between countries will encourage such trade.

Intra-firm trade in service components consist largely of information flows and these generally occur in one of three ways: firstly through a telecommunications network; secondly, in tangible form, for example, through group wide reports and manuals; and thirdly through the movement of staff either temporarily or on a longer term basis, for example, for the length of a particular project or on secondment for a set period of time. International business service firms are increasingly making use of ICTs to enhance their group wide communications. Skills and information from all over the company can thus be tapped to solve a problem and offer maximum service quality to clients. The ability to maximise the capabilities of the company through accessing skills and information dispersed throughout the group is an important source of competitive advantage for international business service firms.

As noted earlier, in some cases trade is not possible without a physical presence in the overseas market. This may be required because of the importance of client producer contact necessary during the provision of the service. Once an overseas presence is established any trade between it and the home firm is regarded as intra-firm trade. It is possible to regard certain overseas establishments as *transaction specific assets*, since they exist solely to facilitate the export of particular services. The survey provided clear evidence of the existence of such transaction specific assets. A presence of this type may be viewed as similar to a sales subsidiaries established by manufacturing firms. The final touches to the service are made in the country of sale by the firm's local representatives.

Intra-firm trade then is an important element in the internationalisation of business service firms. Theoretical and empirical research is required to develop a closer understanding of such trade. It is difficult to quantify intra-firm trade, it is only possible at this stage to recognise its existence within business service firms and that its volume looks set to increase as ICTs are increasingly utilised in the production and distribution of business services. The rapid growth in telecommunications highlighted by Ducatel and Miles (1992) can in part be attributed to the growth in intra-firm service trade both within the service and manufacturing sectors. It has been estimated that one third of world trade in manufactures is intra-firm (Gilroy, 1989), the proportion of intra-firm trade in services (both within the manufacturing and service sector) may well be higher. It is then necessary to look beyond traditional trade theories to explain the growth in trade generally, and service trade in particular.

10.5 Multinational organisational structures in the business services sector

From an examination of the business services sector it is clear that a variety of organisational structures are present. However, the holding group, and hybrids of this form, appear to be the most common organisational structure adopted by those firms which are internationally active. Advertising firms use this structure in order to expand by adding new networks, and thus avoid the problem of client conflicts. Among accountancy firms the organisational structure is similar to that of a holding group. This is particularly the case with the more globally integrated firms, where an international firm is responsible for strategy and individual firms within the organisation are concerned with day to day management. Independent computer service companies also tend to be organised on a holding group basis, although it is clear that some firms in this sector are developing more integrated organisational forms.

The multinational structures among business service firms are clearly a function of the strategy pursued. For example, as advertising firms become international and choose to add another network to the organisation in their pursuit of growth, a holding group structure is required. This research then confirms Chandler's (1962) view that structure follows strategy. Furthermore, in a period of rapid expansion through acquisition the holding group is the most appropriate form. New companies are added to the group with integration, when it does occur, following after a certain time lag. Channon (1978) identified the use of the holding group structure in the early stages of internationalisation among the service industries he studied, with the M-form structure often being adopted at a later stage. Perhaps a similar pattern will occur in the organisational development of international business service firms. There is clear evidence that the business service firms studied in-depth are seeking more integrated organisational structures.

It is important to highlight the significance of local autonomy among business service firm subsidiaries. The local presence is better informed than the head office with respect to local markets, and therefore in a position to make appropriate decisions. For example, the local presence will have a more detailed knowledge of local regulations and customs. Cultural sensitivity is highly important for a sector in

261

which client relations play a vital role, by virtue of the need for the customer to participate in the production of the service. The importance of cultural awareness in international business has been widely recognised (Ferrero, 1994; Casson, 1991; Terpstra, 1978; inter alia).

Despite the increasing harmonisation of the international economy, separate and distinctive cultural identities remain. Thus the ability to cater for specific cultural needs can be seen as an important source of competitive advantage. Local offices must be in touch with the local economy and culture. Indigenous firms and staff are well positioned in this respect, hence the tendency for multinational business service firms to expand through acquisition. It is important though that in becoming a part of a large international group the local firm does not lose the ability to service local clients. For example, in the advertising sector local knowledge is highly important. Despite the attention given to the idea of global advertising it is only possible in rare cases (Chapter 6). The reality of most global advertising involves the coordination of global campaigns made up of various different advertisements depending upon the nature and cultural characteristics of national markets. The ability to offer clients advertising skills which are culturally sensitive on a global basis must be regarded as an important source of competitive advantage for international advertising firms. Business services generally are dependent upon client relations and interaction between the provider and client, hence the need for cultural sensitivity. Without good client relations a business service firm cannot hope to survive.

Local autonomy also provides a greater incentive for local staff to remain with the company, giving rise to greater opportunities for promotion, and advancement. Retaining high quality local staff is very important because for many information intensive business service firms skilled personnel are one of their most important assets, if not the most important asset. The benefits of an acquisition have to accrue to both sides in the process. The international organisation obtains a quality local representative. The local firm gains opportunities for growth through its links with the international group and the transfer of knowledge assets such as established brand names.

Given the need for local autonomy in the business service sector the holding group structure would appear to be highly appropriate. With the holding company determining overall strategy, and individual firms within the group operating as semi autonomous units or profit centres. The survey results clearly indicated that internationally active business service firms do give a higher level of autonomy to their subsidiaries than those whose activities were confined to the UK (Chapter 8).

The rapid development of the business services sector in the past 25 years and the speedy development of multinational business service firms is reflected in the instability and volatility of the organisational structures present within the sector. There appears to be a trend towards greater integration among computer service firms, clearly visible in the case study of Logica. Within the accountancy sector the disintegration of the UK BDO firm Binder Hamlyn in 1994 with a major part of it merging with Andersens into a more integrated group serves to highlight the weaknesses of the less integrated federal structure. The more fully integrated accountancy firms clearly have an advantage. Integration is also occurring within the subsidiaries of the advertising holding companies. Although, GGT claims that retaining the independence of agencies is important to maintain creativity and entrepreneurial skills. Among the large international advertising groups, however, integration within separated networks appears to be increasing.

There appear to be two opposing forces at work which influence the organisational structures adopted by multinational business service firms. On the one hand, there is the drive for increased integration with the aim of achieving organisational economies of scale and scope, on the other, there is the need to retain independence and autonomy at a local level. The organisational structures which develop provide a balance between these two opposing forces.

As with all multinationals there is a global/local dilemma (Prahalad and Doz, 1987; Humes, 1993), but for business service firms the problem is perhaps more acute. Multinational clients are increasingly demanding integrated global services, whilst servicing the subsidiaries of multinational clients requires that local sensitivities are continuously taken into account.

The organisational structure of business service firms do not necessarily depend on wholly owned subsidiaries. The multinational accountancy firm provide a useful example of an integrated global organisation where ownership is disintegrated, remaining with the partners of individual firms. Ownership is not essential in the development of business service firm organisations, although, the accountancy firm provides a somewhat idiosyncratic example. Among the other sectors studied ownership of foreign subsidiaries is important, especially in the computer service sector. There appeared to be a clear preference for majority ownership as firms become increasingly international.

Ownership provides control over the firm's assets. Especially important to business service firms are the intangible assets of reputation, goodwill, brand name, firm specific methodologies, and R&D. Control over such assets is essential because of the experience nature of services. Brand names, for example, provide a signal of the level of quality which can be expected. The firm must ensure that quality throughout the group is harmonised at the highest level through the use of training programmes, common methodological approaches and other group wide schemes. Without full ownership there is always the risk of opportunism, that is, information assets, for example, may be used in ways which have not been paid for. If business service firms are explored within the context of Williamson's (1986) governance structures, then we might regard the investment in training programmes, R&D, quality control, and so on, to be firm specific assets. The benefits of such investments can be easily disseminated hence the need for an internal governance structure without which there is scope for opportunism among the various parties using such assets. With information assets there is less incentive to use the market due to the high transaction costs incurred. The market serves to disseminate information assets

263

giving the creator less chance to recoup R&D costs or obtain monopoly rents from the exploitation of a knowledge asset. Only in cases where the knowledge is easily codifiable is it possible to share information assets through a contractual relationship. The subsidiaries of a multinational business service firm must be examined as a system of transaction specific asset through which information can be shared for mutually beneficial advantage whilst being protected from universal dissipation (Chapter 4).

It is necessary to distinguish between ownership and control, and to recognise that these do not always coincide. Full ownership may exist but central control may be limited. On the other hand ownership may be decentralised and yet a high degree of central control may exist. The development of common objectives and priorities between the various parts of a multinational business service firm is essential. This is as important, if not in some cases more important, for the maintenance of control as central ownership.

Recognition of the influence of the environment upon the organisational form of business service firms is also important. A highly competitive environment, for example, may force the rapid establishment of an international network without full ownership. The regulatory environment is also important, and may prevent the entry of a foreign firm into a particular market therefore necessitating the use of contractual governance relations such as licensing or franchising. In addition, the nature of the service to be provided will influence the organisational structure of the service provider. For example, some computer service projects are very large, where for example a MNE wants to integrate its ICT network globally. Such projects are relatively infrequent thus there is insufficient market demand to justify the establishment of a firm of the size capable of carrying out the project. In such cases computer service firms may work together with other computer service providers and hardware manufacturers in a consortium for the duration of the project, whilst competing for business from other clients.

In terms of the organisational structure of business service firms the two opposing forces of the desire for central control and the need for local autonomy have been identified. The various factors which influence the choice of organisational structure among business service firms are summarised in Table 10.4. The greater the importance of factors leading to centralisation the more likely it is that the firm will be highly integrated. It is clear that the sector displays a variety of organisational forms, although, at present the holding group structure appears common. The sector has developed rapidly and its dynamic character is reflected in the manner in which organisations have been evolving over time. This organisational change is set to continue and can be regarded as a result of a balance between the various factors listed in Table 10.4. Particularly important among these is the balance between firm specific knowledge and local knowledge required to provide the service.

Table 10.4
Factors influencing the choice of organisational structure among business service firms

Forces for the centralisation of control:

- Firm specific knowledge advantages.
- Experience nature of the service.
- Cultural proximity between home and host countries.
- High market transaction costs.
- High level of integration.
- High level of resource commitment.

Forces for the decentralisation of control:

- Local knowledge requirement.
- Cultural distance between home and host countries.
- Low market transaction costs.
- Local regulation.
- Low level of integration.

10.6 Conclusion

When examining the multinationalisation of the business service firm it is important to recognise the significance of the firm's strategy. Is the firm looking for continued growth through internationalisation? Does it prefer to remain small servicing a niche market? To a great extent the market environment will influence the firm's strategy in terms of providing strategic options. But choices are made by the individual firms. Increasingly, in all three sectors studied in-depth there is a trend towards polarisation between a small number of very large and international firms and a large number of small mainly national firms. Thus business service firms make a choice they either remain small servicing local or niche markets, or if they wish to grow they must aspire to join the small group of large international firms which face an increasingly concentrated international competitive environment.

In this chapter a framework for the internationalisation of business services has been proposed which identifies various stages in the development of the multinational business service firm. This evolutionary model recognises the importance of service exports as a stage, brief as it may be, in the overall internationalisation process. The factors influencing the internationalisation process

265

have been identified as both internal and external to the firm.

The theory of international transactions, reviewed in Chapter 3, can clearly contribute to the understanding of the internationalisation of business services. However, as highlighted above, intra-firm trade plays an important role in the multinational development of business service firms. As a consequence, it is necessary to look beyond trade and investment theories to gain a full appreciation of the internationalisation process. An organisational perspective is useful, it is for example possible in certain cases to view overseas subsidiaries as transaction specific assets which facilitate intra-firm trade in business services.

Having explored the organisation of multinational business service firms a number of factors have been identified which influence the organisational structure adopted. These can be grouped into those which favour the centralisation of control and those which favour decentralisation. By drawing together these factor with the various other elements considered in this chapter it is possible to provide a framework for the multinational development of business services firms (Figure 10.3).

It is clear that the model presented here requires further empirical testing and development. However, it provides a valuable basis for future research, presenting as it does a fresh perspective on the internationalisation of services. A range of important elements within the internationalisation process are highlighted. Indeed, the framework developed here can be used in conjunction with others, such as the conceptual framework proposed by Edvardsson et al. (1993) for analysing the internationalisation of knowledge-intensive service companies, which stresses a creative management perspective on the development and internationalisation of companies.

The heterogeneity of the service sector must be recognised and as a result the limitations upon the usefulness of the model developed here for other service activities. Undoubtedly, though, it would be possible to adapt the various elements to suit the service of specific interest. Even within the business services sector there is great diversity and hence the wide range of factors which influence the internationalisation of the sector. The broader relevance of the model developed in this chapter will be considered further in the next and final concluding chapter.

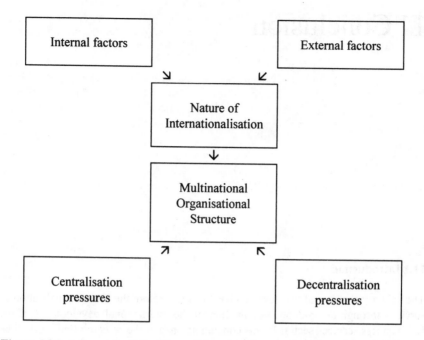

Figure 10.3 A framework for the multinational development of business service firms

11 Conclusion

11.1 Introduction

The primary concern of this research has been to explore the internationalisation of services through an in-depth examination of the international development of the UK business services sector. In this concluding chapter the research findings will be assessed in terms of their relevance to the internationalisation of the UK service sector in general. Clearly the service sector includes a diverse range of activities and the research results may hold more relevance to services which display similar characteristics to those supplied by business service firms. In particular, the findings will no doubt have greater significance for other information intensive services and producer services. However, in certain areas the research does have broader relevance and where possible generally applicable results will be highlighted.

This research has drawn upon a wide and diverse body of literature. The internationalisation of the service sector has been considered through an exploration of literature and secondary data. In order to fully appreciate the process of international expansion among service sector firms it has been necessary to draw on a range of theoretical literature including that concerned with trade and FDI, as well as the organisation of the firm. The review of literature serves to highlight the growing importance of service sector activity in advanced industrialised countries, both in terms of employment and as a source of GDP. In particular, the significance of the internationalisation of the service sector has been emphasised.

The UK business services sector has been explored at a number of levels. Firstly, at a general level the sector has been reviewed with attention being paid to the international position of the UK relative to other countries. It has been illustrated that the UK holds a fairly competitive position in the provision of many business services (Chapter 7). The business services sector itself consists of a wide range of activities from cleaning services to management consultancy. This research has focused upon information intensive business services. In order to develop a closer understanding of such business services three sub-sectors have been examined in detail at both a national and international level. This sub-sectoral research included the use of secondary data sources, together with primary data generated through a postal survey and interviews. Further research was conducted at the level of the individual firm with the in-depth exploration of two firms from each of the three sub-sectors. Thus the research has been conducted at the broad level of the business services sector, on a sub-sectoral level and at the level of the individual firm. Such a research approach provides a clear picture of the operation and internationalisation of a cross section of UK business services sector firms.

The findings of the empirical research presented in this study make an important contribution to the appreciation of business service sector internationalisation. A clear picture of the process of international expansion is provided from which a model has been developed that can be used to predict the internationalisation process through which business service firms can expect to pass.

In this concluding chapter the major findings of the research will be summarised, and assessed in terms of their relevance to other service sectors. Having evaluated the research findings it will then be useful to highlight the policy implications at both a national and international level. Finally, the contribution of this research will be considered, and the questions which it raises highlighted. Suggestions for the direction of future research will be considered. However, prior to this, it is useful to assess the international competitiveness of the UK business services sector in the light of the research findings.

11.2 The international competitiveness of the UK business services sector

As has been shown earlier (Chapter 7) the UK business service sector is well developed employing nearly 8 per cent of the total workforce at the end of 1994 (Employment Gazette, July 1995) and making an important contribution to GDP. From an international perspective the UK appears to have a competitive advantage in the provision of services in general and business services in particular, having a positive current account balance in these areas. Within the European Union the UK appears to have one of the most advanced business service sectors which employs 31 per cent of all persons employed in the sector in the EUR (12) (EUROSTAT, 1994, p.194).

It has been shown (Chapters 6, 7 & 8) that many UK business service firms are involved in providing services in an international market. The UK is home to a number of highly successful business service sector MNEs, for example, in the advertising sector WPP Group Plc. and Cordiant Plc.. In the accountancy sector many of the top companies have British origins although today by virtue of the dominance of US partners they may no longer be referred to as fully British. The UK has also been the source of some highly successful computer service firms a

269

number of which in recent years have been acquired by foreign companies, for example, Hoskyns acquired by Cap Gemini Sogeti and ICL acquired by Fujitsu. In all the sectors studied in-depth a polarisation between a small number of very large international firms and a large number of small firms was found. The healthy level of new firm formation in the sector provides a source of innovative ideas and services, as well as a pool of skilled labour from which the larger firms can draw, either through poaching workers, employing a small firm on a contractual basis, or through acquisition.

The competitiveness of the UK business services sector can be viewed in terms of firms exploiting their ownership advantages including: specialised skills; international networks; brand names; reputation; among others. The research findings serve to highlight the importance of the internalisation of ownership advantages among information intensive services firms. Locational advantages, are also important, which derive from originating in the UK, these include: the regulatory environment; the level of economic activity; the strong domestic demand for business services; the availability of skilled professional labour, and so on. For example, in the UK, the sectors examined are largely self regulating, this provides firms with an added advantage of greater independence and freedom. Also the general business environment in the UK is liberal relative to other countries. Britain also has the infrastructure necessary for the efficient provision of business services, including effective telecommunication networks. The process of industrial restructuring and externalisation of non-core activities also contributes to the expansion of the business services sector.

The UK's business services sector has developed ahead of those in other countries, apart from the US. As a result, the UK has a competitive lead in the provision of such services. British firms have the advantage of experience from which they have developed good reputations giving them a competitive advantage in relation to their foreign counterparts. In addition, those firms which are successful in developing international networks have in effect created barriers at the international level for new market entrants.

Furthermore, the use of the English language gives an advantage to UK firms since it is accepted as the main language in which international business is conducted. As a result of this, together with other locational advantages, the UK is a major recipient of US and Asian FDI seeking to establish a presence in the European market. The UK then benefits form a high level of inward FDI, as well as being a major source of FDI. Consequently, UK business service companies have many opportunities to work with clients which have overseas interests, and so are more likely to become involved with the international supply of services than firms in countries which have lower levels of both inward and outward FDI.

Business services in the UK are heavily concentrated in the South, and in particular in the South East. There is a connection here between the headquarters location of many large and multinational companies, which are attracted to centres of agglomeration where they can be assured of the supply of services and

270

infrastructure which they require. The important relationship between business service firms and their multinational clients has been highlighted in the research findings.

Having explored the UK business service sector it is clear that the sector is highly competitive, confirming Porter's (1990) view that the UK has a leading competitive position in a range of business service activities. The growth of the UK business services sector provides further evidence of its competitive strength.

11.3 The development of a theory for the internationalisation of service activity

Can the model of business service internationalisation developed in this book be of equal relevance to other service activities? As noted earlier the service sector includes a heterogeneous group of activities and as a result the finding of this research are likely to be of greater relevance to certain sub-sectors than to others. Different sections of the service sector have different levels of internationalisation. The provision of personal services, for example hair dressing, are largely provided domestically. For such sectors there are less benefits to be acquired through large scale production, and consequently, these services are generally provided by small local or region based firms. Clearly then the model developed here is of less relevance to service activities with low levels of internationalisation.

For service firms which are international in scope this research predicts that overseas expansion will occur in an evolutionary manner. The stages identified within the international development of business service firms may be of less relevance for other internationally provided services. Nevertheless, it is likely that stages of some sort can be identified. For other service activities there may be more, or indeed, less stages in the internationalisation process, and undoubtedly the role of exports will vary.

A trade and investment perspective

This research has highlighted the importance of trade in the business services sector, however, it is clear that trade is also likely to be important to many other service sector activities. Almost all services can be provided to foreign clients in the form of domestically located service exports, and many services can be provided either in the form of embodied service exports, transhuman service exports, or wire exports. Clearly exports have potential importance throughout the services sector despite the commonly accepted view that services are non-tradable. Indeed, technological developments are likely to increase the tradability of many services activities, primarily those which are information intensive, although with the development of sophisticated machinery and robotics, together with virtual reality, the scope for the exportation of services will increase. For example, research is currently taking place

271

which will, in time, enable doctors to perform 'tele-presence surgery', that is surgeons will be able to operate at a distance from patients using robots guided by remote control (The Economist, 19.3.94). Trade in services is then likely to become more important. The findings of this research would suggest that a reassessment of international trade in services is required.

It is helpful to explore trade in services within the context of the available trade theory. The theories of absolute and comparative advantage, for example, are useful tools with which to analyse service sector trade. Clear though, for many service activities, trade and investment occur together. It is therefore necessary to explore the relevance of theories of FDI. The theories of the MNE explored clearly can be used to understand a wide range of multinational service sector activity. However, this research highlights the need to explore beyond trade and FDI. Service sector firms engage in a wide variety of arrangements to service foreign markets, including trade and FDI, but also joint ventures, contractual arrangements, franchise agreements, licensing among others. To fully appreciate the internationalisation of services it is necessary to recognise and examine all the diverse forms of cross border activity.

The exploration of trade and FDI highlighted the importance of intra-firm trade which occurs in the international operations of firms in all sectors. It is felt that this is of particular importance in some service activities, since in many cases independent trade is not possible so an overseas presence is established to facilitate trade. The survey provided evidence of the existence of transaction specific overseas presences. Lack of data prevents further analysis of intra-firm trade at this stage. However, clearly intra-firm trade is a vital element in the internationalisation of service sector firms and as such it warrants further investigation.

An organisational perspective

Internationalisation among service firms usually occurs, after perhaps an initial phase of exporting, through the extension of the organisation into foreign markets. Thus an appreciation of the organisation of service firms is essential to fully understand the internationalisation of service firms. The importance of intra-firm trade can also be explored from an organisational perspective, with trade being internalised in order to minimise transaction costs. This research has found Williamson's (1975, 1979) transaction cost approach to organisations together with internalisation theory (Buckley and Casson, 1976) to be useful theoretical tools with which to explore the international development of service firms. They hold particular relevance for business services because of the significance of information assets, and the need to protect these through the process of internalisation.

By tracing the organisational development of a number of business service firms an understanding of the organisational dynamics of service firms has been gained. Among the multinational business service firms studied the holding company or variations of this organisational form proved dominant. However, organisational structures are clearly evolving. There is particular scope for the development of new innovative and flexible organisational forms within information intensive service sectors. New ICTs would appear to hold as much significance for the organisational development of international service firms as they do for the internationalisation of services through trading mechanisms.

The conflicting pressures for centralisation of control and those for decentralisation of control within business service firms have been highlighted as factors influencing the choice of organisational form. Structures do vary even within the business services sector, for example the desire for majority ownership is stronger among computer service firms than among advertising firms. In contrast, the accountancy sector illustrates the achievement of a high level of central control with decentralised ownership. Although the accountancy sector may be regarded as somewhat idiosyncratic in this respect, the organisational structures utilised in this sector do hold wider relevance.

The model developed to understand and predict the process of internationalisation and level of centralisation or decentralisation among business service sector firms can be extended to other service sector MNEs. The weight given to the variables may differ and this would lead to distinct internationalisation sequences and levels of centralisation among the international organisation of service firms from other sub-sectors.

An assessment of the internationalisation of services model

The framework for the multinational development of business service firms elaborated upon in Chapter 10 makes a useful contribution to the developing body of literature concerned with the internationalisation of service sector activity. Through the detailed examination of three business service sub-sectors valuable insights into the internationalisation process have been gained. Clearly, a model built upon findings from an examination of the internationalisation of business services is of limited value when applied to other service activities given the heterogeneity of the sector. Nevertheless it is quite possible that the model could be adapted to the specific characteristics of other service sectors and still retain explanatory value. Indeed, it would be interesting to test whether this is the case by examining the internationalisation of a number of other service activities.

Clearly, the framework forwarded in this book adds to a developing body of academic literature concerned with the internationalisation of service activity. On a practical level it is a helpful model for decision-makers in the business services sector considering embarking upon a strategy of international expansion or reassessing their international position and organisational structure. Policy makers concerned with the regulation of services, and in particular business services, both at a national and international level will also find this research useful.

The theoretical approach taken in the examination of the business services sector is clearly of value when exploring other service activities. The combination of trade and investment theory with organisational theory is highly suitable given the importance of internationalisation through the establishment of overseas presences, together with the role of intra-firm trade in the internationalisation of services.

11.4 Policy implications

The UK clearly has a competitive advantage in the provision of a number of business services, and, consequently, should seek to maintain and even extend such advantages. It is necessary to sustain and enhance the sources of such competitive advantage elaborated upon earlier. For example, the supply of well educated labour must be ensured through appropriate educational policies. In addition, the UK would do well to maintain its relatively liberal business and regulatory environment. Investment in appropriate infrastructure is vital to the success of economic activity generally. For business services and other information intensive services telecommunications infrastructures are of particular importance given their role in the transportation of information.

Information and communications technologies are vital to facilitate the most efficient and flexible organisation and operation of business service firms. The ability of ICTs to enhance the organisational capacities of firms reaches far beyond the service sector since for all organisations the major limitation is related to the ability to collect analyse and disseminate information.

At a global level the internationalisation of business service firms and services generally can lead to welfare gains in terms of specialisation and the gains from trade. Furthermore, the internationalisation of firms lead to the transfer of technology, in a broad sense. For example, the transfer of new and more efficient organisational techniques. Increased efficiency of service production is likely to have a significant impact on other sectors of the economy, for example, contributing to the effective production and distribution of manufactured goods. Welfare gains from the internationalisation of services are likely to permeate through the economy in general. As Quinn and Doorley (1988, p.214) note:

> ...the services- and goods-producing sectors are so intertwined that it is counterproductive to think of policy mechanisms for one without carefully considering the impact on the other. The interactions between services and manufacturing cover a broad, and often unrecognized, spectrum of activities and profoundly affect the performance and competitiveness of US manufacturing enterprises.

The boundary between services and manufactures is fluid and varies widely over time, this must be recognised in domestic economic, and international trade and investment policies.

In general it can be assumed that a competitive market place will provide the optimal environment for the successful development of services. Government intervention would seem justified only in those situations where market imperfections or externalities make it unlikely that private initiatives can meet the challenge.

At an international level one of the major barriers to the development of international service providers is the high level of regulation which many service activities attract. Deregulation is not appropriate in many cases but harmonisation of the regulatory environment on a global scale would clearly enable a more efficient provision of services. If the full benefits from the internationalisation of the service sector are to be attained it is necessary to ensure free trade and the free flow of investment in the sector. This task is now being addressed within the World Trade Organisation following the General Agreement on Trade in Services (GATS), concluded at the Uruguay Round of GATT negotiations. The GATS agreement is in its early days, nevertheless, it represents the start of a process which in time will hopefully lead to a more liberal international trade and investment environment for services.

A further factor inhibiting the internationalisation of some service activities concerns the protection of intellectual property rights. For example, many information intensive services can be easily replicated, consequently, without adequate protection at an international level, there is little incentive for firms producing such services to supply overseas markets. The 1993 GATT agreement on trade related aspects of intellectual property rights (TRIPS) goes some way towards addressing this problem with, for example, the extension of copyright protection and clarification over the protection of trademarks and service marks among other measures. Clearly, the protection of knowledge intensive assets at an international level is essential if the full benefits of internationalisation and specialisation in the provision of services is to be achieved. Further effort is required at an international level to ensure the necessary level of protection.

A major difficulty in the examination of trade and investment in services is the lack of adequate data. The collection of statistics has in the past been focused upon material production, with the increased importance of service sector activity steps are being taken to address this problem. In time hopefully it will be possible to obtain similar data for services as is now available for manufactured goods. Of course, service activity does present some measurement difficulties which are not easily overcome. Indeed, there is the whole problem of the blurring of activities making it difficult to distinguish what is a good and what is a service. Furthermore, this research has highlighted the significance of intra-firm trade in services and this presents specific measurement problems, since it occurs within the boundaries of the firm it is necessary to secure the cooperation of service firms to facilitate the collection of data regarding this type of transaction. Governments certainly have a role to play in sponsoring the development of improved systems for the collection of service sector data at a national level and no doubt institutions such as the WTO can help ensure that such systems are comparable at an international level.

275

11.5 Final conclusions

The research findings reported in this book provide fresh insights into the internationalisation of service activities. Though the focus has been upon the UK business services sector, it is clear that the findings have relevance to other service sectors. The approach to internationalisation has been one which incorporated trade and investment with organisational factors. It has been found that this approach is highly suitable to service activities which are most often, though not always, internationalised through the extension of the service organisation across national borders.

In the process of this research many more questions have arisen than have been answered. Clearly, there are many further lines of enquiry which require attention if the process of service internationalisation is to be fully understood. In particular, ICTs undoubtedly have a major impact on the tradability of many services as well as on the organisational design of international firms. Given the speed with which technology is evolving, together with the nature of services, particularly, those which are information-intensive, any model of service sector internationalisation must be dynamic in character. The framework developed in this study attempts to address this requirement, however, further refinements are necessary. Additional research is necessary to test and improve upon the model presented here. It would be useful, for example, to explore other service activities and indeed to make cross country comparisons.

The research presented here provides a valuable record of the development of the UK business services sector through the 1980s and into the 1990s. A number of important insights into the internationalisation of business service activities have been highlighted, and a model for the multinational development of business service firms has been forwarded. The in-depth study of the UK business services sector has proved useful in terms of building an understanding of the internationalisation of service activities in general. As such, it makes a valuable contribution to research into the multinational development of service sector firms. Clearly, though, further investigation is required.

Appendices

Research techniques and data analysis

1 Introduction

The research methods employed in this study have been given consideration in Chapters 1 and 7, it is the intention of this appendix to elaborate upon certain details of the discussion presented earlier. Furthermore, the main characteristics of the data analysis, from which the results reported in Chapter 8 are derived, will be briefly outlined. Consideration will be given to the use of postal questionnaires and case study work as means of data collection. The use of scales in questionnaires will be explored, since a number of questions in the survey employed this technique. The representativeness of the sample surveyed will also be assessed. Finally, conclusions will be drawn with respect to the validity of the research, with its strengths and weaknesses being highlighted.

2 Questionnaires and case studies

Questionnaires

Questionnaires have become a common method of gathering information. Postal surveys enable the collection of data from a large number of respondents. The biggest problem with the postal questionnaire is that it is only somewhat tenuously

277

a primary data gathering method (Howard and Sharp, 1983). The investigator may have no direct contact with the respondents who may interpret the questions very differently from his/her intentions. A pilot study, as utilised in this research project, is therefore essential to test the questionnaire and minimise the scope for misunderstanding on the part of respondents. Clearly, the strength of the postal questionnaire is its capacity to reach a wide range of respondents, and provide a large body of data, in a cost effective manner.

Sample surveyed The sample surveyed cannot be seen as a completely random sample of the UK business services sector. Firstly it was subdivided in to six sub-sectors, in order to ensure a range of activities were represented in the sample. The particular sub-sectors were selected to provide a cross section of information intensive business services activities. In addition, the six sub-sectors selected showed a high level of inter relatedness resulting from diversification within the sectors. Secondly, the purpose of the research being to study the internationalisation of business service firms, it was necessary to ensure a fair proportion of the sample were likely to be engaged in overseas activity. Given the number of business service firms, 117,732 in 1990 (Business Monitor SDA29 1995), compared to the level of resources available for the research project, a completely random sample of 1019 firms would no doubt have led to responses being dominated by small local and national firms with few firms with international interests being surveyed. Thus, although a truly random sample would have been preferred, funding limitations necessitated a careful selection of firms for the survey.

As a consequence, the top 30 firms from each of the sub-sectors were included in the survey sample. Since the larger the firm is the more likely it is to be international, it was felt that this selection of firms would ensure that a high level of internationally active firms were surveyed. The remainder of the sample were selected at random and would therefore consisted of a large number of small firms, ensuring that internationalisation among small firms could also be explored.

Response rate Of a total of 1019 postal questionnaires sent out 409 were returned, giving a total response rate of 40.1 percent. However, of these total usable returns amounted to 328, a response rate of 32.2 per cent. Postal surveys have produced response rates in excess of 90 per cent, but responses as low as 10 per cent are encountered (Dixon and Leach, 1978). Clearly, a variety of factors influence the level of response, including the interests of respondents and the level of follow up. The postal survey was followed up with a second letter and further copy of the questionnaire and this did lead to further responses. However, again resource limitations restricted the level of follow up. The larger the non-response, the less meaningful the conclusions that can be drawn from the survey data. This is further exacerbated by the tendency for certain types of respondent to select themselves leading to the possibility that the response sample may incorporate some form of

278

bias. Despite this, a response rate of 32.2 per cent, providing a sample that appears to reflect accurately the wider population of business service firms (Chapter 7), does serve as a valuable source of data from which it is possible to draw conclusions of a general nature.

Use of scales in questionnaires A number of questions asked in the postal survey made use of scales. With the use of such a technique the researcher is assuming a dimension that goes from the most negative rating possible to the most positive. The way the researcher gets respondents into ordered categories is to put designations or labels on such a continuum. Respondents are then asked to consider the labels and place themselves in the proper category.

There are two points which should be noted about the kind of data that results from such questions. Firstly, respondents will differ in their understanding of what the labels or categories mean. The only assumption that is necessary in order to make meaningful analysis, however, is that, on the whole the people who give a rating of 'extremely important' give a higher priority to a factor than those who give a rating 'important'. To the extent that people differ in their understanding of the criteria for 'extremely important' and 'important' there is unreliability in the measurement, but the measurement still may have meaning. Secondly, an ordinal scale measurement like this is relative. The distribution of people choosing a particular label or category depends on the particular scale that is presented.

Case studies

The case studies were used in this research to provide a detailed insight into the operations of individual firms. The selection of case study firms was determined by a number of factors. Where possible UK owned firms were selected, this proved a particular limitation in the computer services sector where in recent years a number of UK firms have been acquired by foreign companies. The two firms in each sub-sector were selected where possible to illustrate alternative organisational strategies, and different levels of development. To some extent the firms were self selecting in that the companies studied were willing to provide relevant information. The case studies were compiled from material obtained directly from the companies concerned, generally in the form of company reports and accounts. In addition, a variety of secondary sources were also used.

Clearly, the weakness of a case study approach is the narrow sample of firms studied which reduces the scope for making valid generalisations concerning all firms in the sector. However, by combining this approach with the postal survey it is possible to provide a detailed exploration of the UK business services sector.

3 Statistical techniques

The postal survey gave rise to a large quantity of data, consisting as it did of some 19 main question and many more sub-questions. The SPSS/PC+ V2.0 and Data Entry computing programmes were used to help analyse this data. Many of the survey results arise from the use of descriptive statistics, in addition, methods of statistical inference were employed, namely correlation coefficients and the chi square. These two statistical measurements will be considered briefly here.

Correlation coefficients

Correlation studies are concerned with investigating the relationship between pairs of variables. This does not mean establishing cause and effect relations, since correlation coefficients only indicate the strength of relations between variables. Correlation analysis attempts to measure the strength of such relationships between two variables by means of a single number called a correlation coefficient (denoted by *r*), the higher this number the stronger the association. The correlation coefficient is calculated in the following manner:

$$r = \frac{\sum_{i=1}^{N} (X_i - \bar{X})(Y_i - \bar{Y})}{(N-1) S_x S_y}$$

Where N is the number of cases and S_x and S_y are the standard deviations of the two variables. The absolute value of *r* indicates the strength of the linear relationship, that is, *r* measures the extent to which the points cluster about a straight line. The largest possible absolute value is 1, which occurs when all points fall exactly on the line. When the line has a positive slope, the value of *r* is positive, and when the slope of the line is negative, the value of *r* is negative. It is important to remember that the correlation coefficient between two variables is a measure of their linear relationship, and a value of *r*=0 implies a lack of linearity and not a lack of association.

   Correlation coefficients should be tested to see if they are statistically significant, to determine whether or not they occurred by chance alone, but this still has nothing to do with proving causation.

Chi-square

The Pearson Chi-square (χ^2) is a statistic often used to test the hypothesis that the row and column variables are independent. It is calculated by summing over all cells the square residuals divided by the expected frequencies:

280

$$\chi^2 = \sum_i \sum_j \frac{(O_{ij} - E_{ij})^2}{E_{ij}}$$

The calculated chi-square is compared to the critical points of the theoretical chi-square distribution to produce an estimate of how likely (or unlikely) this calculated value is if the two variables are in fact independent. Since the value of the chi-square depends on the number of rows and columns in the table being examined, one must know the degrees of freedom. The degrees of freedom can be viewed as the number of cells of a table that can be arbitrarily filled when the row and column totals (marginals) are fixed. For a R × C table, the degrees of freedom are (R - 1) × (C - 1), since once (R - 1) rows and (C - 1) columns are filled, frequencies in the remaining row and column cells must be chosen so that marginal totals are maintained. If the probability of the chi-square result is small enough (usually 0.05 or 0.01), the hypothesis that the two variables are independent is rejected. This probability is also known as the observed significance level of the test.

The chi-square is a test of independence; it provides little information about the strength or form of the association between two variables. The magnitude of the observed chi-square depends not only on the goodness of fit of the independence model, but also on the sample size. If the sample for a particular table increases n-fold, so does the chi-square value. Thus large chi-square values can arise in applications where residuals are small relative to expected frequencies but where the sample size is large.

Certain conditions must be met for the chi-square distribution to be a good approximation of the distribution of the statistic in the equation given above. The data must be random samples from multinomial distributions and the expected values must not be too small. While it has been recommended that all expected frequencies be at least 5, studies indicated that this is probably too stringent and can be relaxed (Everitt, 1977).

To improve the approximation in the case of a 2 × 2 table, Yates' correction for continuity is sometimes applied. Yates' correction for continuity involves subtracting 0.5 from positive differences between observed and expected frequencies (the residual) and adding 0.5 to negative differences before squaring.

4 Conclusion

In this appendix further consideration has been given to the research techniques employed in this project. Clearly, a major factor accounting for the choice of research techniques adopted has been the limitation of resources. As noted earlier, the postal survey provides a cost effective method of generating a large body of data. To have employed a questionnaire administered by an interviewer would have given rise to higher quality data, however, this would also have involved extensive travel and accommodation costs far beyond the scope of the available resources.

The weaknesses inherent in the data generated through the postal survey must be recognised when considering the results and conclusions of this study. Nevertheless, the information provided in this book is of value, bases as it is upon the responses from 328 business service firms together with the detailed examination of 6 individual firm. As such, it makes an important contribution to the knowledge of an area which has as yet received little attention.

International Standard Industrial Classification: classification of business services

Divi-sion	Major group	Group	
83			*Real Estate and Business Services*
	831	8310	Real estate
			This group does not include operators of hotels, rooming houses, camps, trailer camps, and other lodging places, who are classified in group 6320.
	832		Business services except machinery and equipment rental and leasing
		8321	Legal services
		8322	Accounting, auditing, and book keeping services
		8323	Data-processing and tabulation services
		8324	Engineering, architectural, and technical service. Medical and dental laboratories are classified in group 9331 (Medical, dental, and other health services); and research and scientific institutes). Engineering and technical services carried on in association with manufacturing, construction, or other activities are classified in the group appropriate to the activity with which the developmental or testing work is associated.
		8325	Advertising services
			Market research services provided to others on a fee or contractual basis are included in this group.
		8329	Business services, except machinery and equipment rental and leasing not elsewhere classified.
			Establishments primarily engaged in furnishing business services not elsewhere classified to others on a fee or contract basis, such as credit rating agencies; adjustment and collection agencies; duplicating, addressing, blueprinting, photocopying, mailing list and stenographic services; employment agencies; news gathering and reporting agencies; business management and consulting services; fashion designers; bondsmen; fingerprint services; detective agencies and protective services.
	833	8330	Machinery and equipment rental and leasing
			The leasing of agricultural or construction equipment with drivers is classified in group 1120 or 5000 respectively. The renting or leasing of transport equipment is classified in the appropriate group of division 71(Transport and storage); renting clothing, furniture, pillows, lockers, and most other personal and household goods is classified in group 6200(Retail trade); and the renting of pleasure boats and canoes, motorcycles and bicycles, saddle horses, and similar recreational goods is included in group 9490 (Amusement and recreation services not elsewhere classified).

Detailed descriptions of items are not reproduced in full.

Source: Compiled from United Nations 1968 International Standard Industrial Classification of All Economic Activities, New York: United Nations.

Bibliography

Aaronovitch, S. and Samson, P. (1985), *The Insurance Industry in the Countries of the EEC: Structure, Conduct and Performance*, Commission of the European Communities: Luxembourg.

Aaronovitch, S. and Sawyer, M.C. (1975), *Big Business*, Macmillan: London.

Accountancy (1989), 'What's in a name - firms' simplified family trees', Feb. p.137-8.

Accountancy (1994), 'Thumbs-up from the partners', Sept. p.11.

Advertising Association The (1994), *Advertising Statistics Yearbook 1994*, NTC Research/ Register MEAL Ltd.

Advertising Association The (1995), *Advertising Statistics Yearbook 1995*, NTC Research/ Register MEAL Ltd.

Aglietta, M.C. (1979), *A Theory of Capitalist Regulation: the US experience*, New Left Books: London.

Aharoni, Y. (1966), *The Foreign Investment Decision Process*, Harvard University Press: Boston, Mass.

Aharoni, Y. (ed.) (1993), *Coalitions and Competition: The Globalization of Professional Business Services*, Routledge: London.

Alchian, A.A. and Demsetz, H. (1972), 'Production, information costs and economic organization', *American Economic Review*, Vol. 62, pp. 777-95.

Aliber, R.Z. (1970), 'A theory of foreign direct investment', in C.P. Kindleberger (ed.) *The International Corporation: a Symposium*, MIT Press: Cambridge, Mass.

Alic, J.A., Miller, J.R., and Hart, J.A. (1991), 'Computer software: strategic industry', *Technology Analysis and Strategic Management*, Vol. 3, No. 2, pp.177-90.

Alter, S. (1987), 'Backer, Ted Bates Form New Agency', *Advertising Age*, 20th. June p.52.

284

Anderson, E. and Gatignon, H. (1986), 'A Transaction Cost Approach to Modes of Market Entry', *Journal of International Business Studies*, Vol. 17, Fall.

Anderson, M.H. (1984), *Madison Avenue in Asia: Politics and Transnational Advertising*, Associated University Press Inc.

Ansoff, H.I. (1987), *Corporate Strategy*, revised edition, Penguin.

Aronson, J.D and Cowhey, P.F. (1984), *Trade in Services: A Case for Open Markets*, American Enterprise Institute for Public Policy Research: Washington D.C.

Arrow, K.J. (1969), 'The Organization of Economic Activity: Issues Pertinent to the Choice of Market Versus Nonmarket Allocation', in *The Analysis and Evaluation of Public Expenditure: the PPB System*, Vol. 1, US Joint Economic Committee, pp. 59-73, US Government Printing Office: Washington DC .

Ascher, B. and Whichard, O.G. (1986), 'Improving Service Trade Data', in *Services World Economy Series No. 1*, Pergamon Press: Oxford.

Atinc, T., Behnam, A., Cornford, A., Glasgow, R., Shipper, M. and Yusuf, A. (1984), 'International Transactions in Services and Economic Development', *Trade and Development*, No. 5, pp.141-214.

Bailly, A.S., Boulianne, L. and Maillat, D. (1987), 'Services and production : for a reassessment of economic sectors', *Annals of Regional Sciences*, Vol. 21, No. 2, pp.45-59.

Bailly, A.S., Coffey, W.J., Paelink, J.H.P. and Polese, M. (1992), *Spatial Econometrics of Services*, Avebury: Aldershot.

Balassa, B. (1979), 'The Changing Pattern of Comparative Advantage in Manufactured Goods', *Review of Economics and Statistics*, Vol. 61.

Barras, R. (1986), 'Towards a theory of innovation in services', *Research Policy*, Vol. 15, pp.161-73.

Barras, R. and Swann, J. (1984), *The Adoption and Impact of Information Technology in the UK Accountancy Profession*, The Technical Change Centre: London.

Bartlett, C.A. and Ghoshal, S. (1989), *Managing Across Borders: The Transnational Solution*, Harvard Business School Press: Boston.

Baumol, W.J. (1959), *Business Behaviour, Value and Growth*, Macmillan.

Bavishi, V.B. and Wyman H.E. (1983), *Who Audits the World ?*, School of Business Administration, University of Connecticut.

BDO Binder Hamlyn (1991), *Annual Review 1991*.

BDO Binder Hamlyn (1991), *Annual Report 1991*.

BDO Binder Hamlyn (1992), *Annual Review 1992*.

BDO Binder Hamlyn (1993), *Annual Review 1993*.

Beaverstock, J.V. (1990), 'New International Labour Markets: the case of professional and managerial labour migration within large chartered accountancy firms', *Area*, Vol. 22, No. 2, pp.151-158.

Beaverstock, J.V. (1991), 'Skilled international migration: an analysis of the geography of international secondments within large accountancy firms',

Environment and Planning A, Vol. 23, No. 8, pp.1133-46.

Bell, D. (1974), *The Coming of Post-industrial Society, a venture in social forecasting*, Heinmann Education.

Berle, A.A. and Means, G.C. (1932), *The Modern Corporation and Private Property*, Macmillan.

Benz, S.F. (1985), 'Trade Liberalization and the Global Service Economy', *Journal of World Trade Law*, March-April, pp. 95-120

Bhagwati, J.N. (1964), 'A survey of the theory of international trade', *Economic Journal*, 74, pp.1-84.

Bhagwati, J.N. (1984), 'Splintering and Disembodiment of Services and Developing Nations', *World Economy*, Vol. 7.

Bhagwati, J.N. (1987), 'International Trade in Services and its Relevance for Economic Development', in: Giarini, O., ed., *The Emerging Service Economy*, Pergamon Press.

Binder Hamlyn (1988), *Binder Hamlyn Chartered Accountants*.

Binder Hamlyn (1995), *Creating Opportunity: Annual Review 1995*, Binder Hamlyn.

Boddewyn, J.J.(1981), 'The Global Spread of Advertising Regulation', *MSU Business Topics*, Spring, pp.5-13.

Boddewyn, J.J., Baldwin Halbrich, M. and Perry, A.C. (1986), 'Service Multinationals: Conceptualization, Measurement and Theory', *Journal of International Business Studies*, Vol. 17, No. 3, pp. 41-57.

Brander, J. and Krugman, P. (1983), 'A Reciprocal Dumping Model of International Trade', *Journal of International Economics*, Vol. 13.

Brander, J. and Spence, B. (1984), 'Tariff protection and imperfect competition in the presence of oligopoly over economies of scale', in Kierzkowski, H., (ed.), *Monopolistic Competition and International Trade*, Oxford University Press: Oxford, pp.313-21.

Bressand, A. (1983), 'Mastering the World Economy', *Foreign Affairs*, Vol. 61, No. 4.

Briston, R.J. (1979), 'The UK Accountancy Profession: The Move Towards Monopoly Power', *The Accountants Magazine*, Nov.

Brooke, M.Z. (1984), *Centralization and Autonomy*, Holt, Rinehard & Winston.

Brooke, M.Z. (1986), *International Management: A Review of Strategies and Operations*, Hutchinson.

Brooke, M.Z. and Remmers, H.L. (1978), *The Strategy of Multinational Enterprise*, Second Edition, Pitman.

Browne, L.E. (1983), 'High Technology and Business Services', *New England Economic Review*, July/August .

Browning, H.L, and Singelmann, J. (1975), *The Emergence of a Service Society*, National Technical Information Services: Springfield, Virginia.

Bryson, J., Keeble, D. and Wood, P. (1993), 'The Creation, Location and Growth of Small Business Service Firms in the United Kingdom', *The Service Industries*

Journal, Vol. 13, No. 2, pp.118-31.

Buckley, P.J. (1983), 'New theories of international business: some unresolved problems', in M. Casson (ed.) *The Growth of International Business*, George Allen & Unwin.

Buckley, P.J. (1992), *Studies in International Business*, St.Martin's Press.

Buckley, P.J. and Casson, M.C. (1976), *The Future of the Multinational Enterprise*, Macmillan, London.

Buckley, P.J. and Casson, M.C. (1981), 'The Optimal Timing of Foreign Direct Investment', *The Economic Journal*, Vol. 91, March, pp.75-87.

Buckley, P.J. and Casson, M.C. (1985), *The Economic Theory of the Multinational Enterprise*, Macmillan: London.

Burger,W. (1988), 'The Message Merchants', *Newsweek*, 21st. March, p.32.

Business, The (1995), The Virtual Office, BBC 2.

Business Week (1986), 'Supplement: The Hollow Corporation', 3rd. March.

Cairns, D., Lafferty, M. and Mantle, P. (1984), *IAB Survey of Accounts and Accountants 1983-84*, Lafferty Publications: London.

Campaign (1993), 'The Campaign Report: Technology in Advertising', August 6th. pp.33-40.

Canton, I.D. (1984), 'Learning to Love the Services Economy', *Harvard Business Review,* May-June.

Casas, F.R. (1983), 'International Trade with producer Transport Services', *Oxford Economic Papers*, Vol. 35, No. 1, pp.89-109.

Cassing, J. (1978), 'Transportation Costs in International Trade Theory: A comparison with the analysis of Non-traded goods', *Quarterly Journal of Economics*, Nov. pp.535-50.

Casson, M.C. (1979), *Alternatives to the Multinational Enterprise*, Macmillan: London.

Casson, M.C. (ed.) (1983), *The Growth of International Business*, Allen & Unwin: London.

Casson, M.C. (1990), *Enterprise and Competitiveness: A Systems View of International Business*, Clarendon Press: Oxford.

Casson, M.C. (1991), *Economics of Business Culture: Game Theory, Transaction Costs and Economic Performance*, Clarendon Press: Oxford.

Casson, M.C. (ed.) (1992), *International Business and Global Integration: Empirical Studies*, Macmillan Press.

Casson, M.C. and Associates (1986), *Multinationals and World Trade: Vertical Integration and the Division of Labour in World Industries*, Allen & Unwin: London.

Castle, L.V. and Finlay, C. (eds.) (1988), *Pacific Trade in Services*, Allen & Unwin.

Caves, R.E. (1971), 'International Corporations: The Industrial Economics of Foreign Investment', *Economica*, Vol. 38, p.1-27.

Caves, R.E. (1980), 'Industrial Organization, Corporate Strategy and Structure', *Journal of Economic Literature*, Vol. 18, pp.64-92.

Caves, R.E. (1982), *Multinational Enterprise and Economic Analysis*, Cambridge University Press: Cambridge.

Centre-file (1993), *Annual Report and Accounts*.

Chandler, A.D. (1962), *Strategy and Structure: Chapters in the History of the Industrial Enterprise*, The MIT Press: Cambridge Massachusetts.

Channon, D.F. (1973), *The Strategy and Structure Of British Enterprise*, Graduate School of Business Administration, Harvard University.

Channon, D.F. (1978), *The Service Industries: Strategy, Structure and Financial Performance*, The Macmillan Press Ltd.

Channon, D.F. and Jalland, M. (1979), *Multinational Strategic Planning*, MacMillan Press.

Chudson,W.A. (1981), 'Intra-Firm Trade And Transfer Pricing', in R. Murray (ed.) *Multinationals Beyond The Market*, The Harvester Press.

Clairmonte, E. and Cavanagh, J. (1984), 'Transnational corporations and services: the final frontier', *Trade and Development*, Vol. 5, pp. 215-73.

Clairmonte, F.F. (1986), 'Transnational Conglomerates: Reflections on Global Power', in: Ahooja-Patel, K., Gordon Darbek A., and Nerfin M., (eds.), *World Economy in Transition*, Pergamon Press.

Clark, C. (1957), *The Conditions of Economic Progress*, Macmillan: London.

Coase, R.H. (1937), 'The Nature of the Firm', *Economica*, Vol. 4, pp.386-405.

Coffey, W.J. and Polese, M. (1987), 'Intrafirm Trade In Business Services: Implications For The Location Of Office-Based Activities', *Papers Of The Regional Science Association*, Vol. 62, pp.71-80.

Computing Services Association (1993), *The Computing Services Association Handbook 1993*, Sterling Publications Ltd.

Computing Services Association (1994), *The Computing Services Association Handbook 1994*, Sterling Publications Ltd.

Cordiant Plc. (1995a), *Report and Accounts 1994*, Cordiant Plc.

Cordiant Plc. (1995b), *Proposed one for one rights issue of 221,633,792 New Ordinary Shares of 25 pence at 60 pence per share*, Cordiant Plc.

Cyert, R.M. and March, J.G. (1963), *A Behavioural Theory of the Firm*, Prentice Hall: Englewood Cliffs, New Jersey.

Dahlman, C.J. (1979), 'The Problem of Externality', *Journal of Law and Economics*, Vol. 22, No. 1, pp.141-62.

Daniels, P.W. (1982), *Service industries: growth and location*, Cambridge University Press: Cambridge.

Daniels, P.W. (1985), 'Service Industries: Some New Directions', in M. Pacione (ed.) *Progress in Industrial Geography*, Croom Helm.

Daniels, P.W. (1993), *Service Industries in the World Economy*, Blackwell.

Daniels, P.W. and Moulaert, F. (1991), *The Changing Geography of Advanced Producer Services: Theoretical and empirical perspectives*, Belhaven Press: London.

Daniels, P.W., Thrift, N.J. and Leyshon, A. (1989), 'Internationalization of

Professional Services: Accountancy Conglomerates' in P. Enderwick (ed.) *Multinational Service Firms*, Routledge: London.

Datamation (1994), 'Datamation 100: Overview', June 15th.

Datamation (1995), 'Datamation 100: Overview', June 1st.

Davies, H. (1977), 'Technology Transfer through Commercial Transactions', *Journal of Industrial Economics*, Vol. 26, Dec. pp.161-75.

Davis, S.M. and Lawrence, P.R. (1977), *Matrix*, Addison-Wesley: Reading, Mass.

Deardorff, A.V. (1980), 'The general validity of the Law of Comparative Advantage', *Journal of Political Economy*, Vol. 88, No. 5.

Deardorff, A.V. (1982), 'The general validity of the Heckscher-Ohlin Theorem', *American Economic Review*, Vol. 72, pp.683-94.

Deardorff, A.V. (1985), 'Comparative advantage and international trade in investment in services', in R.M. Stern (ed.) *Trade and Investment in Services: Canadian/US Perspectives*, Toronto: Ontario Economic Council, pp.39-71.

Deloitte, Plender, Griffiths & Co. (1958), *Deloitte & Co.: 1845-1956*, Deliotte, Plender, Griffiths & Co.: London.

Dick, R. and Dicke, H. (1979), 'Patterns of Trade in Knowledge', in *International Economic Development and Resource Transfer*, (ed.) H. Giersch, Institut fur Weltwirtschaftander.

Dicken, P. (1992), *Global Shift: The Internationalization of Economic Activity*, 2nd. edition, Paul Chapman Publishing Ltd.: London.

Dietrich, M. (1994), *Transaction Cost Economics And Beyond*, Routledge: London & New York.

Djajic, S and Kierzkowski, H. (1989), 'Goods, Services and Trade', *Economica*, Vol. 56, pp.83-95.

Dornbusch, R., Fischer, S., and Samuelson, P.A. (1977), 'Comparative Advantage, Trade, and Payments in a Ricardian Model with a Continuum of Goods', *American Economic Review*, Vol. 67, pp. 823-39.

Doyle, P. (1968), 'Economic Aspects of Advertising: A Survey', *Economic Journal*, Vol. 78, Sept.

Douma, S. and Schreuder, H. (1991), *Economic Approaches To Organisations*, Prentice Hall: London.

Ducatel, K. and Miles, I. (1992), 'Internationalisation of information technology services and public policy implications', *World Development*, Vol. 20, No. 12, pp.1843-1857.

Dunning, J.H. (1979), 'Explaining changing patterns of international production: in defence of the eclectic theory', *Oxford Bulletin of Economics and Statistics*, Vol. 41, No. 4, pp.269-95.

Dunning, J.H. (1981), *International Production and the Multinational Enterprise*, Allen and Unwin: London.

Dunning, J.H. (1988), *Multinationals, Technology and Competitiveness*, Unwin Hyman.

Dunning, J.H. (1989), 'Multinational Enterprises and the Growth of Services: Some

Conceptual and Theoretical Issues', *The Service Industries Journal*, Vol. 9, No. 1, pp.5-39.

Dunning, J.H. (1993a), *Multinational Enterprise and the Global Economy*, Addison Wesley.

Dunning, J.H. (1993b), *The Globalization of Business*, Routledge: London.

Dunning, J.H. and McQueen, M. (1982), 'The Eclectic Theory of the Multinational Enterprise and the International Hotel Industry', in A.M. Rugman (ed.) *New Theories of the Multinational Enterprise*, Croom Helm.

Dyas, G.P. and Thanheiser, H.T. (1976), *The Emerging European Enterprise, Strategy and Structure in French and German Industry*, Macmillan.

Economist The (1993), 'A Survey Of The Computer Industry', Feb. 27th.

Economist The (1994), 'A Survey of the Future of Medicine', March 19th.

Economist The (1995), 'Accountancy firms: A glimmer of hope', April 1st., pp.100-05.

Economist The (1995), 'British accountant's liability: Big Six PLC', Oct. 7th. pp. 135-38.

Edvardsson, B., Edvinsson, L. and Nystrom, H. (1993), 'Internationalisation in Service Companies', *The Service Industries Journal*, Vol. 13, No. 1, January, pp.80-97.

Edvinsson, L. (1985), *Services Internationalization: Trade in Thoughtware*, Consultus International A.B.: Stockholm.

Elfring, T. (1993), 'Structure and growth of business services in Europe', In, *The Structure of European Industry*, H.W. de Jong (ed.), Kluwer Academic Publishers: Dordrecht.

Elfring, T. and Baven, G. (1994), 'Outsourcing Technical Services: Stages of Development', *Long Range Planning*, Vol. 27, No. 5, pp.42-51.

Elliott, B.B.(1962), *A History of English Advertising*, Business Publications Ltd.

Enderwick, P. (1987), 'The Stategy and Structure of Service-sector Multinationals: Implications for Potential Host Regions', *Regional Studies*, Vol. 21, No. 3, pp.215-23.

Enderwick, P. (1989), *Multinational Service Firms*, Routledge: London.

Enderwick, P. (1992), 'The Scale and Scope of Service Sector Multinationals', in *Multinational Enterprise in the World Economy: Essays in Honour of John Dunning*, Edward Elgar.

Erramilli, M.K. and Rao, C.P. (1990), 'Choice of foreign entry modes by service firms: role of market knowledge', *Management International Review*, Vol. 30, pp.135-150.

Erramilli, M.K. and Rao, C.P. (1993), 'Service firm's international entry-mode choice: a modified transaction-cost analysis approach', *Journal of Marketing*, Vol. 57, July, pp.19-38.

Erramilli, M.K. (1991), 'The experience factor in foreign market entry behaviour of service firms', *Journal of International Business Studies*, Vol. 22, No. 3, pp.479-501.

290

Erramilli, M.K. (1992), 'Influence of some external and internal environmental factors on foreign market entry mode choice in service firms', *Journal of Business Research*, Vol. 25, pp.263-76.

Esperanca, Jose-Paulo (1992), 'International Strategies in the European Service Sector: A Comparative Study', in M. Casson (ed.) *International Business and Global Integration: Empirical Studies*, Macmillan Press.

Ethier, W. (1982), 'National and International Returns to Scale in the Modern Theory of International Trade', *American Economic Review*, Vol. 72, pp.389-405.

Ethier, W.J. (1986), 'The Multinational Firm', *The Quarterly Journal of Economics*, Nov.

European Commission (1988), *Panorama of EC Industry 1988*, European Commission: Luxembourg.

European Commission (1994), *Panorama of EU Industry 1994*, European Commission: Luxembourg.

EUROSTAT (1994), *International Trade In Services: EUR 12 from 1983 to 1992*, Office for Official Publications of the European Communities: Luxembourg.

EUROSTAT (1995), *Business Services in Europe*, Office for Official Publications of the European Communities: Luxembourg.

Everitt, B.S. (1977), *The Analysis of Contingency Tables*, Chapman and Hall.

Eyeions, D. (1993), 'The Computing Services Association', in *The Computing Services Association Handbook 1993*, pp.13-16.

Falvey, R. (1976), 'Transportation costs in the pure theory of international trade', *Economic Journal*, Sept., pp.536-50.

Farbey, D. (1979), *The Business of Advertising*, Associated Business Press: London.

Feketekuty, G. (1985), 'Negotiating Strategies for Liberalizing Trade and Investment in Services', in R.M. Stern (ed.) *Trade and Investment in Services/; Canada/U.S. Perspectives*, Toronto, pp.203-14.

Feketekuty, G. (1988), *International Trade in Services: An Overview and Blueprint for Negotiations*, Ballinger: Cambridge,Mass.

Findlay, R. and Kierzkowski, H. (1983), 'International Trade and Human Capital: A Simple General Equilibrium Model', *Journal of Political Economy*, Vol. 91, Dec., pp.957-78.

Findlay, C. (1985), 'A framework for services trade policy questions', *Pacific Economic Papers*, Sept.

Fischer, A. (1939), 'Primary, secondary and tertiary production', *Economic Record*, June.

Fischer, S. (1977), 'Long-term contracting, sticky prices and monetary policy: a comment', *Journal of Monetary Economics*, Vol. 3, pp. 317-23.

Forge, S. (1991), 'Why the computer industry is restructuring now', *Futures*, Vol. 23, No. 9, pp.960-77.

Forge, S. (1993), 'Business models for the computer industry for the next decade:

when will the fast eat the largest?', *Futures*, Vol. 25, No. 9, pp.923-48.

Forsgren, M. (1989), *Managing the Internationalisation Process: a Swedish case*, Routledge: London.

Fraser, W.H. (1981), *The Coming of the Mass Market 1985-1914*, Macmillan: London.

Fuchs, V.R. (1968), *The Service Economy*, Columbia University Press.

Gatignon, H. and Anderson, E. (1988), 'The multinational degree of control over foreign subsidiaries: an empirical test of a transaction cost explanation', *Journal of Law Economic and Organisation*, Vol. 4, No. 2, pp.305-35.

GATT (1992), *International Trade 1990-1*, GATT Secretairiat: Geneva.

GATT (1994), *International Trade: 1994 Trends and Statistics*, GATT Secretairiat: Geneva.

Gentle, C.J., Marshall, J.N. and Coombes, M.G. (1991), 'Business reorganization and regional development: The case of the British Building Societies Movement', *Environment and Planning A*, Vol. 23, pp.1759-77.

Gentle, C. and Howells, J. (1994), 'The Computer Services Industry: Restructuring for a Single Market', *Tijdschrift voor Economische en Sociale Geografie*, Vol. 85, No. 4, pp.311-21.

Gershuny, J.I. and Miles, I.D. (1983), *The New Services Economy: The Transformation of Employment in Industrial Societies*, Praeger Publishers: New York.

Gershuny, J.I. (1978), *After Industrial Society? The Emerging Self Service Economy*, Macmillan Press.

Giarini, O. (ed.) (1987), *The Emerging Service Economy*, Pergamon Press.

Gibbs, M. (1986), 'Services, development and TNC's', *The CTC Reporter*, No. 21, Spring.

Giddy, I.H. (1978), 'The demise of the product cycle in international business theory', *Columbia Journal of World Business*, Vol. 13, pp.90-7.

Goe, W.R. (1990), 'Producer Services, Trade and the Social Division of Labour', *Regional Studies*, Vol. 24, No. 4, pp. 327-242.

Gold Greenlees Trott PLC (1988), *Report and Accounts 1988*.

Gold Greenlees Trott PLC (1992), *Report and Accounts 1992*.

Gold Greenlees Trott PLC (1993), *Report and Accounts 1993*.

Gold Greenlees Trott PLC (1994), *Report and Accounts 1994*.

Gonenc, R. (1988), 'Changing Economics of International Trade in Services', in Guile, B.R. and Quinn, J.B., *Technology in Services: Policies for growth, trade and employment*, National Academy Press: Washington D.C.

Gray, H.P. (1990), 'The role of services in global structural change', in A. Webster and J. Dunning (eds.) *Structural Change in the World Economy*, Routledge: London.

Grubel, H.G. and Lloyd, P.J. (1975), *Intra-Industry Trade*, Macmillan: London.

Grubel, H.G. (1987), 'All Traded Services are Embodied in Materials or People', *World Economy*, Vol. 10, No. 3, pp. 319-30.

292

Grubel, H.G. and Walker, M.A. (1989), *Service Industry Growth: Causes and Effects*, Fraser Institute: Vancouver.

Guile, B.R. and Quinn, J.B. (1988), *Technology in Services: Policies for growth, trade and employment*, National Academy Press: Washington D.C.

Harris, C. (1988), 'Saatchi rises to £63m and shuns financial services' *Financial Times*, 26th. May.

Harris, G. (1984), 'The Globalization of Advertising', *International Journal of Advertising*, Vol. 3, P. 223-34.

Heckscher, E. (1919), 'The effect of foreign trade on the distribution of income', in Ellis, H. and Metzler, L.A. (eds.)(1950), *Readings in the Theory of International Trade*, Allen and Unwin, London, pp.272-300.

Hedlund, G. and Kverneland, A. (1984), *Are Establishment and Growth Patterns for Foreign Markets Changing? The Case of Swedish Investment in Japan*, Institute of International Business, Stockholm School of Economics.

Hedlund, G. and Rolander, D.(1990), 'Action in heterarchies: new approaches to managing the MNC', in C.A.Bartlett, Y.Doz and G.Hedlund (eds.) *Managing the Global Firm*, Routledge: London.

Helleiner, G.K. (1981), 'Intra-Firm Trade And The Developing Countries: An Assessment Of The Data', in R. Murray (ed.) *Multinationals Beyond The Market*, The Harvester Press.

Helpman, E. (1984), 'A Simple Theory of International Trade with Multinational Corporations', *Journal of Political Economy*, Vol. 92, No. 3.

Helpman, E. (1985), 'Multinational Corporations and Trade Structure', *Review of Economic Studies*, LII, pp.443-57.

Helpman, E. and Krugman, P.R. (1985), *Market Structure and Foreign Trade, Increasing Returns, Imperfect Competition, and the International Economy*, The MIT Press: Cambridge, Massachusetts/London.

Hegarty, J. (1994), 'GATS: a chance to take the lead', *Accountancy*, Feb. pp.73-4.

Hennart, J.F. (1986), 'What is internalisation ?' *Weltwirtschaftliches Archiv*, Vol. 122, pp.791-804.

Hennart, J.F. (1991), 'The transaction cost theory of the multinational enterprise', in Pitelis, C.N. and Sugden, R. (eds.), *The Nature of the Transnational Firm*, Routledge: London.

Herman, B. and Van Holst, B. (1981), *Towards a Theory of International Trade in Services*, Netherlands Economic Institute: Rotterdam.

Herman, B. and Van Holst, B. (1984), *International Trade in Services: Some Theoretical and Practical Problems*, Netherlands Economic Institute: Rotterdam.

Heskett, J. (1986), *Managing the Service Economy*, Harvard Business School Press: Cambridge, MA.

Hill, P.T. (1977), 'On Goods and Services', *Review of Income and Wealth*, Vol. 23, No. 4, pp.315-38.

Hindley, B., and Smith, A. (1984), 'Comparative Advantage and Trade in Services',

World Economy, Vol. 7.

Hirsch, S. (1975), 'The Product Cycle Model of International Trade: a multi-country cross-section analysis', *Oxford Bulletin of Economics and Statistics*, Vol. 37, pp.305-17.

Hite, R. and Fraser, C. (1988), 'International advertising strategies of multinational companies', *Journal of Advertising Research*, Vol. 28, pp.9-17.

Hodgson, G.M. (1988), *Economics And Institutions*, Polity Press.

Hoekman, B.M. (1990), 'Service-Related Production, Employment, Trade, and Factor Movements', in Messerlin, P.A. and Sauvant, K.P. (eds.) *The Uruguay Round: Services in the World Economy*, United Nations: New York.

Holmes, J. (1986), 'The organization and locational structure of production subcontracting', in A.J. Scott and M. Storper (eds.) *Production, Work and Territory: The Geographical Anatomy of Industrial Capitalism*, Allen & Unwin: London.

Hood, N. and Young, S. (1979), *The Economics of Multinational Enterprise*, Longman: London.

Hood, N. and Young, S. (1983), *Multinational Investment Strategies in the British Isles: A study of MNEs in the Assisted Areas and in the Republic of Ireland*, HMSO, London.

Howard, K. and Sharp, J.A. (1983) *The Management of a Student Research Project*, Gower.

Howells, J. (1988), *Economic, Technological and Locational Trends in European Services*, Gower: Aldershot.

Howells, J. (1989), *Trade in Software, Computer Services and Computerised Information Services*, Report to the Directorate for Science Technology and Industry, Paris: Organisation for Economic Cooperation and Development (DST/ICCP/TISP/-89.16).

Howells, J., and Green, A. (1988), *Technological Innovation, Structural Change and Location in U.K. Services*, Avebury: Aldershot.

Hufbauer, G.C. (1966), *Synthetic Materials and the Theory of International Trade*, Duckworth: London.

Hufbauer, G.C. (1970), 'The impact of national characteristics and technology on the commodity composition of trade in manufactured goods', in Vernon, R. (ed.) *The Technology Factor in International Trade*, Columbia U.P.: New York.

Hume, S. (1993), *Managing the Multinational: Confronting the Global-Local Dilemma*, Prentice Hall: London.

Hymer, S.H. (1960), *The International Operation of National Firms: A Study of Direct Foreign Investment*, MIT Press: Cambridge, Mass (published 1976).

Illeris, S. (1989), *Services and Regions in Europe*, Avebury: Aldershot.

Inman, R.P. (ed.) (1985), *Managing the Service Economy: Prospects and Problems*, Cambridge University Press.

James Capel (1989), *The Global Advertising Marketplace*, Second Edition, James Capel: London.

294

James, B.G. (1985), 'Alliance: the new strategic focus', *Long Range Planning*, Vol. 18, pp.76-81.

Jensen, M.C. and Meckling, W.H. (1976), 'The theory of the firm: managerial behaviour, agency costs and ownership structure', *Journal of Financial Economics*, Vol. 3, pp. 305-60.

Johanson, J. and Wiedensheim-Paul, F. (1975), 'Internationalization of the Firm - Four Swedish Cases', *Journal of Management Studies*, Oct., pp.305-22.

Johanson, J. and Vahlne, J.E. (1977), 'The internationalization process of the firm - a model of knowledge development and increasing foreign market commitments', *Journal of International Business Studies*, Vol. 8, No. 1, pp.23-32.

Johnson, H.J. (1970), 'The efficiency and welfare implications of the international corporation', in Kindleberger, C.P., (ed.) *The International Corporation*, MIT Press: Cambridge Mass.

Jones, E. (1981), *Accountancy and the British Economy, 1840-1980. The Evolution of Ernst Whinney*, Batsford: London.

Jones, P. and Ricks, S. (1989), 'Service organisations - structure and performance', in P. Jones, (ed.) *Management in Service Industries*, Pitman: London.

Jones, P. (ed.) (1989), *Management in Service Industries*, Pitman: London.

Jones, R.W. and Ruane, F. (1990), 'Appraising The Options For International Trade In Services', *Oxford Economic Papers*, Vol. 42, pp.672-87.

Kakabadse, M. (1987), *International Trade in Services: Prospects for Liberalisation in the 1990s*, Atlantic Paper No. 64, Atlantic Institute for International Affairs, Croom Helm: Paris.

Kaldor, N. (1950), 'The economics aspects of advertising', *Review of Economic Studies*, Vol. 18, pp.1-27.

Kay, N.M. (1984), *The Emergent Firm*, Macmillan.

Kaynak, E. (1989), *The Management of International Advertising: A handbook and guide for professionals*, Quorum Books: New York.

Kelly, J. (1994), 'Andersen Confirms Merger', *Financial Times*, 27th. Sept..

Key, T.S.T. (1985), 'Services in the U.K. Economy', *Bank of England Quarterly Bulletin*, Vol. 25 No. 3 Sept.

Key Note (1992), *Computer Services - A Report*, Key Note Publications.

Key Note (1995), *Computer Services - A Report*, Key Note Publications.

Kierzkowski, H. (1986), *Modelling International Transportation Services*, I.M.F. Research Paper, DM/86/35.

Kierzkowski, H. (1987), 'Recent Advances in International Trade Theory: A Selective Survey', *Oxford Review of Economic Policy*, Vol. 3, No. 1.

Kindleberger, C.P. (1969), *American Business Abroad: Six Lectures on Direct Investment*, Yale University Press: New Haven, Conn.

Klein, R.W. (1973), 'A Dynamic Theory of Comparative Advantage', *American Economic Review*, Vol. 63, No. 1, pp.173-84.

Knickerbocker, F.T. (1973), *Oligopolistic Reaction and Multinational Enterprise*,

Harvard Business School: Boston.

Kojima, K. (1978), *Direct Foreign Investment: a Japanese Model of Multinational Business Operations*, Croom Helm: London.

Kojima, K. and Ozawa, T. (1985), *Japan's General Trading Companies: Merchants of Economic Development*, OECD Development Centre: Paris.

Kravis, I.B. (1956), 'Wages and foreign trade', *Review of Economics and Statistics*, Vol. 38, p.14-30

Kravis, I. (1983), *Services in the Domestic Economy and in World Transactions*, Working Paper No. 1124, National Bureau of Economic Research: Cambridge, Mass.

Krommenacker, R.J. (1984), *World-Traded Services: The Challenge of the Eighties*, Artech House: Dedham, MA.

Krugman, P.R. (1979), 'Increasing Returns, Monopolistic Competition, and International Trade', *Journal of International Economics*, Vol. 9, pp.469-79.

Lakha, S. (1994), 'The new international division of labour and the Indian computer software industry', *Modern Asian Studies*, Vol. 28 No. 2, pp.381-408.

Landefeld, J.S. (1987), 'International Trade in Services: Its Composition, Importance and Links to Merchandise Trade', *Business Economics*, Vol. 22, No. 2, pp.25-31.

Landesmann, M.A. and Petit, P. (1995), 'International Trade in Producer Services: Alternative Explanations', *The Service Industries Journal*, Vol. 15, No. 2, pp.123-161.

Lanigan, D. (1984), 'Agency alignment', *Marketing*, Nov. pp. 97-98.

Leamer, E.E. (1974), 'The commodity composition of international trade in manufactures: an empirical analysis', *Oxford Economic Papers*, Vol. 26, pp.351-74.

Leamer, E.E. (1984), *Sources of International Comparative Advantage: Theory and evidence*, MIT Press: Cambridge, Mass.

Leontief, W. (1953), 'Domestic production and foreign trade: the American capital position re-examined', *Proceeding of the American Philosophy Society*, Vol. 97, pp.332-49.

Leslie, D.A. (1995), 'Global Scan: The Globalization of Advertising Agencies, Concepts, and Campaigns', *Economic Geography*, Vol. 71, No. 4, pp.402-26.

Levitt, T. (1983), 'The Globalization of Markets', *Harvard Business Review*, Vol. 61, No. 3, May-June pp.92-102.

Levitt, T. (1986), *The Marketing Imagination*, The Free Press: New York.

Lewis, R. (1973), *The Service Society*, Longman.

Leyshon, A., Daniels, P.W. and Thrift, N.J. (1987a), 'Internationalization of Professional Producer Services: The Case of Large Accountancy Firms', *Working Papers on Producer Services 3*, St. Davids University College, Lampeter and University of Liverpool.

Leyshon, A., Daniels, P.W. and Thrift, N.J. (1987b), 'Large Accountancy firms in the U.K.: Operational Adaptation and Spatial Development', *Working Papers on*

Producer Services 2, St. Davids University College, Lampeter and University of Liverpool.

Linder, S.B. (1961), *An Essay on Trade and Transformation*, John Wiley: London.

Liston, D. and Reeves, N. (1988), *The Invisible Economy: A Profile of Britain's Invisible Exports*, Pitman Publishing.

Logica PLC (1988), *Annual Review 1988*.

Logica PLC (1989), *Interim Report For The Six Months Ended 31 December 1989*.

Logica PLC (1990), *Annual Review 1990*.

Logica PLC (1991), *Annual Review 1991*.

Logica PLC (1992), *Annual Report 1992*.

Logica PLC (1993), *Annual Report 1993*.

Logica PLC (1994), *Annual Report 1994*.

M.A.C.E. (1992), *Europe 1992 Impact On The Worldwide Computer Industry*, M.A.C.E.

Machlup, F. (1984), *The Economics of Information and Human Capital*, Vol.III, University Press: Princeton.

Magee, S.P. (1977), 'Information and the multinational corporation: an appropriability theory of direct foreign investment', in Bhagwati, J.H. (ed.) *The New International Economic Order*, MIT Press: Cambridge, Mass., pp.317-40.

Malmgren, H.B. (1985), 'Negotiating International Rule for Trade in Services', *World Economy*, Vol. 8.

Margerion, T. (1980), *The Making of a Profession*, The Institute of Chartered Accountants in England and Wales: London.

Markusen, J.R. (1989), 'Trade in Producer Services and in Other Specialized Intermediate Inputs', *The American Economic Review*, Vol. 79, No. 1, pp.85-95.

Markusen, J.R. (1989), 'Services trade by the multinational enterprise', in P. Enderwick (ed.) *Multinational Service Firms*, Routledge: London.

Marris, R. (1964), *The Economic Theory of Managerial Capitalism*, Macmillan: London.

Marshall, J.N. (1985), 'Business Services, the Regions and Regional Policy', *Regional Studies*, Vol. 19, No. 4, pp.353-63.

Marshall, J.N., Damesick P., and Wood, P.A. (1987), 'Understanding the location and role of producer services in the United Kingdom', *Environment and Planning A*, Vol. 19, pp.575-96.

Marshall, J.N., Wood, P., Daniels, P.W., McKinnon, A., Bachtler, J., Damesick, P., Thrift, N., Gillespie, A., Green, A. and Leyshon, A. (1988), *Services and Uneven Development*, Oxford University Press: Oxford.

Martinelli, F. (1991a), 'A demand-orientated approach to understanding producer services', in *The Changing Geography of Advanced Producer Services: Theoretical and Empirical Perspectives*, (eds.) P.W. Daniels and F. Moulaert, Belhaven Press: London.

Martinelli, F. (1991b), 'Producer services, location and regional development', in *The Changing Geography of Advanced Producer Services: Theoretical and*

297

Empirical Perspectives, (eds.) P.W. Daniels and F. Moulaert, Belhaven Press: London.

Mattelart, A. (1979), *Multinational Corporations and the Control of Culture*, Harvester Press: Brighton.

Mattelart, A. (1992), *Internationalisation of Advertising*, Routledge: London.

May, T. (1995), 'Publicis joins 'New Saatchi' in BA pitch', *The Guardian*, 4th April.

Mayere, A. and Vinot, F. (1993), 'Firm Structures and Production Networks in Intellectual Services', *Service Industries Journal*, Vol. 13, No. 2, pp.76-90.

McManus, J.C. (1972), 'The theory of the multinational firm', in G. Paquet (ed.) *The Multinational Firm and the Nation State*, : Collier-Macmillan: Don Mills, Ont.

Meier, G.M. (1980), *International Economics: The Theory of Policy*, Oxford University Press.

Melvin, J.R. (1989), 'Trade in Producer Services: A Heckscher-Ohlin Approach', *Journal of Political Economy*, Vol. 97, No. 5, pp.1180-96.

Messerlin, P.A. and Sauvant, K.P. (eds.) (1990), *The Uruguay Round: Services in the World Economy*, United Nations: New York.

Michell, P. (1988), *Advertising Agency-Client Relations: A Strategic Perspective*, Croom Helm: London.

Miles, I. (1987), 'Information technology and the service economy', in (ed) P. Zorkoczy, *Oxford Surveys in Information Technology*, No. 4, Oxford University Press.

Miles, I. (1993), 'Services in the new industrial economy', *Futures*, July/August, pp.653-72.

Miles, R.E. and Snow, C.C. (1986), 'Organizations: new concepts for new forms', *California Management Review*, Vol. XXVIII, pp.62-73.

Morris, B. and Johnston, R. (1987), 'Dealing with inherent variability: the difference between manufacturing and services?', *International Journal of Operations and Production Management*, Vol. 7 No. 4.

Morris, J.L. (1988), 'Producer Services and the Regions: The Case of Large Accountancy Firms', *Environment and Planning A*, Vol. 20, No. 6, pp.741-59.

Mundell, R.A. (1957a), 'A Geometry of Transport Costs in International Trade Theory', *Canadian Journal of Economics and Political Science*, (August) pp.331-48.

Mundell, R.A. (1957b), 'International Trade and Factor Mobility', *American Economic Review*, Vol. 47, pp.321-25.

Nayyar, D. (1988), 'The Political Economy of International Trade in Services', *Cambridge Journal of Economics*, Vol. 12, No. 2, pp.279-98.

Nevett, T.R. (1982), *Advertising in Britain: A History*, Heinemann: London.

Nicholas, S.J. (1983), 'Agency Contract, Institutional Modes, and the Transition of Foreign Direct Investment By British Manufacturing Multinationals before 1939', *Journal of Economic History*, Vol. 43.

Nicholas, S.J. (1986), 'Multinationals, transaction costs and choice of institutional form', *University of Reading Discussion Papers in International Investment and*

Business Studies, No. 97.

Nicolaides, P. (1989), *Liberalizing Service Trade*, Routledge: London.

Normann, R. (1991), *Service Management: Strategy and Leadership in Service Business*, second edition, John Wiley and Sons: Chichester.

Nusbaumer, J. (1987a), *The Services Economy: Lever to Growth*, Kluwer -Nijhoff Publishing: Boston.

Nusbaumer, J. (1987b), *Services in the Global Market*, Kluwer Academic Publishers: Boston.

Ochel, W., and Wegner, M. (1987), *Service Economies in Europe - Opportunities for Growth*, Pinter Publishers, London.

O'Connor, K. (1987), 'The Location of Services Involved with International Trade', *Environment and Planning A*, Vol. 19, No. 5, pp.687-700.

OECD (1989), *The Internationalisation of Software and Computer Services*, Information Computer Communications Policy Series No. 17, OECD: Paris.

OECD (1990), *Trade in Information, Computer and Communication Services*, Information Computer Communications Policy Series No. 21, OECD: Paris.

O'Farrell, P.N. and Hitchens, D.M. (1990), 'Producer services and regional development: key conceptual issues of taxonomy and quality measurements', *Regional Studies*, Vol. 24, pp.163-71.

O'Farrell, P.N., Wood, P.A. (1993), *A holistic conceptual framework of international entry mode choice by business service firms*, Paper presented to RESER Conference, Sicily; copy available from the authors.

O'Farrell, P.N., Moffat, L.A.R. (1995), 'Business Services and their Impact upon Client Performance: An Exploratory Interregional Analysis', *Regional Studies*, Vol. 29, No. 2, pp.111-24.

O'Farrell, P.N., Moffat, L. and Wood, P.A. (1995), 'Internationalisation by business services: a methodological critique of foreign-market entry-mode choice', *Environment and Planning A*, Vol. 27, pp.683-97.

Ohlin, B. (1933), *International and Inter-regional Trade*, Harvard University Press.

Panzar, J.C. and Willig, R.D. (1981), 'Economies of scope', *American Economic Review*, Vol. 71, pp.268-72.

Pavan, J. (1972), *The Strategy and Structure of Italian Enterprise*, unpublished DBA thesis, Graduate School of Business Administration, Harvard University.

Peebles, D and Ryans, J. (1984), *Management of International Advertising*, Allyn & Bacon: Boston, MA.

Penrose, E.T.(1959), *The Theory of the Growth of the Firm*, Blackwell: Oxford.

Perry, M. (1989), *The international and regional context of the advertising industry in New Zealand*, Occasional Publications 24 Dept. of Geography University of Auckland.

Perry, M. (1990a), 'The internationalization of advertising', *Geoforum*, Vol. 21, pp.35-50.

Perry, M. (1990b), 'Business services specialisation and regional economic change', *Regional Studies*, Vol. 24, pp.195-210.

Perry, M. (1991), 'The capacity of producer services to generate regional growth: some evidence from a peripheral metropolitan economy', *Environment and Planning A*, Vol. 23, pp.1331-47.

Perry, M. (1992), 'Flexible Production, Externalisation and the Interpretation of Business Service Growth', *The Service Industries Journal*, Vol. 12, No. 1, pp.1-16.

Peterson, J. and Barras, R. (1987),'Measuring International Competitiveness in Services', *Service Industries Journal*, Vol. 7, No. 2.

Peterson, J. (1989), 'International Trade in Services: The Uruguay Round and Cultural and Information Services', *National Westminster Bank Quarterly Review*, August.

Petit, P. (1986), *Slow Growth and the Service Economy*, Frances Pinter Publishers: London.

Pitelis, C. and Sugden, R. (eds.) (1991), *The Nature of the Transnational Firm*, Routledge: London.

Porter, M.E. (1985), *Competitive Advantage*, Free Press: New York.

Porter, M.E. (ed.) (1987), *Competition in Global Industries*, Harvard Business School Press: Boston, MA.

Porter, M.E. (1990), *The Competitive Advantage of Nations*, Free Press: New York.

Posner, M.W. (1961), 'International trade and technical change', *Oxford Economic Papers*, Vol. 13, pp.323-41.

Prahalad, C.K. and Doz, Y. (1987), *The Multinational Mission: Balancing local demands and global vision*, Free Press: New York.

Price Waterhouse (1985), *Annual Review 1984-85*.

Price Waterhouse (1986), *Annual Review 1985-86*.

Price Waterhouse (1987), *Annual Review 1986-87*.

Price Waterhouse (1988), *Annual Review 1987-88*.

Price Waterhouse (1989), *Annual Review 1988-89*.

Price Waterhouse (1990), *Annual Review 1989-90*.

Price Waterhouse Worldwide (1993), *Facts and Figures 1992/1993*.

Quinn, J.B. and Doorley, T.L. (1988), 'Key Policy Issues Posed by Services', in Guile, B.R. & Quinn, J.B., *Technology in Services: Policies for growth, trade and employment*, National Academy Press: Washington D.C.

Quinn, J.B. and Paquette, P.C. (1990), 'Technology in services: creating organizational revolutions', *Sloan Management Review*, Vol. 11 No. 2, pp.67-78.

Quinn, J.B., Doorley, T.L., and Paquette, P.C. (1990), 'Technology in services: rethinking strategic focus', *Sloan Management Review*, Vol. 11, No. 2, pp.79-88.

Quinn, J.J., and Dickson, K. (1995), 'The Co-location of Production and Distribution: Emergent Trends in Consumer Services', *Technology Analysis and Strategic Management*, Vol. 7, No. 3, pp.343-52.

Rada, J.F. (1984), 'Advanced Technologies And Development: Are Conventional

Ideas About Comparative Advantage Obsolete?', *Trade and Development*, No, 5, pp.275-96.

Rajan, A. (1987), *Services: The Second Industrial Revolution*, Butterworths: London.

Reynolds, B. (1993), *Excellence in Accountancy*, Macmillan: London.

Ricardo, D. (1817), *On the Principles of Political Economy and Taxation*, Harmondsworth: Penguin, 1971.

Richards, A.B. (1981), *Touche Ross and Co 1899-1981*, Touche Ross and Co.: London.

Richardson, J.B. (1986), 'A sub-sectoral approaches to services in trade theory', *Services World Economy Series No. 1*, Pergamon Press: Oxford.

Richardson, J.B. (1987), 'Approaches to services in trade theory', in O.Giarini, *The Emerging Service Economy*, Pergamon Press: Oxford.

Ricketts, M. (1994), *The Economics Of Business Enterprise*, Second Edition, Harvester Wheatsheaf: London.

Riddle, D. (1986), *Service-Led Growth: The Role of the Service Sector in World Development*, Praeger: New York.

Rimmer, P.J. (1988), 'The internationalization of engineering consultancies: problems of breaking into the club', *Environment and Planning A*, Vol. 20, pp.761-88.

Rosen, B.N., Boddewyn J.J. and Louis E.A. (1988), 'Participation By U.S. Agencies in International Brand Advertising: An Empirical Study', *Journal of Advertising*, Vol. 17, No. 4, pp.14-22.

Rowland, C. (1993), 'An international future for IT services', in *The Computing Services Association Handbook 1993*, pp.17-19.

Rugman, A.M. (1979), *International Diversification and the Multinational Enterprise*, Lexington Books: Lexington, Mass.

Rugman, A.M. (1981), *Inside the Multinationals: The Economics of Internal Markets*, Croom Helm: London.

Rugman, A.M. (ed.) (1982), *New Theories of the Multinational Enterprise*, Croom Helm: London.

Rugman, A.M. (1987), 'Multinationals and Trade in Services: A Transaction Cost Approach', *Weltwirtschaftliches Archiv*, Vol. 123, No. 4, pp.651-67.

Rumelt, R.P. (1974), *Strategy, Structure and Economic Performance*, Harvard University Press: Boston, Mass..

Ryan, C. (1988), 'Trade in Services: An Introductory Survey', *The Economic and Social Review*, Vol. 20, No. 1, pp.37-48.

Rybczynski, T.M. (1955), 'Factor Endowment and Relative Commodity Prices', *Economica*, Vol. 22, Nov., pp.336-41.

Saatchi & Saatchi Company PLC (1987), *Annual Report and Accounts 1987*, Saatchi & Saatchi, London.

Saatchi & Saatchi Company PLC (1988), *Annual Report and Accounts 1988*, Saatchi & Saatchi, London.

301

Saatchi & Saatchi Company PLC (1990), *Annual Report and Accounts 1990*, Saatchi & Saatchi, London.

Saatchi & Saatchi Company PLC (1991), *Report and Accounts 1991*, Saatchi & Saatchi, London.

Saatchi & Saatchi Company PLC (1992), *Report and Accounts 1992*, Saatchi & Saatchi, London.

Saatchi & Saatchi Company PLC (1993), *Report and Accounts 1993*, Saatchi & Saatchi, London.

Sampson, G.P. and Snape, R.H., (1985), 'Identifying the Issues in Trade in Services', *World Economy*, Vol. 8.

Samuelson, P.A. (1948), 'International trade and the equalisation of factor prices', *Economic Journal*, Vol. 58, pp.163-84.

Samuelson, P.A. (1949), 'International factor price equalisation once again', *Economic Journal*, Vol. 59, pp.181-97.

Samuelson, P.A. (1954), 'The Transfer Problem and Transport Costs; II: Analysis of Effects of Trade Impediments', *Economic Journal*, (June), pp.264-69.

Sapir, A. and Lutz, E. (1980), *Trade in Non-Factor Services: Past Trends and Current Issues*, The World Bank: Washington, D.C.

Sapir, A. and Lutz, E. (1981), *Trade in Services: Economic Determinants and Development-Related Issues: A Background Study for World Development Report 1981*, Staff working Paper No. 480, World Bank: Washington, D.C.

Sapir, A. (1985), 'North South Issues in Trade in Services', *World Economy*, Vol. 8.

Sasser, W.E., Wyckoff, D.D. and Olsen, R.P. (1978), The Management of Service Operations, Allyn and Bacon inc.: Newton, M.A.

Sauvant, K.P. (1986), *International Transactions in Services: The Politics of Transborder Data Flows*, Westview Press.

Sauvant, K.P. and Zimmy, Z. (1985), 'FDI and TNC's in Services', *The CTC Reporter*, No. 20, Autumn.

Schmalansee, R. (1972), *The Economics of Advertising*, North Holland: Amsterdam.

Schott, J.J. (1983), 'Protectionist Threat to Trade and Investment in Services', *World Economy*, Vol. 6.

Scott, A.J. (1988), 'Flexible production systems and regional development', *International Journal of Urban and Regional Research*, Vol. 12, pp.171-85.

Segebarth, K. (1990), 'Some Aspects of the Trade in Services: An Empirical Approach', *The Service Industries Journal*, Vol. 10, No. 2.

Sema Group PLC (1988), *Annual Report 1988*.

Sema Group PLC (1989), *Annual Report 1989*.

Sema Group PLC (1990), *Annual Report 1990*.

Sema Group PLC (1992), *Annual Report 1992*.

Sema Group PLC (1993), *Annual Report 1993*.

Sema Group PLC (1994), *Annual Report 1994*.

Sharma, D.D, and Johanson, J. (1987), 'Technical Consultancy in

Internationalisation', *International Marketing Review*, Winter, pp. 20-29.

Shelp, R.K. (1981), *Beyond Industrialisation: Ascendancy of the Global Service Economy*, Praeger publishers.

Shelp, R.K., Stephenson J.C. et al., (1984), *Service Industries and Economic Development: Case Studies in Technology Transfer*, Praeger.

Shirley-Beaven, M. (1979), 'Success story of the first Euro-accountants', *Accountancy Age*, Feb. pp.26-27.

Simon, H.A. (1955), 'A behavioural model of rational choice', *Quarterly Journal of Economics*, Vol. 69, pp.99-118.

Singlemann, J. (1978), *From Agriculture to Services: The Transformation of Industry and Employment*, Sage Publications: London.

Sinclair, J. (1987), *Images Incorporated: Advertising as Industry and Ideology*, Croom Helm: London.

Smith, A. (1776), *An Enquiry into the Nature and Causes of the Wealth of Nations*, Harmondsworth: Penguin, 1982.

Sowels, N. (1989), *Britain's Invisible Earnings*, Gower: Aldershot.

Stern, R.M. and Hoekman, B.M. (1988), 'Conceptual Issues Relating to Services in the International Economy', in C.H.Lee and S.Naya (eds.) *Trade and Investment in Services: in the Asia-Pacific Region*, Pacific and World Studies No. 1, Westview Press.

Stigler, G.J. (1956), *Trends in Employment in the Service Industry*, National Bureau for Economic Research, Princetown University Press: New York.

Stopford, J.M. and Wells. L.T. (1972), *Managing the Multinational Enterprise: Organization of the Firm and Ownership of the Subsidiaries*, Longman: London.

Teece, D.J. (1981), 'Internal organisation and economic performance: an empirical analysis of the profitability of principal firms', *Journal of Industrial Economics*, Vol. 30, pp.173-200.

Teece, D.J. (1983), 'Technological and organisational factors in the theory of the multinational enterprise', in M. Casson (ed.) *The Growth of International Business*, George Allen & Unwin.

Teece, D.J., (1986), 'Transaction cost economics and the multinational enterprise: an assessment', *Journal of Economic Behaviour and Organisation*, Vol. 7, pp.21-45.

Terpstra, V. (1978), *Cultural Environment of International Business*, South-Western: Cincinnati, Ohio.

Terpstra, V. and Yu, C. (1988), 'Determinants of foreign investment of US advertising agencies', *Journal of International Business Studies*, Vol. 19, pp.33-46.

Thompson, S. and Wright, M. (eds.) (1988), *Internal Organisation, Efficiency and Profit*, Philip Allan: Oxford.

Trapp, R. (1994), 'Fears grow among auditors as the liability claims soar', *Independent on Sunday*, 6th. March.

303

Turnbull, P.W. (1987), 'A challenge to the stages theory of the internationalization process', in P.J. Rosson and S.D. Reed (eds.) *Managing Export Entry and Expansion*, Prager: New York.

Turner, E.S. (1952), The Shocking History of Advertising!, Michael Joseph: London.

UNCTAD (1983), *Production and Trade in Services, Policies and Their Underlying Factors Bearing Upon International Service Transactions*, (TD/B/941), United Nations: New York.

UNCTC (1979), *Transnational Corporations in Advertising*, United Nations: New York.

UNCTC (1984), *Transnational Corporations and Transborder Data Flows: Background and Overview*, Elsevier-North Holland: Amsterdam and New York.

UNCTC (1988), *Transnational Corporations and World Development, Trends and Prospects*, United Nations: New York.

UNCTC (1990), *Transnational Corporations, Services and the Uruguay Round*, United Nations: New York.

UNCTC (1991), *World Investment Report 1991: The Triad in Foreign Direct Investment*, United Nations: New York.

UNCTC (1992), *World Investment Report 1992: Transnational Corporations as Engines of Growth*, United Nations: New York.

UNCTC (1993), *World Investment Report 1993: Transnational Corporations and Integrated International Production*, (ST/CTC/156) United Nations: New York.

UN Economic and Social Council (1978), Transnational Corporations in World Development, Commission on Transnational Corporations, 4th. session, E/C.10/38, United Nations: New York.

Van Grasstek, C. (1987), 'Trade in Services: Obstacles and Opportunities', *Economic Impact*, Vol. 58, pp.46-51.

Van Rens, J.H.P. (1982), *Multinational in the Transport Industry*, paper produced for Conference on Multinationals in Transition, Paris: I.R.M., 15-16 November 1982.

Vandermerwe, S. (1987), 'Deregulation in Services and the Marketing Challenge', *The Service Industries Journal*, Vol. 7, No. 1.

Vandermerwe, S. and Chadwick, M. (1989), 'The internationalization of services', *Service Industry Journal*, Vol. 9, pp.79-93.

Vernon, R. (1966), 'International investment and international trade in the product cycle', *Quarterly Journal of Economics*, Vol. 80, pp.190-207.

Vernon, R. (1979), 'The product cycle hypothesis in a new international environment', *Oxford Bulletin of Economics and Statistics*, Vol. 41, pp.255-68.

Weinstein, A.K. (1974), 'The International Expansion of US Multinational Advertising Agencies', *MSU Business Topics*, Summer, pp.29-35.

Weinstein, A.K. (1977), 'Foreign Investment By Service Firms: The Case Of Multinational Advertising Agencies', *Journal of International Business Studies*, Vol. 8, Spring/Summer, pp.83-91.

304

Wells, P.E. and Cooke, P.N. (1991), 'The geography of international strategic alliances in the telecommunications industry: the case of Cable and Wireless, Ericsson and Fujitsu', *Environment and Planning A*, Vol. 23, pp.87-106.

Williamson, J. and Milner, C. (1991), *The World Economy*, Harvester Wheatsheaf.

Williamson, O.E. (1964), *The Economics of Discretionary Behaviour: Managerial Objectives in a Theory of the Firm*, Prentice-Hall.

Williamson, O.E. (1975), *Markets and Hierarchies: Analysis and Anti-trust Implications*, Free Press: New York.

Williamson, O.E. (1979), 'Transaction cost economics: the governance of contractual relations', *Journal of Law and Economics*, Vol. 22, pp.233-62.

Williamson, O.E. (1981), 'The modern corporation: origins, evolution, and attributes', *Journal of Economic Literature*, Vol. 19, pp.1537-68.

Williamson, O.E. (1985), *The Economic Institutions of Capitalism: Firms, Markets, Relational Contracting*, Macmillan: London.

Williamson, O.E. (1986), *Economic Organisation: Firms, Markets and Policy Control*, Wheatsheaf Books.

Winsbury, R. (1977), *Thomson McLintock & Co. - A First Hundred Years*, Thomson Mclintock: London.

Wise, T.A. (1981), *Peat Marwick Mitchell & Co.: 85 years*, Peat Marwick Mitchell: New York.

Wolf, B.M. (1977), 'Industrial diversification and internationalisation: some empirical evidence', *Journal of Industrial Economics*, Vol. 26, December, pp.177-91.

World Bank (1988), *World Development Report*, Oxford University Press: Oxford.

Wrigley, L. (1970), *Diversification and Divisional Autonomy*, Unpublished PhD dissertation, Harvard Business School.

Yannopoulos, G.N. (1983), 'The growth of transnational banking', in M. Casson (ed.) *The Growth of International Business*, George Allen & Unwin.

Yoshino, M.Y., and Lifson, T.B. (1986), *The Invisible Link, Japan's Sogo Shosha and the Organisation of Trade,* MIT Press: Cambridge, Mass.

Young, A.K. (1979), *The Sogo Shosha: Japan's Multinational Trading Companies*, Westview Press: Boulder.

Young, S., Hamill, J., Wheeler, C. and Davies, J.R. (1989), *International Market Entry and Development: Strategies and Management*, Harvester Wheatsheaf.

Zweifel, P. (1986), 'On the tradeability of services', *Deuxiemes journees annuelles d'etude sur l'economie de service*, Geneva. Institut universitaire d'etudes europeennes, unpublished.